Human Impact on Security and Privacy:

Network and Human Security, Social Media, and Devices

Rajeev Kumar
Moradabad Institute of Technology, India

Saurabh Srivastava
Moradabad Institute of Technology, India

Ahmed A. Elngar
Beni-Suef University, Egypt

IGI Global
Publishing Tomorrow's Research Today

Published in the United States of America by
IGI Global
701 E. Chocolate Avenue
Hershey PA, USA 17033
Tel: 717-533-8845
Fax: 717-533-8661
E-mail: cust@igi-global.com
Web site: https://www.igi-global.com

Library of Congress Cataloging-in-Publication Data

CIP PENDING

ISBN13: 9798369392355
Isbn13Softcover: 9798369392362
EISBN13: 9798369392379

Vice President of Editorial: Melissa Wagner
Managing Editor of Acquisitions: Mikaela Felty
Managing Editor of Book Development: Jocelynn Hessler
Production Manager: Mike Brehm
Cover Design: Phillip Shickler

British Cataloguing in Publication Data
A Cataloguing in Publication record for this book is available from the British Library.

Table of Contents

Detailed Table of Contents

This chapter explores the crucial influence that human behavior and decision-making have on information system security. Human factors continue to be a major source of weaknesses in cybersecurity plans, even while technology measures constitute its core. This study looks into the several ways that human factors—such as social engineering, cognitive biases, and insufficient training—affect cybersecurity risks. The chapter illustrates how human errors, such as weak password practices, and phishing vulnerability, can undermine even the strongest technology defenses by looking at case studies. It emphasizes the significance of strategy for cybersecurity. To lower the risks associated with people, it suggests extensive training plans, approachable system designs, and organizational guidelines. In an effort to reduce human error, the chapter also examines new developments in the field, such as behavioural biometrics and AI-driven monitoring systems. In the end, this chapter highlights how important it is to address human elements in order to improve overall cybersecurity resilience

Addressing human factors in cybersecurity is essential due to the prevalent exploitation of human errors and behaviors by attackers. This approach involves continuous education and engaging training programs tailored to various roles, emphasizing interactive and personalized learning. Implementing strong security policies with clear guidelines and simplified procedures, backed by regular audits and enforcement, enhances compliance. Technological solutions such as automation, user-friendly security tools, and behavioral analytics play a critical role in reducing human errors and detecting anomalies. Cultivating a security-conscious culture, with leadership commitment and encouraging non-punitive incident reporting, fosters proactive security practices. Limiting the attack surface through different principles minimizes vulnerabilities. Enhancing incident response capabilities ensures effective handling and mitigation of security breaches. This holistic approach integrates education, policy, technology, and culture to strengthen organizational resilience against cybersecurity threats.

Advancements in affordable computing and communication technologies have led to the widespread proliferation of interconnected devices, giving rise to a new era characterized by devices that sense, compute, and share information, forming loosely connected Cyber-Physical Systems (CPS). Managing data and making intelligent decisions are the primary areas of research within CPS. Traditionally, cloud-based centralized computation has been the dominant architecture due to its ease of implementation and enhanced control. However, the explosion of data, scalability challenges, and privacy concerns are increasingly highlighting the limitations of such centralized systems. Therefore, there is a growing interest in decentralizing control and distributing computing tasks among the devices as a more promising approach for sharing intelligence. Investigating novel decentralization mechanisms is a central focus of this chapter.

Keyloggers are malicious programs that record keystrokes and jeopardize the security of personal and business data. These sneaky malwares grab vital information while evading user discovery. Keyloggers conceal their existence by using techniques like rootkits to bypass antivirus and other security measures. Once installed, they are not visible on the process monitor . Attackers may unlawfully access sensitive information, such as banking credentials. One major worry regarding keyloggers is that around 90% of them now function in the user's environment without express authorization, leaving the user unaware that their device is being watched. Although there are hazards, addressing the keylogger threat necessitates preventative actions. This article proposes ways to improve the prevention of assaults, such as hacking. It advocates employing strong security tools and increasing cybersecurity awareness. Additionally, the following discussion suggests methods to understand the capabilities of keyloggers, develop detection methods, and rigorously evaluate countermeasures accordingly.

Cloud computing deals with the dynamic allocation of resources on demand from any location. Load balancing is the phenomenon of ensuring the distribution of traffic and the operation of loads on multiple servers. There are security considerations where the load balancers are potential targets for Distributed Denial of Service (DDoS) attacks. This occurs when the attacker overwhelms the system with a flood of traffic, causing it to become unresponsive. The paper discusses the security challenges and attacks that affect workload distribution across servers dealing with access control mechanisms and concerns about multi-tenancy risks. The analysis involves identifying attacks in load-balancing systems from pre-existing frameworks by utilizing tools like Snort, Wireshark, and MATLAB for DDoS attacks. Furthermore, the paper does a comparative study on the established works. It addresses the best mitigation strategies for different types of DDoS attacks, such as Smurfing and TCP-SYN attacks, thus enhancing resilience with SDN architecture and multi-layered defense mechanisms.

The Internet of Things (IoT) represents a network of interconnected devices that collect and exchange data, while deep learning, a subset of artificial intelligence involves algorithms that model high-level abstractions in data through neural networks. The fusion of these technologies has transformed various sectors, from healthcare and agriculture to smart cities and autonomous vehicles. However, this convergence has also created new avenues for cybercrime, posing significant challenges to data security and privacy. The combination of deep learning and the Internet of Things has resulted in new vulnerabilities that hackers may take advantage of in addition to creative uses. This chapter looks at legal approaches to enhanced data analysis as well as practical methods for fighting cybercrime in the context of new technologies. With a focus on deep learning, legal frameworks and forward-thinking solutions, this study attempts to convey a thorough knowledge of the confluence of deep learning, cybercrime, and IoT.

E-Health applications enable one to acquire, process, and share patient medical data to improve diagnosis, treatment, and patient monitoring. Despite the undeniable benefits brought by the digitization of health systems, the transmission of and access to medical information raises critical issues, mainly related to security and privacy. This paper describes a safe e-health data management system that employs the MERN stack (MongoDB, Express, React, and Node.js) and strong encryption algorithms. The solution improves security by using client-side encryption with the AES-256-CBC technique to encrypt e-health files before uploading them to MongoDB. To improve security, encrypted files and keys are stored separately. User authentication employs bcryptjs for password hashing and JSON Web Tokens (JWT) for permission, ensuring that only authorized users can access and decrypt data. The study demonstrates the efficiency of coupling MERN stack development with encryption in protecting sensitive patient information, establishing confidence, and boosting the adoption of e-health solutions.

The objective of this article is to recognize facial features from images using face recognition approaches. For preprocessed face images with equalized histograms, the suggested solution employs a local binary pattern histogram (LBPH). One of the long-standing issues with computer vision is accurate face detection and recognition. The Local Binary Pattern (LBP) is a better facial descriptor in face recognition, in recent study. A person's identity, sentiments, and ideas may be more easily discernible from their face. Everyone wants to feel safe from unauthorized authentication in the current world. To improve security, face detection and recognition have joined the scene and are tackling the most challenging challenge of effectively recognizing faces without creating any false identities. The histogram values are extracted and joined into a single vector. After applying these methods, the training loss decreases and the validation of accuracy rise by over 96.5%. This vector compares the facial likenesses and produces the most advantageous outcome.

Kinship verification involves determining the relatedness between individuals by analysing their genetic or phenotypic characteristics or traits. The realm of kinship research has garnered substantial attention particularly in computer vision, with broad applications spanning forensic analysis, genealogy exploration, immigration law and more. This chapter introduces a five-stage methodology for kinship verification through facial images, employing Convolutional Neural Networks (CNNs). The process involves dataset acquisition, preprocessing with FaceNet and Res-Net-50, feature extraction, and CNN model development utilizing Inception Resnet V1 and ResNet-50. The proposed model attains a remarkable accuracy exceeding 85% on a substantial dataset, showcasing its efficacy in identifying kinship relations. Thus, the proposed work contributes to reshaping the methodology for kin verification, enhancing human surveillance through the development of facial image analysis techniques with immense potential for practical applications.

The field of exploring social models of smart home appliances aims to understand how these technologies interact with mobility and security issues, highlighting their broader social implications. This research has emerged due to the ubiquity of smart home devices and the need to comprehend their social impact. It focuses on the interplay between technology and its effects on equity and privacy concerns, aiming to develop policies that prioritize users over technology providers, while ensuring the protection of both smart home technologies and user privacy. The main challenge is understanding the integrated social safety functionality of these appliances. By examining the relationships between different countries, the research seeks to address differences through an approach that includes cultural norms, technological infrastructure, legal expertise, and user education. This anticipates a shift in smart home research towards a holistic approach, considering complex interactions. The goal is to provide insights for developing flexible and socially responsive smart home technologies.

The chapter explores the transformative journey of social media and its impact on contemporary society, highlighting both challenges and opportunities. From its origins to its global ubiquity, social media has redefined communication, transcending geographical and cultural barriers. While it empowers global sharing and creativity, it also raises issues like privacy breaches, data security, and misinformation. Despite these challenges, social media drives social movements, political engagement, and revolutionizes marketing. It influences agriculture by spreading innovative techniques and bioinformatics by enhancing research collaboration. Emerging technologies like AR, VR, and AI will further shape its future. Integrating bioinformatics and agricultural analytics into social media can address global challenges, fostering positive societal change and connectivity.

Along with human evolution, communication has continued to change. Social media has surfaced as yet another revolution in the vast spheres of mass media and communication in general in the modern day. Social media has completely changed how people connect and communicate with each other. It has brought the diversity of the world onto one platform, transcending time, national boundaries, racial and cultural divides, and more. Nevertheless, the other aspect of this information society's development—its insatiable thirst for knowledge—cannot be ignored. The risk of social engineering is one of the main weaknesses of social media. The practice of influencing someone's thoughts through deft communication techniques are known as social engineering or social manipulation, and it has existed for as long as communication itself. It combines creativity and science. The primary issue with social media is that people tend to overshare. This, however, simply makes it easier for a social engineer to prepare an assault.

Preface

In an era defined by rapid technological advancements and an increasingly interconnected world, the challenges and opportunities presented by digitalization demand a new approach. The digital world, characterized by optimized, sustainable, and digitally networked solutions, necessitates the integration of intelligence systems, machine learning, deep learning, blockchain methods, and robust cybersecurity measures. This book, *Human Impact on Security and Privacy: Network and Human Security, social media, and Devices*, delves into these complex challenges, offering insights into the synergistic utilization of cutting-edge technologies and their implications for modern living.

As we navigate the digital era, cybersecurity has emerged as a critical concern. Every individual and organization is becoming increasingly reliant on digital tools, and the future must aspire to seamlessly integrate technology into our daily lives. This integration spans modern living, knowledge-based workforces, factory automation, and even the virtual-real social behaviors that are becoming more prevalent. At the strategic intersection of these diverse disciplines lies cyber informatics, a field that promises to realize a comprehensive vision of smart technology.

This book provides a global perspective on current and future trends concerning the integration of intelligent systems with cybersecurity applications. It aims to offer a comprehensive exploration of ethical considerations within the realms of security, artificial intelligence, agriculture, and data science. Key topics include the evolving landscape of cybersecurity, social engineering perspectives, algorithmic transparency, data privacy, and the broader societal implications of AI and data science.

The impact of this book on the research community will be profound. By consolidating and advancing the discourse on AI and data science ethics, it contributes to the ongoing dialogue on these critical issues, helping researchers, professionals, and policymakers develop a deeper understanding of the ethical challenges that are becoming increasingly vital in their work.

This publication is particularly valuable for researchers and academics in fields such as agriculture, cybersecurity, AI, data science, computer science, and ethics. It also serves as a crucial resource for graduate and postgraduate students, tech industry professionals, data analysts, AI developers, and policymakers concerned with regulatory and ethical aspects of AI and data science. The book offers guidance on developing AI and data science solutions that not only perform well but also align with ethical standards and societal values.

In today's industrial informatics landscape, this book stands at the crossroads of multiple disciplines, offering case studies and real-world examples that demonstrate the practical applications of deep learning, machine learning, and other advanced technologies. We believe that the insights provided here will serve as a valuable resource for a wide range of readers, including researchers, industry experts, students, and anyone with a vested interest in the future of our digital world.

ORGANIZATION OF THE BOOK

Chapter 1: The Role of Human Factors in Cybersecurity Vulnerabilities

In this chapter, we delve into the critical role that human behavior and decision-making play in the security of information systems. Despite the robustness of technological safeguards, human factors remain a persistent source of vulnerability in cybersecurity. This chapter thoroughly investigates how social engineering, cognitive biases, and inadequate training contribute to these risks, presenting case studies that reveal how human errors, such as weak password practices and susceptibility to phishing, can compromise even the most sophisticated defenses. We emphasize the need for a strategic approach to cybersecurity that includes comprehensive training programs, user-friendly system designs, and well-defined organizational policies to mitigate these human-induced risks. Additionally, we explore emerging innovations, such as behavioral biometrics and AI-driven monitoring systems, aimed at reducing the impact of human error. Ultimately, this chapter underscores the necessity of addressing human factors to bolster overall cybersecurity resilience.

Chapter 2: Understanding and Addressing Human Factors in Cybersecurity Vulnerabilities

Addressing human factors in cybersecurity is paramount, given the persistent exploitation of human errors and behaviors by malicious actors. This chapter presents a holistic approach that combines continuous education, engaging and role-specific training programs, and robust security policies. We highlight the importance of interactive and personalized learning to reinforce security practices and discuss the role of strong security policies, clear guidelines, and simplified procedures in enhancing compliance. Technological solutions, including automation, user-friendly security tools, and behavioral analytics, are also explored as crucial elements in reducing human errors and detecting anomalies. By fostering a security-conscious culture with leadership commitment and encouraging non-punitive incident reporting, organizations can cultivate proactive security practices. The chapter also discusses limiting the attack surface through strategic principles and enhancing incident response capabilities to effectively manage and mitigate security breaches.

Chapter 3: Understanding the Human Factors in the Psychology of Cyber Threats

This chapter explores the intricate relationship between human psychology and cybersecurity vulnerabilities, focusing on how psychological and behavioral factors influence susceptibility to and mitigation of cyber threats. We delve into the psychological tactics used in social engineering, the motivations behind insider threats—whether driven by malice or incompetence—and the cognitive biases that skew cybersecurity judgments. By applying principles of behavioral economics, the chapter demonstrates how organizations can design security interventions that effectively promote safer behavior. Through empirical case studies, including significant incidents in India, we illustrate the real-world consequences of these human factors. The chapter stresses the importance of fostering a culture of cybersecurity awareness and resilience through comprehensive training, stringent access controls, and well-designed behavioral interventions. By integrating technical measures with a deep understanding of human behavior, organizations can enhance their defenses against the evolving landscape of cyber threats.

Chapter 4: Comparative Analysis of Traditional vs. AI-Driven Network Security

The sophistication of cyber threats has necessitated the evolution of network security mechanisms. In this chapter, we compare traditional methods, such as firewalls, IDS, and antivirus software, which rely on established guidelines and signature-based detection, with the emerging paradigm of AI-driven network security. AI introduces new capabilities through machine learning, behavioral analytics, and automated threat detection, offering significant improvements in efficiency, accuracy, response time, adaptability, scalability, and cost-effectiveness. By analyzing large datasets, AI systems can detect patterns, recognize anomalies, and respond to threats in real time, reducing false positives and addressing zero-day attacks. Despite the complexity and cost of AI systems, their integration with traditional methods can enhance security, creating a proactive defense strategy against the continually evolving cyber threats.

Chapter 5: Cyber-Physical Systems for Enhancing Security in Cyber Environments

The advent of affordable computing and communication technologies has led to the widespread adoption of interconnected devices, marking the rise of Cyber-Physical Systems (CPS). These systems, which sense, compute, and share information, are central to the discussion in this chapter, particularly in the context of security. We explore the traditional reliance on cloud-based centralized computation for managing data and making intelligent decisions and highlight the limitations posed by the explosion of data, scalability challenges, and privacy concerns. The chapter advocates for the decentralization of control and the distribution of computing tasks among devices as a more promising approach to sharing intelligence within CPS. By investigating novel decentralization mechanisms, we aim to offer insights into enhancing the security and efficiency of these increasingly prevalent systems.

Chapter 6: Keyloggers and the Prevention of Security Breaches

Keyloggers represent a significant threat to the security of personal and business data, operating covertly to capture vital information while evading user detection. In this chapter, we examine the stealthy techniques employed by keyloggers, such as rootkits that bypass antivirus measures and remain hidden from process monitors. The chapter highlights the alarming statistic that around 90% of keyloggers function within the user's environment without their knowledge, leading to unauthorized access to sensitive information, including banking credentials. To address this pervasive threat, we propose several preventive measures, including the use of robust security tools and enhanced cybersecurity awareness. Additionally, the chapter discusses strategies for detecting keyloggers and rigorously evaluating countermeasures, emphasizing the need for continuous vigilance and advanced detection methods to safeguard against these insidious attacks.

Chapter 7: Security Considerations of SDN Networks During DDoS Attacks in Load Balancing

The dynamic allocation of resources in cloud computing presents unique challenges, particularly in the context of load balancing—a crucial process that ensures the distribution of traffic and operations across multiple servers. This chapter focuses on the security considerations surrounding load balancers, which are prime targets for Distributed Denial of Service (DDoS) attacks. We explore the methods attackers use to overwhelm systems with excessive traffic, rendering them unresponsive, and discuss the implications for access control mechanisms and multi-tenancy risks. By analyzing attacks on load-balancing systems using tools like Snort, Wireshark, and MATLAB, the chapter provides a comparative study of established mitigation strategies for various DDoS attack types, including Smurfing and TCP-SYN attacks. We emphasize the importance of enhancing resilience through Software-Defined Networking (SDN) architecture and multi-layered defense mechanisms.

Chapter 8: Exploring Effective Strategies for Combatting Cybercrime: The Intersection of IoT, Deep Learning, and Legal Standpoints

The convergence of the Internet of Things (IoT) and deep learning technologies has revolutionized numerous sectors, from healthcare and agriculture to smart cities and autonomous vehicles. However, this fusion has also opened new avenues for cybercrime, creating significant challenges for data security and privacy. In this chapter, we examine the vulnerabilities introduced by the integration of IoT and deep learning and the innovative approaches hackers may exploit. We explore legal frameworks and progressive data analytics to combat cybercrime, with a focus on deep learning's role in enhancing security measures. The chapter aims to provide a comprehensive understanding of the intersection between deep learning, cybercrime, and IoT, offering practical strategies for mitigating risks and ensuring the secure implementation of these transformative technologies.

Chapter 9: A Security and Privacy Validation Methodology for e-Health Systems Using Cloud Storage

The digitization of health systems has brought tremendous benefits, enabling the acquisition, processing, and sharing of patient medical data to improve diagnosis, treatment, and monitoring. However, this digital transformation also raises critical concerns regarding the security and privacy of medical information. In this chapter, we propose a secure e-health data management system utilizing the MERN stack

(MongoDB, Express, React, and Node.js) coupled with strong encryption algorithms. We detail the implementation of client-side encryption using the AES-256-CBC technique to protect e-health files before uploading them to MongoDB, and discuss the separation of encrypted files and keys to enhance security. User authentication methods, including bcryptjs for password hashing and JSON Web Tokens (JWT) for authorization, are also examined to ensure that only authorized users can access and decrypt sensitive data. The chapter demonstrates the effectiveness of combining MERN stack development with encryption techniques in safeguarding patient information, thereby building trust and promoting the adoption of e-health solutions.

Chapter 10: Improving the Quality of Face Recognition Using LBPH in Machine Learning

Facial recognition technology has long been a challenge in computer vision, with the accurate detection and identification of faces being a critical security concern. In this chapter, we present an approach that leverages the Local Binary Pattern Histogram (LBPH) method for recognizing facial features from images. By applying LBPH to preprocessed face images with equalized histograms, we achieve significant improvements in training loss reduction and validation accuracy, exceeding 96.5%. The chapter details the extraction of histogram values and their integration into a single vector, which is then used to compare facial likenesses and generate optimal outcomes. We highlight the importance of face detection and recognition in enhancing security, particularly in preventing unauthorized authentication, and discuss the broader implications of these technologies in safeguarding personal identities in an increasingly digital world.

Chapter 11: Kinship Verification by Analyzing Facial Images to Ensure Human Security

Kinship verification, the process of determining the relatedness between individuals through the analysis of genetic or phenotypic traits, has garnered significant attention, particularly in the field of computer vision. This chapter introduces a five-stage methodology for kinship verification using facial images, employing advanced techniques such as Convolutional Neural Networks (CNNs). The process involves the acquisition of datasets, preprocessing with FaceNet and Res-Net-50, feature extraction, and the development of CNN models utilizing Inception Resnet V1 and ResNet-50. The proposed model demonstrates remarkable accuracy, exceeding 85% on a substantial dataset, underscoring its efficacy in identifying kinship relationships. We discuss the implications of this work for reshaping kin verification methodologies and enhancing human surveillance through facial image analysis, with potential applications in forensic analysis, genealogy exploration, and immigration law.

Chapter 12: Exploring the Social Model of Smart Home Devices: An In-Depth Analysis of Social Impact and Security Issues

As smart home devices become increasingly ubiquitous, understanding their social impact and the security issues they introduce is essential. This chapter explores the interplay between technology and its broader social implications, with a focus on how smart home devices interact with mobility and the changing workplace dynamics. The chapter also addresses the heightened need for security and privacy in environments where personal information is constantly collected and processed. We provide a detailed analysis of the potential risks posed by smart home devices, such as data breaches and unauthorized access, and offer strategies for mitigating these threats. Through a combination of case studies, theoretical insights, and practical recommendations, this chapter aims to equip readers with a comprehensive understanding of the social and security challenges associated with the proliferation of smart home technologies.

Chapter 13: Social Media Revolution - Unraveling the Threads of Connectivity and Influence

This chapter embarks on a detailed exploration of the evolution of social media and its profound impact on modern society. It traces the journey from the inception of social media platforms to their current global dominance, emphasizing how these platforms have redefined communication by transcending geographical and cultural barriers. While social media empowers users to share and create content globally, it also introduces significant challenges, such as privacy breaches, data security risks, and the spread of misinformation. Despite these concerns, social media remains a powerful driver of social movements, political engagement, and a revolution in marketing strategies. The chapter further examines how social media influences sectors like agriculture by promoting innovative techniques and in bioinformatics by enhancing research collaboration. Emerging technologies such as AR, VR, and AI are poised to shape the future of social media further. The integration of bioinformatics and agricultural analytics into social media is proposed as a means to tackle global challenges, fostering positive societal change and enhanced connectivity.

Chapter 14: Cybersecurity Concerns in Social Media and Online Interactions

This chapter delves into the cybersecurity challenges that have emerged alongside the evolution of social media and online communication. As social media has revolutionized the way people connect, bringing global diversity onto a single platform, it has also introduced significant vulnerabilities. One of the primary risks is social engineering, where attackers manipulate users through subtle communication tactics. This long-standing practice of influencing others is now amplified by the widespread use of social media, making it easier for bad actors to prepare and execute attacks. The chapter discusses how the inherent tendency of users to overshare personal information on these platforms exacerbates the risk, providing social engineers with the data they need to carry out their schemes. The discussion highlights the need for increased awareness and robust strategies to mitigate these cybersecurity threats.

Chapter 15: Theoretical Insights into User Security and Privacy in Social Media Environments

In this chapter, the editors present a comprehensive analysis of user security and privacy within social media environments, focusing on the complex interplay of socio-cultural, psychological, and technological factors that influence user experiences. Through an exploratory design and qualitative approach, the research examines how users perceive and respond to security and privacy threats on social media platforms. The study is grounded in a theoretical framework that draws from multiple disciplines, including sociology, psychology, communication studies, and computer science. The findings reveal a diverse range of user concerns, including data privacy, the threat of cyber attacks, misinformation, and the responsibility of platforms to protect users. The chapter concludes with recommendations for enhancing user education, promoting platform accountability, advocating for stronger regulatory frameworks, encouraging interdisciplinary collaboration, and supporting continuous research to address these ongoing challenges.

IN CONCLUSION

As editors of this comprehensive reference book, we are honored to present a collection of scholarly contributions that delve into the multifaceted issues surrounding social media, cybersecurity, and user privacy. The chapters within this volume collectively offer a rich tapestry of insights, theoretical perspectives, and practical solutions that address the critical challenges of our time.

Throughout this book, we have explored the transformative power of social media, acknowledging its role as a catalyst for global connectivity and influence. Yet, we have also confronted the inherent risks and vulnerabilities that accompany this digital revolution, particularly in the realms of cybersecurity and user privacy. The discussions presented here reflect the urgency of addressing these concerns, highlighting the need for interdisciplinary collaboration, robust regulatory frameworks, and innovative approaches to safeguard user rights in an increasingly interconnected world.

As we conclude this volume, it is our hope that the knowledge and perspectives shared by our esteemed contributors will serve as a valuable resource for researchers, practitioners, policymakers, and anyone invested in the future of digital communication. The challenges outlined in these chapters are not insurmountable; rather, they offer opportunities for collective action and innovation. By embracing the insights provided in this book, we can work together to build a safer, more inclusive digital environment that respects the privacy and security of all users.

We extend our deepest gratitude to the contributors for their rigorous research and thought-provoking analyses, and to the readers who will carry forward the ideas and solutions discussed within these pages. Together, we can navigate the complexities of the digital age, ensuring that social media and online interactions continue to enrich our lives while safeguarding the fundamental principles of security and privacy.

Chapter 1
The Role of Human Factors in Cybersecurity Vulnerabilities

Harish Chandra Verma
https://orcid.org/0000-0002-5085-2004
ICAR-Central Institute for Subtropical Horticulture, Lucknow.India

Saurabh Srivastava
https://orcid.org/0000-0001-7654-0220
Moradabad Institute of Technology, India

ABSTRACT

This chapter explores the crucial influence that human behavior and decision-making have on information system security. Human factors continue to be a major source of weaknesses in cybersecurity plans, even while technology measures constitute its core. This study looks into the several ways that human factors—such as social engineering, cognitive biases, and insufficient training—affect cybersecurity risks. The chapter illustrates how human errors, such as weak password practices, and phishing vulnerability, can undermine even the strongest technology defenses by looking at case studies. It emphasizes the significance of strategy for cybersecurity. To lower the risks associated with people, it suggests extensive training plans, approachable system designs, and organizational guidelines. In an effort to reduce human error, the chapter also examines new developments in the field, such as behavioural biometrics and AI-driven monitoring systems. In the end, this chapter highlights how important it is to address human elements in order to improve overall cybersecurity resilience

DOI: 10.4018/979-8-3693-9235-5.ch001

INTRODUCTION

As the globe grows more digitally connected, cybersecurity is becoming a top priority for all parties—individuals, businesses, and governments. In accordance with the Computer Misuse Act (legislation.gov.uk, 1990), the UK National Cyber Security Centre (NCSC) defines a cyber-security incident as a violation of a system's security policy that affects its availability or integrity, as well as any unauthorised access or attempted access to a system or systems. Generally speaking, the following behaviours are acknowledged as violations of a standard security policy: 1) Unauthorised access attempts to systems and/or data; 2) Unauthorised data processing or storage on systems; 3) Modifications to a system's hardware, software, or firmware without the system owner's permission; and 4) Malevolent interference and/or suppression. Furthermore, by deploying several levels of security between computer systems, networks, and any data that needs to be kept private, the cybersecurity method can be successfully applied (Upadhyay & Sampalli, 2020. Cybersecurity incidents range from large-scale malevolent cyberattacks on businesses or government institutions to individuals using social engineering to get access to their social media accounts.

A cyberattack known as "social engineering" is used to psychologically manipulate a target into disclosing confidential information(Krombholz *et al.*, 2015). Because the human inclination to trust is more easily exploited than other hacking software, criminals deploy social engineering techniques. Social engineering techniques account for over 95% of online attacks. A malevolent hacker initially investigates the intended victim in order to gather background data for the assault. The thief then makes an effort to win over the victim's trust and convince them to do other acts, including providing access to a personal profile or disclosing critical personal information, that will ultimately lead to breathing security (Contel, and Schmick, 2016).

Even though intrusion detection systems, firewalls, and encryption are crucial technological solutions, they are not perfect. The human element is among the most important—yet sometimes disregarded—aspects of cybersecurity. According to a study by Alsharif *et al.*(2022), the degree of awareness about cybersecurity issues has reached 61%, which is a startlingly low level that needs to be raised as much as possible. The findings demonstrate a lack of knowledge of email usage (22%), phishing (30%), social media (35%), social engineering (37%), antivirus (33%), and data protection (29%).

This chapter examines the several ways that organisational culture, psychology, and human behaviour affect cybersecurity vulnerabilities. We seek to clarify the crucial role that human factors play in both generating and reducing cybersecurity threats by an examination of case studies, psychological theories, and organisational practices.

UNDERSTANDING HUMAN FACTORS IN CYBERSECURITY

The various ways that human behaviour and decision-making affect the security of information systems are referred to as human factors in cybersecurity. This covers a wide range of topics, including as social engineering, insider threats, user mistake, and how corporate culture affects security procedures.

A significant amount of cyber security issues are ascribed to insider threats or human error. As per the findings of Cybint Solutions (2020), human error is responsible for 95% of cyber security breaches. Similarly, IBM reported that 13% of all OT (Operational Technology)-related incidents in 2020 involved insider incidents, of which 60% involved malicious insiders and 40% involved negligence (Anonymous, 2021).

User Error And Un-Intentional Actions

Three types of behaviour are described by Rasmussen's basic taxonomy of human error: skill-based, rule-based, and knowledge-based. During routine, familiar tasks, skill-based behaviours occur. They are usually carried out instinctively and with minimal conscious thinking(Rasmussen,1983) . Rule-based errors include applying rules or operating procedures incorrectly, applying the wrong rules, or failing to apply the correct rules. Errors based on knowledge arise when someone lacks experience or expertise in a particular scenario, or when they fail to adapt their current knowledge to a novel circumstance. One of the most frequent causes of cybersecurity vulnerabilities is user error. These mistakes can be as basic as misconfiguring a security option or as complicated as using bad password management techniques or falling for phishing schemes. Studies reveal that almost 95% of cybersecurity breaches are the result of human error.

The 2013 Target data breach serves as one example, in which hackers used credentials they had stolen from a third-party HVAC provider to enter the retailer's network. Human error played a major role in this breach, which led to the theft of 40 million credit and debit card details. The vendor's inadequate security procedures and Target's tardiness in identifying and addressing the attack were two major contributing factors.

Insider Threats

Insider threats are a serious concern to cybersecurity, regardless of their motivation. Because insiders have access to private data and systems, their possible actions could be more harmful. Malicious actions like data theft, sabotage, or espionage by resentful workers or others with hidden agendas are examples of intentional threats.

Conversely, unintentional hazards occur when staff members unintentionally jeopardise security due to careless actions or straightforward errors.

The three primary requirements for crime, according to routine activity theory (Cohen, & Felson, 1979), are a motivated offender, an appropriate target (such as a project or the organisation as a whole), and the lack of a capable guardian. It's crucial to keep in mind that after any preliminary screening during recruitment, people can change. The 2017 Equifax hack, which made 147 million people's personal information public, emphasises the significance of insider threats. An unpatched vulnerability in the company's web application framework was largely blamed for this breach in this instance; this omission was probably the result of human error in maintaining and updating the programme.

Social Engineering

Cybercriminals continue to employ social engineering as a common technique to take advantage of the human factor in cybersecurity. Attackers use psychological manipulation, such as phishing emails, pretexting, or baiting, to trick people into disclosing private information or taking activities that jeopardise security. Strong incident response protocols, user awareness training, and technological controls must all be used to reduce the risks brought on by social engineering.

Decision-making can be hampered by exhaustion, burnout, and cognitive overload, which can also reduce the effectiveness of security measures. Prioritising employee well-being and providing sufficient resources and support are essential for organisations to avoid weariness and sustain peak performance. Furthermore, cultivating a culture of cooperation and information exchange helps strengthen cybersecurity teams' overall resistance to changing threats.

The human factor in cybersecurity extends beyond individual users and organizations to encompass broader societal issues. Cybersecurity policies and regulations must strike a delicate balance between protecting privacy and promoting security, ensuring that measures designed to enhance security do not infringe upon individual rights and freedoms. Moreover, addressing the root causes of cybercrime, such as economic inequality and geopolitical tensions, requires a multifaceted approach that goes beyond technical solutions.

Social engineering uses psychological tricks to coerce people into disclosing private information or taking activities that jeopardise security. Strategies like baiting, tailgating, phishing, and pretexting rely on human emotions like trust, fear, and curiosity. Participants in a poll attested to the fact that attack techniques are developing to become more complex and that the amount of security breaches aimed at individual and organisational data is still unchecked, (Rishi, 2020).

For instance, phishing is a common social engineering assault in which attackers send phoney emails pretending to be trustworthy organisations in an attempt to fool recipients into divulging personal information or clicking on harmful links. The 2020 Twitter hack, which let hackers to use popular accounts to spread a Bitcoin fraud, (Dell, 2017), was set up as a result of a phone spear-phishing campaign directed at Twitter staff members.

Organizational Culture And Security Practices

An entity's approach to and management of cybersecurity is greatly influenced by its organisational culture. Vulnerabilities can be decreased by fostering a culture that values security awareness and promotes preventative actions. On the other hand, dangers can be increased in a society that disregards security or gives it little priority.

Studies have indicated that companies with a robust security culture experience fewer data breaches. This is frequently accomplished by leadership that exemplifies best practices, frequent training, and clear communication of security standards.

Phishing Awareness

The weakest link in cybersecurity is frequently people. Attackers that use phishing techniques to deceive people into disclosing personal information rely on human weaknesses. Users can detect and thwart such attempts with the use of training programmes.

Security Education

The general security of the company can be improved by giving staff members regular education and training on cybersecurity best practices, new risks, and the value of safe behaviour.

Compliance Training

Ensuring that personnel comprehend and adhere to industry-specific standards is crucial in regulated businesses to prevent legal complications and preserve a secure atmosphere. For businesses in a variety of sectors, cybersecurity is a top priority. Technology has advanced, bringing with it many advantages as well as new risks and vulnerabilities. Because of this, businesses are starting to understand how important it is for staff to keep up cybersecurity defences.

Employee cybersecurity training is crucial because it gives people the information and abilities they need to recognise and counteract online threats. Consider your staff to be your first line of defence against dishonest people. Cybersecurity is an issue that affects the entire Employees play a more important role in cybersecurity than just adhering to procedures; they function as a human firewall, actively protecting critical information and systems by being informed, watchful, and proactive. The possibility of successful cyberattacks can be considerably decreased by promoting a cybersecurity culture.organisation, not just the IT division.

THE RISKS AND REPERCUSSIONS OF NOT PROVIDING EMPLOYEE CYBERSECURITY TRAINING

Ignoring cybersecurity training for employees can put firms at risk and have dire repercussions. An elevated susceptibility to cyberattacks is one of the main dangers associated with insufficient staff training. Employees who lack the necessary information and awareness may unintentionally click on phishing emails or download dangerous attachments.

Data breaches have long-lasting effects on an organization's reputation in addition to their immediate financial impact. Employee ignorance of security risks compromising client data, which undermines trust and harms the company's reputation. Regaining the trust of customers may be an arduous and frequently expensive task.

PSYCHOLOGICAL THEORIES RELEVANT TO CYBERSECURITY

It is crucial to investigate pertinent psychological theories in order to comprehend how human factors contribute to cybersecurity vulnerabilities. These theories shed light on the reasons behind people's actions and how they may unintentionally compromise security.

Cognitive Load Theory

According to the cognitive load theory, people's ability to process information is restricted. Errors become more likely when this capacity is exceeded. When it comes to cybersecurity, consumers frequently encounter convoluted security procedures, confusing interfaces, and an abundance of notifications, which can cause cognitive overload. This may lead to errors like incorrectly configuring settings, missing crucial security updates, or failing to detect phishing attempts.

Complex password restrictions that necessitate frequent changes and a variety of characters, for example, may overload users and result in the generation of weak passwords that are simple to guess or the reuse of passwords across several websites, both of which increase susceptibility.

Theory of Planned Behaviour

The Theory of Planned Behaviour (TPB) describes how people's intentions and behaviours are influenced by their attitudes, perceived behavioural control, and subjective norms. TPB can be applied to cybersecurity to comprehend why users may choose to take risks even when they are aware of the possible repercussions. Employees may put convenience ahead of security, for instance, if the culture of the company encourages taking shortcuts to save time. This could result in careless behaviour like circumventing security measures. The idea that security regulations are unimportant can be strengthened by an organization's inconsistent enforcement of them, which can further erode adherence to safe practices.

Prospect Theory

According to prospect theory, people frequently choose risk-averse or risk-seeking behaviours because they base their judgements more on the potential worth of losses and gains than on the actual result. This hypothesis in cybersecurity helps explain why people would take unwarranted risks, such clicking on dubious links, if they believe the possible benefit (like swiftly accessing a restricted website) outweighs the perceived risk (like the minimal chance of running into virus). By changing the perceived balance of potential advantages and losses, training and awareness programmes that highlight the real and immediate hazards of cyber attacks can help prevent such dangerous behaviour.

MITIGATING HUMAN FACTORS IN CYBERSECURITY

Human factors can be used to improve security even if they can greatly contribute to cybersecurity risks. A mix of organisational transformation, technology, training, and policy creation are used as risk-mitigation strategies.

Enhancing Security Awareness and Training

In order to mitigate the human aspects that lead to cybersecurity vulnerabilities, security awareness training is essential. Employees that participate in effective training programmes learn about safe online activities, the nature of cyber risks, and the significance of following security procedures. Training ought to be interactive and ongoing, highlighting the effects of cyberthreats through simulations and actual situations. For instance, phishing simulators can assist staff members in identifying and properly handling phishing attacks. Frequent revisions to training programmes guarantee that staff members are informed about new security procedures and developing dangers.

Implementing User-Friendly Security Solutions

User-friendliness should be considered while designing security systems in order to minimise cognitive strain and user mistake. Clear explanations, automatic updates, and simplified interfaces can all assist users in adhering to security procedures without feeling overburdened. For example, password management software can make it easier to remember complicated passwords by safely storing and automatically filling in login information. An extra degree of security can be offered by multifactor authentication (MFA) without requiring a major increase in user effort.

Fostering a Security-Conscious Organizational Culture

Leadership commitment, policy communication that is clear, and the integration of security into day-to-day operations are all necessary to foster a security-conscious organisational culture. It is imperative for leaders to exemplify sound security practices and underscore the significance of cybersecurity via consistent outreach and inducements. Policies that encourage secure behaviour can also be implemented by organisations. Some examples of these policies are regular security audits, incident response drills, and MFA requirements. Positive security culture can be strengthened even more by praising and rewarding staff members who follow security best practices.

Policy Development and Enforcement

In order to mitigate human issues, strong cybersecurity policies must be developed and enforced. Data security, incident response, and password management are just a few of the topics that should be covered by explicit, thorough, and enforced policies. Conducting routine audits and compliance checks guarantees adherence to policies and pinpoints opportunities for enhancement. A clear incident response plan can help minimise damage and speed up recovery in the case of a breach.

Leveraging Behavioural Analytics

Using behavioural analytics, users' conduct is tracked and analysed to look for patterns that can point to a security risk. Organisations can detect potential insider threats or compromised accounts by identifying deviations from baseline patterns of typical conduct. An anomaly can be set off for additional examination, for instance, if an employee who usually logs in from a certain place suddenly logs in from another nation. Because behavioural analytics may see possible dangers early, it can offer an extra layer of security.

CASE STUDIES IN HUMAN FACTORS AND CYBERSECURITY

Case Study 1: The 2017 WannaCry Ransomware Attack

Using a Microsoft Windows vulnerability, the WannaCry ransomware outbreak of 2017 infected over 200,000 systems in 150 countries. Numerous organisations failed to implement a fix that was available months prior to the attack, indicating human factors including carelessness and subpar patch management procedures (Dell, 2017). This instance shows how crucial it is to update software on schedule and how crucial organisational policies are to maintaining compliance. WannaCry's effects might have been lessened by automated patch management systems and training, which would have lessened the need for individual security maintenance.

Case Study 2: The 2013 Yahoo Data Breach

A data breach at Yahoo in 2013 resulted in the exposure of all 3 billion users' personal data. Weak security procedures, such as the use of antiquated encryption techniques and insufficient incident response mechanisms, contributed to the breach(Stempel, & Finkle, 2017). The example of Yahoo shows how leadership attitudes about security and organisational culture can lead to vulnerabilities. Regular audits and a greater focus on preventive security measures might have helped to find and fix the vulnerabilities that were exploited in the hack.

Case Study 3: The 2020 SolarWinds Supply Chain Attack

Malicious code was introduced into the company's software upgrades during the 2020 SolarWinds attack, which had an impact on a number of public and private institutions. This intricate supply chain assault took use of both technological and human elements, such as faith in software suppliers and a lack of due diligence on independent vendors(Yang *et al.,* 2022). The SolarWinds case emphasises the necessity of strict oversight and all-encompassing supply chain security procedures.

CONCLUSION

Understanding and minimising cybersecurity vulnerabilities depend heavily on human factors. Organisations can create training programmes and security protocols that are more effective by acknowledging the limitations and inclinations of human behaviour. This chapter seeks to clarify these important points and offer a road map for improving cybersecurity usi Consequently, human aspects are essential to the accomplishment of any cybersecurity project. Organisations can greatly improve their cybersecurity defences by comprehending human behaviour, offering efficient training, and fostering a security-aware culture.employing a human-centered approach.

Organisations may create more effective risk mitigation and digital asset protection strategies by comprehending the nuances of human behaviour. Integrating the human aspect into cybersecurity activities is crucial for defending against emerging threats in an increasingly digital world. This includes anything from improving awareness and fostering a culture of security consciousness to tackling insider threats and resisting social engineering tactics.

The main points and sections of the suggested book chapter are summarised in this conclusion, which also highlights the useful solutions that may be used to overcome the difficulties presented by the diverse effects of human factors on cybersecurity.

REFERENCES

legislation.gov.uk. (1990). Computer Misuse Act [online] Available at: http://www.legislatin.gov.uk/ukpga/1990/18/sectin/3ZA

Alsharif, M., Mishra, S., & AlShehri, M. (2022). Impact of Human Vulnerabilities on Cybersecurity. *Computer Systems Science and Engineering*, 40(3), 1153–1166. DOI: 10.32604/csse.2022.019938

Anonymous. (2020). Cybersecurity Risk Report for Businesses, Cybint Solutions, https://www.cybintsolutions.com/2020-cybersecurity-risk-report-for-businesses

Anonymous. (2021). IBM X-Force Threat Intelligence Index 2021 https://enterprise.verizon.com/resources/reports/2020-data-breach-investigations-report.pdf

Cohen, L. E., & Felson, M. (1979). Social change and crime rate trends: A routing activity approach. *American Sociological Review*, 44(4), 588–608. DOI: 10.2307/2094589

Contel, N. Y., & Schmick, P. J. (2016). Cybersecurity: Risks, Vulnerablities and countermeasures to prevent social engineering attacks. *International Journal of Advanced Computer Research*, 6(23), 31–38. DOI: 10.19101/IJACR.2016.623006

Dell, C. (2017). Today's Massive Ransomware Attack Was Mostly Preventable; Here's How To Avoid It. Gizmodo. https://www.gizmodo.com.au/2017/05/todays-massive-ransomware-attack-was-mostly-preventable-heres-how-to-avoid-it. Retrieved 13 May 2017.

Krombholz, H. H., Huber, M., & Weippl, E. (2015). Advanced social engineering attacks. *Journal of Information Security and Applications*, 22, 113–122. DOI: 10.1016/j.jisa.2014.09.005

Rasmussen, J. (1983). Skills, Rules, and Knowledge: Signals, Signs, and Symbols, and other Distinctions in Human Performance Models. *IEEE Transactions on Systems, Man, and Cybernetics*, 13(3), 257–266. DOI: 10.1109/TSMC.1983.6313160

Rishi, I.(2020). Twitter accounts of Joe Biden, Barack Obama, Elon Musk, Bill Gates, and others apparently hacked. CNN Business. Archived from the original on July 16, 2020. Retrieved July 15, 2020.

Stempel, J., & Finkle, J. (2017). *Yahoo Says All Three Billion Accounts Hacked in 2013*. Data Theft.

Upadhyay, D., & Sampalli, S. (2020). SCADA (Supervisory control and data acquisition) systems: Vulnerability assessment and security recommendations. *Computers & Security*, 89, 1–18. DOI: 10.1016/j.cose.2019.101666

Yang, J., Lee, Y., & McDonald, A. P. (2022). SolarWinds Software Supply Chain Security: Better Protection with Enforced Policies and Technologies. In Yang, J., Lee, Y., & McDonald, A. P. (Eds.), *Cyber.* Supply Chain Security. DOI: 10.1007/978-3-030-92317-4_4

Chapter 2
Understanding and Addressing Human Factors in Cybersecurity Vulnerabilities

Lingala Thirupathi
Sreenidhi Institute of Science and Technology, India

Vijaya Bhaskar Ch
Sreenidhi Institute of Science and Technology, India

B. Vasundara
Sreenidhi Institute of Science and Technology, India

Ravi Gugulothu
Sreenidhi Institute of Science and Technology, India

Dheeraj Sundaragiri
Sreenidhi Institute of Science and Technology, India

Radhika Pulyala
https://orcid.org/0000-0002-3991-098X
Sreenidhi Institute of Science and Technology, India

ABSTRACT

Addressing human factors in cybersecurity is essential due to the prevalent exploitation of human errors and behaviors by attackers. This approach involves continuous education and engaging training programs tailored to various roles, emphasizing interactive and personalized learning. Implementing strong security policies with clear guidelines and simplified procedures, backed by regular audits and enforcement, enhances compliance. Technological solutions such as automation, user-friendly security tools, and behavioral analytics play a critical role in reducing human errors and detecting anomalies. Cultivating a security-conscious culture, with leadership commitment and encouraging non-punitive incident reporting,

DOI: 10.4018/979-8-3693-9235-5.ch002

fosters proactive security practices. Limiting the attack surface through different principles minimizes vulnerabilities. Enhancing incident response capabilities ensures effective handling and mitigation of security breaches. This holistic approach integrates education, policy, technology, and culture to strengthen organizational resilience against cybersecurity threats.

I INTRODUCTION

Addressing human factors in cybersecurity has become increasingly imperative in today's digital landscape, where attackers frequently exploit vulnerabilities stemming from human errors and behaviors. This multifaceted approach involves implementing strategies that encompass continuous education and engaging training programs tailored to various organizational roles. By emphasizing interactive and personalized learning experiences, organizations can effectively empower their workforce to recognize and mitigate cyber risks proactively.

Central to this approach is the establishment of robust security policies characterized by clear guidelines and simplified procedures. Regular audits and stringent enforcement mechanisms serve to bolster compliance across the organization, ensuring that security measures remain robust and up-to-date in the face of evolving threats.

Technological innovations such as automation, user-friendly security tools, and advanced behavioral analytics are pivotal in mitigating human errors and swiftly detecting anomalous activities within networks and systems. These tools not only enhance operational efficiency but also contribute significantly to the overall security posture of the organization by preemptively identifying potential threats.

Cultivating a security-conscious culture is equally vital in fortifying defenses against cyber threats. Leadership commitment to cybersecurity initiatives and fostering an environment of trust and transparency are fundamental in promoting proactive security practices among employees. Encouraging non-punitive incident reporting ensures that potential security breaches are promptly addressed and remediated, minimizing their impact on organizational operations and reputation.

Limiting the attack surface through strategic principles and proactive measures is essential in reducing vulnerabilities that could be exploited by malicious actors. This involves adopting a layered security approach that encompasses network segmentation, least privilege access controls, and regular patch management to safeguard critical assets and data.

Furthermore, enhancing incident response capabilities is crucial for effectively managing and mitigating security breaches when they occur. Establishing clear protocols and response procedures, coupled with regular drills and simulations, ensures that the organization can swiftly contain threats and minimize their impact on business continuity.

Ultimately, a holistic approach that integrates education, stringent policy enforcement, cutting-edge technology, and a supportive organizational culture is paramount in strengthening resilience against the ever-evolving landscape of cybersecurity threats. By fostering a unified and proactive cybersecurity strategy, organizations can better safeguard their assets, maintain trust with stakeholders, and navigate the complexities of the digital age with confidence.

II LITERATURE REVIEW

Cybersecurity vulnerabilities often stem from human factors, ranging from social dynamics to cognitive biases. Understanding and addressing these human elements is crucial in devising effective cybersecurity strategies.

(Emmanuel et al., 2024)In the realm of cybersecurity, businesses often prioritize technological solutions while overlooking human factors. Despite robust firewalls and encryption, human error and behaviour can still expose vulnerabilities. This paper explores the critical role of human factors in cybersecurity, encompassing user behaviours, training, and awareness. Understanding these aspects is crucial for enhancing defences against digital threats. By addressing human vulnerabilities through comprehensive training programs and awareness initiatives, organizations can significantly bolster their cybersecurity posture. Changing behaviours and fostering a culture of vigilance among employees are essential steps towards a safer digital environment. Ultimately, integrating human-centric approaches alongside technical measures is paramount for mitigating risks effectively and ensuring a resilient defence against evolving cyber threats.

(William et al., 2022) This article identifies human factors within workplaces that pose challenges for cybersecurity leadership in organizations. It discusses strategic communication, human-computer interaction, organizational factors, social environments, and security awareness training. Cybersecurity extends beyond IT systems to encompass how humans interact with information systems, potentially leading to vulnerabilities. As cyber leaders recognize human behaviors and processes and coleffectively; actively, organizational strategies can significantly improve. Human error, whether due to inaccurate strategic implementations or insufficient plan execution, remains a critical issue. A systematic literature review underscores human fallibility as a weak point in securing data transmission, exacerbated by complacency and unintentional behaviors stemming from leaders' and employees' ignorance. Thus, cybersecurity efforts emphasize education, awareness, and communication. The study advocates for interdisciplinary research to further understand

and mitigate these human-centric cybersecurity risks, proposing a comprehensive research agenda. This approach offers a novel perspective by highlighting the role of human factors in cybersecurity incidents and prevention.

(Wang Shuo et al., 2018) The paper addresses inefficiencies in warehouse delivery by integrating theoretical analysis and mathematical modeling with extensive data collection from single-storehouse operations. Qualitative and quantitative analyses are based on real operational data, culminating in a discriminant model for outbound mode selection using EIQ analysis. Verification results demonstrate that the model achieves outbound time difference errors of less than ±25 seconds, confirming its practicality and reliability in decision-making for warehouse outbound strategies and batch order selection. Ultimately, the study yields an optimized scheme for warehouse outbound operations, significantly enhancing overall efficiency in warehouse management and logistics.

(Alessandro et al., 2021) This paper challenges the prevalent technology-centric approach to Computer and Information Security (CIS), which often neglects the human elements within sociotechnical systems, viewing them as weak links without considering cognitive characteristics, needs, and motivations of end users. It advocates for a holistic Human Factors (HF) approach, demonstrated in pilot healthcare organizations, to highlight how HF vulnerabilities impact cybersecurity risks. The methodology integrates top-down and bottom-up approaches using qualitative and quantitative research methods to assess organizational readiness against cyber threats. Emphasizing a user-centered perspective involving management and employees, the study reveals that a strong cybersecurity culture doesn't always translate into rule-compliant behavior and identifies conflicts within cybersecurity protocols that exacerbate human vulnerabilities. The paper concludes that integrating HF principles into CIS systems can enhance cybersecurity through non-technical measures like user awareness, providing a comprehensive strategy for managing cyber risks in organizations.

(Esmeralda et al., 2021) In the mobile and digital era, technological advancements have greatly enhanced information dissemination, education, remote work, and monitoring capabilities. However, these systems also pose significant risks of breaches at both individual and organizational levels, as cyber threats continuously evolve. This article underscores the critical role of human factors in cybersecurity. Initially, it provides a concise overview of the topic's relevance, emphasizing the growing importance of understanding human behavior in securing digital assets. It then identifies common cybersecurity risks and their wide-ranging impacts. The third section delves into the specific vulnerabilities introduced by human factors and discusses behavioral approaches to mitigate these risks. Conclusions drawn highlight the necessity for integrating behavioral science theories to deepen insights into human behavior's influence on cybersecurity. Future research aims to further explore these theories, enhancing strategies for effectively managing and reducing cyber threats in an increasingly interconnected world.

(Maher et al., 2021) Security challenges in computer networks are exacerbated by evolving cyber-attacks, including viruses, internet vulnerabilities, communications breaches, and hacking. The proliferation of Internet of Things (IoT) devices enhances efficiency in government and business operations but also escalates risks such as password breaches and social engineering. Human factors significantly contribute to cybersecurity vulnerabilities, with over 39% of risks and 95% of successful attacks stemming from human error, notably insider threats. A critical issue is the widespread lack of user awareness regarding cyber threats. This study focuses on mitigating risks through understanding human behavior and responses to cybersecurity incidents. Findings reveal widespread ignorance among participants regarding cybersecurity threats and protective measures. Lack of awareness about phishing, password attacks, and social engineering highlights urgent needs for comprehensive education and training programs. Addressing these gaps is crucial for improving cybersecurity resilience across organizations and individuals.

(Umair Shah et al., 2023) This paper provides an extensive overview of cybersecurity awareness in the young, educated, and technology-savvy population of the United Arab Emirates (UAE), compared to the United States ofAmerica (USA) for advancing the scholarship and practice of global cyber governance. They conducted comparative empirical studies to identify differences in specific human factors that affect cybersecurity behaviour in the UAE and the USA. In addition, they employed several control variables to observe reliable results. They used Hofstede's theoretical framework on culture to advance our investigation. The results show that the targeted population in the UAE exhibits contrasting interpretations of cybersecurity awareness of critical human factors as compared to their counterparts from the USA. They identify possible explanation sfor this relatively different behaviour in the UAE population. Our key contributions are to provide valuable information for cybersecurity policymakers in the UAE and Gulf Cooperation Council (GCC) region tofurther enhance cyber safety, governance, awareness, and trust among citizens.

(Ani et al., 2019) In the evolving landscape of industrial cybersecurity, human factors play a pivotal role as primary vectors for cyber-attacks. Efforts must prioritize human-centered security strategies to effectively mitigate these threats. The knowledge and skills of the industrial workforce in cybersecurity are critical for creating a resilient and compliant environment. Historical data highlight that successful compromises in industrial control systems exploit security weaknesses among personnel, particularly those lacking adequate cybersecurity aptitude. Securing industrial domains and networks now demands collective responsibility across all workforce levels, not solely cybersecurity professionals. Non-security-specialized personnel in industrial operations must acquire substantial knowledge and skills in adopting appropriate security behaviors and responses, given their heightened vulnerability as targets. Strengthening cybersecurity awareness and capabilities among all industrial personnel is essential to bolstering defenses against ongoing and emerging cyber threats in operational environments.

(Mahesh et al., 2022) This investigation aims to explore cyber infrastructure attacks, threats, and vulnerabilities across hardware, software systems, networks, intranets, and cyber intrusions. It emphasizes the significance of governance in combating network invasions and cyber-theft, while delving into the rapid expansion of cybercrime. The paper defines cyber security and its pivotal role in preventing community infiltration and cyber theft, examining the factors contributing to the surge in cybercrime and their consequences. Practical preventative measures and remedies against cyber security threats are also discussed. Despite the importance of technological expertise in mitigating cyberattacks, the paper asserts that human behavior and psychological tendencies are crucial vulnerabilities. Organizational education programs are proposed as crucial investments to address these psychological vulnerabilities and enhance resilience against cyber threats.

(Andrew et al., 2019) This paper applies the System-Theoretic Accident Models and Processes (STAMP) technique to analyze the 2013/2014 Target Corporation data breach, aiming to uncover causal factors through a systemic approach and demonstrate its value in information security. The study identifies several critical control flaws: insufficient external and internal communication and coordination regarding new threats and vulnerabilities, inadequate organizational learning from past incidents, a deficiency in proactive security management to leverage successes and failures, and ineffective coordination within the supply chain. These findings underscore the importance of systemic analyses like STAMP in understanding and addressing human and organizational factors that contribute to information security vulnerabilities, highlighting areas where improvements in communication, learning, proactive management, and supply chain coordination can enhance overall cybersecurity resilience.

(Maalem et al., 2020) Cyberattacks have become alarmingly routine, with perpetrators employing increasingly sophisticated methods to exploit networks. Cybercriminals capitalize on online anonymity, operating lucrative business models with impunity. This dire situation necessitates a paradigm shift in current defensive strategies. Given that human factors contribute significantly to cyber incidents, expanding research into overlooked areas such as behavioral aspects of cybersecurity are crucial. Emphasizing social and behavioral issues is now paramount for improving cybersecurity defenses. This paper reviews pertinent theories and principles while proposing an interdisciplinary framework that integrates behavioral cybersecurity, human factors, and modeling and simulation. By focusing on these aspects, the paper seeks to enhance understanding and develop more effective strategies to mitigate cyber threats in today's interconnected digital environments.

(Bruce et al., 2016) Today, cybersecurity initiatives predominantly center around deploying and managing technologies that govern cyberspace operations. Government and commercial sectors invest heavily in cybersecurity technologies such as firewalls and intrusion prevention systems. However, this exclusive emphasis on technological solutions overlooks a critical component of any system: human users. While technology is pivotal, neglecting human factors can result in significant vulnerabilities. Therefore, there is a pressing need to adopt a more comprehensive cybersecurity education strategy that bridges the gap between technology-centric approaches and human behaviors. This approach acknowledges that effective cybersecurity requires not only robust technological defenses but also an understanding of human behaviors and vulnerabilities. Integrating human-centered approaches into cybersecurity education can better safeguard systems against evolving cyber threats in both government and commercial sectors.

(Mitchell et al., 2015) proposed and analyzed a behavior-rule specification-based technique for intruding detection in medical devices embedded within a Medical Cyber Physical System (MCPS), prioritizing patient safety. Our methodology involves transforming behavior rules into state machines, enabling straightforward monitoring of device behavior against the transformed state machine to detect deviations from specifications. Using vital sign monitors as a case study, they illustrate that our intrusion detection technique effectively balances minimizing false positives while ensuring high detection probability, essential for countering sophisticated and covert attackers in ultra-safe MCPS applications. Furthermore, through comparative analysis, they demonstrate that our behavior-rule specification-based Intrusion Detection System (IDS) outperforms two existing anomaly-based techniques in identifying abnormal patient behaviors within pervasive healthcare settings. This approach enhances the security and reliability of MCPS by focusing on behavior rules tailored to medical device operations, thereby safeguarding critical healthcare environments more effectively.

(Cohen et al., 1990) addressed unique modeling and simulation challenges in information protection, followed by an explanation of our chosen model and simulation methodology. Results from individual simulations and several thousand runs within specific attack scenarios, both with and without defenses, are presented. Explored parallel simulation issues and showcase outcomes from large-scale simulations utilizing numerous processors, examining various parameters. Findings include insights into how detection and reaction times impact success rates, the influence of defender capabilities on outcomes, non-linear relationships between strength and time, and the efficacy of defensive measures under different threat profiles. analyzed costs, providing expected loss and cost outcomes, and evaluate the impact of strategies on results. They reviewed metric limitations, sensitivity to parameter variations, and briefly discuss result validation, emphasizing comprehensive exploration of simulation outcomes in the realm of information protection.

III METHODOLOGY

1. **To Enhance Organizational Preparedness**: To enhance organizational preparedness against cybersecurity threats through continuous education and tailored training programs. By prioritizing interactive and personalized learning experiences, organizations aim to empower their workforce to recognize and mitigate cyber risks effectively. This objective focuses on building a proactive security mindset among employees and equipping them with the necessary skills to uphold robust security practices.

Interactive and Personalized Learning Experiences: Organizations prioritize interactive and personalized learning to cater to different roles and levels of expertise within the workforce. This approach includes simulations, scenario-based training, and hands-on workshops that simulate real-world cyber threats and incidents. By engaging employees directly in these experiences, organizations can effectively demonstrate the consequences of security lapses and reinforce best practices.

Technical Skill Development: The training programs focus on developing technical skills relevant to cybersecurity, such as understanding common attack vectors (e.g., phishing, malware), secure coding practices, network security fundamentals, and incident response protocols. Technical personnel may receive advanced training in areas like penetration testing, vulnerability assessment, and secure configuration management to bolster defensive capabilities.

Awareness of Emerging Threats and Trends: Continuous education ensures that employees remain updated on emerging cybersecurity threats, trends, and regulatory changes. This includes providing regular updates on new attack techniques, vulnerabilities in commonly used software and systems, and evolving compliance requirements (e.g., GDPR, CCPA). By staying informed, employees can adapt their practices to mitigate new risks effectively.

Promoting a Proactive Security Mindset: Beyond technical skills, the training programs aim to instill a proactive security mindset among employees. This involves fostering a culture where cybersecurity is seen as everyone's responsibility, from the CEO to the front-line staff. Training emphasizes the importance of vigilance, prompt reporting of suspicious activities, and adherence to security policies and procedures.

Measuring Effectiveness and Continuous Improvement: Effective training programs include mechanisms for measuring their impact on organizational preparedness. This may involve conducting pre and post-training assessments to gauge knowledge retention and behavior change. Feedback loops from employees and incident reports also provide insights into areas needing improvement, allowing organizations to refine their training content and delivery methods continuously.

Integration with Incident Response Planning: Training efforts are closely integrated with incident response planning. Employees are educated on their roles and responsibilities during a security incident, ensuring a coordinated response that minimizes downtime and mitigates damages. This integration reinforces the practical application of cybersecurity knowledge gained through training.

Enhancing organizational preparedness through continuous education and tailored training programs involves not only imparting technical knowledge but also cultivating a proactive security culture and readiness to respond effectively to cyber threats. By investing in these initiatives, organizations can significantly strengthen their resilience against cybersecurity risks and empower their workforce to protect critical assets and data proactively.

Developing a structured algorithm for enhancing organizational preparedness against cybersecurity threats through continuous education and tailored training programs involves several key steps and considerations. Below is an outline of an algorithmic approach:

Algorithm: Enhancing Organizational Preparedness through Cybersecurity Training

1. Assess Organizational Needs and Risks

    Identify critical assets, sensitive data, and potential cybersecurity risks specific to the organization.

    Conduct a gap analysis to determine current cybersecurity knowledge and skill levels across different roles and departments.

2. Define Training Objectives and Goals

    Establish clear objectives for cybersecurity training, aligned with organizational goals and compliance requirements.

    Define specific learning outcomes for different employee roles, considering technical skills, awareness, and incident response readiness.

3. Design Tailored Training Programs

    Develop customized training modules based on assessed needs and objectives.

    Incorporate interactive and personalized learning experiences

    Simulation Exercises: Create simulated cyber-attack scenarios (e.g., phishing, ransomware) to test employee responses.

    Hands-on Workshops: Provide practical exercises in secure coding, network security, and incident response.

Scenario-Based Learning: Present realistic scenarios to demonstrate consequences of security lapses and best practices.

4. Select Delivery Methods and Tools

    Choose appropriate delivery methods based on workforce demographics, accessibility, and preferred learning styles (e.g., online courses, in-person workshops, blended learning).

    Utilize learning management systems (LMS) or training platforms to track progress, assessments, and certification.

5. Implement Training Across Organization

    Roll out training programs in phases or cohorts to manage workload and ensure effective participation.

    Schedule regular sessions and make training sessions mandatory for all employees, adjusting timing to minimize operational disruptions.

6. Promote a Proactive Security Culture

    Emphasize the importance of cybersecurity as everyone's responsibility from leadership to front line staff.

    Encourage reporting of suspicious activities and adherence to security policies through interactive training modules and real-world examples.

7. Measure Effectiveness and Continuous Improvement

    Conduct pre and post-training assessments to evaluate knowledge retention and behavior change.

    Solicit feedback from participants to identify strengths and areas for improvement in training content and delivery.

    Adjust training programs based on assessment results and emerging cybersecurity threats.

8. Integrate Training with Incident Response Planning

    Ensure training content includes incident response protocols and procedures.

    Conduct drills and simulations to practice incident response scenarios, involving employees in realistic exercises to reinforce learning.

9. Monitor and Maintain Training Efforts

    Establish a schedule for ongoing cybersecurity training and updates to keep employees informed of new threats and best practices.

    Regularly review and update training materials to reflect changes in technology, regulations, and organizational needs.

10. Evaluate Return on Investment (ROI)

    Assess the impact of training on reducing cybersecurity incidents, improving response times, and enhancing overall organizational resilience.

    Compare costs associated with training against potential losses from cyber incidents to demonstrate ROI.

2. **To Strengthen Policy Framework and Compliance**: It involves strengthening the organization's policy framework and enhancing compliance through the implementation of strong security policies with clear guidelines and simplified procedures. Regular audits and stringent enforcement mechanisms ensure that these policies remain effective and aligned with evolving cyber threats. This objective aims to establish a secure operational environment by minimizing vulnerabilities and maintaining regulatory adherence.

Developing Strong Security Policies

Policy Creation: Begin by defining comprehensive security policies that cover all aspects of cybersecurity relevant to the organization. This includes policies on data protection, access control, incident response, network security, and acceptable use of technology resources.

Clear Guidelines: Ensure that each policy is accompanied by clear guidelines and procedures that specify how employees should adhere to the policy requirements in their daily activities. This clarity helps in eliminating ambiguity and ensures consistent application across the organization.

Simplified Procedures

User-Friendly Documentation: Simplify policy documents and procedures to make them easily understandable for all employees, regardless of their technical expertise. Use plain language and avoid excessive jargon to facilitate comprehension and compliance.

Training Integration: Integrate policy awareness and compliance training into the overall cybersecurity training programs. Ensure that employees understand the policies and know how to apply them in their respective roles.

Regular Audits and Assessments

Scheduled Audits: Conduct regular audits of security policies, procedures, and controls to evaluate their effectiveness and identify any gaps or areas needing improvement. Audits should be conducted at predefined intervals (e.g., annually, or bi-annually) or triggered by significant organizational changes.

Compliance Checks: Perform compliance checks against industry standards (e.g., ISO 27001, NIST Cybersecurity Framework) and regulatory requirements (e.g., GDPR, HIPAA) to ensure that policies align with current best practices and legal obligations.

Stringent Enforcement Mechanisms

Policy Enforcement: Implement robust enforcement mechanisms to ensure adherence to security policies throughout the organization. This may include disciplinary actions for non-compliance and incentives for proactive adherence.

Monitoring and Reporting: Utilize monitoring tools and systems to track policy compliance and detect deviations or violations promptly. Establish reporting channels for employees to report potential policy breaches or security incidents without fear of reprisal.

Aligning with Evolving Threat Landscape

Continuous Improvement: Regularly review and update security policies in response to emerging threats, technological advancements, and changes in regulatory requirements. Ensure that policies remain relevant and effective in mitigating new and evolving cyber risks.

Incident Learning: Incorporate insights from security incidents and audits into policy updates to address weaknesses and enhance resilience against similar incidents in the future.

Minimizing Vulnerabilities and Regulatory Adherence

Risk Mitigation: The ultimate goal of this objective is to minimize vulnerabilities by establishing proactive measures outlined in policies. This includes enforcing access controls, data encryption standards, and secure coding practices to protect sensitive information.

Regulatory Compliance: Ensure that security policies adhere to relevant laws, regulations, and industry standards. This not only helps in avoiding legal penalties but also enhances trust with customers and partners by demonstrating commitment to protecting their data and privacy.

Here's an algorithmic approach for strengthening an organization's policy framework and enhancing compliance through the implementation of strong security policies:

Algorithm: Strengthening Security Policies and Enhancing Compliance

1. Assessment of Current Policies and Compliance Needs

Objective: Evaluate existing security policies, procedures, and compliance status.
Steps:
Identify all current security policies and associated procedures.

Conduct a gap analysis to determine areas where policies may be lacking or outdated.

Assess compliance with relevant regulations and industry standards (e.g., GDPR, HIPAA, ISO 27001).

2. Policy Development and Enhancement

Objective: Develop and refine security policies to establish a robust framework.

Steps:

Define comprehensive security policies covering data protection, access control, incident response, etc.

Ensure policies include clear guidelines and procedures for implementation.

Simplify policy documentation to enhance readability and understanding among employees.

3. Integration with Training and Awareness Programs

Objective: Educate employees on security policies and promote compliance.

Steps:

Integrate policy awareness into cybersecurity training programs.

Provide regular updates and refresher courses on policy changes and new regulations.

Use interactive training methods to reinforce understanding and practical application of policies.

4. Implementation of Regular Audits and Assessments

Objective: Ensure ongoing adherence to security policies and identify areas for improvement.

Steps:

Schedule regular audits of security policies, procedures, and controls.

Conduct compliance checks against industry standards and regulatory requirements.

Use audit findings to identify gaps and prioritize improvements.

5. Enforcement Mechanisms

Objective: Establish mechanisms to enforce policy adherence throughout the organization.

Steps:

Implement disciplinary actions for policy violations.
Provide incentives for proactive compliance.
Monitor and track compliance through automated tools and reporting systems.

6. Continuous Improvement and Adaptation

Objective: Evolve policies in response to changing threats and regulatory landscape.
Steps:
Regularly review and update security policies based on audit findings and incident leanings.
Incorporate emerging cybersecurity threats and technological advancements into policy updates.
Ensure policies remain aligned with organizational goals and industry best practices.

7. Documentation and Reporting

Objective: Maintain accurate records of policy implementation and compliance efforts.
Steps:
Document all changes to policies and procedures.
Generate reports on compliance status and audit outcomes for stakeholders.
Ensure transparency and accountability in policy management and enforcement.

8. Monitoring and Feedback Loop

Objective: Monitor the effectiveness of policies and adjust as needed.
Steps:
Monitor key metrics related to policy adherence and security incidents.
Solicit feedback from employees on policy effectiveness and clarity.
Use data-driven insights to continuously improve policy frameworks and compliance efforts.

3. TO OPTIMIZE TECHNOLOGICAL DEFENSES AND INCIDENT RESPONSE

This includes leveraging automation, user-friendly security tools, and advanced behavioral analytics to reduce human errors and swiftly detect anomalies. Enhancing incident response protocols ensures the organization can effectively handle and mitigate security breaches, thereby minimizing potential damages and disruptions. This objective focuses on leveraging technological advancements to fortify the organization's resilience against cyber threats and ensure a swift and coordinated response to incidents.

3.1 Advanced Threat Detection and Prevention

Objective: Implement proactive measures to detect and prevent cyber threats before they cause harm.

Techniques:

Behavioral Analytics: Utilize advanced analytics to monitor user and system behavior for anomalous activities that may indicate a security breach.

Machine Learning and AI: Deploy machine learning algorithms to analyze vast amounts of data and identify patterns indicative of potential threats.

Threat Intelligence: Integrate threat intelligence feeds to stay updated on current threats and apply this knowledge to enhance defensive strategies.

3.2 Automation and Orchestration

Objective: Streamline and automate security processes to improve response times and efficiency.

Techniques:

Security Orchestration, Automation, and Response (SOAR): Implement SOAR platforms to automate incident response workflows, including threat detection, investigation, and remediation.

Automated Vulnerability Management: Utilize automated tools to scan and prioritize vulnerabilities across IT assets, ensuring timely patching and mitigation.

3.3 User-Friendly Security Tools

Objective: Provide intuitive tools that enhance user experience while maintaining robust security measures.

Techniques:

Single Sign-On (SSO) and Multi-Factor Authentication (MFA): Implement user-friendly authentication methods to secure access to systems and applications without compromising usability.

Secure Email Gateways: Deploy solutions that detect and block phishing attempts and malicious attachments, reducing the risk of successful email-based attacks.

Endpoint Detection and Response (EDR): Utilize EDR solutions to monitor endpoint activities in real-time and respond swiftly to suspicious behavior or threats.

3.4. Continuous Monitoring and Incident Response

Objective: Maintain real-time visibility into IT infrastructure to detect and respond to security incidents promptly.

Techniques:

Security Information and Event Management (SIEM): Implement SIEM solutions to aggregate and analyze security event data from across the organization, enabling proactive threat detection and incident response.

Incident Response Playbooks: Develop and regularly update incident response playbooks that outline predefined steps and procedures for different types of security incidents.

Threat Hunting: Proactively search for signs of advanced threats within the network using specialized tools and techniques to identify and mitigate potential risks before they escalate.

3.5. Integration and Collaboration

Objective: Foster collaboration between security teams and other departments to strengthen overall cybersecurity posture.

Techniques:

Cross-Functional Training: Provide cybersecurity awareness training to employees across all departments to promote a culture of security and ensure everyone understands their role in incident response.

Integration with IT Operations: Integrate security tools and processes with IT operations to facilitate rapid deployment of security patches and updates.

Collaboration Tools: Use collaboration platforms to facilitate communication and coordination during security incidents, ensuring swift resolution and minimal impact on operations.

3.6. Scalability and Resilience

Objective: Ensure that technological defenses and incident response capabilities can scale with organizational growth and evolving cyber threats.

Techniques:

Cloud Security: Implement robust cloud security measures, such as cloud access security brokers (CASBs) and encryption, to protect data and applications hosted in cloud environments.

Scalable Infrastructure: Design and deploy IT infrastructure that supports scalability and resilience, allowing for rapid expansion or contraction of security resources as needed.

Redundancy and Disaster Recovery: Maintain redundant systems and disaster recovery plans to ensure business continuity in the event of a security incident or breach.

By leveraging advanced technologies, automation, user-friendly tools, continuous monitoring, and collaborative practices, organizations can optimize their technological defenses and incident response capabilities. This proactive approach not only strengthens defenses against cyber threats but also enhances the organization's overall resilience and ability to mitigate potential impacts of security incidents effectively.

IV CASE STUDIES

In the digital age, cybersecurity vulnerabilities have become a pressing concern for organizations and individuals alike. While technological advancements have bolstered defenses against cyber threats, human factors remain a significant and often overlooked aspect of cybersecurity vulnerabilities. This paper explores case studies that illustrate the importance of understanding and addressing human factors in cybersecurity, ranging from phishing attacks to insider threats.

1. The Target Data Breach

In 2013, Target Corporation, a retail giant, experienced one of the most significant data breaches in history, compromising the personal and financial information of millions of customers. The breach was initiated through a phishing attack on a third-party HVAC contractor, exploiting human factors such as lack of cybersecurity awareness and susceptibility to social engineering. The attacker sent a malicious email containing malware to the contractor, which allowed them to gain access to Target's network. This incident underscored the importance of comprehensive cybersecurity training for employees and third-party vendors to mitigate the risk of similar attacks.

2. The Equifax Breach

In 2017, Equifax, one of the largest credit reporting agencies, suffered a devastating data breach that exposed sensitive personal information, including Social Security numbers, of over 147 million individuals. The breach was attributed to the company's failure to patch a known vulnerability in its systems, highlighting the human factor of neglecting security protocols and best practices. Despite being aware of the vulnerability months before the breach, Equifax failed to take appropriate action, allowing cybercriminals to exploit the flaw and exfiltrate vast amounts of data. This case emphasizes the importance of proactive vulnerability management and regular security updates to prevent cybersecurity incidents.

3. Business Email Compromise (BEC) Scams

Business Email Compromise (BEC) scams have become increasingly prevalent in recent years, targeting organizations across industries. These attacks involve cybercriminals impersonating company executives or employees to trick employees into transferring funds or sensitive information. BEC scams exploit human factors such as trust in email communication and authority figures, as well as the desire to comply with requests from higher-ups. Various organizations have fallen victim to BEC scams, resulting in significant financial losses and reputational damage. Mitigating these vulnerabilities requires robust email security protocols, user training on identifying phishing attempts, and implementing verification processes for financial transactions.

4. Insider Threats at Snowden and Manning

Edward Snowden and Chelsea Manning are notable examples of insider threats who leaked classified information from government agencies, highlighting the human factor of insider risks in cybersecurity. Snowden, a former contractor for the National Security Agency (NSA), leaked classified documents revealing the agency's mass surveillance programs. Manning, a former Army intelligence analyst, leaked hundreds of thousands of classified documents to WikiLeaks. These incidents demonstrated the potential damage caused by individuals with authorized access to sensitive data who exploit their privileges for malicious purposes. Addressing insider threats requires a combination of technical controls, such as access monitoring and data loss prevention systems, as well as employee monitoring, training, and fostering a culture of security and trust within organizations.

5. Ransomware Attacks on Healthcare Organizations

Healthcare organizations have become prime targets for ransomware attacks, which often exploit human factors such as staff members clicking on malicious links or downloading infected attachments. These attacks can disrupt critical healthcare services, compromise patient data privacy, and pose significant risks to patient safety. In 2017, the WannaCry ransomware attack impacted healthcare organizations worldwide, encrypting patient records and demanding ransom payments for their release. Similarly, in 2020, the Ryuk ransomware attack targeted Universal Health Services (UHS), a major hospital chain in the United States, disrupting operations across its network. Mitigating ransomware vulnerabilities in healthcare requires robust cybersecurity training for employees, regular security assessments, network segmentation, and implementing effective backup and recovery procedures.

These case studies highlight the diverse ways in which human factors contribute to cybersecurity vulnerabilities, ranging from phishing attacks to insider threats and ransomware attacks. Understanding and addressing these factors are essential for organizations and individuals to effectively mitigate the risks posed by cyber threats. By implementing comprehensive cybersecurity training programs, strengthening security protocols, and fostering a culture of security awareness, organizations can better protect themselves against cyber-attacks and safeguard sensitive information from unauthorized access or disclosure.

V CHALLENGES

Understanding and addressing human factors in cybersecurity vulnerabilities present several challenges:

1. Complexity of Human Behavior

Human behavior is complex and often unpredictable, making it challenging to anticipate and mitigate cybersecurity vulnerabilities effectively. Individuals may exhibit varying levels of cybersecurity awareness, susceptibility to social engineering, and adherence to security protocols, making it difficult to implement one-size-fits-all solutions.

2. Lack of Cybersecurity Awareness

Many individuals lack basic cybersecurity awareness and education, leading to behaviors that increase the risk of cyber threats. Addressing this challenge requires comprehensive training programs and awareness campaigns to educate users about common threats, best practices, and the importance of cybersecurity hygiene.

3. Social Engineering Tactics

Cybercriminals increasingly employ sophisticated social engineering tactics to manipulate human behavior and exploit vulnerabilities. Phishing emails, pretexting, and baiting are just a few examples of social engineering techniques used to deceive individuals into disclosing sensitive information or performing unauthorized actions.

4. Insider Threats

Insider threats pose a significant challenge to cybersecurity, as individuals with authorized access to systems and data may intentionally or inadvertently compromise security. Detecting and mitigating insider threats require a delicate balance between protecting sensitive information and respecting employees' privacy and trust.

5. Technological Limitations

While technology plays a crucial role in cybersecurity, it also has limitations in addressing human factors. Technical solutions such as antivirus software and firewalls cannot fully protect against vulnerabilities stemming from human error or manipulation. Integrating behavioural analytics and user-centric design principles into cybersecurity tools can help bridge this gap.

6. Resistance to Change

Changing human behaviour and organizational culture is often met with resistance, particularly in environments where cybersecurity is perceived as an inconvenience or hindrance to productivity. Overcoming resistance to change requires effective communication, leadership support, and incentivizing security-conscious behaviour.

7. Privacy Concerns

Balancing cybersecurity measures with individuals' privacy rights is a persistent challenge. Monitoring user behaviour and implementing security controls may encroach on privacy rights and erode trust within organizations. Striking the right balance between security and privacy requires careful consideration of legal, ethical, and regulatory frameworks.

8. Resource Constraints

Many organizations face resource constraints, including limited budgets, personnel, and expertise, which can impede efforts to address human factors in cybersecurity vulnerabilities. Investing in cybersecurity training, technology, and personnel is essential but may not always be feasible for smaller organizations or those operating in resource-constrained environments.

9. Evolution of Threat Landscape

The cybersecurity threat landscape is constantly evolving, with cybercriminals developing new tactics and techniques to exploit human vulnerabilities. Staying ahead of emerging threats requires continuous monitoring, threat intelligence sharing, and adapting cybersecurity strategies to mitigate evolving risks.

10. Global Nature of Cyber Threats

Cyber threats transcend geographical boundaries, posing challenges for international cooperation and coordination in addressing human factors in cybersecurity vulnerabilities. Achieving a unified approach to cybersecurity requires collaboration among governments, industry stakeholders, and international organizations to share information, resources, and best practices effectively.

Addressing these challenges requires a multi-faceted approach that encompasses technological, organizational, and human-centric strategies to mitigate cybersecurity vulnerabilities effectively. By recognizing the complexities of human behaviour and adopting proactive measures to address them, organizations can strengthen their cybersecurity defenses and better protect against cyber threats.

VI RISKS

1. Overreliance on Technology

Focusing solely on technological solutions may lead to an underestimation of the role of human factors in cybersecurity vulnerabilities. Relying too heavily on technology can create a false sense of security and overlook the importance of addressing human behavior and psychology in mitigating cyber risks.

2. Inadequate Training and Education

Insufficient training and education programs may fail to effectively address human factors in cybersecurity vulnerabilities. Without proper awareness and understanding of cyber threats, individuals may continue to engage in risky behaviors, such as clicking on suspicious links or sharing sensitive information, leaving organizations vulnerable to attacks.

3. Complacency and Overconfidence

Successfully addressing human factors in cybersecurity vulnerabilities may lead to complacency and overconfidence within organizations. Believing that human vulnerabilities have been adequately addressed may result in neglecting ongoing training, awareness campaigns, and security measures, leaving organizations susceptible to emerging threats.

4. Privacy and Ethical Concerns

Monitoring and analyzing human behavior for cybersecurity purposes raise privacy and ethical concerns. Intrusive monitoring practices may infringe on individuals' privacy rights and erode trust within organizations. Striking the right balance between security and privacy is essential to avoid unintended consequences and maintain ethical standards.

5. Resistance to Change

Addressing human factors in cybersecurity vulnerabilities often requires cultural and organizational changes, which may encounter resistance from employees, stakeholders, and leadership. Resistance to change can hinder the adoption of new security measures, impeding efforts to strengthen cybersecurity defenses and leaving organizations vulnerable to attacks.

6. Insider Threats and Misuse of Information

Implementing measures to address human factors in cybersecurity vulnerabilities may inadvertently increase the risk of insider threats or misuse of information. Employees with malicious intent or disgruntled individuals may exploit access to sensitive data or circumvent security controls, posing significant risks to organizations' security and integrity.

7. False Positives and Misinterpretation

Behavioral analytics and monitoring tools used to detect human factors in cybersecurity vulnerabilities may generate false positives or misinterpret normal behavior as suspicious. False alarms can overwhelm security teams and lead to fatigue, resulting in legitimate threats being overlooked or ignored, thereby undermining the effectiveness of security measures.

8.Regulatory and Legal Compliance

Implementing measures to address human factors in cybersecurity vulnerabilities must align with regulatory requirements and legal frameworks governing data protection and privacy. Non-compliance with regulations such as GDPR, HIPAA, or CCPA can result in legal liabilities, financial penalties, and reputational damage for organizations.

9. Vendor and Third-Party Risks

Third-party vendors and service providers may introduce additional risks related to human factors in cybersecurity vulnerabilities. Outsourcing services or relying on third-party solutions without adequate security measures in place can expose organizations to supply chain attacks, data breaches, and regulatory violations.

10. Emerging Threats and Evolving Tactics

Cyber threats and attack vectors are constantly evolving, requiring organizations to continuously adapt their strategies for addressing human factors in cybersecurity vulnerabilities. Failure to anticipate and respond to emerging threats effectively may leave organizations vulnerable to sophisticated attacks and exploitation of human vulnerabilities.

Understanding and addressing these risks is essential for developing comprehensive cybersecurity strategies that effectively mitigate human factors in cybersecurity vulnerabilities while minimizing potential negative impacts on individuals, organizations, and society.

VII CONCLUSION

In conclusion, addressing human factors in cybersecurity is crucial due to the frequent targeting of human errors and behaviors by attackers. A comprehensive approach that includes continuous education, engaging and role-specific training, clear and enforceable security policies, and the use of advanced technological solutions can significantly reduce vulnerabilities. By fostering a security-conscious culture with committed leadership and encouraging non-punitive incident reporting, organizations can promote proactive security practices. Additionally, limiting the attack surface and enhancing incident response capabilities further strengthens the organization's resilience against cybersecurity threats. This integrated strategy ensures a robust defense against the evolving landscape of cyber risks.

REFERENCES

Alsharif, M., Mishra, S., & AlShehri, M. (2022). Impact of Human Vulnerabilities on Cybersecurity. *Computer Systems Science and Engineering*, 40(3).

Ani, U. D., He, H., & Tiwari, A. (2019) Human factor security: evaluating the cybersecuritycapacity of the industrial workforce. Journal of Systems and Information Technology, 21(1). pp. 2-35. ISSN 1328-7265https://doi.org/DOI: 10.1108/JSIT-02-2018-0028

Cohen, F. (1999). Simulating Cyber Attacks, Defences, and Consequences Modeling, Simulation, and Data Limitations in Information Protection. *Computers & Security*, 18(6), 479–518. DOI: 10.1016/S0167-4048(99)80115-1

Kadena, E., & Gupi, M. (2021). Human factors in cybersecurity: Risks and impacts. Security science journal, 2(2), 51-64.

Leis, R., Badillo-Urquiola, K., Caulkins, B. D., & Bockelman, P. (2016). Modeling and Simulation Education for Behavioral Cybersecurity. In Interservice/Industry, Training, Simulation and Education Conference (I/ITSEC), in review, Orlando, FL.

Maalem Lahcen, R. A., Caulkins, B., Mohapatra, R., & Kumar, M. (2020). Review and insight on the behavioral aspects of cybersecurity. *Cybersecurity*, 3, 1–18.

Mitchell, R., & Chen, R. (2014). Behavior rule specification-based intrusion detection for safety critical medical cyber physical systems. *IEEE Transactions on Dependable and Secure Computing*, 12(1), 16–30.

Pollini, A., Callari, T. C., Tedeschi, A., Ruscio, D., Save, L., Chiarugi, F., & Guerri, D. (2022). Leveraging human factors in cybersecurity: An integrated methodological approach. *Cognition Technology and Work*, 24(2), 371–390.

Shah, M. U., Iqbal, F., Rehman, U., & Hung, P. C. (2023). A comparative assessment of human factors in cybersecurity: Implications for cyber governance. *IEEE Access : Practical Innovations, Open Solutions*.

Shuo, W. (2018, September). Design and Verification of Outbound Mode Strategy Based on EIQ Analysis. In *2018 International Symposium in Sensing and Instrumentation in IoT Era (ISSI)* (pp. 1-6). IEEE.

Triplett, W. J. (2022). Addressing human factors in cybersecurity leadership. *Journal of Cybersecurity and Privacy*, 2(3), 573–586.

Wright, A., & Thomas, G. (2019). *Human and organisational factors incybersecurity: applying STAMP to explorevulnerabilities.Contemporary Ergonomics and Human Factors* (Charles, R., & Golightly, D., Eds.). CIEHF.

Chapter 3
Understanding the Human Factors in the Psychology of Cyber Threats

Mohd Saleem
Teerthanker Mahaveer University, India

Rajeev Kumar
Moradabad Institute of Technology, India

Chanchal Chawla
TMIMT, India

Mahendra Singh
Moradabad Institute of Technology, India

ABSTRACT

This chapter examines how human factors play a crucial part in cybersecurity vulnerabilities, highlighting the important influence of psychological and behavioral aspects on the vulnerability to and mitigation of cyber threats. It explores the psychological tricks used in social engineering, insider threats motivated by malice or incompetence, and the cognitive biases that affect cybersecurity judgment. The chapter demonstrates how businesses can create security interventions that effectively encourage safer behavior by utilizing behavioral economics concepts. Empirical case studies, encompassing significant episodes in India, demonstrate the pragmatic consequences of these human elements. The chapter emphasizes how crucial it is to create a culture of cybersecurity awareness and resilience through

DOI: 10.4018/979-8-3693-9235-5.ch003

thorough training, strict access controls, and well-thought-out behavioral interventions. Through the integration of technical measures and an understanding of human behavior, companies may strengthen their defences against the constantly changing cyber threat scenario.

I. OVERVIEW OF HUMAN FACTORS IN CYBERSECURITY

Human factors are an important, but frequently disregarded, component of cybersecurity. Human behavior is still a major susceptibility to cyber threats even with advances in technology security. This chapter explores the psychological aspects of cybersecurity, specifically how behavioural patterns, decision-making processes, and cognitive biases lead to security breaches. We can create more thorough and successful cybersecurity plans that address both technological and human-centric threats by comprehending these human components. Human factors continue to be one of the most important yet frequently disregarded components in the constantly changing field of cybersecurity. Although technological progress has greatly strengthened defences against cyberattacks, human error remains a serious vulnerability. The problem of cybersecurity is not just technological; it is also psychological (Salahdine & Kaabouch, 2019). This chapter explores the complex psychological aspects of cybersecurity and how behavioural patterns, decision-making processes, and cognitive biases lead to security breaches. There are many different factors that affect human behavior in the context of cybersecurity, including as psychological, social, and cultural dimensions. Overconfidence and the propensity to undervalue hazards are two examples of cognitive biases that frequently cause people to make decisions that jeopardize security. Convenience and an underestimating of the possible risks are two reasons why it's normal practice to reuse passwords across many accounts.

Understanding decision-making procedures is also essential to comprehending cybersecurity flaws. People frequently make snap decisions when under duress or with insufficient information, which can result in mistakes that cybercriminals can take advantage of. Phishing attacks, for instance, take advantage of people's innate inclination to reply to urgent requests without properly confirming the legitimacy of the source (Krombholz et al., 2015). Behavioural patterns can highlight how vulnerable people are to cyberattacks. Because routine tasks like downloading attachments or clicking links in emails are frequently carried out carelessly, they are frequently the focus of cyberattacks. It is possible to design ways to reduce these hazards by using behavioral interventions and awareness campaigns when these patterns are understood (Hadnagy, 2010).

Furthermore, social engineering uses psychological tricks on people to access systems and data without authorization. Attackers employ deception and manipulation to trick people into disclosing private information or doing activities that jeopardize security. They do this by appealing to emotions like fear, curiosity, and trust. Organizations can better prepare and safeguard their staff against social engineering attacks by knowing the psychological strategies employed in the attack (Abraham & Chengalur-Smith, 2010). Acknowledging the significant influence of human factors on cybersecurity makes it clear that finding technological fixes alone won't be enough to address these problems. A thorough cybersecurity plan needs to incorporate human-centric strategies, stressing the value of training, education, and creating user-friendly security measures. Through the cultivation of a security-conscious culture and a comprehension of the psychological foundations of human conduct, entities can greatly augment their cybersecurity resistance (Mouton et al., 2016). With the goal of bridging the gap between human-centric approaches and technology protections, this chapter offers a comprehensive overview of cybersecurity vulnerabilities.

II. SOCIAL ENGINEERING: THE ALTERATION OF HUMAN EMOTIONS

Cybercriminals frequently use social engineering as a means of taking advantage of people's psychological vulnerabilities to obtain illegal access to systems and data. This section looks at different social engineering strategies that take advantage of authority, curiosity, and trust. These strategies include phishing, pretexting, and baiting (Gupta et al., 2016). Readers will learn how these strategies work by controlling human emotions and behaviors through in-depth case studies. The analysis emphasizes how important it is to raise awareness and provide education so that people can spot and thwart attempts at social engineering. Cybersecurity concerns include social engineering, which leverages human psychology to compromise systems that are otherwise safe (Gragg, 2003). Social engineering, as opposed to traditional hacking, which depends on technological exploits, uses deception and manipulation to persuade people into disclosing private information or taking activities that jeopardize security. Gaining an understanding of these strategies is crucial for creating strong defences and increasing awareness among possible targets (Tetri & Vuorinen, 2013).

A. **Social Engineering Techniques and Strategies:** Attacks using social engineering can take many different shapes, each taking advantage of unique facets of human nature. The most popular strategies consist of:

- **Phishing:** It is the practice of sending phony emails or other correspondence that looks to be from reliable sources. The intention is to fool the receivers into clicking on dangerous links or disclosing private information like credit card details or passwords. Phishing emails frequently inspire a sense of urgency by taking advantage of the recipient's curiosity or terror to demand quick action.
- **Pretexting:** This tactic involves the attacker fabricating a situation, or pretext, in order to interact with the victim and obtain private data. An attacker might, for example, pretend to be an IT specialist for the organization who needs login credentials to resolve a technical problem.
- **Baiting**: It is the practice of luring someone into a trap by making an alluring offer. Baiting can take two forms: offline, like dropping a USB drive loaded with malware for someone to take and use, or online, like downloading malware under the premise of a free software update.
- **Tailgating**: It is a physical social engineering technique in which an attacker follows an authorized individual closely in order to obtain unauthorized entry to a secure place. It takes use of the societal custom of opening doors for people.

B. **Case Studies and Practical Illustrations:** Examining actual instances of successful social engineering implementation is necessary to comprehend the efficacy of this tactic:

- **The Cosmos Bank Cyber Heist (2018):** One of the biggest cooperative banks in India, Cosmos Bank, was the target of a highly skilled cyberattacks in August 2018 that combined malware and phishing. Over the course of two days, the attackers gained access to the bank's computers and carried out fraudulent transactions, stealing almost INR 94 crore (USD 13.5 million). The attackers were able to take advantage of ATM withdrawals in more than 28 countries and duplicate debit card details by breaking into the bank's internal computers through the use of a phishing email (Deshpande et al., 2022).
- **The UIDAI Aadhaar Data Leak (2018):** A significant data breach that occurred in January 2018 resulted in the exposure of millions of Indian residents' personal data from the Unique Identification Authority of India (UIDAI)-managed Aadhaar database. The Tribune's journalists revealed that they could get database access for as low as INR 500 (USD 7). Social engineering allowed people acting as authorized users to access private information, which enabled this compromise (Tyagi et al., 2018).
- **Malware Attack on Canara Bank ATM (2018):** One of the biggest public sector banks in India, Canara Bank, experienced a malware as-

sault in July 2018 that was directed at its ATMs. The software, which was distributed to bank staff members via phishing emails, infiltrated more than 20 ATMs and resulted in unapproved transactions totalling INR 20 lakh (USD 30,000). The hack made use of malware and skimming devices to record card details, which were subsequently used to duplicate cards and make cash withdrawals (Shah, 2020).

- **SBI Data Leak (2019):** Millions of consumers' financial information was compromised in a significant data breach that occurred in January 2019 at the largest bank in the nation, State Bank of India (SBI). An unsecured server that held private client information, such as account numbers, balances, and transaction information, was the source of the breach. A misconfiguration left the server vulnerable, allowing anyone with an internet connection to access it (Garg, 2022).
- **The Cyberattacks on the Indian Nuclear Power Plant in 2019:** The Kudankulam Nuclear Power Plant in Tamil Nadu was the victim of a cyberattacks in October 2019 that was allegedly started by a phishing email. The plant's administrative network was the source of data collection for the malware known as DTrack. Despite reports that the key systems were undamaged, the hack caused grave worries about India's critical infrastructure's cybersecurity (Tripathi et al., 2021).
- **The Phishing Scam of "Google Docs" (2017):** In this extensive phishing attempt, emails seemed to be requests for cooperation on a Google Doc. Users who received the emails were taken to a phony login page where their credentials were harvested. Because Google Docs is widely used, and the assault seemed legitimate, it was especially successful (Mehendele et al., 2017).

C. **Psychological Manipulation in Social Engineering:** Attacks using social engineering are successful because they take advantage of basic facets of human nature. Important components consist of:

- **Trust:** To win over the victim's trust, attackers frequently pose as reputable organizations like banks, service providers, or co-workers. One major risk is the innate human desire to trust authority individuals and well-known businesses.
- **Emotion:** Strong motivators include feelings of fear, greed, and curiosity. For example, phishing emails often incite panic by threatening to suspend accounts or take legal action, which causes recipients to react without hesitation.
- **Cognitive Overload:** Due to time restrictions or cognitive overload, social engineering assaults frequently target busy people who might not

carefully consider the legitimacy of a request. It is simpler for attackers to succeed when there is a lack of focus.

D. **Strategies to Combat Social Engineering:** Techniques for Countering Social Engineering

A combination of technical controls, regulations, and educational initiatives are used to reduce the danger of social engineering attacks:

- **Education and Awareness:** Staff members can identify typical social engineering techniques and take necessary action by attending regular training sessions. Exercises that simulate phishing might be especially useful in reiterating this information (Saleem et al., 2021).
- **Robust Policies and Procedures:** Unauthorized access can be avoided by putting in place stringent verification procedures for information requests. For instance, many social engineering tactics can be thwarted by demanding various forms of verification before providing access to sensitive information (Bullée et al., 2015).
- **Technical defences:** Multi-factor authentication (MFA), intrusion detection systems, and email filters can all dramatically lower the success rate of social engineering attempts. An attacker must get beyond additional security levels added by these methods (Bhusal, 2021).
- **Culture of Security Consciousness:** Proactive cybersecurity is facilitated by motivating staff members to raise red flags about requests and report possible security breaches (Saleem & Khan, 2021).

Organizations can greatly lessen their susceptibility to social engineering attacks by comprehending the psychological dynamics underlying these techniques and putting in place thorough plans to counter them. The significance of incorporating psychological knowledge into cybersecurity procedures is emphasized in this section, which will ultimately increase an organization's defences' overall resilience.

III. INSIDER THREATS AND HUMAN ERROR

Although outside cyber threats frequently make the news, insider threats and human error can present serious hazards that have the potential to be just as harmful. Insiders have the ability to seriously hurt a company, whether through carelessness or malevolent intent (Ismail & Widyarto, 2022). The nature of insider threats, the causes of human mistake, and risk-reduction techniques are all covered in this section.

A. **Recognizing Insider Threats:** Insider threats are security hazards that come from within the company and are typically carried out by workers, subcontractors, or business associates who have been granted permission to access the company's assets. There are two primary categories of insider threats ***Figure 1***:

Figure 1. Forms of insider threats

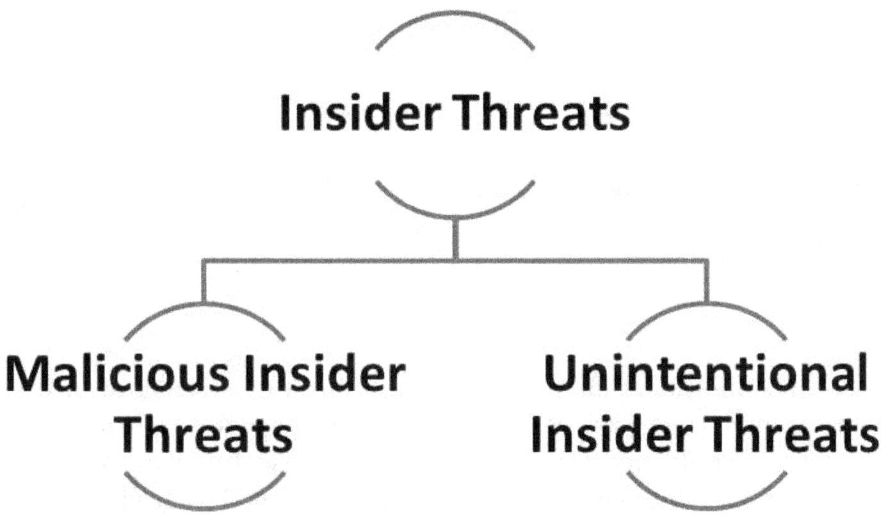

- **Malicious Insider Threats:** These people purposefully abuse their access for their own benefit, retaliation, or to support outside attacks. Financial gain, ideological convictions, or employment issues are a few examples of motivations. An insider planting malware to disrupt operations, or a dissatisfied employee taking confidential data to sell to rival companies (Greitzer et al., 2014).
- **Unintentional Insider Threats:** These risks result from carelessness, incompetence, or ignorance. Typical reasons include misconfigurations, falling for phishing scams, and unintentional data spills. A worker may unintentionally send private emails to the incorrect address or may click on a link that leads to the installation of malware on the company network (Abdelsadeq et al., 2019).

B. **Factors Associated with Human Error:** The primary source of cybersecurity incidents is human mistakes (Bailey et al., 2018). These mistakes are caused by a number of factors ***Figure 2***:

Figure 2. Factors associated with human error

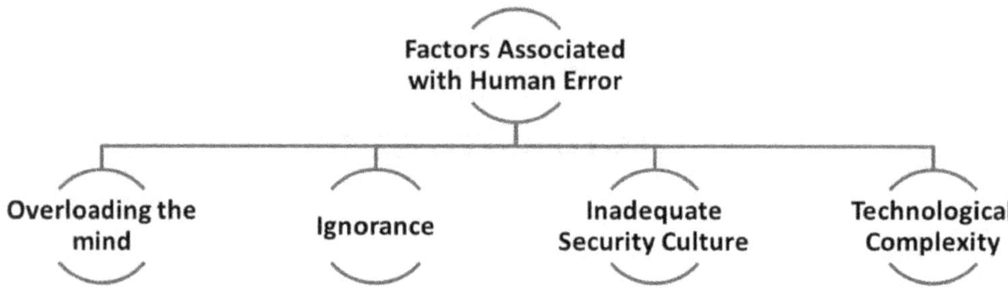

- **Overloading the mind:** Workers frequently mix up assignments and deadlines, which cause errors. People who experience cognitive overload may fail to notice security precautions or make bad choices when under duress.
- **Ignorance:** Inadvertent security breaches may result from inadequate cybersecurity threat and best practice training and awareness. For example, employees who are ignorant of phishing strategies are more susceptible to these kinds of attacks.
- **Inadequate Security Culture:** An organizational culture that does not prioritize cybersecurity can result in lax security practices. If security is seen as a secondary concern, employees may not adhere to necessary protocols.
- **Technological Complexity:** Complex systems and software can be challenging for employees to use correctly, leading to configuration errors or misuse.

C. **Strategies for Mitigating Insider Threats and Human Error:** Among the practical methods for reducing insider risks and human error are:

- **Comprehensive Training and Awareness Programs:** Frequent cybersecurity training aids staff members in identifying and addressing risks. Programs for raising awareness ought to address subjects including social engineering, phishing, and safe data handling techniques (Ismail & Yusof, 2018).
- **Robust Access Controls:** Ensuring that employees only have access to the information required for their responsibilities is ensured by putting the con-

cept of least privilege into practice. Access permissions should be routinely audited in order to find and remove any unused rights (Takabi et al., 2018).

- **Monitoring and Analytics:** Unusual activity that can point to an insider threat can be found by using behavioral analytics and sophisticated surveillance techniques. Potential breaches can be avoided by careful study of abnormalities and real-time alarms (Greitzer et al., 2014).
- **Strong Organizational Culture:** It is imperative to cultivate a culture of security consciousness throughout the organization. Leadership needs to stress the value of cybersecurity and make sure that it permeates every employee's everyday work and way of thinking (Abdelsadeq et al., 2019).
- **Incident Response Planning:** Creating and maintaining an incident response strategy guarantees that the company is ready to react to security events quickly and efficiently. Employees can better grasp their roles and duties during an incident by participating in simulated drills.

The fields of cybersecurity are greatly challenged by insider attacks and human mistake. Organizations can create focused plans to reduce these risks by knowing the reasons behind malevolent insiders and the elements that lead to inadvertent mistakes. A successful protection against insider threats must include solid security procedures, thorough training, and strict access limits. In the end, strengthening overall cybersecurity resilience and defending against the variety of threats that businesses confront depend heavily on addressing the human factor.

IV. BEHAVIOURAL ECONOMICS AND CYBERSECURITY DECISION-MAKING

An important viewpoint on cybersecurity decision-making comes from behavioral economics, which acknowledges that people frequently stray from logical action due to cognitive biases, heuristics, and emotional factors. Vulnerabilities result from traditional models' inability to capture these subtleties (Saleem & Chawla, 2023). People's perceptions and reactions to cyber risks are influenced by biases such as confirmation bias, overconfidence, and the availability heuristic. For instance, people may underestimate the hazards associated with phishing due to overconfidence, and estimates of risk may be skewed by recent high-profile breaches. Organizations can use behavioral economics to encourage people to adopt safer habits by implementing techniques like frequent security reminders and stronger password defaults. Certain decision-making errors can be addressed by introducing focused interventions, streamlining security procedures, and rewarding good practices. Real-world examples of security enhancements that don't overwhelm users are Facebook's Security

Check-up and Google's easy-to-use two-step verification. Organizations can increase defences against complex threats by fostering a culture of cybersecurity awareness and resilience through the identification of critical behaviors, comprehension of contextual factors, and iterative testing of strategies.

V. CONCLUSION

Human factors have a significant and diverse role in cybersecurity weaknesses, impacting both the vulnerability to and the ability to counteract cyber assaults. Robust cybersecurity measures require an understanding of the psychological and behavioral components that support human interactions with technology (Khan & Matloob Ullah Khan, 2022). Internal risks must be addressed, as human mistake and insider threats underscore, while social engineering takes advantage of basic human psychology. Behavioral economics offers significant perspectives on decision-making procedures, which facilitates the creation of more efficient security measures. Organizations can cultivate a culture of awareness and resilience by incorporating these lessons into cybersecurity strategies. Vulnerabilities can be greatly decreased by thorough training, robust access controls, and well-timed behavioral interventions. It is still crucial to address the human factor in order to improve security and safeguard sensitive data as cyber threats continue to change. Organizations can more effectively protect themselves against the wide range of constantly evolving cyber threats by adopting a comprehensive strategy that blends technological controls with human behavior knowledge.

REFERENCES

Abdelsadeq, Z. A., Omar, S. N., Basir, N., & Rafei, N. F. N. B. M. (2019). Unintentional Insider Threats Countermeasures Model (UITCM). *2019 International Conference on Cybersecurity (ICoCSec)*, 53–58. https://ieeexplore.ieee.org/abstract/document/8970986/

Abraham, S., & Chengalur-Smith, I. (2010). An overview of social engineering malware: Trends, tactics, and implications. *Technology in Society*, 32(3), 183–196. DOI: 10.1016/j.techsoc.2010.07.001

Bailey, T., Kolo, B., Rajagopalan, K., & Ware, D. (2018). Insider threat: The human element of cyberrisk. *The McKinsey Quarterly*, 1–8.

Bhusal, C. S. (2021). Systematic review on social engineering: Hacking by manipulating humans. *Journal of Information Security*, 12(1), 104–114. DOI: 10.4236/jis.2021.121005

Bullée, J.-W. H., Montoya, L., Pieters, W., Junger, M., & Hartel, P. H. (2015). The persuasion and security awareness experiment: Reducing the success of social engineering attacks. *Journal of Experimental Criminology*, 11(1), 97–115. DOI: 10.1007/s11292-014-9222-7

Deshpande, K., Dam, L. B., & Pandey, N. (2022). *Cyberattack at cosmos bank: Regaining customer trust*. SAGE Publications: SAGE Business Cases Originals. https://sk.sagepub.com/cases/cyberattack-at-cosmos-bank-regaining-customer-trust

Garg, H. (2022). Financial Regulators and the Need for Data Privacy and Protection-Issues, Opportunities and Challenges. *International Journal Of Legal Developments And Allied Issues*, 8(1), 290–301.

Gragg, D. (2003). A multi-level defense against social engineering. *SANS Reading Room*, 13, 1–21.

Greitzer, F. L., Strozer, J., Cohen, S., Bergey, J., Cowley, J., Moore, A., & Mundie, D. (2014). Unintentional insider threat: Contributing factors, observables, and mitigation strategies. *2014 47th Hawaii International Conference on System Sciences*, 2025–2034. https://ieeexplore.ieee.org/abstract/document/6758854/

Gupta, S., Singhal, A., & Kapoor, A. (2016). A literature survey on social engineering attacks: Phishing attack. *2016 International Conference on Computing, Communication and Automation (ICCCA)*, 537–540. https://ieeexplore.ieee.org/abstract/document/7813778/

Hadnagy, C. (2010). *Social engineering: The art of human hacking*. John Wiley & Sons. https://books.google.com/books?hl=en&lr=&id=9LpawpklYogC&oi=fnd&pg=PT7&dq=Social+Engineering&ots=vdfsJTf3VP&sig=4U3wYfau3ptMGpQSR4cDFUTIC1E

Ismail, W. B. W., & Widyarto, S. (2022). *A Classification Of Human Error Factors In Unintentional Insider Threats*. 667–676. DOI: 10.15405/epms.2022.10.63

Ismail, W. B. W., & Yusof, M. (2018). Mitigation strategies for unintentional insider threats on information leaks. *International Journal of Security and Its Applications*, 12(1), 37–46. DOI: 10.14257/ijsia.2018.12.1.03

Khan, M. K., & Matloob Ullah Khan, D. M. U. (2022). Analysis the Growth & Linkage b/w Crypto-currency and Stock Market Indices: Evidence from the US and Indian Stock Market. *CEMJP*, 30(4), 1912–1920.

Krombholz, K., Hobel, H., Huber, M., & Weippl, E. (2015). Advanced social engineering attacks. *Journal of Information Security and Applications*, 22, 113–122. DOI: 10.1016/j.jisa.2014.09.005

Mehendele, D. K., Masurekar, R. S., Takawale, N., & Kulkarni, S. (2017). Review of Phishing Attacks and Anti Phishing Tools. [IJRCCE]. *International Journal Of Innovative Research In Computer And Communication Engineering*, 5, 15132.

Mouton, F., Leenen, L., & Venter, H. S. (2016). Social engineering attack examples, templates and scenarios. *Computers & Security*, 59, 186–209. DOI: 10.1016/j.cose.2016.03.004

Salahdine, F., & Kaabouch, N. (2019). Social engineering attacks: A survey. *Future Internet*, 11(4), 89. DOI: 10.3390/fi11040089

Saleem, M., & Chawla, C. (2023). Blockchain-Powered Decentralized Finance (DeFi): Transforming Financial Inclusion & Investment Landscapes. *2023 12th International Conference on System Modeling & Advancement in Research Trends (SMART)*, 342–346. https://ieeexplore.ieee.org/abstract/document/10428666/

Saleem, M., & Khan, M. U. (2021). Green finance for sustainable development: A bibliometric review of current status, development and prospects. *International Journal of Advanced Research in Commerce* [IJARCMSS]. *Management & Social Science*, 4(4), 1–9.

Saleem, M., Khan, M. U., & Ather, D. (2021). Fintech startups and banks: Adoption, incentives, competition, and regulations. *International Journal on Global Business Management & Research*, 10(2), 21–28.

Shah, I. (2020). *Analysis of Cyber Crime in Banking Sector*. http://103.85.141.163:8071/jspui/bitstream/123456789/182/1/46%20%20IMTISHAL%201190997022.pdf

Takabi, H., Hashem, Y., & Dantu, R. (2018). Prediction of human error using eye movements patterns for unintentional insider threat detection. *2018 IEEE 4th International Conference on Identity, Security, and Behavior Analysis (ISBA)*, 1–8. https://ieeexplore.ieee.org/abstract/document/8311479/

Tetri, P., & Vuorinen, J. (2013). Dissecting social engineering. *Behaviour & Information Technology*, 32(10), 1014–1023. DOI: 10.1080/0144929X.2013.763860

Tripathi, D., Singh, L. K., Tripathi, A. K., & Chaturvedi, A. (2021). Model based security verification of Cyber-Physical System based on Petrinet: A case study of Nuclear power plant. *Annals of Nuclear Energy*, 159, 108306. DOI: 10.1016/j.anucene.2021.108306

Tyagi, A. K., Rekha, G., & Sreenath, N. (2018). Is your privacy safe with Aadhaar?: An open discussion. *2018 Fifth International Conference on Parallel, Distributed and Grid Computing (PDGC)*, 318–323. https://ieeexplore.ieee.org/abstract/document/8745836/

Chapter 4
Comparative Analysis of Traditional vs. AI-Driven Network Security

Nobhonil Roy Choudhury
https://orcid.org/0009-0009-1046-7492
Brainware University, India

Shyamalendu Paul
https://orcid.org/0009-0008-1028-4867
Brainware University, India

ABSTRACT

The increasing sophistication of cyber threats has driven the evolution of network security mechanisms. Traditional methods like firewalls, IDS, and antivirus software, which rely on established guidelines and signature-based detection, are now limited in addressing new and unknown threats. AI has introduced a new paradigm in network security, utilizing machine learning, behavioral analytics, and automated threat detection. AI-driven methods offer improved efficiency, accuracy, response time, adaptability, scalability, and cost-effectiveness. They analyze large data sets to detect patterns, recognize anomalies, and respond to threats in real time. While AI systems are costly and complex, their advantages in reducing false positives and handling zero-day attacks make them essential. The integration of AI with traditional methods can enhance security, combining strengths for a proactive defense against evolving cyber threats.

DOI: 10.4018/979-8-3693-9235-5.ch004

INTRODUCTION

Network security has been an essential component of information technology since the inception of computer networks. Ensuring the safety and integrity of data as it traverses these networks is critical for both organizations and individuals. Traditional network security measures, such as firewalls, intrusion detection systems (IDS), and antivirus software, have served as primary defence mechanisms against cyber threats for decades. These approaches, relying heavily on predefined rules and signature-based detection, have proven effective in mitigating known threats. However, the landscape of cyber threats has evolved dramatically, exposing the limitations of these traditional methods (Anderson & Brown, 2018; Harris & White, 2020).

The rise of sophisticated attacks, such as zero-day exploits and advanced persistent threats (APTs), has highlighted the inadequacies of traditional security measures (Zhao et al., 2021). These threats often bypass conventional defences by exploiting unknown vulnerabilities that are not covered by existing rules and signatures. The growing complexity and frequency of these cyber-attacks necessitate more advanced and dynamic security solutions. In response to these challenges, the cybersecurity industry has increasingly turned to artificial intelligence (AI) and machine learning (ML) to enhance network security (Jones & Patel, 2019).

AI-driven network security leverages advanced algorithms to analyze vast amounts of data, identify patterns, and predict potential threats. Unlike traditional methods, AI-driven approaches can adapt to new threats in real-time, providing a more proactive and dynamic defence mechanism (Nguyen & Lee, 2020). AI technologies, including machine learning, deep learning, and behavioural analytics, enable systems to learn from data, improving their detection capabilities over time and reducing the reliance on human intervention. This evolution represents a significant shift in how organizations approach network security, moving from reactive to proactive strategies (Tripathi et al., 2024).

The primary objective of this paper is to explore the differences, advantages, and limitations of traditional and AI-driven network security methods. By examining various aspects such as efficiency, accuracy, response time, adaptability, scalability, and cost-effectiveness, this study seeks to provide a comprehensive understanding of these two approaches.

Traditional Network Security Methods

Traditional network security methods have long been the cornerstone of network defence strategies. Firewalls, IDS, and antivirus software are some of the most commonly used tools. Firewalls act as a barrier between trusted and untrusted networks, filtering traffic based on predefined rules. They are effective in blocking unauthorized access and preventing certain types of attacks. Intrusion detection systems monitor network traffic for suspicious activities and known attack patterns. When an anomaly is detected, IDS alerts administrators to potential security breaches. Antivirus software scans files and programs for known malware signatures, quarantining or removing malicious software.

While these traditional methods have been effective against known threats, their limitations become apparent when dealing with more sophisticated attacks. Signature-based detection methods, for instance, are only effective against known malware. As new threats emerge, it takes time to develop and distribute signatures, leaving networks vulnerable in the interim. Furthermore, these systems often generate a high number of false positives, leading to alert fatigue among security personnel and potentially causing genuine threats to be overlooked (Harris & White, 2020).

Challenges of Traditional Network Security

The primary challenge of traditional network security measures is their reliance on predefined rules and known signatures. This approach makes it difficult to detect and respond to new, unknown threats. Zero-day exploits, which target previously unknown vulnerabilities, can bypass traditional defenses because there are no existing signatures to detect them. Advanced persistent threats (APTs) represent another significant challenge. APTs are highly sophisticated, multi-stage attacks that are often carried out by well-funded adversaries. These threats can remain undetected for long periods, infiltrating networks and exfiltrating data without triggering traditional security alarms (Zhao et al., 2021).

Moreover, the volume of network traffic and the increasing complexity of attacks have outpaced the capabilities of traditional security measures. The manual processes involved in updating rules and signatures cannot keep up with the rapid evolution of cyber threats. This has led to a growing need for more automated and intelligent security solutions that can adapt in real-time.

The Advent of AI in Network Security

In response to the limitations of traditional security methods, the cybersecurity industry has turned to AI and machine learning to enhance network security. AI-driven network security utilizes advanced algorithms to analyze large datasets, identify patterns, and predict potential threats. Machine learning, a subset of AI, involves training algorithms on historical data to recognize normal and anomalous behaviours. These systems can then detect deviations from the norm, flagging potential security incidents (Nguyen & Lee, 2020).

One of the key advantages of AI-driven security is its ability to adapt to new threats in real-time. Unlike traditional methods that rely on predefined rules and signatures, AI systems continuously learn from new data. This dynamic learning capability allows them to identify and respond to previously unknown threats more effectively. Behavioural analytics, another important aspect of AI-driven security, involves analyzing user behaviour to detect anomalies that may indicate malicious activities. By understanding normal behaviour patterns, AI systems can identify deviations that suggest a security breach.

Comparative Advantages of AI-driven Network Security

AI-driven network security offers several advantages over traditional methods. In terms of efficiency, AI systems can process and analyze vast amounts of security data much faster than human analysts. This capability is crucial in identifying and mitigating threats in real-time, reducing the window of vulnerability. Additionally, AI systems can handle big data more effectively, filtering out false positives and focusing on genuine threats. This improves the overall efficiency and accuracy of threat detection (Jones & Patel, 2019).

Accuracy is another critical area where AI-driven methods excel. Traditional methods are limited by their reliance on known signatures and rules, making them less effective against zero-day attacks and sophisticated malware. AI-driven systems, however, continuously learn from new data, improving their ability to detect previously unknown threats with greater precision. This dynamic learning capability enhances the overall security posture of an organization.

Response time is crucial in mitigating the impact of cyber threats. Traditional methods, with their manual processes, often have slower response times compared to AI-driven approaches. AI systems can automatically respond to threats, isolating affected systems and mitigating damage almost instantaneously. This rapid response capability is essential in minimizing the potential impact of security incidents.

Adaptability and scalability are also significant advantages of AI-driven network security. Traditional security systems can be rigid and difficult to scale, requiring significant manual effort to update and expand. AI-driven approaches, on the other hand, are inherently more adaptable and scalable. They can automatically adjust to new threats and expanding network environments without extensive manual intervention. This makes AI-driven security solutions more suitable for modern, dynamic network environments.

Cost-effectiveness of AI-driven Network Security

Cost-effectiveness is another key consideration when comparing traditional and AI-driven network security methods. While the initial implementation of AI-driven security systems can be expensive, their ability to reduce the need for human intervention and improve threat detection efficiency can lead to cost savings in the long run. Traditional methods, with their ongoing maintenance and manual monitoring requirements, may incur higher operational costs over time. By automating many aspects of threat detection and response, AI-driven systems can help organizations optimize their security budgets and allocate resources more effectively (Evans & Jones, 2019; Tatomur, 2020).

Challenges and Ethical Considerations

Despite the numerous advantages of AI-driven security, there are challenges associated with their implementation. The complexity of AI systems can pose significant hurdles, requiring specialized skills and knowledge to manage and maintain. Organizations may need to invest in training and hiring skilled personnel to effectively leverage AI technologies. Additionally, ethical concerns regarding the use of AI in security, such as data privacy issues and potential biases in AI algorithms, need to be addressed to ensure responsible deployment.

Data privacy is a critical concern in AI-driven network security. The vast amounts of data collected and analyzed by AI systems can include sensitive information, raising questions about how this data is stored, processed, and protected. Ensuring compliance with data protection regulations and implementing robust privacy measures are essential to maintaining trust and safeguarding user data.

Algorithmic bias is another ethical issue that must be considered. AI systems are only as good as the data they are trained on. If the training data is biased, the AI system may produce biased outcomes, potentially leading to unfair or discriminatory practices. Addressing these biases and ensuring that AI algorithms are transparent and fair is crucial for the ethical deployment of AI-driven security solutions.

Future Trends and Integration Strategies

The integration of AI with traditional security measures, the development of more sophisticated AI algorithms, and the implementation of robust ethical guidelines are suggested as ways to create a more secure digital environment. By combining the strengths of both traditional and AI-driven approaches, organizations can achieve a more resilient and proactive security posture, better equipped to face the evolving landscape of cyber threats.

Future research should focus on addressing the ethical and practical challenges of AI in network security, ensuring that these technologies are used responsibly and effectively. The ongoing evolution of cyber threats and security technologies will continue to shape the future of network security, highlighting the need for continuous innovation and adaptation. By staying ahead of the curve and embracing advanced security solutions, organizations can better protect their networks and data in an increasingly interconnected world.

LITERATURE REVIEW

Overview of Traditional Network Security

Traditional network security methods have been the cornerstone of protecting digital assets for many years. These methods include firewalls, which act as barriers between trusted and untrusted networks; intrusion detection systems (IDS), which monitor network traffic for suspicious activity; antivirus and anti-malware software, which detect and remove malicious software; encryption techniques, which protect data confidentiality; and virtual private networks (VPNs), which provide secure communication channels (Smith et al., 2020; Anderson & Brown, 2018).

Firewalls

Firewalls are one of the oldest and most widely used network security tools. They function by controlling the incoming and outgoing network traffic based on predetermined security rules. Firewalls may consist of hardware, software, or a mixture of the two. They are effective in preventing unauthorized access to network resources but may struggle with sophisticated and rapidly evolving threats (Davis & Smith, 2016).

Types of Firewalls

1. **Packet-Filtering Firewalls**: These firewalls inspect packets at the network layer and filter traffic based on predefined rules.
2. **Stateful Inspection Firewalls**: These firewalls observe active connection states and make decisions depending on the traffic context.

3. **Proxy Firewalls**: These firewalls act as intermediaries between users and the internet, providing an additional layer of security by masking internal network details.

Intrusion Detection Systems (IDS)

Intrusion detection systems are created to track network traffic to detect any indications of harmful behavior. There are two main types: network-based IDS (NIDS) and host-based IDS (HIDS). NIDS monitor traffic across the entire network, while HIDS focus on individual devices. IDS can detect a wide range of attacks, including signature-based and anomaly-based threats, but they often generate a high number of false positives (Clark & Turner, 2017; Ghafir et al., 2018).

Types of IDS

1. **Signature-Based IDS**: These systems detect attacks by comparing network traffic to known attack signatures.
2. **Anomaly-Based IDS**: These systems establish a baseline of normal network behaviour and detect deviations from this baseline.

Antivirus and Anti-malware

Antivirus and anti-malware software are essential for protecting individual devices from malicious software. These tools rely on signature-based detection to identify known threats. While effective against known malware, they are less capable of detecting new or unknown threats, particularly those that use obfuscation techniques (Evans & Jones, 2019).

Encryption

Encryption is a critical security measure for protecting data confidentiality. It involves converting data into a coded format that can only be read by authorized parties with the correct decryption key. Encryption is widely used for securing sensitive information in transit and at rest but requires proper key management practices to be effective (Harris & White, 2020).

VPNs

VPNs offer protected channels for communication on shared networks. They encrypt data transmitted between the user's device and the VPN server, protecting it from interception and eavesdropping. VPNs are commonly used for remote access to corporate networks and for securing internet connections (Davis & Smith, 2016).

Overview of AI-Driven Network Security

AI-driven network security represents a significant advancement over traditional methods. Machine learning algorithms have the ability to examine large volumes of data in order to detect patterns and irregularities that could signal a potential security risk. Behavioural analytics focuses on understanding the normal behaviour of users and systems to detect anomalies. Automated threat detection systems use AI to identify and respond to threats in real time, reducing the need for human intervention. These technologies promise to enhance the effectiveness and efficiency of network security (Jones & Patel, 2019; Nguyen & Lee, 2020).

Machine Learning Algorithms

Machine learning algorithms are the foundation of AI-driven network security. These algorithms can analyze large datasets to identify patterns and anomalies that may indicate a security threat. Supervised learning algorithms require labeled training data, while unsupervised learning algorithms can detect anomalies without prior knowledge of what constitutes a threat (Zhao et al., 2021).

Types of Machine Learning Algorithms

1. **Supervised Learning**: Algorithms that learn from labelled training data and make predictions based on that data.
2. **Unsupervised Learning**: Algorithms that identify patterns and anomalies in data without labelled training data.
3. **Reinforcement Learning**: Algorithms that learn by interacting with an environment and receiving feedback based on their actions.

Behavioral Analytics

Behavioural analytics involves monitoring the behaviour of users and systems to establish a baseline of normal activity. Deviations from this baseline can indicate potential security threats. Behavioral analytics can detect insider threats, compromised accounts, and other types of attacks that may not be identifiable through traditional methods (Clark & Turner, 2017).

Automated Threat Detection

Automated threat detection systems use AI to identify and respond to security threats in real time. These systems can analyze network traffic, user behaviour, and other data sources to detect and mitigate threats without human intervention. Automated threat detection can significantly reduce response times and improve the overall efficiency of network security (Nguyen & Lee, 2020).

AI in Incident Response

AI can also have a significant impact on incident response. AI-driven systems can automate the investigation of security incidents, identifying the root cause and suggesting remediation steps. This can help organizations respond to incidents more quickly and effectively, minimizing the impact of security breaches (Harris & White, 2020).

Comparative Studies

Several studies have compared traditional and AI-driven network security methods. For example, research conducted by Smith et al. (2020) found that AI-driven systems could detect threats with greater accuracy and speed compared to traditional IDS. Another study by Jones and Patel (2019) highlighted the scalability and adaptability of AI-driven security in dynamic environments.

COMPARATIVE ANALYSIS

Efficiency and Accuracy

AI-driven network security systems often outperform traditional methods in terms of efficiency and accuracy. Machine learning algorithms can quickly analyze vast amounts of data and identify patterns that human analyst might miss. Behavioural analytics can detect subtle deviations from normal activity that could indicate a security threat. Automated threat detection systems can respond to threats in real time, reducing the need for human intervention and minimizing the impact of security incidents (Smith et al., 2020).

In contrast, traditional network security methods such as firewalls, IDS, and antivirus software rely heavily on predefined rules and signatures. These methods can be effective at blocking known threats but are less capable of detecting new or evolving threats. Additionally, traditional methods often generate a high number of false positives, which can overwhelm security teams and reduce their overall efficiency (Jones & Patel, 2019; Zhao et al., 2021).

Table 1. Efficiency and accuracy

Metric	Traditional Security	AI-Driven Security
Threat Detection Speed	Moderate	High
Accuracy	Moderate	High
False Positives	High	Low
Adaptability	Low	High

Response Time

Response time to security incidents is pivotal in minimizing the damage from cyber-attacks. AI-driven network security systems exceed in this area by detecting and responding to pitfalls in real-time, significantly reducing response times. These systems use automated trouble discovery and response mechanisms to take immediate action, similar as segregating compromised bias or blocking vicious business, thereby mollifying pitfalls fleetly and effectively (Nguyen & Lee, 2020).

In discrepancy, traditional network security styles frequently calculate on homemade intervention to address pitfalls. This reliance can lead to longer response times, especially if the security platoon is overwhelmed by a high number of false cons. The homemade nature of these styles means that relating and responding to pitfalls is slower, adding the eventuality for damage during a security incident. The detention in response can allow bushwhackers further time to exploit vulnerabilities, performing in more significant detriment to the association's network and data (Clark & Turner, 2017; Cardoso, 2022).

Table 2. Response time

Metric	Traditional Security	AI-Driven Security
Detection Speed	Seconds to Minutes	Real-Time
Response Speed	Minutes to Hours	Seconds to Minutes
Automation	Low	High
Human Involvement	High	Low

Adaptability and Scalability

AI- driven network security systems stand out for their rigidity and scalability, making them largely effective in moment's dynamic cybersecurity geography. Machine literacy algorithms, a core element of these systems, continuously learn from new data, enabling them to acclimatize to arising and evolving pitfalls fleetly. This constant literacy process allows AI-driven security systems to fete and respond to new attack patterns that traditional styles might miss. Also, behavioral analytics play a pivotal part in these systems by covering and conforming to changes in stoner gesture and network exertion. This rigidity ensures that AI-driven systems remain effective over time, indeed as the trouble geography and network surroundings change (Jones & Patel, 2019).

The scalability of AI-driven network security systems is another significant advantage. These systems can efficiently cover and manage large and complex networks, making them ideal for associations with expansive IT architectures. AI can handle vast quantities of data and network business without compromising performance, furnishing harmonious security content across all corridors of an association. This scalability is particularly salutary for large enterprises and institutions with complex network infrastructures, as AI can seamlessly integrate into being systems and gauge up as the association grows.

In discrepancy, traditional network security styles, similar to firewalls and Intrusion Discovery Systems (IDS), warrant the same position of rigidity and scalability. These conventional styles calculate heavily on predefined rules and autographs to descry pitfalls, which means they need regular homemade updates to stay current. Addressing new pitfalls frequently requires security brigades to continuously develop and apply new rules, a process that's both time-consuming and resource-ferocious. This reliance on homemade updates can lead to gaps in security, as there's always a pause between the emergence of new trouble and the perpetration of a corresponding rule.

Also, traditional network security styles struggle with scalability. Monitoring and managing large and complex networks can overwhelm these systems, making them less effective for associations with expansive IT architectures. The fixed nature of predefined rules and the homemade trouble needed to modernize them can limit the capability of traditional styles to keep up with fleetly growing and changing networks. This limitation can affect in reduced effectiveness and increased vulnerability to attacks (Smith etal., 2020).

Thus, the superior rigidity and scalability of AI-driven network security systems make them a more suitable choice for ultramodern associations. By continuously learning from new data and conforming to changes in network exertion, AI-driven systems give a robust and flexible defense against evolving cyber pitfalls. Their capability to gauge efficiently ensures comprehensive security content, making them well-suited for associations with expansive and complex IT architectures (Jones & Patel, 2019; Smith et al., 2020).

Table 3. Adaptability and scalability

Metric	Traditional Security	AI-Driven Security
Adaptability	Low	High
Scalability	Moderate	High
Continuous Learning	No	Yes

Cost-Benefit Analysis

Enforcing AI-driven network security systems can be a significant investment due to the need for technical tackle, advanced software, and expert labor force. Despite these high original costs, the advantages handed by AI-driven security can justify the expenditure. The primary benefits include enhanced effectiveness, bettered delicacy, and briskly response times to pitfalls. AI systems are able of automating routine monitoring tasks, significantly reducing the necessity for homemade intervention. This robotization helps lower the threat of security breaches by enabling hastily and more precise identification and mitigation of implicit pitfalls. Also, AI can continuously learn and acclimatize to new trouble geographies, icing that security measures remain effective against evolving cyber pitfalls (Evans & Jones, 2019).

AI-driven systems offer substantial advancements over traditional network security styles, which, although less expensive to apply, may not be as effective in the ultramodern cyber trouble terrain. Traditional styles, similar as firewalls and Intrusion Discovery Systems (IDS), frequently induce a high number of false cons. These inaccuracies can overwhelm security brigades, leading to alert fatigue and potentially causing genuine pitfalls to be overlooked. Also, traditional systems calculate heavily on homemade intervention to respond to detected pitfalls. This homemade process not only increases response times but also elevates the threat of significant damage due to slower trouble mitigation.

In discrepancy, AI-driven security systems can reuse vast quantities of data in real-time, allowing them to descry anomalies and implicit pitfalls with a position of delicacy and speed that traditional styles cannot match. The capability of AI to give nonstop monitoring and real-time analysis means that implicit pitfalls can be linked and addressed much more fleetly, reducing the window of occasion for bushwhackers to exploit vulnerabilities. Likewise, AI systems can gauge more efficiently than mortal-operated systems, handling increased network business and more complex attack vectors without a corresponding increase in mortal labor. The cost-benefit analysis therefore favors AI-driven security results when considering the long-term benefits. While the original investment is advanced, the reduction in homemade labor, dropped liability of successful breaches, and minimized impact of security incidents contribute to lower overall costs in the long run. Organizations can achieve advanced functional effectiveness, reduce the burden on their security brigades, and ameliorate their overall security posture. Traditional styles may still have a part, particularly in lower associations with limited budgets. Still, the growing complication of cyber pitfalls makes the integration of AI into network security decreasingly essential. As the cyber trouble geography evolves, the capability of AI-driven systems to acclimatize and respond snappily will be critical in maintaining robust network security (Clark & Turner, 2017; Gill, 2022).

Table 4. Cost-benefit analysis

Metric	Traditional Security	AI-Driven Security
Implementation Cost	Low to Moderate	High
Maintenance Cost	Moderate	Moderate
Efficiency Gains	Moderate	High
Long-Term Savings	Moderate	High

CASE STUDIES

Traditional Network Security Case Studies

1. **Company A**: Implemented a traditional network security system that included firewalls, IDS, and antivirus software. The system was effective at blocking known threats but struggled to detect new and evolving threats. The high number of false positives generated by the IDS overwhelmed the security team, resulting in longer response times and increased risk of damage (Smith et al., 2020).

2. **Company B**: Relied on traditional network security methods to protect its network. A sophisticated cyber-attack bypassed the company's defences, resulting in a significant data breach. The manual intervention required to respond to the attack delayed the company's response, increasing the impact of the breach (Clark & Turner, 2017).

AI-Driven Network Security Case Studies

1. **Company C**: Implemented an AI-driven network security system that included machine learning algorithms, behavioural analytics, and automated threat detection. The system was able to detect and respond to threats in real time, reducing the need for manual intervention and minimizing the impact of security incidents. The company experienced fewer false positives and improved overall efficiency (Nguyen & Lee, 2020).
2. **Company D**: Adopted an AI-driven network security approach to protect its network. The system was able to continuously learn from new data, adapting to new and evolving threats. The company's response time to security incidents was significantly reduced, and the impact of security breaches was minimized (Jones & Patel, 2019).

Table 5. Case studies

Company	Security Approach	Effectiveness	Response Time	False Positives	Adaptability
Company A	Traditional Security	Moderate	Long	High	Low
Company B	Traditional Security	Low	Long	High	Low
Company C	AI-Driven Security	High	Short	Low	High
Company D	AI-Driven Security	High	Short	Low	High

CHALLENGES AND LIMITATIONS

Traditional Network Security Challenges

1. **Limited ability to detect new and evolving threats**: Traditional methods rely on predefined rules and signatures, which can be bypassed by sophisticated attackers (Smith et al., 2020).

2. **High number of false positives**: Traditional methods often generate a high number of false positives, which can overwhelm security teams and reduce their overall efficiency (Jones & Patel, 2019).
3. **Manual intervention required**: Traditional methods often require manual intervention to respond to threats, resulting in longer response times and increased risk of damage (Clark & Turner, 2017).
4. **Difficulty scaling to large and complex networks**: Traditional methods may struggle to monitor large and complex networks, making them less suitable for organizations with extensive IT infrastructure (Davis & Smith, 2016).

AI-Driven Network Security Challenges

1. **High implementation cost**: AI-driven systems can be expensive to implement due to the need for specialized hardware, software, and expertise (Evans & Jones, 2019).
2. **Complexity**: AI-driven systems can be complex to set up and maintain, requiring specialized knowledge and skills (Harris & White, 2020).
3. **Data privacy concerns**: AI-driven systems often require access to large amounts of data, raising concerns about data privacy and security (Nguyen & Lee, 2020).
4. **Ethical considerations**: The use of AI in network security raises ethical questions about the potential for bias and discrimination in automated decision-making processes (Jones & Patel, 2019).

FUTURE TRENDS

Emerging Technologies

Several emerging technologies have the potential to enhance network security in the future. These technologies include:

1. **Quantum computing**: Quantum computing has the potential to revolutionize encryption and decryption processes, making it possible to secure data more effectively (Kumar & Singh, 2021).
2. **Blockchain**: Blockchain technology can be used to create secure, tamper-proof records of transactions and data, making it more difficult for attackers to alter or delete information (Harris & White, 2020).

3. **IoT security**: As the number of Internet of Things (IoT) devices continues to grow, new security solutions are being developed to protect these devices from cyber threats (Evans & Jones, 2019).

Integration of AI with Traditional Methods

Integrating AI with traditional network security styles is a promising trend, offering enhanced protection capabilities. This community leverages the strengths of both AI and conventional approaches to develop more robust and effective security results. Traditional styles like firewalls and Intrusion Discovery Systems (IDS) form the backbone of network security, furnishing foundational defenses against pitfalls. Still, their effectiveness can be significantly stoked through AI integration.

AI-driven systems exceed at assaying large volumes of data in real-time, relating patterns, and prognosticating implicit pitfalls with a speed and delicacy that traditional styles alone cannot match. By enhancing firewalls and IDS with AI, associations can ameliorate trouble discovery and response times. For case, AI can dissect business patterns to describe anomalies reflective of cyber-attacks that traditional systems might overlook. Also, AI can give nonstop literacy and adaption, allowing security systems to evolve in response to new pitfalls without taking constant homemade updates.

This combined approach not only strengthens overall security but also reduces the workload on IT security brigades by automating routine tasks and flagging only significant pitfalls for mortal intervention. By employing the capabilities of both AI and traditional security measures, associations can achieve a more flexible and responsive security posture (Jones & Patel, 2019).

Policy and Ethical Considerations

As AI- driven network security advances, addressing policy and ethical counter-accusations becomes pivotal. Crucial enterprises include data sequestration, security, and the fair and transparent use of AI systems. Guarding sensitive information is consummate, as AI technologies frequently reuse vast quantities of particular data, raising the threat of breaches and unauthorized access. Icing robust data security measures is essential to maintaining trust and compliance with sequestration regulations.

Inversely important is the fairness and translucency of AI-driven security systems. These technologies must operate without bias, furnishing indifferent protection for all druggies and avoiding discriminative practices. Transparent AI operations help make stoner trust and enable effective oversight, icing that opinions made by AI systems can be understood and scanned.

To address these challenges, policymakers and assiduity leaders must unite to produce comprehensive guidelines and norms for AI use in network security. These norms should encompass stylish practices for data protection, ethical AI deployment, and responsibility mechanisms. By fostering a collaborative approach, stakeholders can develop a nonsupervisory frame that supports invention while securing ethical principles and public trust. This cooperative trouble will insure that AI-driven network security technologies are both effective and aligned with societal values (Harris & White, 2020).

CONCLUSION

In conclusion, both traditional and AI-driven network security methods have their strengths and weaknesses. Traditional methods, such as firewalls, intrusion detection systems (IDS), and antivirus software, have been the backbone of network security for many years. These tools are designed to protect against known threats by relying on predefined rules and signature-based detection. Firewalls, for instance, monitor and control incoming and outgoing network traffic based on predetermined security rules. IDS analyze network traffic for suspicious activities and known attack patterns, alerting administrators when anomalies are detected. Antivirus software scans files and programs for known malware signatures, quarantining or removing malicious software to prevent infection.

While these traditional methods have been effective in mitigating known threats, their limitations become apparent when dealing with the dynamic nature of modern cyber threats. The rise of sophisticated attacks, such as zero-day exploits and advanced persistent threats (APTs), has exposed the weaknesses of traditional security measures (Zhao et al., 2021). Zero-day exploits target previously unknown vulnerabilities, making it difficult for traditional defenses to detect and mitigate these threats. APTs, which are often carried out by well-funded adversaries, involve long-term, targeted attacks that can remain undetected for extended periods. These sophisticated threats can bypass conventional defenses by exploiting unknown vulnerabilities not covered by existing rules and signatures.

In response to these challenges, the cybersecurity industry has increasingly turned to artificial intelligence (AI) and machine learning (ML) to enhance network security (Jones & Patel, 2019). AI-driven network security leverages advanced algorithms to analyze vast amounts of data, identify patterns, and predict potential threats. Unlike traditional methods, AI-driven approaches can adapt to new threats in real-time, providing a more proactive and dynamic defense mechanism (Nguyen & Lee, 2020).

AI technologies, including machine learning, deep learning, and behavioral analytics, enable systems to learn from data, improving their detection capabilities over time and reducing the reliance on human intervention. This dynamic learning capability allows AI systems to identify and respond to previously unknown threats more effectively. Machine learning algorithms, for instance, can analyze patterns in network traffic and detect anomalies that may indicate a security breach. Behavioral analytics involves analyzing user behavior to detect anomalies that may suggest malicious activities. By understanding normal behavior patterns, AI systems can identify deviations that indicate potential security incidents.

AI-driven network security offers significant advantages in terms of efficiency, accuracy, response time, adaptability, and scalability. In terms of efficiency, AI systems can process and analyze vast amounts of security data much faster than human analysts. This capability is crucial in identifying and mitigating threats in real-time, reducing the window of vulnerability. Additionally, AI systems can handle big data more effectively, filtering out false positives and focusing on genuine threats, improving overall efficiency (Jones & Patel, 2019).

Accuracy is another critical area where AI-driven methods excel. Traditional methods are limited by their reliance on known signatures and rules, making them less effective against zero-day attacks and sophisticated malware. AI-driven systems, however, continuously learn from new data, improving their ability to detect previously unknown threats with greater precision. This dynamic learning capability enhances the overall security posture of an organization.

Response time is crucial in mitigating the impact of cyber threats. Traditional methods, with their manual processes, often have slower response times compared to AI-driven approaches. AI systems can automatically respond to threats, isolating affected systems and mitigating damage almost instantaneously. This rapid response capability is essential in minimizing the potential impact of security incidents.

Adaptability and scalability are also significant advantages of AI-driven network security. Traditional security systems can be rigid and difficult to scale, requiring significant manual effort to update and expand. AI-driven approaches, on the other hand, are inherently more adaptable and scalable. They can automatically adjust to new threats and expanding network environments without extensive manual intervention. This makes AI-driven security solutions more suitable for modern, dynamic network environments.

Cost-effectiveness is another key consideration when comparing traditional and AI-driven network security methods. While the initial implementation of AI-driven security systems can be expensive, their ability to reduce the need for human intervention and improve threat detection efficiency can lead to cost savings in the long run. Traditional methods, with their ongoing maintenance and manual monitoring requirements, may incur higher operational costs over time. By automating many aspects of threat detection and response, AI-driven systems can help organizations optimize their security budgets and allocate resources more effectively (Evans & Jones, 2019; Lange & Kettani, 2019).

Despite the numerous advantages of AI-driven security, there are challenges associated with their implementation. The complexity of AI systems can pose significant hurdles, requiring specialized skills and knowledge to manage and maintain. Organizations may need to invest in training and hiring skilled personnel to effectively leverage AI technologies. Additionally, ethical concerns regarding the use of AI in security, such as data privacy issues and potential biases in AI algorithms, need to be addressed to ensure responsible deployment.

Data privacy is a critical concern in AI-driven network security. The vast amounts of data collected and analyzed by AI systems can include sensitive information, raising questions about how this data is stored, processed, and protected. Ensuring compliance with data protection regulations and implementing robust privacy measures are essential to maintaining trust and safeguarding user data. For instance, data anonymization techniques can be employed to protect individual privacy while still allowing for comprehensive analysis.

Algorithmic bias is another ethical issue that must be considered. AI systems are only as good as the data they are trained on. If the training data is biased, the AI system may produce biased outcomes, potentially leading to unfair or discriminatory practices. Addressing these biases and ensuring that AI algorithms are transparent and fair is crucial for the ethical deployment of AI-driven security solutions. This requires continuous monitoring and updating of AI models to reflect the latest threat landscapes and ensure unbiased decision-making.

By understanding the comparative strengths and weaknesses of these two approaches, organizations can make informed decisions about how to enhance their cybersecurity posture. The integration of AI with traditional methods represents a promising trend that can help organizations create more robust and effective security solutions. For example, AI-driven systems can analyze vast amounts of data to identify potential threats, while traditional methods can provide a fallback mechanism for detecting known attacks. This hybrid approach can improve overall threat detection and response capabilities, reducing the risk of security breaches (Jones & Patel, 2019).

The future of network security lies in leveraging emerging technologies such as quantum computing, blockchain, and IoT security solutions (Kumar & Singh, 2021; Harris & White, 2020; Evans & Jones, 2019). These technologies have the potential to revolutionize how organizations protect their digital assets and mitigate cyber threats. Quantum computing offers the promise of exponentially faster processing speeds, which could enable more robust encryption algorithms that are resistant to brute-force attacks. By harnessing the principles of quantum mechanics, quantum computers can perform complex calculations that are infeasible for classical computers. This could lead to significant advancements in encryption technologies, making it more difficult for attackers to compromise sensitive data (Kumar & Singh, 2021).

Blockchain technology provides a tamper-proof and decentralized ledger that can be used to create secure records of transactions and data. By storing information in a distributed and immutable manner, blockchain can prevent unauthorized modifications and ensure data integrity. This technology has applications in various industries, including finance, healthcare, and supply chain management, where data security and transparency are paramount (Harris & White, 2020). For instance, in supply chain management, blockchain can ensure the authenticity of products by providing a traceable record from the point of origin to the end consumer.

IoT security is becoming increasingly important as the number of connected devices continues to grow. IoT devices are often vulnerable to cyber-attacks due to their limited processing power and lack of built-in security features. However, new security solutions are being developed to address these challenges, including device authentication, data encryption, and intrusion detection systems specifically designed for IoT environments. Securing the IoT ecosystem is essential for protecting critical infrastructure and personal privacy (Evans & Jones, 2019). For example, in smart homes, IoT security can prevent unauthorized access to connected devices such as security cameras, thermostats, and home assistants, ensuring the safety and privacy of residents. (Jernejcic & Kettani, 2019).

The integration of AI with traditional network security methods represents a promising approach for enhancing cybersecurity. By leveraging the strengths of both AI-driven and traditional approaches, organizations can create more resilient and adaptive security solutions. This hybrid approach can improve overall threat detection and response capabilities, reducing the risk of security breaches. For example, AI-driven systems can analyze vast amounts of data to identify potential threats, while traditional methods can provide a fallback mechanism for detecting known attacks. This combined strategy enhances the overall security posture by ensuring comprehensive coverage against a wide range of threats.

However, the adoption of AI-driven network security also raises important policy and ethical considerations. Organizations must ensure that AI systems are trained on unbiased and representative data to avoid perpetuating existing biases or discrimination. Additionally, the collection and processing of large amounts of data by AI systems raise concerns about data privacy and security. Organizations must implement robust data protection measures to safeguard sensitive information and comply with relevant regulations (Harris & White, 2020). For example, data anonymization techniques can be employed to protect individual privacy while still allowing for comprehensive analysis.

REFERENCES

Anderson, J., & Brown, L. (2018). Emerging cybersecurity challenges in the age of digital transformation. *Journal of Cybersecurity Research*, 2(1), 45–58. DOI: 10.1000/jcr.2018.045

Cardoso, P. (2022, June 20). Internet of Things: Security Challenges and Solutions. DOI: 10.31224/2420

Clark, R., & Turner, S. (2017). An overview of intrusion detection systems. *Cybersecurity Review*, 5(2), 78–92. DOI: 10.1000/csr.2017.078

Davis, M., & Smith, P. (2016). Understanding the role of firewalls in network security. *Journal of Network Security*, 12(3), 210–225. DOI: 10.1000/jns.2016.210

Evans, T., & Jones, K. (2019). The impact of emerging technologies on network security. *Journal of Information Security*, 8(4), 300–315. DOI: 10.1000/jis.2019.300

Ghafir, I., Hammoudeh, M., & Prenosil, V. (2018, June 15). Defending against the advanced persistent threat: Detection of disguised executable files. DOI: 10.7287/peerj.preprints.2998v2

Gill, H. (2022, June 21). Malware: Types, Analysis and Classifications. DOI: 10.31224/2423

Harris, B., & White, A. (2020). AI-driven incident response: Challenges and solutions. *Journal of Incident Response*, 7(2), 150–167. DOI: 10.1000/jir.2020.150

Jernejcic, T., & Kettani, H. (2019, October 23). On the Intersection of Big Data and Privacy. *Proceedings of the 4th International Conference on Big Data and Internet of Things*. DOI: 10.1145/3372938.3372939

Jones, R., & Patel, S. (2019). Enhancing network security with AI: A review. *International Journal of Artificial Intelligence in Network Security*, 6(3), 180–195. DOI: 10.1000/ijains.2019.180

Kumar, R., & Singh, T. (2021). Quantum computing and its impact on network security. *Future Technologies Journal*, 4(1), 65–80. DOI: 10.1000/ftj.2021.065

Lange, T., & Kettani, H. (2019). On Security Challenges of Future Technologies. *Journal of Communication*, •••, 1002–1008. DOI: 10.12720/jcm.14.11.1002-1008

Nguyen, H., & Lee, J. (2020). Leveraging AI for network security: Opportunities and challenges. *Journal of AI Applications in Cybersecurity*, 2(2), 85–100. DOI: 10.1000/jaics.2020.085

Smith, D.. (2020). The future of AI in cybersecurity. *Cybersecurity Futures*, 3(3), 210–225. DOI: 10.1000/cf.2019.210

Tatomur, I. (2020, March). UNIVERSITY CYBER SECURITY AS A METHOD FOR ANTI-FISHING FRAUD. *The Economic Discourse*, 1(1), 59–67. DOI: 10.36742/2410-0919-2020-1-7

Tripathi, S., Vardhan Reddy Baddam, S., Kumar Dhadige, P., Singh, S., Abhishek, T., Vijendar Reddy, G., & Kumar Singla, A. (2024). Cyber Watch an Comprensive Security Tool. MATEC Web of Conferences, 392, 01094. DOI: 10.1051/matecconf/202439201094

Chapter 5
Cyber Physical System for Enhancement in Security While Using Cyber

Abhay Bhatia
https://orcid.org/0000-0001-7220-692X
Roorkee Institute of Technology, India

Anil Kumar
Ajay Kumar Garg Engineering College, India

Devendra Sood
Tulas Institute, Dhoolkot, India

ABSTRACT

Advancements in affordable computing and communication technologies have led to the widespread proliferation of interconnected devices, giving rise to a new era characterized by devices that sense, compute, and share information, forming loosely connected Cyber-Physical Systems (CPS). Managing data and making intelligent decisions are the primary areas of research within CPS. Traditionally, cloud-based centralized computation has been the dominant architecture due to its ease of implementation and enhanced control. However, the explosion of data, scalability challenges, and privacy concerns are increasingly highlighting the limitations of such centralized systems. Therefore, there is a growing interest in decentralizing control and distributing computing tasks among the devices as a more promising approach for sharing intelligence. Investigating novel decentralization mechanisms is a central focus of this chapter.

DOI: 10.4018/979-8-3693-9235-5.ch005

1. INTRODUCTION TO CYBER PHYSICAL SYSTEM

Helen Gill coined the phrase "Cyber-Physical System" (CPS) in 2006, and it describes the fusion of the cyber (digital) and physical worlds. A theoretical framework called CPS treats each of its constituents as a model. It includes a wide variety of gadgets linked together through a network. In CPS, the software that manages and runs its physical counterpart is referred to as the cyber component. A CPS is created by the connectivity of different heterogeneous devices. These CPS components usually have constrained processing power and network capacity.

According to references, the first research roadmap for CPS included a number of core study fields, including computing and networking, security, and resource scheduling. Given the resource limitations, energy efficiency is another important issue in CPS research; as a result, CPS must make sure that participating devices are energy-efficient. Parolini et al. (reference) suggested a strategy to reduce data centre energy utilization while still fulfilling user demands. Scalable middleware or platforms that can adapt to the changing needs of CPS are becoming more and more important as the number of networked devices grows. Kim and Kumar are quoted (reference),

It is a significant challenge to design extensible, scalable, and adaptable software platforms that can operate in distributed, heterogeneous, time-critical, and safety-critical contexts because of the scale, structure, and behavioural complexity of today's and tomorrow's CPS. As they all include the fusion of digital and physical systems for diverse applications and industries, CPS has significant ties to modern paradigms including the Internet of Things (IoT), Industry 4.0, Networked Robotics, Machine-to-Machine (M2M) communication, and Edge computing.

Fog computing, Vehicular Networks (VANETs), Network of Things, and Web of Things are all related concepts in the realm of networked systems and Cyber-Physical Systems (CPS). According to Lee, CPS is a theoretical framework that is more enduring and adaptable compared to its specific implementations (such as IoT) and applications (like Machine-to-Machine or M2M communication). While CPS serves as a foundational term, industrial marketing standards have popularized the term "Internet of Things" (IoT) as the prevailing representation of networked devices. However, IoT can have different interpretations, often leading to overlaps with other paradigms and causing confusion.

Among the various definitions of IoT released by IEEE (reference), the one provided by the National Institute of Standards and Technology (NIST) in the US states: "Cyber-physical systems (CPS) - sometimes referred to as the Internet of Things (IoT) - involves connecting smart devices and systems in diverse sectors like transportation, energy, manufacturing and health care in fundamentally new ways."

In alignment with this perspective, this work encompasses all contemporary paradigms within the overarching concept of a Cyber-Physical System (CPS) and treats them interchangeably. For clarity and educational purposes, the chapter delves into the specifics of an Internet of Things (IoT) and its various incarnations in the following subsections. Additionally, a concise introduction to networked robotics is provided for a comprehensive understanding of these emerging technologies and their interconnections.

1.1 Decentralized CPS

According to Kuwahara, autonomous decentralized systems are an integration of multiple subsystems, each of which is autonomous and capable of carrying out its functions on its own. Together, the subsystems can perform maintenance and prevent total breakdowns. Even though Kuwahara's description predates us by more than 20 years, it nevertheless applies to today's decentralized and distributed computing. Mark Zuckerberg, the creator of Facebook and its current CEO, offers a democratic perspective in a new year's resolution.

"The most interesting questions in the technology right now is about centralizing and decentralizing with government using such technology to watch their citizens in broad way, many people in the field now believe technology only centralization of power rather than decentralizing it."

Due to their simplified architecture and relatively low initial cost of investment, centralized networks have long been a widely used technology in deployment. The owner has more authority and control thanks to centralization, which makes it easier to update rules and policies quickly. However, as Zuckerberg said, centralized systems are vulnerable to single point failures, provide privacy problems, and present a significant scalability challenge.

A decentralized CPS (dCPS) is a group of physically connected subsystems that are remotely controlled by cyber units. This type of CPS is made up of devices that are networked together and transmit information and make judgments based on their collective experience. Semwal et al. list a few benefits of hop-to-hop local knowledge exchange establishing such CPS:

1. Trust: Instead of a central server with no control, the data in a decentralized CPS is distributed across the nodes closer to the user and is governed by his/her own rules. The users thus can have more trust since there is limited or no third-party involvement.
2. Reduced network latency: The in-network processing on the nodes which is closer to the user reduces the delays which may occur when the same happens at the remote server side.

3. Single-point of no failure: Failure of the centralized server can cause the complete system to go down. For instance, if Google's email server goes down, productivity (at least to some parts of the world) can come to a stand-still. This may not be the case in a decentralized system where the application could be running at multiple nodes.
4. Running cost: The cost of traditional cloud services rises as storage and communication needs grow because they use a "pay-as-you-go" business model. Decentralized CPS favors in-node data processing, which lowers data traffic.
5. Easy to scale: To be precise, centralized systems should be favored for small or controlled scales. However, decentralized systems only need to connect a node to any of the nodes in the network which make them scalable without affecting the performance.

Decentralization thus offers a set of benefits that can support more advanced and intelligent CPS and IoT-based applications. A decentralized architecture for IoT devices to store and offer consumers email services has been suggested by the author kilobot et al paper. Jha et al. have presented ways to offer sharing and learning in multi-robot systems connected in a decentralized fashion, and the same has been evaluated on a system consisting of Pi. The authors have also provided a stigmergy-based method for managing a population of mobile, autonomous agents that move between nodes in a network.

A prime example of decentralized decision-making is seen in nature. For instance, in insect colonies, an individual's local contacts with its peers allow it to communicate the information it has learned. Common examples are pheromone communication in ants and the trophallaxis displayed by bees. Such local interactions result in intriguing global behaviors, such as the construction of mounds by termites and the construction of intricate nests by social wasps. Researchers have created algorithms that enable robots to emulate such distributed capabilities by modelling them after the social behavior of insects and other animals. Some of the outstanding decentralized multi-robot systems are Werfel et al.'s termite-inspired robots building structures and Rubenstein et al.'s thousands of Kilobots shape formation. The development of decentralized CPS research opens up potential opportunities for new applications as the number of devices and robots rises. However, putting such systems into practice brings up a long list of problems that must be resolved before they can be used in the real world.

1.2 Research Challenges in Decentralized CPSs

Though decentralized CPSs have advantages over their centralized counterparts they pose their own set of research challenges, some of which have been described below:

1. Choice of Communication method: Since there is no concept of a central node to which all other nodes are connected, methods that ensure efficient message communication become mandatory. Broadcasting is one such widely used method.
2. Middleware: As pointed in one research, the development of middle wares that can meet the current needs of a CPS poses to be a significant challenge.
3. Dynamic nature of the network: Unlike conventional IoTs and sensor networks, a decentralized CPS includes mobile entities such as robots and vehicles which can at any point of time connect to or disconnect from the network. This calls for mechanisms that cope up with such dynamism, during run-time.
4. Scalability: One of the prime reasons behind using a decentralized approach is scalability. Hence, mechanisms designed for such a CPS should provide the appropriate performance while also facilitating scalability.
5. On-the-fly (run-time) Alteration: Upgradation in centralized servers necessarily mean a downtime during which most services may need to be halted. A decentralized CPS is favoured in such scenarios since new nodes can be added or existing ones deleted, in run-time. Providing seamless on-the-fly modifications is a challenging task.
6. In-network Information Processing: In order to reduce data size and thus minimize communication cost, in-network processing is carried out wherein data is processed within the nodes itself and only the relevant information is forwarded. However, execution of remote procedures which can carry and process the data is non-trivial.
7. Distributed knowledge sharing: A single node which is part of the *d*CPS may not have the global perception about a task. Thus, knowledge distributed among the nodes needs to be shared. However, what and how to share form some of the crucial questions that need to be answered in such scenarios.
8. Task Ordering and Mutual Exclusion: Tasks delegated to a *d*CPS of robots may require resources which are shared by them. Thus, a mechanism which can ensure mutual exclusion of resources by ordering the execution of tasks is crucial for such decentralized systems. Formulating such methods remains a great challenge.

9. Selection of the best solutions (algorithms, heuristics, mechanism, etc.): Any intelligent CPS must focus on finding the best solution for a specific issue. Finding the optimal solution, without any centralized or globally accessible data on the nodes' performance scores, becomes a difficult task due to the fact that diverse problems are scattered among the nodes. To accommodate dCPSs, mechanisms that can search the mappings to choose the best answer to a particular problem must be developed.
10. Self-adaptation and Organization: The dynamics of the environment and the nature of the problem can change over time. This demands that the algorithms be self-adaptive to such changes and organize or align themselves towards the course that leads to better performances.
11. Security and Privacy: In a *d*CPS, the data is stored and processed across the nodes. Algorithms that can ensure authorization and authentication and cater to such distributed environments are thus needed. A typical example includes the adaptation of blockchain technology in decentralized scenarios.
12. Generation of new solutions and their evolution: A *d*CPS should be self- sustainable in the sense that it not only selects the best solution but also generates and evolves a new set of solutions as and when required. Thus, for a stream of new problems, the system should be capable of adapting and learning.
13. Life-long Learning: Unlike conventional systems which have a separate training and testing phase, life-long learning facilitates the continuous learning of patterns of incoming problems and devises the best possible solution. Embed- ding such life-long learning into a decentralized CPS will boost its learning ability.

This work aims to just to lay a foundation for catering to the challenges that have been discussed earlier as above. The initial half of the chapter involves the development of a middleware suitable for a decentralized CPS followed by a real-world comparison against a centralized system. The latter half of it propounds mechanisms inspired by the Biological Immune System; a classical decentralized system found in vertebrates. This makes use of mobile agents to provide task ordering, mutual exclusion, solution selection and evolution and finally tries to wrap up the whole as a *d*CPS capable of decentralized and distributed learning. A brief review of mobile agents is presented in the next section. A short introduction to the Biological Immune System is also presented in the following section.

1.3 Mobile Agents

Computer programs known as agents can complete a task or set of tasks on behalf of the user. They are capable of making their own decisions and moving on independently. Maes et al. define agents as computational systems that have the ability to sense their surroundings and act autonomously to accomplish a set of goals. In the cyberspace, these agents function similarly to people and robots as they do in the actual one. The agents are typically static, which means they do their task(s) while perched atop a computing device and collaborate with other static agents to accomplish a common goal.

On the other hand, the mobile agents belong to a certain class of agents that are as the added capability of mobility to the system. A mobile agent is just as a tiny piece of software with having the capacity to travel to a different node while still carrying its data and code, pause the execution of a job, and resume it there. After doing its work on the distant side, it can also return the results to the source node. According to Outtagarts, there are several applications for mobile agents, including e-commerce, smart grids, energy efficiency and metering, network management, e-learning, and web services. The author also emphasizes the superiority of mobile agents over more conventional message transmission techniques like client-server architecture, Remote Procedure-Call (RPC), CORBA, etc.

(a) In addition to moving, a mobile agent can replicate itself, it also carries the payload (such as data or any program), making choices locally, runs a program on a separate node or even on locations etc. Mobile agents can also be used as for generation and transmission of intelligence as they travel across any network. Only a few of the numerous applications for which they have been used include wireless sensor network, e-commerce, robot control, e-learning, security, networked robotics, and IoT. Several important advantages of employing mobile agents include:
(b) Reduced bandwidth and latency: A mobile agent can easily send the calculation as code to a remote site. By moving to this site and processing the data there, the computing program or logic can avoid having to retrieve all of the raw or unprocessed data from a faraway location. Network traffic and latency are thereby reduced.
(c) Discrete operations: In the dynamic network with the mobile devices, it is as unusual for a continuous and regular connection that is to be maintained between two nodes for the lengthy period of time. In a conventional client-server system, an unexpected disconnect could compel the server to broadcast all the data again, which would be costly. In contrast, in a mobile agent-based the scenarios, migrants only take place after a connection has been established. Until a link to the following node is made, the mobile agent remains in the new node. The agent of the mobile is far less demanding to process than big amounts of data. As a result, a migration failure does not result in appreciable bandwidth or time losses.

(d) Cloning: Using a mobile agent's ability to clone, many copies of the program can be made in the nodes making up a decentralized CPS. This makes some parallelism possible and, as a result, speeds up CPS execution. According to Godfrey et al., cloning can expedite the servicing of such nodes.

(e) Adaptivity and flexibility: A traditional centrally managed system would need to be shut down, the upgrades done, and then the system would need to be restarted. In a system based on mobile agents, upgrades might be stored inside the agent and released into the network. More flexibility is possible with these On-The-Fly Programming (OTFP) features. The ability to monitor and perceive their surroundings allows agents to adapt their behaviour as needed. A mobile agent can modify its behaviour to fit different situations and add new payload behaviour.

Thus, mobile agents could potentially offer a workable distributed solution to problems relating to a dCPS.

In Wireless Sensor Networks (WSN), where it is challenging to maintain constant network connectivity, mobile agents have been a key utility. Godfrey et al.'s platform for IoT applications makes use of mobile agents to offer linked devices emergency services. Mobile agents for the Internet of Things are presented in a resource-oriented way in a recent dissertation by Lappänen. The suggested framework offers a REST-based interface for opportunistic agent-based applications that have been built. An intelligent cart system has been implemented by Kambayashi et al. using mobile agents in multi-robot settings. The system was created using an evolutionary ant clustering technique. In order to offer synchronisation, learning, and dispersed job distribution in a milieu, Jha et al. have developed a mobile agent-based approach.

2. PHYSICAL AND CYBER SYSTEM TOGETHER

Tartarus' capabilities as a multi-agent platform are enhanced to the network with integration of it to the robots with other heterogeneous devices producing a CPS. It has a variety of features, including distributed and decentralized control, intelligence, autonomy, and more, thanks to its integrated agent-based technology. The chapter describes how these functionalities were enhanced to incorporate crucial components that can make it easier for cyber agents to access and operate real-world devices. The chapter explains the creation and integration of software interfaces that provide access to various hardware, including the Raspberry Pi, Intel Galileo, Lego Mindstorm NXT, and others. As a result, Tartarus has become a tool that can be used not only to research and analyses such systems but also to construct them. Thus, this chapter presents Tartarus as a means of bridging the gap between the virtual and real worlds. This chapter describes an implementation of a CPS of robots following an initial rationale, a description of Tartarus' architecture, and several existing and enhanced features.

Currently, the number of devices added to the cyberspace each year is in the millions, and this growth is occurring quickly. Such a surge has encouraged research into putting computers closer to the physical things. A new field of study called Cyber-Physical Systems (CPS) aims to close the gap between computational and physical phenomena. CPS entails the connection of numerous.

It utilizes gadgets like sensor-based nodes, cell phones, embedded system, Personal Computers, routers, switches etc. and focuses on how computational and physical processes interact with real-time information. As a result, a CPS becomes dispersed and diversified. A CPS may also request that the devices be given embedded intelligence in order to make them intelligent. The CPS devices must have autonomy in order for them to independently make local decisions without human intervention. A CPS should naturally be able to accommodate many numbers of devices, grant autonomy to any internal devices, supporting the distributed computing models, and be scalable to it. A platform that permits fast prototyping and CPS programming must be created in order to get over these challenges.

The majority of a CPS might be made up of active robots that communicate with the physical world via sensors and actuators. Robots must be able to make decisions since they are considered autonomous or semi-autonomous beings. As a result, the terms scalability and heterogeneity in a CPS of robots might be combined to create a complex CPS by combining many and different classes of robots. With so many robots interacting with so many other devices, all of which contribute to the distributed or decentralized resolution of problems, it is challenging to realize a CPS.

The Multi-Agents System (MAS) paradigm can be used to computationally solve these issues. The coordinated actions of the processes that result from the local interactions of individual agents are what give the system its overall intelligent behavior. Agents are the terms used in MASs to describe software entities that are carrying out tasks on the behalf of any user, forum, or any type of client-side systems. A number of factors, including as autonomy, reactive to things, proactiveness, social interaction capability, adaptability, rationality, specialization, etc. set an agent apart from any other conventional piece of software. It is believed that most agents are static objects. However, their portability adds a new level to their utility, especially in such distributed and decentralized types of systems. Mobile Agents (MA) are types of agents that can travel between nodes in a network. Mobile agents have been used by researchers in a variety of applications, including robotics, network manager, electronic commerce, energy efficiency and metering, wireless sensors, grid computing, distributed data mining, security, and e-learning.

Tartarus is changed into a piece of software with special properties that allow cyber agents to quickly and easily access and control real-world things. Tartarus was created using the whole open-source SWI-Prolog ecosystem. Tartarus (Figure 1) is now able to utilized for all Prolog-based features which includes dynamic databases, retraction with rule assertion, etc.

Figure 1. Architecture of Tartarus

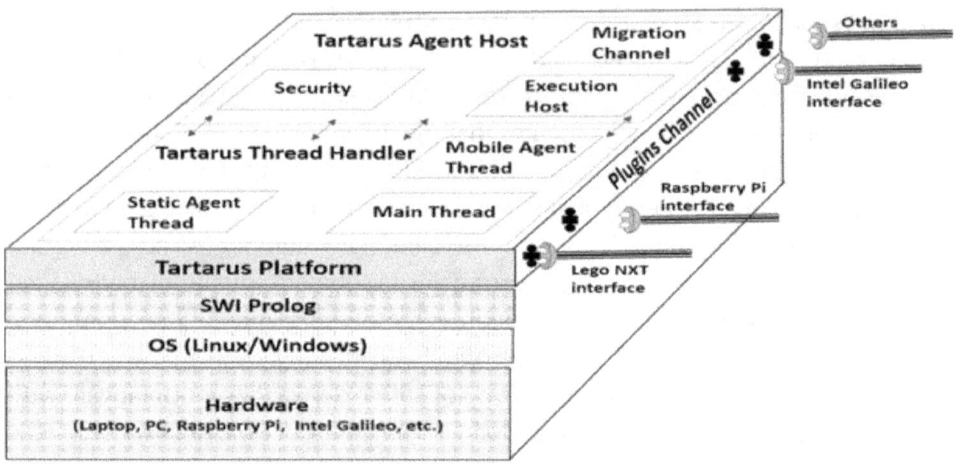

Table 1. Important redicates of Tartarus

Function of the Predicate	Description	Syntax
Creating Agent	Generating a name using any random alphabet or creating a new agent with the provided name.	*create_static_agent*(AgentName,(IP,Port), HandlerName) *create_mobile_ agent*(AgentName,(IP,Port), HandlerName)
Migration of Agent	Enables the transfer of an agent from a Tartarus source host to a Tartarus destination host, enabling the agents' mobility.	*move_agent*(AgentName,(IP, Port)).
Agent Payload	user-defined predicates and data can be added.	*add_payload*(AgentName, ListOfPredicates).
Agent Communication	Message passing between static agents stationed at several Tartarus hosts.	*agent_post*(AgentName,(DestinationIP, Des-tinationPort),ListOfPredicates).

continued on following page

Table 1. Continued

Function of the Predicate	Description	Syntax
Agent Clone	creates a copy of the original agent at the specified IP address and port.	*clone_agent*(AgentName,(DestinationIP, DestinationPort),CloneName).
Agent Kill	Kills the specified agent.	*kill_agent*(AgentName).

The TCP/IP protocol stack is used by the Tartarus agent platform to facilitate communication via wired or wireless channels in a LAN/WAN. For the purpose of creating the communication interface with other Tartarus systems that are reachable within the network, each Tartarus platform creates a TCP/IP socket. Both static and mobile agents can be created using the Tartarus platform. Moving and stationary agents can converse with one another. A distinct TCP/IP socket and thread are created by each static agent for use in communication and execution. Mobile agent communication is always done over the same Tartarus platform socket. The SWI-Prolog environment-based development environment Tartarus offers the flexibility of writing interpreted code. Tartarus can thus support dynamic programming, as will be discussed in more detail later.

Multiple Tartarus platforms that have been configured (Figure 2) as a CPS can be roughly shown in Figure 2.2. A Pi controller board (Node 1), a laptop (Node 2), and desktop computers (Nodes 3, 4, 5, and 6) are some of these platforms. Additionally, a LEGO ® MINDSTORMS ® NXT robot is connected via Bluetooth to each of nodes 2 and 3. The graphic shows that the nodes have wired or wireless communication options.

Static agents Si (S1, S2, and S3) and mobile agents Mi (M1 and M2) are shown to reside on Tartarus platforms. The mobile agents that are migrating are referred to by the abbreviation MuMi. Node 1 houses S1 and S2, while Node 3 houses S3. In addition, Mobile Agent 3 (MuM3) is travelling across a wireless link from Node 2 to Node 1 while M1 and M2 are operating at Nodes 2 and 3, respectively. The intra-node communication between a stationary agent (S3) and a moving agent (M2) is shown in node 3.

Figure 2. CPS Config on Tartarus platform

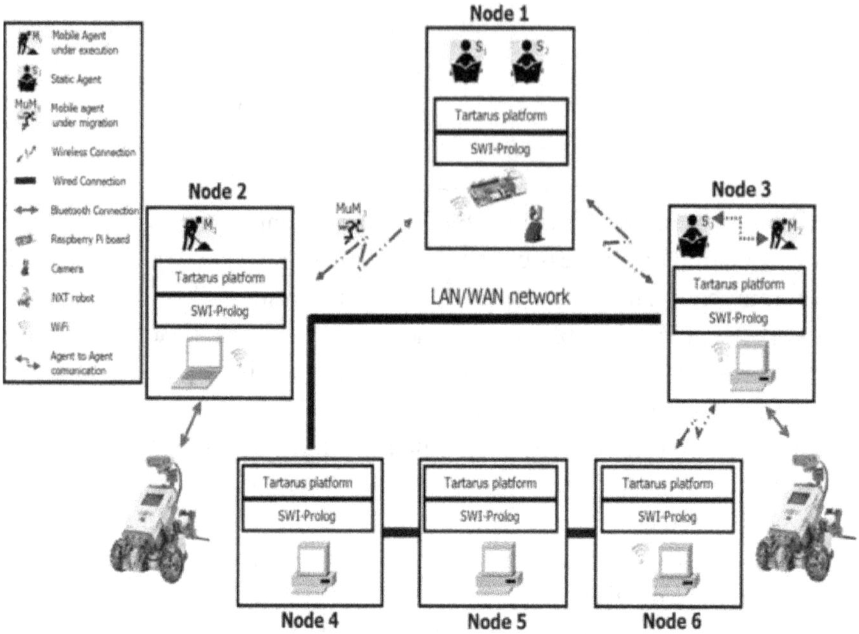

3. DECENTRALIZATION OF CYBER PHYSICAL SYSTEM

The price of embedded hardware has dramatically decreased as a result of the rapid advancement in VLSI technology research. The development of computer ecosystems that are both ubiquitous and widespread is made possible by embedded devices, such mobile phones, being able to conduct far more complex computations than their older counterparts. While realizing IoTs and CPSs, networking capabilities have expanded the use of these devices and given rise to new paradigms and viewpoints. These physical devices produce enormous volumes of data, which are typically transferred to a distant server, which then handles the necessary calculations and decision-making. Even while such a centralized solution is simple and relatively simple to implement, it endangers the confidentiality and integrity of personal data and raises the cost of usage by causing irrational uploads and downloads. In military and medical applications, the utilization of a centralized system becomes extremely delicate. The current situation calls for a framework that may enable data processing and decision making in a decentralized and distributed manner among the devices linked to a network in order to significantly lessen the aforementioned practical challenges. A mobile agent-based implementation of Decentralized and Distributed CPS (dCPS), incorporating IoT, is shown in this chapter. The method converts a centralized system into a fairly distributed system with no or little centralization by fusing local peer-to-peer communication with ideas from multi-agent abstraction.

An indoor implementation of the CPS application LATS which is acronym for Location-Aware and Tracking Service has been used to demonstrate the use of mobile agent-based approaches that share and process data locally within the participating nodes. Thus, the work presented in this chapter is built on top of these systems. The network's agents keep an eye on and track anybody who enters. Providing LATS in a dynamic environment is challenging. When this happens, it's necessary to inquire about a person's whereabouts, when they entered the monitored area, how they are travelling, etc. Sending requests to a centrally stored database of related data is comparatively simple. However, if the person being tracked moves around a lot, finding gets challenging because the database becomes dynamic. The difficulty increases when a large number of persons are being tracked. The situation worsens when there are multiple tracking and data storage devices present with limited computational and storage resources. In these cases, data is disseminated throughout a network and is dynamic. As more informational queries are fired simultaneously and asynchronously, the issue gets worse. In this chapter, the significance and value of dCPS are emphasized, and a mobile agent-based implementation strategy is shown. The strategy attempts to address and resolve the aforementioned problems.

The static agents as well as mobile agent in this cyber environment are responsible for the actual decision-making and intelligence-gathering process. These are applications that run on the embedded devices that are connected.

The development of any computing environment such as Fog Computing environment is quite similar to the idea of deploying agents (Figure 3) in to Intranet of Things. The cloud is generally extended towards user side, consisting of a collection of decentralized, computer nodes (distributed) that make up the network's edge. An idea like this provides a number of benefits, which includes:

Figure 3. Agent and cyber world

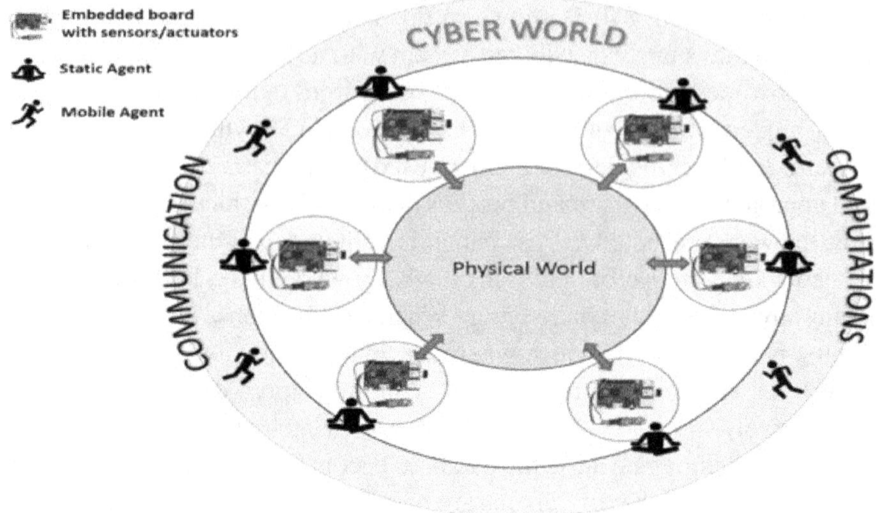

- *Privacy*: Multinational firms like Amazon, Google, Microsoft, Cisco, and others own the majority of the cloud servers, which are constantly receiving data from the user side. When all data of any user is collected for analytics purposes at the cloud, personal information leakage and data ownership become a serious problem. A safer substitute would be a local infrastructure over which the user has more control than a cloud server. This would make it possible to filter and process local data before transferring it to the cloud. A system based on agents might offer a more effective way to protect privacy.
- *Cost*: A "Pay-as-you-go" model is used for cloud services, which raises the price as storage and network communication grow. These expenses can be minimized in a model of local computational infrastructure, if only pertinent data is sent to the cloud after the acquired data has been locally filtered.
- *Network Latency*: Because of its inherent latency problems, a cloud may not be an appropriate solution for applications that call for quick responses, such as real-time data analytics in smart grids, live video streaming in linked cars, etc. On the other hand, an Intranet of Things powered by agents can deliver quick local calculations, reducing latency.

- *Energy*: Agents, in an environment of Intranet of Things can filter the collected data before sending it to the cloud, as was already described. This decreases communication overheads, which in turn decreases energy consumption and prolongs the battery life of the network's devices.

A quick overview of the topic is also included, since the work presented employs LATS as an agent-based software implemented on a Pi.

A dynamic model with location-dependent services is one where the object, the observer, or both, may be mobile with respect to their geolocation. Among the traditional methods for tracking moving objects are cameras, RFIDs, GPS, and other devices. The most often used tool for self-finding is a cell phone's GPS. But outside, where the device can have a satellite connection, is where this strategy works best. Such an approach can be used for indoor localization, although GPS is unreliable due to room geometry and erratic and weak satellite reception. This necessitates the development of a dependable, reasonably priced indoor positioning and tracking system.

4. METHODOLOGY AND WORKING CULTURE

Wolfson et al.'s early work on location-aware services offers a database-based approach for tracking moving items. On top of an existing database, they provide a Database for Moving Objects (DOMINO), which enables the database management system to forecast the future location of the moving object. The predicted position is updated each time the moving object moves from its current location.

In order to model the moving item, Wolfson et al. have also presented a trajectory location management system. The main problems with the point-location management paradigm are outlined. A point-location paradigm is erroneous when it comes to the extrapolation or interpolation of position data for moving objects. An estimate of a moving object's source and destination can be obtained using a trajectory location model. A trajectory is created using this data and an electronic map created using the journey time data. In the actual world, essential information isn't often concentrated in one place. According to Wolfson et al., their model has to be modified to take into consideration scenarios in which data is made available in a scattered fashion.

Figure 4. How the system works with Tartarus platform

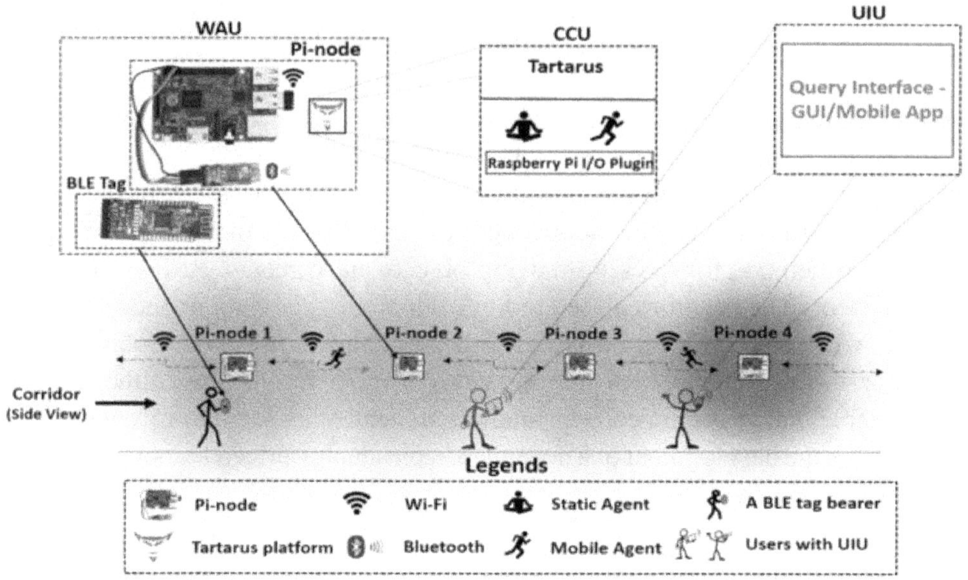

A complex system can be divided into more manageable, separately controllable components. This kind of abstraction facilitates system design and implementation. This section covers the Location Aware and Tracking Service (Figure 4) (LATS) use case, detection technique, and essential application components. We wrap off by discussing a mobile agent-based algorithm to process user requests.

This device's wearable Bluetooth Low Energy (BLE) beacon emitter, the HM-10, sends out data packets on a consistent basis. Using the on-board UART module, a BLE receiver connected to a Raspberry Pi receives these packets. An acquisition unit that serves as a BLE receiver is equipped with a wearable BLE tag that is set up as a beacon transmitter (made up of a BLE device and a battery) and a Pi-node (a Pi attached to a BLE device). Additionally, the Pi comes with a USB Wi-Fi adapter. The wearable BLE device transmits data in 30-byte packets that each contains five fields of data as listed below.

1. Prelude: The manufacturer's information is contained in this 9-byte read-only field.
2. Universally Unique Identifier (UUID): This 16-byte field can be pre-configured to include the name as of the BLE device.

3. Major: This field majorly, which is editable by users, aids in locating specific examples of these devices within a larger group.
4. Minor: A subset of the Major field may be specified in this writable field.
5. Tx Power: The signal intensity at a distance of 1 m from the device is indicated by a calibrated 2's complement value in this field. To determine the distance between the transmitter and receiver, this field is analogized with the strength of signal measured at the rare end of it.

An intimate link between the offline and online worlds is a CPS. In this example, the physical unit (Pi) is supported by the Tartarus platform, which operates as a cyber-unit on top of it. Tartarus is equipped with a plugin that enables access to the Pi's internal peripherals.

By exploiting the UART interface, a static agent named as the Database agent inside a Tartarus instance, running on a Pi retrieves the beacon data of the BLE receiver from the buffer register. Then the database agent then timestamps that data and stores it in a database of SQL surely on the Pi's memory card. If a person spends a lot of time in a zone, a lot of data will gather; most of this data could

Data is only logged as a result when the beacon's Received Signal Strength (RSS) has significantly changed. Additionally, if we talk about regions than they are 3 in number—Distant, Beyond and Close—have been utilized for the position characterizing of a user within a zone rather than basing a choice on the typically noisy RSS readings. The following definitions apply to the three regions:

(i) Beyond: When the value of RSS value is '0', indication is purely the person is beyond the concerned zone and has not been identified.
(ii) Distant: In this scenario, the target of the tracking is located far from the Pi-node. This is indicated at the Pi-node by a low RSS value of the affected zone, which indicates that the BLE tag holding is between 2 to 5 meters away that is from the associated Pi-node.
(iii) Close: In the present situation, less than 2 meters, it is having a strong RSS value which indicates that the individual is well and is within the range.

The above given fields that are as six in number with the names UUID, Timestamps, Minors, Major, Region, and RSS, making up each SQL entry.

Only when the value of the field Region changes is an entry made in the SQL database. An entry is registered with the new Region, for instance, if the field switches from beyond to close. No record is to be made into the database to the subsequent items after it is also close. Likewise, if the sixth field becomes, there is a record, either distinct or beyond. It can be seen that the database makes it simple to compute information about a user's time spent in a given region or zone. A person may also be followed as they transition between zones. One may also readily guess the precise time at which they entered a zone, how long they were there, and the moment they left it. As a result, each Pi-node keeps track of the next zone a person enters as they go down a corridor made up of several such zones. This is accomplished using the Motion Vector notion, which has been outlined feature of this work and is as the concluder to this chapter.

5. CONCLUSION

Although the goal of this chapter was to create the groundwork for the use of decentralization in CPS and IoT systems, it must be noted that the absence of a central governing body makes it difficult to really put these ideas into effect. The same holds true for physically controlled cyber-weakly connected systems. Among the difficult problems faced by networked robotic systems include synchronization, population control of mobile agents, and task distribution. The majority of these challenges have been attempted to be covered in this chapter.

REFERENCES

Bhatia, A., Kumar, A., Jain, A., Kumar, A., Verma, C., Illes, Z., Aschilean, I., & Raboaca, M. S. (2022). Networked control system with MANET communication and AODV routing. *Heliyon*, 8(11), 11. DOI: 10.1016/j.heliyon.2022.e11678 PMID: 36439715

Bhatia, P., GRD-IMT, D., Bhatia, A., & India, U. (2023). POTENTIAL ROLE OF ICTS IN. *Social Development.*

Capodieci, N., Hart, E., & Cabri, G. (2013, September). Designing self-aware adaptive systems: from autonomic computing to cognitive immune networks. In 2013 IEEE 7th International Conference on Self-Adaptation and Self-Organizing Systems Workshops (pp. 59-64). IEEE.

Catarinucci, L., De Donno, D., Mainetti, L., Palano, L., & Patrono, L. (2015). M. L. Ste- fanizzi, and L. Tarricone. An iot-aware architecture for smart healthcare sys- tems. *Internet ofThings Journal, IEEE*, 2(6), 515–526. DOI: 10.1109/JIOT.2015.2417684

Chandy, K. M., & Misra, J. (1984, October). The Drinking Philosophers Problem. *ACM Transactions on Programming Languages and Systems*, 6(4), 632–646. DOI: 10.1145/1780.1804

Chen, M., Gonzalez, S., & Leung, V. (2007). Applications and design issues for mobile agents in wireless sensor networks. *IEEE Wireless Communications*, 14(6), 20–26. DOI: 10.1109/MWC.2007.4407223

Chen, R., Liu, C. M., & Chen, C. (2012). An artificial immune-based distributed intrusion detection model for the internet of things. *Advanced Materials Research*, 366, 165–168.

Chertov, R., Fahmy, S., & Shroff, N. B. (2006, March). Emulation versus simulation: A case study of TCP-targeted denial of service attacks. In 2nd International Conference on Testbeds and Research Infrastructures for the Development of Networks and Communities, 2006. TRIDENTCOM 2006. (pp. 10-pp). IEEE.

Chess, D., Harrison, C., & Kershenbaum, A. (1996, July). Mobile agents: Are they a good idea? In International Workshop on Mobile Object Systems (pp. 25-45). Berlin, Heidelberg: Springer Berlin Heidelberg.

Chetty, M., Sung, J.-Y., & Grinter, R. E. How smart homes learn: The evolution of the networked home and household. In *International Conference on Ubiquitous Computing*, pages 127–144. Springer, 2007. DOI: 10.1007/978-3-540-74853-3_8

Chu, H. N., Glad, A., Simonin, O., Sempe, F., Drogoul, A., & Charpillet, F. Swarm approaches for the patrolling problem, information propagation vs. pheromone evaporation. In *19th IEEE International Conference on Tools with Artificial Intelligence(ICTAI 2007)*, volume 1, pages 442–449, Oct 2007. DOI: 10.1109/ICTAI.2007.80

Coello, C. A. C., Rivera, D. C., & Cortes, N. C. Use of an artificial immune system for job shop scheduling. In *International Conference on Artificial Immune Systems*, pages 1–10. Springer, 2003. DOI: 10.1007/978-3-540-45192-1_1

Coffman, E. G., Elphick, M., & Shoshani, A. (1971, June). System deadlocks. *ACM Computing Surveys*, 3(2), 67–78. DOI: 10.1145/356586.356588

Cusumano, M. (2010). Cloud computing and saas as new computing platforms. *Communications of the ACM*, 53(4), 27–29. DOI: 10.1145/1721654.1721667

Dangerfield, J., McCarthy, T., & Ellery, W. (1998). The mound-building termite macrotermes michaelseni as an ecosystem engineer. *Journal of Tropical Ecology*, 14(4), 507–520. DOI: 10.1017/S0266467498000364

Dasgupta, D. (1999). *An Overview of Artificial Immune Systems and Their Applications*. Springer.

de Castro, L. N., & Timmis, J. (2002). Artificial immune systems: a novel approach to pattern recognition.

De Castro, L. N., & Von Zuben, F. J. (2002). Learning and optimization using the clonal selection principle. *IEEE Transactions on Evolutionary Computation*, 6(3), 239–251. DOI: 10.1109/TEVC.2002.1011539

Dhenakaran, S. S., & Parvathavarthini, A. (2013). An overview of routing protocols in mobile ad-hoc network. *International Journal of Advanced Research in Computer Science and Software Engineering*, 3(2).

Dias, M. B., & Stentz, A. A free market architecture for distributed con- trol of a multirobot system. In *6th International Conference on Intelligent Autonomous Systems (IAS-6)*, pages 115–122, 2000.

Dobkin, D. M. (2012). *The RF in RFID: UHF RFID in Practice*. Newnes.

Duarte, M., Gomes, J., Oliveira, S. M., & Christensen, A. L. Evorbc: Evolu- tionary repertoire-based control for robots with arbitrary locomotion complex- ity. In *Proceedings of the Genetic and Evolutionary Computation Conference 2016*, GECCO '16, pages 93–100, 2016. DOI: 10.1145/2908812.2908855

Duarte, M., Oliveira, S., & Christensen, A. L. Hierarchical evolution of robotic controllers for complex tasks. In *Development and Learning and Epigenetic Robotics (ICDL),2012IEEE International Conference on*, pages 1–6. IEEE, 2012. DOI: 10.1109/DevLrn.2012.6400828

Duarte, M., Oliveira, S. M., & Christensen, A. L. Hybrid control for large swarms of aquatic drones. In *Proceedings of the 14th International Conference on the Synthesis & Simulation of Living Systems.MIT Press,Cambridge, MA*, pages 785–792. Citeseer, 2014.

Faragher, R., & Harle, R. An analysis of the accuracy of bluetooth low energy for indoor positioning applications. In *Proceedings of the 27th International Technical Meeting of the Satellite Division of the Institute of Navigation (ION GNSS+ '14)*, 2014.

Farmer, J. D., Packard, N. H., & Perelson, A. S. (1986). The immune system, adaptation, and machine learning. *Physica D. Nonlinear Phenomena*, 22(1), 187–204. DOI: 10.1016/0167-2789(86)90240-X

Fife, L. D., & Gruenwald, L. (2003, June). Research Issues for Data Communication in Mobile Ad-hoc Network Database Systems. *SIGMOD Record*, 32(2), 42–47. DOI: 10.1145/776985.776991

Floreano, D., & Mondada, F. Automatic creation of an autonomous agent: Genetic evolution of a neural-network driven robot. 1994. In *Proceedings of the Third International Conference on Simulation of Adaptive behavior: From Animals to Animats*, volume 3.

Franklin, S., & Graesser, A. (1996). Is it an agent, or just a program?: A taxonomy for autonomous agents. In *Intelligent agents III agent theories, architectures, and languages* (pp. 21–35). Springer.

Freitas, A. A. (2004). A critical review of multi-objective optimization in data mining: A position paper. *SIGKDD Explorations*, 6(2), 77–86. DOI: 10.1145/1046456.1046467

Gaber, J., & Bakhouya, M. Mobile Agent-Based Approach for Resource Dis- covery in Peer-to-Peer Networks. In *Agents and Peer-to-Peer Computing*, pages 63–73, 2008.

Gangwar, N., Semwal, T., & Nair, S. B. Care: An iot based system for passenger service and comfort in railways. In *Communication Systems and Networks (COMSNETS),20179th International Conference on*, pages 55–62. IEEE, 2017.

Gartner. Gartner says 6.4 billion connected "things" will be in use in 2016, up 30 percent from 2015, (2015). [Online; accessed 20-February-2016].

Gerkey, B. P., & Matarić, M. J. (2001). *Principled communication for dynamic multi-robot task allocation*. Springer Berlin Heidelberg.

Gerkey, B. P., & Mataric, M. J. (2003, September). Multi-robot task allocation: Analyzing the complexity and optimality of key architectures. In 2003 IEEE international conference on robotics and automation (Cat. No. 03CH37422) (Vol. 3, pp. 3862-3868). IEEE.

Ghosh, A., Ratasuk, R., Mondal, B., Mangalvedhe, N., & Thomas, T. (2010). Lte- advanced: Next-generation wireless broadband technology. *IEEE Wireless Communications*, 17(3), 10–22. DOI: 10.1109/MWC.2010.5490974

Godfrey, W. W., Jha, S. S., & Nair, S. B. On a mobile agent framework for an internet of things. In *International Conference on Communication Systems and Network Technologies (CSNT),2013*, pages 345–350. IEEE, 2013. DOI: 10.1109/CSNT.2013.79

Godfrey, W. W., Jha, S. S., & Nair, S. B. (2014). On stigmergically controlling a population of heterogeneous mobile agents using cloning resource. In *Trans- actions on Computational Collective Intelligence XIV* (pp. 49–70). Springer. DOI: 10.1007/978-3-662-44509-9_3

Godfrey, W. W., & Nair, S. B. (2008). An immune system based multi-robot mobile agent network. In *Artificial Immune Systems* (pp. 424–433). Springer. DOI: 10.1007/978-3-540-85072-4_37

Godfrey, W. W., & Nair, S. B. (2010). Mobile agent cloning for servicing networked robots. In *Principles and Practice of Multi-Agent Systems* (pp. 336–339). Springer.

Godfrey, W. W., & Nair, S. B. A Mobile Agent Cloning Controller for Ser- vicing Networked Robots. In *International Conference on Future Information Technology IPCSIT*, volume 13, pages 81–85. IACSIT Press, 2011.

Godfrey, W. W., & Nair, S. B. A Pheromone Based Mobile Agent Migration Strategy for Servicing Networked Robots. In *Bio-Inspired Models of Network, Information, and Computing Systems*, pages 533–541. Springer, 2012. DOI: 10.1007/978-3-642-32615-8_52

Gomez, C., Oller, J., & Paradells, J. (2012). Overview and evaluation of bluetooth low energy: An emerging low-power wireless technology. *Sensors (Basel)*, 12(9), 11734–11753. DOI: 10.3390/s120911734

I. Goodfellow, Y. Bengio, A. Courville, and Y. Bengio. *Deep learning*, vol- ume 1. MIT press Cambridge, 2016.

Gray, R. S. Agent tcl: A transportable agent system. In *Proceedings of the ciKM Workshop on intelligent information Agents, Fourth international conference on information and Knowledge Management (ciKM 95), Baltimore, Maryland*, 1995.

Gubbi, J., Buyya, R., Marusic, S., & Palaniswami, M. (2013). Internet of things (iot): A vision, architectural elements, and future directions. *Future Generation Computer Systems*, 29(7), 1645–1660. DOI: 10.1016/j.future.2013.01.010

Guo, H. *Algorithm Selection for Sorting and Probabilistic inference: A ma- chine learning approach*. PhD thesis, Department of Computing and Informa- tion Sciences, College of Engineering, Kansas State University, 2003.

Hadzilacos, V. A note on group mutual exclusion. In *Proceedings of the Twentieth Annual ACM Symposium on Principles of Distributed Computing*, PODC '01, pages 100–106, New York, NY, USA, 2001. ACM. DOI: 10.1145/383962.383997

Harmer, P. K., Williams, P. D., Gunsch, G. H., & Lamont, G. B. (2002, June). An arti- ficial immune system architecture for computer security applications. *IEEE Transactions on Evolutionary Computation*, 6(3), 252–280. DOI: 10.1109/TEVC.2002.1011540

Hart, E., Davoudani, D., & McEwan, C. Immunological inspiration for building a new generation of autonomic systems. In *Proceedings of the 1st international conference on Autonomic computing and communication sys- tems*, page 9. ICST (Institute for Computer Sciences, Social-Informatics and Telecommunications Engineering), 2007. DOI: 10.4108/ICST.AUTONOMICS2007.2229

Heinerman, J., Zonta, A., Haasdijk, E., & Eiben, A. E. On-line evolution of foraging behaviour in a population of real robots. In *European Conference on the Applications of Evolutionary Computation*, pages 198–212. Springer, 2016. DOI: 10.1007/978-3-319-31153-1_14

Ishiguro, A., Kondo, T., Watanabe, Y., & Uchikawa, Y. Dynamic behavior arbitration of autonomous mobile robots using immune networks. In *IEEE International Conference on Evolutionary Computation*, volume 2, pages 722– 727. IEEE, 1995. DOI: 10.1109/ICEC.1995.487474

Jakobi, N. (1997). Evolutionary robotics and the radical envelope-of-noise hypothesis. *Adaptive Behavior*, 6(2), 325–368. DOI: 10.1177/105971239700600205

Jerne, N. K. (1974). Toward a network theory of immune system. *Annales d'Immunologie*, 125(1), 373–389.

Jha, S. S. (2016). On mobile agents for learning and coordination in a networked robotics milieu.

Jha, S. S., Godfrey, W. W., & Nair, S. B. (2014, June). Stigmergy-Based Synchronization of a Sequence of Tasks in a Network of Asynchronous Nodes. *Cybernetics and Systems*, 45(5), 373–406. DOI: 10.1080/01969722.2014.917235

Jha, S. S., & Nair, S. B. (2012, March). A logic programming interface for multiple robots. In 2012 3rd National Conference on Emerging Trends and Applications in Computer Science (pp. 152-156). IEEE.

Jha, S. S., & Nair, S. B. (2015, December). An Idiotypic Solution Sieve for Selecting the Best Performing Solutions in Real-World Distributed Intelligence. In 2015 3rd International Conference on Artificial Intelligence, Modelling and Simulation (AIMS) (pp. 71-76). IEEE.

Jha, S. S., & Nair, S. B. (2015). On a multi-agent distributed asynchronous intelligence-sharing and learning framework. In *Transactions on Computational Collective Intelligence XVIII* (pp. 166–200). Springer Berlin Heidelberg.

Jha, S. S., & Nair, S. B. (2018). Tansa: Task allocation using nomadic soft agents for multirobot systems. *IEEE Transactions on Emerging Topics in Computational Intelligence*, 2(4), 308–318. DOI: 10.1109/TETCI.2017.2764113

Jha, S. S., Shrivastava, K., & Nair, S. B. (2013). On emulating real-world distributed intelligence using mobile agent based localized idiotypic networks. In Mining Intelligence and Knowledge Exploration: First International Conference, MIKE 2013, Tamil Nadu, India, December 18-20, 2013. Proceedings (pp. 487-498). Springer International Publishing.

Johansen, D., van Renesse, R., & Schneider, F. B. (1996, September). Supporting broad internet access to TACOMA. In Proceedings of the 7th workshop on ACM SIGOPS European workshop: Systems support for worldwide applications (pp. 55-58).

Kahn, A. B. (1962). Topological sorting of large networks. *Communications of the ACM*, 5(11), 558–562. DOI: 10.1145/368996.369025

Kahneman, D., & Tversky, A. (2013). Prospect theory: An analysis of decision under risk. In *Handbook of the fundamentals of financial decision making: Part I* (pp. 99–127). World Scientific. DOI: 10.1142/9789814417358_0006

Kambayashi, Y., & Takimoto, M. (2005). Higher-order mobile agents for controlling intelligent robots. [IJIIT]. *International Journal of Intelligent Information Technologies*, 1(2), 28–42. DOI: 10.4018/jiit.2005040103

Kambayashi, Y., Tsujimura, Y., Yamachi, H., Takimoto, M., & Yamamoto, H. (2009, January). Design of a multi-robot system using mobile agents with ant colony clustering. In 2009 42nd Hawaii International Conference on System Sciences (pp. 1-10). IEEE.

Kamei, K., Nishio, S., Hagita, N., & Sato, M. (2012). Cloud networked robotics. *IEEE Network*, 26(3), 28–34. DOI: 10.1109/MNET.2012.6201213

Kant, K., & Mohapatra, P. (2000). Scalable internet servers: Issues and challenges. *Performance Evaluation Review*, 28(2), 5–8. DOI: 10.1145/362883.362891

Khaluf, Y., & Rammig, F. Task Allocation Strategy for Time-Constrained Tasks in Robots Swarms. In *European Conference on Artificial Life*, number 2009, pages 737–744, 2013.

Khan, R., Khan, S. U., Zaheer, R., & Khan, S. (2012, December). Future internet: the internet of things architecture, possible applications and key challenges. In 2012 10th international conference on frontiers of information technology (pp. 257-260). IEEE.

Kim, K.-D., & Kumar, P. (2013). An overview and some challenges in cyber-physical systems. *Journal of the Indian Institute of Science*, 93(3), 341–352.

Kinnunen, J., Krishnamurthy, G., Huhtanen, K., Jussila, P., & Ratschunas, K. (2004). U.S. Patent No. 6,813,501. Washington, DC: U.S. Patent and Trademark Office.

Klusch, M., Lodi, S., & Moro, G. (2003). Agent-based distributed data mining: The KDEC scheme. Intelligent Information Agents: The AgentLink Perspective, 104-122.

Korst, P., & Velthuis, H. (1982). The nature of trophallaxis in honeybees. *Insectes Sociaux*, 29(2), 209–221. DOI: 10.1007/BF02228753

Kumar, A., Bhatia, A., Kashyap, A., & Kumar, M. (2023). LSTM Network: A Deep Learning Approach and Applications. In *Advanced Applications of NLP and Deep Learning in Social Media Data* (pp. 130-150). IGI Global. DOI: 10.4018/978-1-6684-6909-5.ch007

Kumar, A., Bhatia, A., Khan, I., & Kumar, V. (2011). Performance comparison of EW and Genetic Algorithm for Dynamic CMST. International Transactions in Applied Sciences, 3(3).

Kumar, S., & Singh, S. K. (2016). Monitoring of pet animal in smart cities using animal biometrics. *Future Generation Computer Systems*.

Kumar, V., Rus, D., & Sukhatme, G. S. (2008). Networked robots. In *Springer Handbook of Robotics* (pp. 943–958). Springer. DOI: 10.1007/978-3-540-30301-5_42

Kuwahara, H. (1997, April). Experiences teach us the future of autonomous decentralized systems. In *Proceedings of the Third International Symposium on Autonomous Decentralized Systems. ISADS 97* (pp. 169-175). IEEE.

Lange, D. B., & Oshima, M. (1999, March). Seven good reasons for mobile agents. *Communications of the ACM*, 42(3), 88–89. DOI: 10.1145/295685.298136

Lee, J., Bagheri, B., & Kao, H.-A. (2015). A cyber-physical systems architecture for industry 4.0-based manufacturing systems. *Manufacturing Letters*, 3, 18–23. DOI: 10.1016/j.mfglet.2014.12.001

Lee, W. P. (1999). Evolving complex robot behaviors. *Information Sciences*, 121(1-2), 1–25.

Leppänen, T. (2018). Resource-oriented mobile agent and software framework for the Internet of Things.

Liu, C., Yang, J., Chen, R., Zhang, Y., & Zeng, J. (2011, July). Research on immunity-based intrusion detection technology for the Internet of Things. In 2011 Seventh International conference on natural computation (Vol. 1, pp. 212-216). IEEE.

Machado, R. B., Boukerche, A., Sobral, J. B. M., Jucá, K. R. L., & Notare, M. S. M. A. (2005, April). A hybrid artificial immune and mobile agent intrusion detection based model for computer network operations. In 19th IEEE international parallel and distributed processing symposium (pp. 8-pp). IEEE.

Maes, P. (1995). Artificial life meets entertainment: Lifelike autonomous agents. *Communications of the ACM*, 38(11), 108–114. DOI: 10.1145/219717.219808

Maes, P., Guttman, R. H., & Moukas, A. G. (1999). Agents that buy and sell. *Communications of the ACM*, 42(3), 81–91. DOI: 10.1145/295685.295716

Matani, J., & Nair, S. B. (2011). Typhon - A Mobile Agents Framework for Real World Emulation in Prolog. In *Multi-disciplinary Trends in Artificial Intelli- gence* (pp. 261–273). Springer. DOI: 10.1007/978-3-642-25725-4_23

Michalski, R. S., Carbonell, J. G., & Mitchell, T. M. (2013). *Machine learning: An artificial intelligence approach*. Springer Science & Business Media.

Minar, N., Gray, M., Roup, O., Krikorian, R., & Maes, P. (2000). Hive: Distributed agents for networking things. *IEEE Concurrency*, 8(2), 24–33. DOI: 10.1109/4434.846191

Minar, N., Kramer, K. H., & Maes, P. (1998, May). Cooperating mobile agents for mapping networks. MIT Media Lab, to appear in Proceedings of the First Hungarian National Conference on Agent Based Computing.

Minerva, R., Biru, A., & Rotondi, D. (2015). Towards a definition of the internet of things (iot). *IEEE Internet Initiative*, 1, 1–86.

Miskelly, F. G. (2001). Assistive technology in elderly care. *Age and Ageing*, 30(6), 455–458. DOI: 10.1093/ageing/30.6.455 PMID: 11742772

Moioli, R. C., Vargas, P. A., Von Zuben, F. J., & Husbands, P. (2008, June). Towards the evolution of an artificial homeostatic system. In 2008 IEEE Congress on Evolutionary Computation (IEEE World Congress on Computational Intelligence) (pp. 4023-4030). IEEE.

Moyer, S., Maples, D., Tsang, S., & Ghosh, A. (2002). Service portability of networked appliances. *IEEE Communications Magazine*, 40(1), 116–121. DOI: 10.1109/35.978058

Nelson, A. L., Barlow, G. J., & Doitsidis, L. (2009). Fitness functions in evolutionary robotics: A survey and analysis. *Robotics and Autonomous Systems*, 57(4), 345–370. DOI: 10.1016/j.robot.2008.09.009

Nolfi, S. (1998). Evolutionary robotics: Exploiting the full power of self-organization. *Connection Science*, 10(3-4), 167–184.

Null, L., & Lobur, J. (2014). *The essentials of Computer Organization and Architecture*. Jones & Bartlett Publishers.

Outtagarts, A. (2009). Mobile agent-based applications: A survey. *International Journal of Computer Science and Network Security*, 9(11), 331–339.

Papazoglou, M. P. (2001). Agent-oriented technology in support of e-business. *Communications of the ACM*, 44(4), 71–77. DOI: 10.1145/367211.367268

L. E. Parker. Alliance: An architecture for fault tolerant multirobot coopera- tion. *Robotics and Automation, IEEE Transactions on*, 14(2):220–240, 1998.

Parolini, L., Tolia, N., Sinopoli, B., & Krogh, B. H. (2010, April). A cyber-physical systems approach to energy management in data centers. In *Proceedings of the 1st acm/ieee international conference on cyber-physical systems* (pp. 168-177).

Pathirana, P. N., Bulusu, N., Savkin, A. V., & Jha, S. (2005). Node localization using mobile robots in delay-tolerant sensor networks. *IEEE Transactions on Mobile Computing*, 4(3), 285–296. DOI: 10.1109/TMC.2005.43

Peine, H., & Stolpmann, T. (1997). The architecture of the Ara platform for mobile agents. In Mobile Agents: First International Workshop, MA'97 Berlin, Germany, April 7–8, 1997 Proceedings 1 (pp. 50-61). Springer Berlin Heidelberg.

Pham, V. A., & Karmouch, A. (1998, July). Mobile software agents: An overview. *IEEE Communications Magazine*, 36(7), 26–37. DOI: 10.1109/35.689628

Pilkington, M. (2016). Blockchain technology: principles and applications. In *Research handbook on digital transformations* (pp. 225–253). Edward Elgar Publishing.

Pipattanasomporn, M., Feroze, H., & Rahman, S. (2009, March). Multi-agent systems in a distributed smart grid: Design and implementation. In 2009 IEEE/PES Power Systems Conference and Exposition (pp. 1-8). IEEE.

Posadas, J., Poza, J., Simó, J., Benet, G., & Blanes, F. (2008, September). Agent-based distributed architecture for mobile robot control. *Engineering Applications of Artificial Intelligence*, 21(6), 805–823. DOI: 10.1016/j.engappai.2007.07.008

Raynal, M. (1986). *Algorithms for mutual exclusion*. The MIT Press.

Raza, A., & Fernández, B. R. (2018). A multi-tier immuno-inspired framework for heterogeneous mobile robotic systems. *Applied Soft Computing*, 71, 333–352. DOI: 10.1016/j.asoc.2018.06.041

Ren, W., Beard, R. W., & Atkins, E. M. (2005, June). A survey of consensus problems in multi-agent coordination. In *Proceedings of the 2005, American Control Conference*, 2005. (pp. 1859-1864). IEEE.

Rimal, B. P., Choi, E., & Lumb, I. (2009, August). A taxonomy and survey of cloud computing systems. In 2009 fifth international joint conference on INC, IMS and IDC (pp. 44-51). Ieee.

Robles, T., Alcarria, R., de Andrés, D. M., Navarro, M., Calero, R., Iglesias, S., & López, M. (2015). An iot based reference architecture for smart water manage- ment processes. *JoWUA*, 6(1), 4–23.

Rowe, N. C. (1988). *Artificial Intelligence Through Prolog*. Prentice-Hall, Inc.

Rubenstein, M., Ahler, C., & Nagpal, R. (2012, May). Kilobot: A low cost scalable robot system for collective behaviors. In 2012 [IEEE.]. *IEEE International Conference on Robotics and Automation*, •••, 3293–3298.

Rubenstein, M., Cornejo, A., & Nagpal, R. (2014). Programmable self-assembly in a thousand-robot swarm. *Science*, 345(6198), 795–799. DOI: 10.1126/science.1254295 PMID: 25124435

Sadiq, W., & Cummins, F. A. (1998). *Developing Business Systems with CORBA with CD-ROM: The Key to Enterprise Integration* (Vol. 13). Cambridge University Press.

Schreyer, P. (2000). The contribution of information and communication technology to output growth: a study of the G7 countries.

Semwal, T., Bode, M., Singh, V., Jha, S. S., & Nair, S. B. (2015, July). Tartarus: a multi-agent platform for integrating cyber-physical systems and robots. In *Proceedings of the 2015 Conference on Advances in Robotics* (pp. 1-6).

Semwal, T., Jha, S. S., & Nair, S. B. (2016, May). Tartarus: A multi-agent platform for bridging the gap between cyber and physical systems. In *Proceedings of the 2016 International Conference on Autonomous Agents & Multiagent Systems* (pp. 1493-1495).

Semwal, T., Jha, S. S., & Nair, S. B. (2017). On ordering multi-robot task executions within a cyber physical system. [TAAS]. *ACM Transactions on Autonomous and Adaptive Systems*, 12(4), 20. DOI: 10.1145/3124677

Semwal, T., & Nair, S. B. (2016). Agpi: Agents on raspberry pi. *Electronics (Basel)*, 5(4), 72. DOI: 10.3390/electronics5040072

Shi, J., Wan, J., Yan, H., & Suo, H. (2011, November). A survey of cyber-physical systems. In 2011 international conference on wireless communications and signal processing (WCSP) (pp. 1-6). IEEE.

Shi, W., Cao, J., Zhang, Q., Li, Y., & Xu, L. (2016). Edge computing: Vision and challenges. *IEEE Internet of Things Journal*, 3(5), 637–646. DOI: 10.1109/JIOT.2016.2579198

Shrivastava, K., Jha, S. S., & Nair, S. B. (2013, July). Autonomous mobile robot navigation using artificial immune system. In *Proceedings of Conference on Advances In Robotics* (pp. 1-7).

Siano, P. (2014). Demand response and smart grids—A survey. *Renewable & Sustainable Energy Reviews*, 30, 461–478. DOI: 10.1016/j.rser.2013.10.022

Sicari, S., Rizzardi, A., Grieco, L., & Coen-Porisini, A. (2015). Security, privacy and trust in internet of things: The road ahead. *Computer Networks*, 76, 146–164. DOI: 10.1016/j.comnet.2014.11.008

Silva, A., Da Silva, M. M., & Delgado, J. (1998). An overview of agentspace: a next- generation mobile agent system. In *Mobile Agents* (pp. 148–159). Springer. DOI: 10.1007/BFb0057655

Silva, F., Duarte, M., Correia, L., Oliveira, S. M., & Christensen, A. L. (2016). Open is- sues in evolutionary robotics. *Evolutionary Computation*, 24(2), 205–236. DOI: 10.1162/EVCO_a_00172 PMID: 26581015

Silva e Silva, F. J. D., Endler, M., & Kon, F. (2003). A framework for building adaptive distributed applications. In Proceedings.

Sim, K., Hart, E., & Paechter, B. (2015). A lifelong learning hyper-heuristic method for bin packing. *Evolutionary Computation*, 23(1), 37–67. DOI: 10.1162/EVCO_a_00121 PMID: 24512321

Simoes, E. D., & Dimond, K. R. (2001, October). Embedding a distributed evolutionary system into a population of autonomous mobile robots. In 2001 IEEE International Conference on Systems, Man and Cybernetics. e-Systems and e-Man for Cybernetics in Cyberspace (Cat. No. 01CH37236) (Vol. 2, pp. 1069-1074). IEEE.

Tai, H., & Kosaka, K. (1999). The Aglets project. *Communications of the ACM*, 42(3), 100–101. DOI: 10.1145/295685.295882

Takimoto, M., Mizuno, M., Kurio, M., & Kambayashi, Y. (2007). Saving energy consumption of multi-robots using higher-order mobile agents. In Agent and Multi-Agent Systems: Technologies and Applications: First KES International Symposium, KES-AMSTA 2007, Wroclaw, Poland, May 31–June 1, 2007. [Springer Berlin Heidelberg.]. *Proceedings*, 1, 549–558.

Tarau, P. (1992). BinProlog: a continuation passing style Prolog engine. In Programming Language Implementation and Logic Programming: 4th International Symposium, PLILP'92 Leuven, Belgium, August 26–28, 1992 Proceedings 4 (pp. 479-480). Springer Berlin Heidelberg.

Tarau, P. (1999). Jinni: Intelligent mobile agent programming at the intersection of java and prolog. In *Proc. of PAAM* (Vol. 99, pp. 109-123).

Theraulaz, G., & Bonabeau, E. (1995). Modelling the collective building of complex architectures in social insects with lattice swarms. *Journal of Theoretical Biology*, 177(4), 381–400. DOI: 10.1006/jtbi.1995.0255

Timmis, J., Neal, M., & Hunt, J. (2000). An artificial immune system for data analysis. *Bio Systems*, 55(1), 143–150. DOI: 10.1016/S0303-2647(99)00092-1 PMID: 10745118

Tortonesi, M., Morelli, A., Govoni, M., Michaelis, J., Suri, N., Stefanelli, C., & Russell, S. (2016, December). Leveraging Internet of Things within the military network environment—Challenges and solutions. In 2016 IEEE 3rd World Forum on Internet of Things (WF-IoT) (pp. 111-116). IEEE.

Tsipenyuk, G. Y. (2018). *Evaluation of decentralized email architecture and social network analysis based on email attachment sharing (No. UCAM-CL-TR-918)*. University of Cambridge, Computer Laboratory.

Vaquero, L. M., & Rodero-Merino, L. (2014, October). Finding your way in the fog: Towards a comprehensive definition of fog computing. *Computer Communication Review*, 44(5), 27–32. DOI: 10.1145/2677046.2677052

Watanabe, Y., Ishiguro, A., & Uchikawa, Y. (1999). Decentralized behavior arbitration mechanism for autonomous mobile robot using immune network. In *Artificial immune systems and their applications* (pp. 187–209). Springer. DOI: 10.1007/978-3-642-59901-9_10

Watkins, A., Timmis, J., & Boggess, L. (2004). Artificial Immune Recognition System (AIRS): An immune-inspired supervised learning algorithm. *Genetic Programming and Evolvable Machines*, 5(3), 291–317. DOI: 10.1023/B:-GENP.0000030197.83685.94

Watson, R. A., Ficici, S. G., & Pollack, J. B. (2002). Embodied evolution: Dis- tributing an evolutionary algorithm in a population of robots. *Robotics and Autonomous Systems*, 39(1), 1–18. DOI: 10.1016/S0921-8890(02)00170-7

Werfel, J., Petersen, K., & Nagpal, R. (2014). Designing collective behavior in a termite-inspired robot construction team. *Science*, 343(6172), 754–758. DOI: 10.1126/science.1245842 PMID: 24531967

Whitbrook, A., Aickelin, U., & Garibaldi, J. (2008). An idiotypic immune network as a short-term learning architecture for mobile robots. In *International Con-ference on Artificial Immune Systems* (pp. 266–278). Springer. DOI: 10.1007/978-3-540-85072-4_24

Whitbrook, A. M., Aickelin, U., & Garibaldi, J. M. (2007). Idiotypic immune networks in mobile-robot control. *IEEE Transactions on Systems, Man, and Cybernetics. Part B, Cybernetics*, 37(6), 1581–1598. DOI: 10.1109/TSMCB.2007.907334 PMID: 18179075

Whitbrook, A. M., Aickelin, U., & Garibaldi, J. M. (2010). Two-timescale learning using idiotypic behaviour mediation for a navigating mobile robot. *Applied Soft Computing*, 10(3), 876–887. DOI: 10.1016/j.asoc.2009.10.005

Whitley, L. D. (1991). Fundamental principles of deception in genetic search. In *Foundations of genetic algorithms* (Vol. 1, pp. 221–241). Elsevier.

J. Wielemaker, T. Schrijvers, M. Triska, and T. Lager. SWI-Prolog. *Theory and Practice of Logic Programming*, 12:67–96, 1 2012.

Witten, I. H., Frank, E., Hall, M. A., & Pal, C. J. (2016). *Data Mining: Practical machine learning tools and techniques*. Morgan Kaufmann.

Wolfson, O., Chamberlain, S., Kalpakis, K., & Yesha, Y. (2001). Modeling moving objects for location based services. In *Developing an Infrastructure for Mobile and Wireless Systems* (pp. 46–58). Springer.

Wolfson, O., Sistla, P., Xu, B., Zhou, J., Chamberlain, S., Yesha, Y., & Rishe, N. (1999). Tracking moving objects using database technology in domino. In *Next Gen- eration Information Technologies and Systems* (pp. 112–119). Springer. DOI: 10.1007/3-540-48521-X_9

Chapter 6
Key Logger and Prevention of Security Breaches

Aparna Datta
https://orcid.org/0009-0006-2552-9017
Meghnad Saha Institute of Technology, India

Akash Mondal
Meghnad Saha Institute of Technology, India

Arunima Sarkar
Meghnad Saha Institute of Technology, India

ABSTRACT

Keyloggers are malicious programs that record keystrokes and jeopardize the security of personal and business data. These sneaky malwares grab vital information while evading user discovery. Keyloggers conceal their existence by using techniques like rootkits to bypass antivirus and other security measures. Once installed, they are not visible on the process monitor . Attackers may unlawfully access sensitive information, such as banking credentials. One major worry regarding keyloggers is that around 90% of them now function in the user's environment without express authorization, leaving the user unaware that their device is being watched. Although there are hazards, addressing the keylogger threat necessitates preventative actions. This article proposes ways to improve the prevention of assaults, such as hacking. It advocates employing strong security tools and increasing cybersecurity awareness. Additionally, the following discussion suggests methods to understand the capabilities of keyloggers, develop detection methods, and rigorously evaluate countermeasures accordingly.

DOI: 10.4018/979-8-3693-9235-5.ch006

INTRODUCTION

A keystroke logger, often known as a keylogger, is a tool used to systematically track and document each keystroke entered on a device such as a computer or smartphone. It is engineered to surreptitiously record all keyboard interactions on the target device.

Keyloggers are a type of spyware; It is a type of malware designed to spy on users by recording their information without their permission. As spyware, keyloggers work very stealthily, making them difficult for users. It is designed to capture personal information that can be used for malicious purposes such as identity theft, illegal financial transactions, or participation in criminal activities. Keyloggers are regularly used in tandem with other malware to improve the effectiveness of cyberattacks. They are used for both monitoring and harmful activities. The threat of keylogging is not new to users; the first keyloggers were put in U.S. Embassy and Consulate buildings in various nations in the 1970s to collect information for counterterrorism activities in St. Petersburg (Wajahat et al., 2019).

There are many types of keyloggers on the market, such as hardware keyloggers and software keyloggers. Keylogger software is a sort of malware that infects one device and, if built, it can spread to other devices in the same network. Hardware keyloggers, unlike software keyloggers, cannot be transferred from one device to another; yet, they can still be collected by a hacker or group of hackers. This information can then be used to hack a computer or another device that requires authentication to gain access and steal sensitive information.

No physical access to the user's computer is required to install keylogging software programs. Software keyloggers can be classified according to their level of functionality and the way they interact with the system. The main types are kernel-type keyloggers and userspace keyloggers. Kernel-mode keyloggers operate at the kernel level of the system. They have the highest level of authority and can directly interact with hardware and memory. User space keyloggers operate in the user space of the operating system on which most applications run. They are less privileged than kernel-type keyloggers but are easier to create and distribute.

Keylogger software supports the hardware devices used to use keyloggers (Ortolani et al., 2013). Such software is installed on the target machine and is responsible for identifying the user's activity by hiding and storing all keystrokes and some instructions and sending them outside the third party (Zhuang et al., 2009).

Related Work

In the year of 2014, an article was published in the International Journal of Computer Networks and Communications Security titled "An Introduction to Undetectable Keyloggers with Experimental Testing" (Dadkhah et. Al., 2019). In the paper, they showed how keyloggers can be undetectable from security software by changing the structure of the keylogger they made and testing the keylogger on a popular security software in the world.

In 2013, at the 7th International Conference on Intelligent Systems and Control (ISCO), a research paper was published where the prevention and detection of keyloggers were briefly discussed. For monitoring spyware keyloggers, the idea of honeypot-based monitoring was introduced (Wazid et. Al., 2013). To monitor such attacks, a honeypot was installed on the client's network. This honeypot was designed to be easily infiltrated and unnoticed by hackers. When keylogger spyware attacks a user's system, it also infects the honeypot system. The honeypot then observes the malware's behaviour, creates a log file, and sends it to the detection and prevention server. At the detection and prevention server, the file is scanned for risks.

Image authentication schemes were also introduced in the past against key-logger Spyware (Doja et. Al.). An idea was proposed as an alternative to user authentication based on Images resistant to keylogger spyware. A method was developed and implemented that uses a stronger cryptographic hash function to generate fast and safe passwords for an infinite number of accounts while requiring the user to remember only a few memorable places in an image. In addition to being very resistant to keylogger malware, the design successfully protects against brute force and dictionary attacks. This solution enables users to retrieve their passwords from any place as long as they can run the program and remember a short secret.

In October 2019, a paper was published in the International Journal of Computer Applications named "Keylogger Detection Using Memory Forensic and Network Monitoring" (Ahmed et. Al., 2019). Many cybersecurity experts have offered various approaches for detecting keylogger applications, such as API-based detection techniques and network traffic monitoring software. However, as technology advanced, attackers developed sophisticated keyloggers that are difficult to detect using standard approaches. These keyloggers can connect with eavesdroppers without sending attached data, and they employ volatile memory as a buffer. To solve this, the research proposes a memory analysis-based detection method that can identify various forms of keyloggers. This method does not require any specific operating system rights and has been tested on both Linux and Windows with satisfactory results.

Table 1. Reported incidents of keylogger

Year	Loss	Information
2009	$415k	Ukrainian criminals are using keyloggers to steal access to the country's assets. The counterfeit money starts as a list of wire transfers, each with a limit of less than $10,000 and that can be examined by local authorities.
2006	13.9M	Criminals attempted unsuccessfully to get access to the "Sumitomo Mitsui Banks" computer system in London. This infiltration was only possible due to the keylogger installation and 5 recording administrative authorizations. This breached users' privacy, stealing personal information, bank credentials, and account codes. All of their information.
2022	$35M	A popular password manager, "LassPass," was compromised in a security breach that resulted in hackers successfully stealing password vaults containing both encrypted and plaintext data for over 25 million users.
2023	NA	Malicious actors can exploit Apple's "Find My" location network to secretly communicate sensitive information recorded by keyloggers installed in keyboards. The keylogger does not need to use an AirTag or an officially supported chip. If the message is worded correctly, the receiving Apple device will generate a location report and upload it to the Find My network. This allows the numerous reports acquired from the cloud to be concatenated and decoded at the receiving end to retrieve arbitrary data, such as the keylogger's captures.

Basic Workflow of a Keylogger

The way a keylogger works is that it is first installed on the target through a software process, such as a malicious download or physical installation of hardware keyloggers. Once enabled, they capture keystrokes based on user type using methods such as API hooks, driver hooks, or signal intercepts. The captured data is stored locally on the device or sent to the remote control by the attacker. The attacker obtains this information to extract sensitive information.

Effective detection and protection include using up-to-date security software, managing updates, and implementing physical and network security measures. To gain access to your device, a keylogger must be installed on it or, in the case of a hardware keylogger, physically connected to your computer. Keyloggers have numerous ways to target your device.

Phishing is one of the most prevalent methods for virus infections. Phishing emails and links are frequently used to target clients. The connection appears to be real and may have come from a relative or acquaintance. However, when you open an email or click on a link, a keylogger is installed on your computer. Spearphishing assaults can also be used to counter blackmail attempts.

Drive-by downloading refers to the installation of a keylogger on your computer without your knowledge. This is frequently done by rogue websites. When you visit this website, malware gets downloaded onto your computer. It then remains undetected in the background, logging your keystrokes and delivering them to the attacker.

A Trojan horse is a type of Trojan horse that contains a keylogger in a package. The Trojan horse appears to be a benevolent animal, similar to the wooden horses used in Greek mythology. When users enable it, malware containing keyloggers is installed on their devices. Once installed, the malware monitors the user's keystrokes and broadcasts them to the device the hacker has access to.

Figure 1. Workflow of keylogger

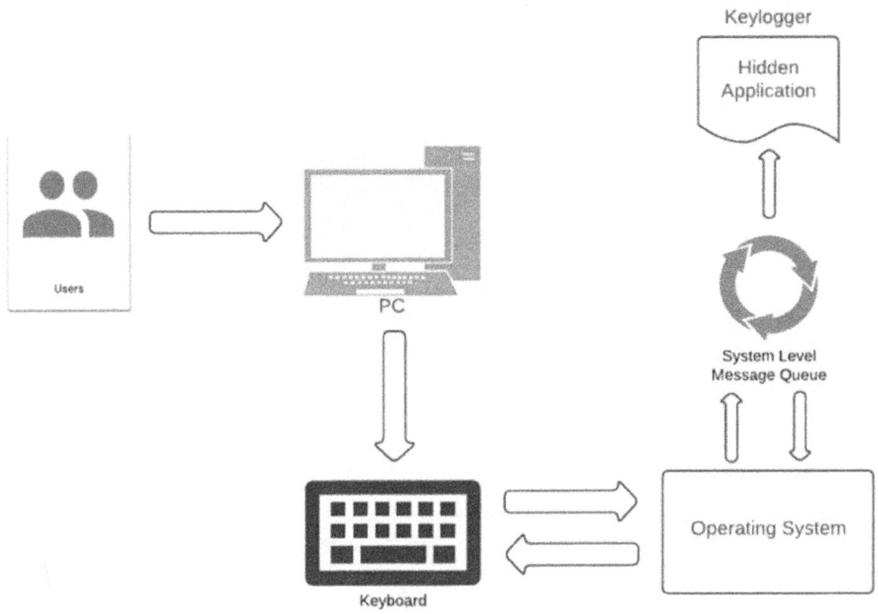

METHODOLOGY

We have made a keylogger to get a better understanding of how keyloggers work on a device and can record keystrokes from a user's device. We chose to use a keylogger written in Python due to its popularity among hackers and its extensive libraries and built-in functions that are well-suited for keylogging tasks. To facilitate its deployment, we converted the Python script into an executable file, enabling it to run as a standalone application. This executable file was then embedded within an image file, creating a seemingly innocuous file. When this file is sent to a potential victim, the true nature of the file remains concealed, making it appear harmless.

Figure 2. Flowchart of a keylogger

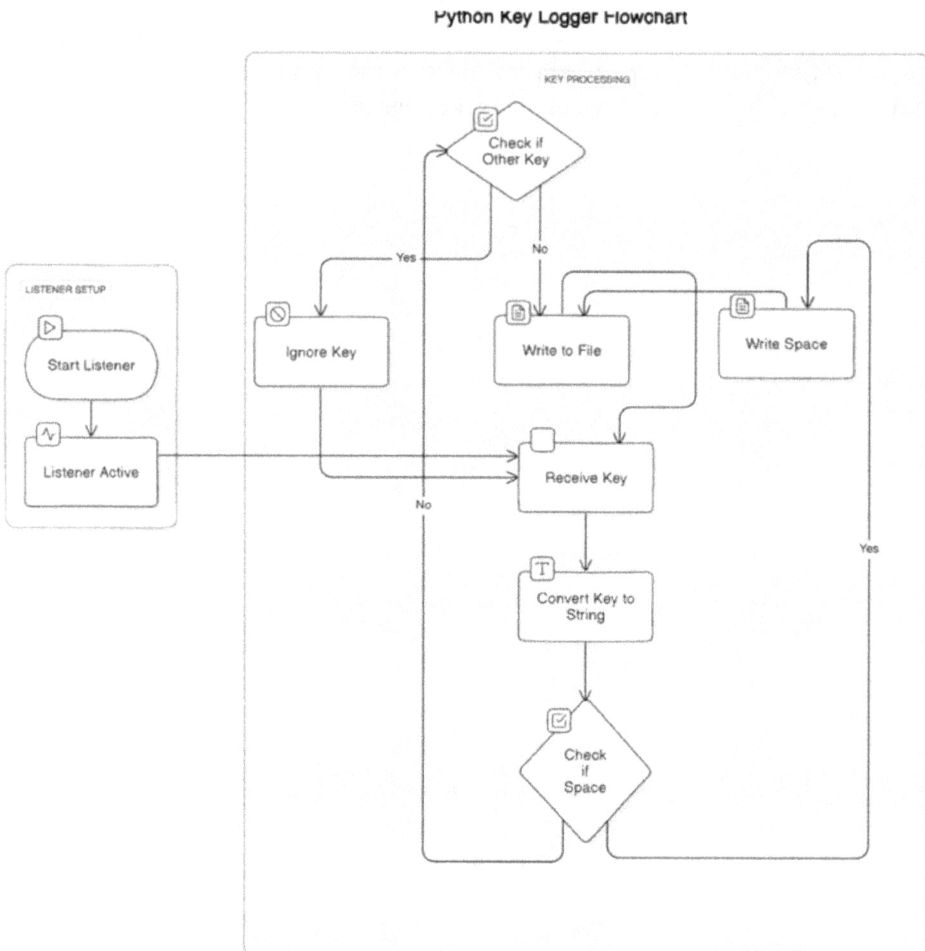

We used Python libraries such as pynput to create a keylogger. This library lets you control and monitor input devices. It includes subpackages for each sort of input device supported, such as a mouse and keyboard controller. In our keylogger, we used the pynput.keylogger package, which includes classes for controlling and monitoring the keyboard. We have also imported the Listener thread, which ensures that listener callbacks are invoked straight from an operating thread on several platforms, most notably Windows. This means that long-running procedures and blocking actions should not be invoked from the callback since they may cause all processes' input to freeze.

The working mechanism of the Keyboard Listener is simple as shown in the figure below:

Figure 3. Keyboard listener

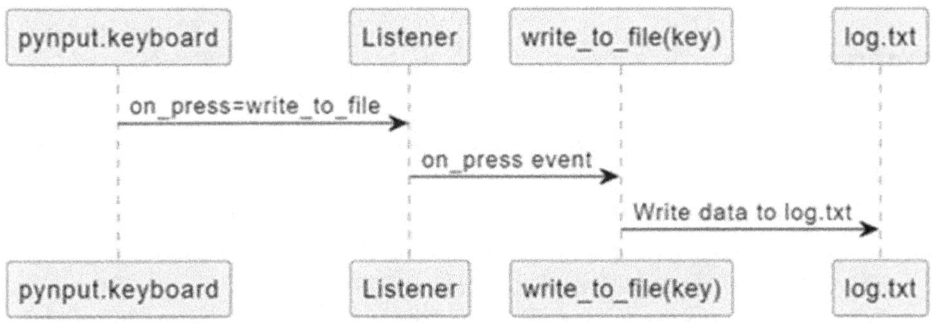

Let us understand the figure with proper implementation details.

- The pynput.keyboard module is used to create a keyboard listener.
- The on_press event of the Listener is set to trigger the write_to_file function whenever a key is pressed.
- When a key is pressed, the on_press event is fired. This event calls the write_to_file function, passing the pressed key as an argument.
- The write_to_file function receives the key press event. The function writes the key data to a file named log.txt.
- The log.txt file is updated with the key press information.

So, in simple words, the diagram shows a keyboard listener that captures key press events and writes the key data to a log file (log.txt) using the pynput library.

Here is the whole process of making a keylogger file:

- **Step-1:** Import the **Listener** class from the **pynput.keyboard** module.
- **Step-2:** Define a function **write_to_file** that takes a key as input.
- **Step-3:** Convert the key to a string and remove any single quotes (').
- **Step-4:** If keydata equals **'Key.space'**, replace it with an actual space character.
- **Step-5:** If keydata contains 'Key' (indicating it is a special key), set keydata to an empty string.
- **Step-6:** Open a file named log.txt in append mode.
- **Step-7:** Write the key data to the file.
- **Step-8:** Close the file.
- **Step-9:** Create an instance of Listener with the **on_press** event linked to the **write_to_file** function.

- **Step-10:** Start the listener and keep it running to continuously capture keystrokes.

Detection

The detection of keyloggers can be a difficult task when it comes to well-coded programs. The Windows Defender can easily detect some keyloggers, but it is only possible if the threat matches known behaviour or signatures. Otherwise, Windows Defender cannot catch the threats due to the constantly evolving nature of malware, as it mainly relies on signature-based detection.

When hackers utilize keyloggers, their objective is to remain untraceable. Victims who are unaware that someone is monitoring their every keyboard continue to submit sensitive information on their devices. However, several warning indications might suggest that you have a keylogger installed.

Three primary warning signs can help you detect keyloggers:

- **A Slow Browser**: When a keylogger is installed in a device and it starts keeping logs, it requires CPU and memory resources. If the keylogger is poorly coded, this extra load on the processor can slow down the ongoing tasks on the device. As a result, the browser becomes slower and takes longer to load web pages and respond to user inputs.
- **A Lag in Mouse Movements And Keystrokes:** Usually, when the user presses a key from the keyboard or moves the mouse, the keylogger quickly records the input. However, if the keylogger is poorly designed, there can be a lag between this process. If the lag is noticeable then the threat can be detected.
- **A Disappearing Cursor:** The keylogger works by hooking into the input handling procedure of the system to log the mouse movement and key press. Sometimes, during the whole process, the cursor vanishes or becomes unresponsive for some time. This issue can be a result of potential threats to the device.

If someone experiences these issues, they should check for keyloggers through the following steps:

- Use Task Manager on PCs or Activity Monitor on Macs. The Task Manager and Activity Monitor are utility tools that display which applications and background processes are currently active. Examine the running programs and processes, and terminate any that appear suspicious.

- Examine all programs and features. Evaluate what applications are installed on your device. If you are unaware of one, search for it online and uninstall it if required.
- Use an antivirus program for scanning your device. The program frequently monitors your devices for malware and promptly removes it from them.

Prevention

Not everyone who is using a computing device is an expert in threats and cybersecurity, and many cannot detect or realize when they are being attacked.

So the first step in preventing the devices from potential keylogging threats should be by educating users about this threat, how it works, and how it can affect a person's private life by violating security breaches. Awareness campaigns and practical training can be conducted as the basic prevention criteria. This can be achieved by distributing easy-to-understand materials that highlight important pieces of information about keyloggers.

Some of the other ways to prevent keylogging attacks which are useful are:

- **Software Updates:** Keeping the Operating System updated is important because the new updates contain patches for security threats that have been discovered since the last update. Cybercriminals usually use these vulnerabilities in their favor. Users should enable automatic updates, periodically check for updates, and also make sure that applications like web browsers and plugins are up to date.
- **Anti-Virus Tools:** Antivirus tools are made to detect and remove malicious software including keyloggers. Though as discussed earlier, Windows Defender cannot detect some of these threats it is possible that poorly coded keyloggers can be detected by it. This is why reliable antivirus programs should be used against these threats.
- **Strong Password and 2FA:** Strong unique passwords for different platforms, make it harder for the cybercriminal to gain unauthorized access. Where on the other hand, 2FA or Two-factor authentication adds an extra layer of security because it requires a second form of verification before accessing. Strong passwords should contain at least 12 characters, both uppercase and lowercase letters, and also numbers and special characters.
- **Phishing Awareness:** One should get proper education to recognize fake emails or, messages that can contain malicious links which will cause installing keyloggers into the device without their knowledge.
- **Utilize Virtual Keyboards:** For particularly sensitive transactions, using an on-screen virtual keyboard can help bypass keyloggers. Virtual keyboards

allow you to click on keys using your mouse rather than typing, which can prevent keyloggers from capturing your input. Many banking and financial websites offer virtual keyboards for this reason.

By implementing these strategies, you can effectively educate people about the dangers of keyloggers, how to prevent them, and how to respond if they suspect their presence, thereby fostering a more secure and vigilant community. A multi-layered approach to security, combining technology and user education, is the most effective way to protect sensitive information from these covert threats.

RESULT AND DISCUSSION

Figure 4. The phishing image file

Figure 4 depicts the phishing image file, within which the keylogger executable is concealed. Upon interaction, this image file not only displays the intended visual content (as illustrated in Figure 5) but also surreptitiously activates the embedded keylogger. This executable subsequently initiates its operation, capturing and logging keystrokes.

Figure 5. Visual content displayed by the phishing image file

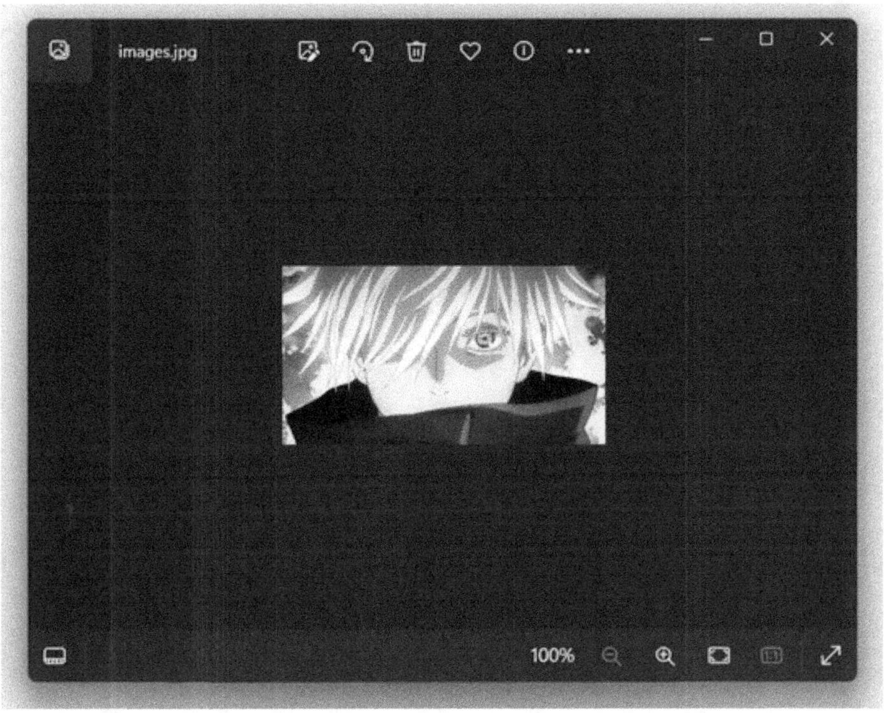

Figure 6. Example of a victim interacting with their device

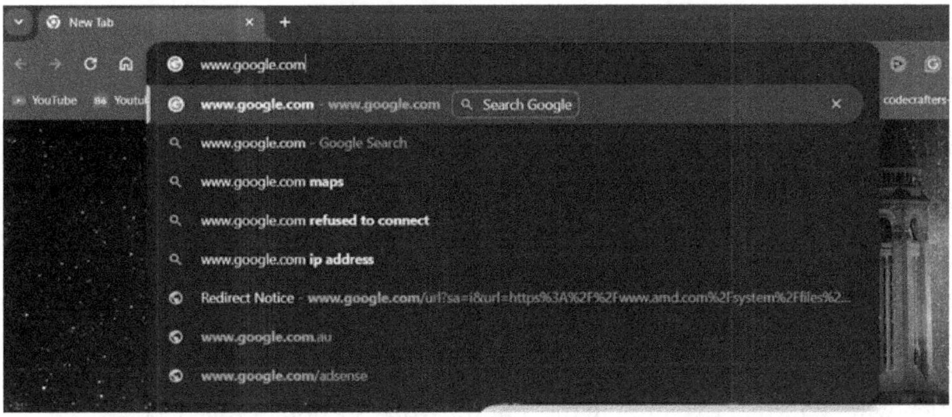

Figure 6 illustrates a scenario wherein the victim, having fallen for the phishing attack, continues to interact with their device. In this example, the victim is shown typing a website URL (google.com), a routine activity. Unbeknownst to the victim, the concealed keylogger executable is actively logging their keystrokes. The logged data is stored in a file, the details of which are depicted in Figure 7.

Figure 7. The stored keystroke log data

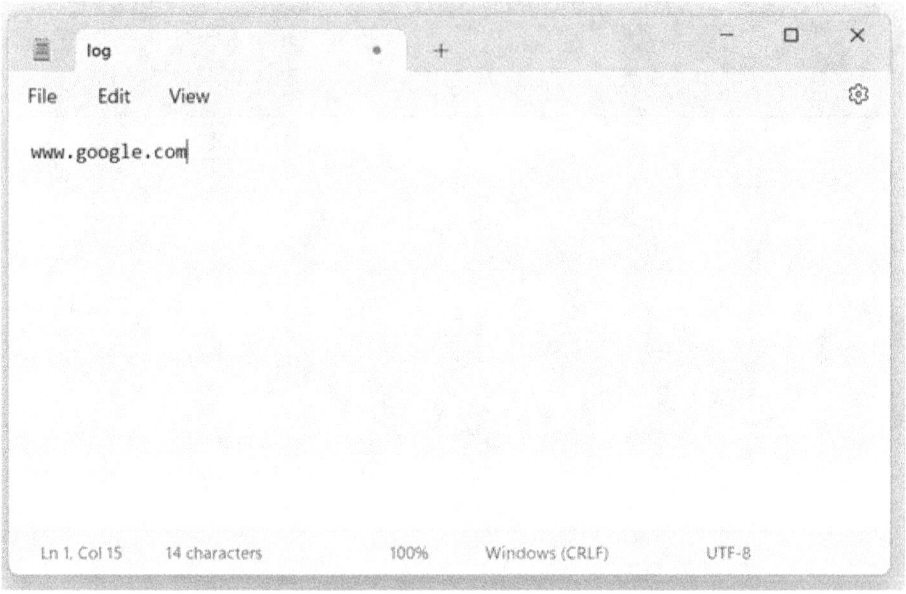

Figure 7 displays the saved keystroke log data, which has been stored in a text file named 'log.txt'.

As demonstrated, creating a keylogger is relatively straightforward, even for individuals with minimal coding knowledge. Following a successful phishing attack—executed via email, MMS, WhatsApp, downloadable links, external storage devices like USB drives, and other methods—the victim remains unaware that the keylogger has been installed on their device. This undetected keylogger logs keystrokes, posing significant risks as it can record and save website credentials, user login information, and potentially sensitive documents, including industry secrets. The log file can be accessed both physically and through various remote means, which will be further explored in the 'Future Work' section of this paper.

Future Work

As demonstrated, creating and deploying a keylogger file is relatively straightforward. However, there are potential improvements that can be made to enhance its stealth and functionality. For example, the keylogger software can be hidden further, and strategies for easier access to log files, such as anonymously transferring recorded data to the attacker via email, can be implemented.

Furthermore, it is critical to develop stronger security measures for possible victims. The prevalence and sophistication of such security threats are growing, and developing them is becoming more accessible. As a result, it is critical to educate people on how to avoid vulnerable websites, stop clicking on strange links, and avoid downloading suspicious files from unverified emails.

Moreover, continual education for new users who are unaware of these types of cyber risks is required. Basic security procedures, such as installing and updating antivirus and anti-malware software regularly, must be prioritized and implemented.

CONCLUSION

Keyloggers constitute a significant cybersecurity danger because of their capacity to steal critical information. Our findings demonstrate the ease with which keyloggers can be built and deployed, underlining the vital need for effective detection and prevention techniques. Updating software, using strong passwords and two-factor authentication, and raising awareness about phishing tactics are all effective preventative measures. As technology advances, fraudsters' methods vary, needing continuous improvements in security policies and user education to fight against these emerging dangers.

REFERENCES

Ahmed, M. B., Shoikot, M., Hossain, J., & Rahman, A. (2019). Key logger detection using memory forensic and network monitoring. *International Journal of Computer Applications*, 975, 8887.

Ahmed, Y. A., Maarof, M. A., Hassan, F. M., & Abshir, M. M. (2014). Survey of Keylogger technologies. International journal of computer science and telecommunications, 5(2).

Bhardwaj, A., & Goundar, S. (2020). Keyloggers: Silent cyber security weapons. *Network Security*, 2020(2), 14–19.

Davarpanah Jazi, M., Ciobotaru, A. M., & Barati, E. (2014). An introduction to undetectable keyloggers with experimental testing. [IJCCN]. *International Journal of Computer Communications and Networks*, 4(3), 1–5.

Doja, M. N., & Kumar, N. (2008, August). Image authentication schemes against key-logger spyware. In *2008 Ninth ACIS International Conference on Software Engineering, Artificial Intelligence, Networking, and Parallel/Distributed Computing* (pp. 574-579). IEEE.

Goring, S. P., Rabaiotti, J. R., & Jones, A. J. (2007). Anti-keylogging measures for secure Internet login: an example of the law of unintended consequences. computers & security, 26(6), 421-426.

Holz, T., Engelberth, M., & Freiling, F. (2009). Learning more about the underground economy: A case-study of keyloggers and dropzones. In Computer Security–ESORICS 2009: 14th European Symposium on Research in Computer Security, Saint-Malo, France, September 21-23, 2009. [Springer Berlin Heidelberg.]. *Proceedings*, 14, 1–18.

Ortolani, S., Giuffrida, C., Crispo, A. B., & Member, S. (2013, January-February). IEEE. *IEEE Transactions on Dependable and Secure Computing*, 10(1).

Singh, A., & Choudhary, P. (2021, August). Keylogger detection and prevention. [). IOP Publishing.]. *Journal of Physics: Conference Series*, 2007(1), 012005.

Solairaj, A., Prabanand, S. C., Mathalairaj, J., Prathap, C., & Vignesh, L. S. (2016, January). Keyloggers software detection techniques. In 2016 10th International Conference on Intelligent Systems and Control (ISCO) (pp. 1-6). IEEE.

Tuli, P., & Sahu, P. (2013). System monitoring and security using keylogger. *International Journal of Computer Science and Mobile Computing*, 2(3), 106–111.

Wajahat, A., Imran, A., Latif, J., Nazir, A., & Bilal, A. (2019, January). A novel approach of unprivileged keylogger detection. In 2019 2nd International Conference on Computing, Mathematics and Engineering Technologies (iCoMET) (pp. 1-6). IEEE.

Wazid, M., Katal, A., Goudar, R. H., Singh, D. P., Tyagi, A., Sharma, R., & Bhakuni, P. (2013, January). A framework for detection and prevention of novel keylogger spyware attacks. In 2013 7th International Conference on Intelligent Systems and Control (ISCO) (pp. 433-438). IEEE.

Wood, C., & Raj, R. (2010, July). Keyloggers in Cybersecurity Education. In Security and Management (pp. 293-299).

Zhuang, L., Zhou, F., & Tygar, J. D. (2009). Keyboard acoustic emanations revisited. *ACM Transactions on Information and System Security*, 13(1), 1–26. DOI: 10.1145/1609956.1609959

Chapter 7
Security Considerations of SDN Networks During DDoS Attacks in Load Balancing

Adrija Das
School of Computer Engineering, KIIT (Deemed to Be) University, Bhubaneswar, India

Tanisha Saini
School of Computer Engineering, KIIT (Deemed to Be) University, Bhubaneswar, India

Pratyasha Nanda
School of Computer Engineering, KIIT (Deemed to Be) University, Bhubaneswar, India

Sneha Bhaskar
School of Computer Engineering, KIIT (Deemed to Be) University, Bhubaneswar, India

Ritika Jain
School of Computer Engineering, KIIT (Deemed to Be) University, Bhubaneswar, India

Hitesh Mohapatra
https://orcid.org/0000-0001-8100-4860
School of Computer Engineering, KIIT (Deemed to Be) University, Bhubaneswar, India

ABSTRACT

Cloud computing deals with the dynamic allocation of resources on demand from any location. Load balancing is the phenomenon of ensuring the distribution of traffic and the operation of loads on multiple servers. There are security considerations where the load balancers are potential targets for Distributed Denial of Service (DDoS) attacks. This occurs when the attacker overwhelms the system with a flood of traffic, causing it to become unresponsive. The paper discusses the

DOI: 10.4018/979-8-3693-9235-5.ch007

security challenges and attacks that affect workload distribution across servers dealing with access control mechanisms and concerns about multi-tenancy risks. The analysis involves identifying attacks in load-balancing systems from pre-existing frameworks by utilizing tools like Snort, Wireshark, and MATLAB for DDoS attacks. Furthermore, the paper does a comparative study on the established works. It addresses the best mitigation strategies for different types of DDoS attacks, such as Smurfing and TCP-SYN attacks, thus enhancing resilience with SDN architecture and multi-layered defense mechanisms.

1. INTRODUCTION

Cloud computing is a popular method to access resources from a shared area referred to as the cloud using a user-friendly interface. It is predicated on the flexible distribution of resources according to need and cost. Because of its lower prices, scalability, remote access, and various other advantages, it is a growing trend in computing. This model's scalability—which allows organizations to only pay for what they use—is one of its greatest benefits, as it may significantly lower manufacturing costs. There are four different kinds of cloud deployment models, depending on the abstraction level offered. A single entity that manages an on-site private cloud infrastructure and provides cloud computing services to users is granted access to private cloud authentication. The organization may also agree via a third-party cloud provider to host and manage dedicated servers off-site. The most popular kind of cloud deployment architecture is the public cloud, which employs shared infrastructure and resources held by a third-party cloud service provider, (Buvaneswari, Loganathan, & Sangeetha, 2017). It stores and controls the accessibility of data and apps via the Internet. This model's primary benefit is that it enables resource scalability, allowing customers to pay for what they use. However, its primary drawback is the safety of the user's data. The benefits of both public and private cloud computing are combined in the hybrid cloud model, allowing users to access shared resources and secure data through the utilization of pre-existing IT infrastructure. It enables businesses to internally store sensitive data that is accessible through apps hosted on public cloud infrastructure. A collection of organizations can access services through the Community Cloud. The members who make up the group are the ones who own, run, and manage it, (He, 2022).

Figure 1. Load balancing architecture

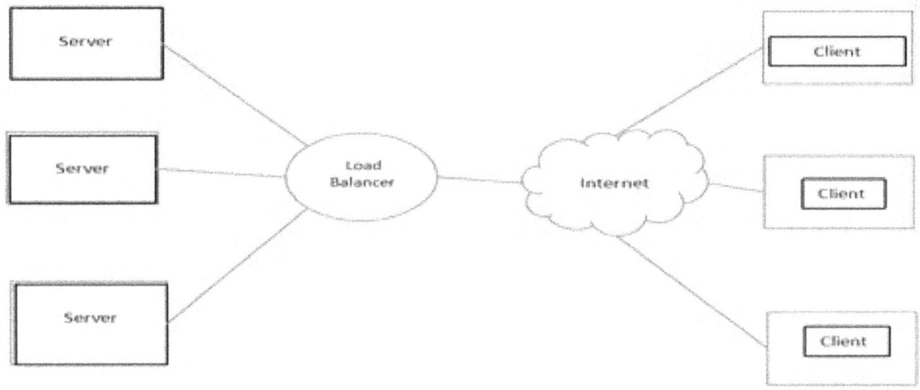

However, system performance suffered as a result of the high volume of users producing enormous amounts of data and tasks. Thus, in cloud environments, load balancing plays a critical role in optimizing the use of resources, improving performance, and guaranteeing high availability by ensuring the allocation and operation of demands across its server nodes. The term "load balancing" refers to a method of efficiently distributing network loads among multiple nodes. Upon receiving a request, the load balancer (shown in Figure 1) allocates it to the server that is available after first verifying server availability. The balancer can respond by increasing the sheer number of servers when there are high requests and decreasing the number of servers when there are low demands, (Mi, Qiu, & Zhang, 2011). For a networking environment to function properly, security measures must be in place. The following security precautions are taken into account: data security during the transfer process, data privacy during storage, privilege levels, access rights, and keeping the network secure from outside intrusions. SSL/TLS and VPN services are essential for secure data transmissions for both cloud service suppliers and customers. Data security in cloud computing does not guarantee total control over the data. In certain situations, data compromise occurs in multi-tenant clouds, and there may be intermediary data loss. Integrity, privacy, dependability, and accessibility of data and applications are requirements for a successful load balancer. Reaching this level is challenging because numerous servers are busy performing multiple jobs whereas some other servers remain idle. In addition to choosing the server that is most appropriate for a given task, the load balancer must make sure the server isn't overworked. Dynamic mitigation techniques, ongoing monitoring, and safe configuration procedures can all help to address security issues with load balancing. Recurring security audits and keeping abreast of developing threats are necessary to maintain a secure load-balancing infrastructure, (Patil & Zade, 2023). The two primary activities of this study are load balancing and security. Secure access to services and resources is ensured by security. To preserve security and stability, load balancing seeks to disperse the load among the firewall nodes in an equal manner, (AlHuwaishel & Zaghloul, 2013).

Figure 2. DDOS attacks

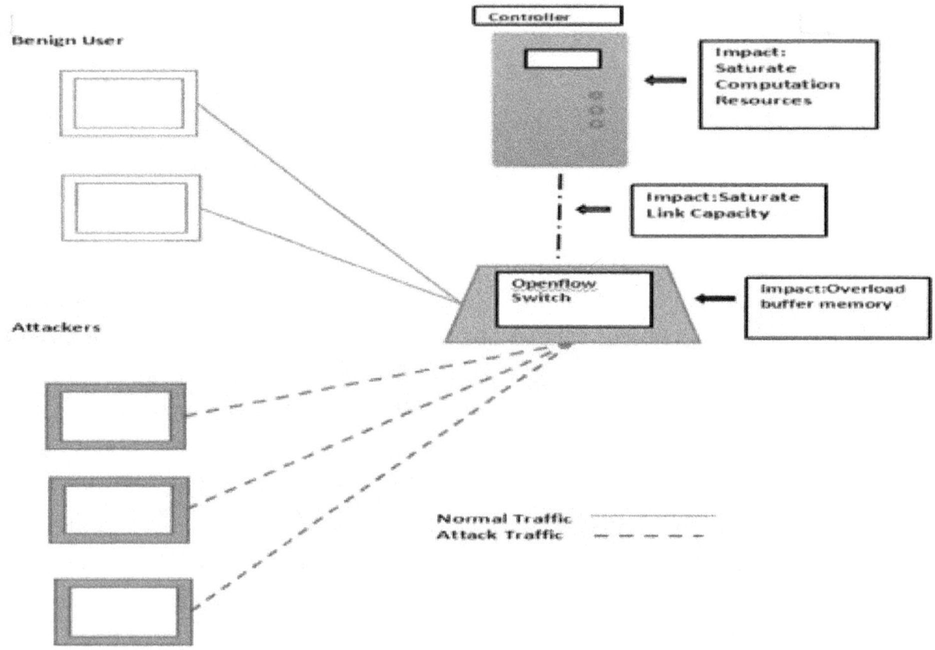

The study continues with an analysis of load-balancing systems' security risks and solutions. DDoS assaults (seen in Figure 2), in which an attacker floods the system with so much traffic that it becomes unresponsive, can target load balancers. They are frequently exposed to potential vulnerabilities in cryptographic protocols and the handling of certificates because they handle SSL/TLS termination. The confidentiality and integrity of information problems could arise from any compromise in the handling of sensitive data. To keep user sessions alive, load balancing frequently needs session persistence, which makes it vulnerable to session hijacking. There are security issues associated with revealing APIs through load balancers, such as illegal access and API abuse. Security incidents may take longer to discover if load balancer operations are not properly recorded and monitored. Unauthorized entry to the load balancer may result from inadequate access controls and insecure setups. It takes a combination of safe setup procedures, continuous surveillance, and proactive mitigation techniques to address security issues with load balancing. A reliable and secure load-balancing system requires regular inspections for safety and keeping up with new threats, (Belyaev & Gaivoronski, 2014a).

2. LITERATURE REVIEW

To ensure optimal resource utilization, responsiveness, and reliability, load balancing is an essential component of distributed computing and network architecture, which helps to distribute incoming network traffic across multiple servers. In addition to enhancing performance, balancing the load also introduces security considerations that need to be considered, (Kaviarasan *et al.*, 2023). Even though cloud research frameworks have a rich literature, there are gaps in the areas that need further research and development to improve the efficacy of cloud security systems. Storing, processing, and accessing data and applications by organizations has been restructured with the help of cloud computing. However, this has also initiated many security challenges that need to be addressed to secure the confidentiality, integrity, and availability of data.

Figure 3. SDN architecture

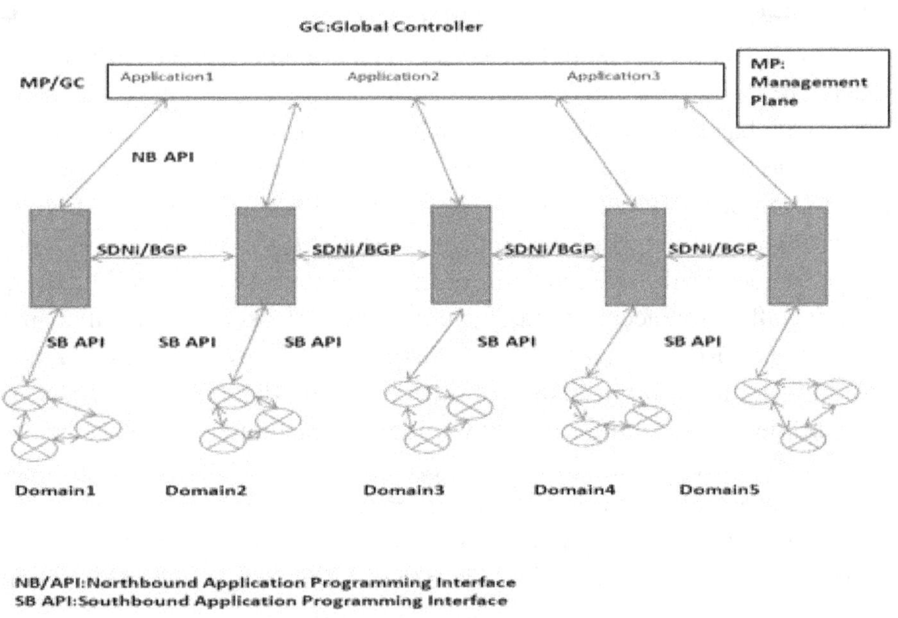

Software Defined Networks (SDN) in Figure 3 are slowly becoming cutting-edge technology on the web. This technology helps solve numerous popular engineering problems efficiently and elegantly as it gives software-defined powered network control. An SDN controller can be enhanced with applications that effectively serve specific purposes and provide flexible network flow management. This opens huge opportunities for network security issues such as properly making, splitting, having privilege control, and attack detection and mitigation. Opportunities of SDN can be considered as a "survival" mitigation during DDoS attacks. Installing a Web Application Firewall to detect and filter traffic, which will protect all web applications from vulnerabilities such as SQL Injection, cross-scripting HTTPSX, or other attacks targeting the application layer vulnerability. To ensure that the load balancer is directing traffic to healthy servers, it periodically tests and monitors server health checks. Ensure that traffic is rerouted from compromised or malfunctioning servers by means of failover mechanisms, (Tayfour, Marsono, & Nadzir, 2020)

The sensitive session data is securely stored and synchronized between the backend servers when session persistence is used. To avoid session hijacking or data corruption, this is essential. Implement rate limiting to protect against brute force attacks and hold in check the number of requests made by the client in a specific interval. This may help to prevent misuse or unauthorized access attempts. Securing APIs with appropriate authentication mechanisms, authorization controls, and encryption are proposed if load balancing involves API. Updating the firmware and software on load balancers with the most recent security fixes. Evaluating vendor security advisories regularly and installing updates as soon as possible to reduce known vulnerabilities. Steps for locating, eradicating, recovering, and learning from security problems should all be part of the approach. By addressing these security considerations, organizations can increase the overall security condition of their load-balancing infrastructure and mediate potential risks associated with the distribution of network traffic. The security issues of the control layer of load balancers can be significant because they play an important role in managing and routing network traffic, (Belyaev & Gaivoronski, 2014b).

Weak authentication mechanisms or misconfigured access control policies can lead to unauthorized access to the control plane. Attackers can use this approach to manipulate load balancing settings, disrupt traffic distribution, or launch new attacks against the network. Like most software, load balancer software may contain vulnerabilities such as buffer overflows, input validation errors, or authentication bypass errors. Exploitation of these vulnerabilities could allow attackers to breach the control plane, which could lead to service interruptions or data breaches. Attackers can use DoS attacks to target the control plane to strain its resources and disrupt its operations. This could mean flooding the load balancer with excessive traffic, using its processing power, or exploiting protocol vulnerabilities to cause service degradation or downtime, (Guirguis *et al.*, 2007).

Misconfigurations of load balancer settings or control plane policies can inadvertently expose security vulnerabilities. For example, misconfigured access lists or routing policies can allow unauthorized access or traffic redirection, compromising network security. Insecure communication channels between the control plane and other network components can be vulnerable to Man-in-the-middle (MitM) attacks. Attackers can intercept and manipulate traffic between the front-end and back-end servers, potentially changing load decisions or stealing sensitive data. Ensuring the integrity and confidentiality of data exchanged at the control plane is critical to maintaining network security. Encryption and encryption protocols should be used to protect sensitive information such as configuration settings, session keys, or authentication information from unauthorized access or modification. To mitigate these security issues, organizations should adopt a multi-layered approach that includes, (Sebbar & Zkik, 2023):

- Deploying strong authentication mechanisms, access control, and encryption protocols to ensure access to the control plane.
- Regular update of load balancer firmware and software to fix known vulnerabilities and security weaknesses.
- Use of intrusion detection and prevention systems to monitor and mitigate potential control layer threats.
- Regular information security assessments and audits can be conducted to identify and rectify errors or mismatches in control-level settings.

Storing, processing, and accessing data and applications by organizations has been restructured with the help of cloud computing. However, this has also initiated many security challenges that need to be taken care of to secure the confidentiality, integrity, and availability of data. Some of the highlighted issues are:

Distributed Denial of Service attacks (DDoS) refer to a condition where malicious vectors try to flood the system with unwanted requests thus making it unavailable for authorized users, (Musa *et al.*, 2024). Thousands or even millions of vulnerable devices such as computers or IOT devices, infected with malware and under the attacker's control can become a cause of this flood of traffic. Load balancing aims to optimize resource usage and refrain from server overload. It can prove to be both a target and a defense mechanism in the context of load balancing. Since during a DDoS attack, a massive volume of traffic is oriented towards the target server, the load balancer can become overloaded if the attack volume exceeds the capacity of the load balancing. This reduces the ability of the load balancer to distribute the traffic to the backend servers efficiently. These attacks can also consume some resources like CPU, memory, etc., thus lowering the performance of the load balancer. Sometimes during a DDoS attack, algorithms designed to detect and block malicious traffic might produce false positives which means they can block legitimate users along with the attackers. Various DDoS attacks that can impede cloud services are presented below, (Ramprasath, Krishnaraj, & Seethalakshmi, 2022):

1. Smurf attacks involve the attacker sending numerous Internet Control Message Protocol (ICP) echo requests to the server. The sender's IP address is identical to the broadcast's, leading to a flood of broadcast addresses on the victim server, causing denial of service to legitimate users. Since it is relatively simpler to execute the attack, it gained popularity in the late 1990s. It happens when the attacker sends packets to a network device that supports the broadcast addressing technique and the return address in these packets is replicated with the victim's address. The network device sends ICMP echo requests packets to all systems in the broadcast IP address range, causing an ICMP echo reply message from all systems to deny the victim's request. An IP spoofing attack occurs when an attacker alters the source IP field headers by an authorized or unreachable IP address. The cloud server is misguided, affecting the genuine user or causing the server to fail due to unreachable IP addresses, impacting the server's sources. Preventing this type of attack can prove to be difficult due to the fake IP address of the source IP. First, the attacker creates packets with a dummy source IP address which appears to be originating from a trusted source. The attacker then sends the spoofed packets to the target system or network by utilizing the weaknesses in the network protocols or the security mechanisms. By doing this the attacker can potentially gain unauthorized access. This can flood the target network with many fake packets, thus preoccupying the resources and causing disturbance. In some cases, IP spoofing can also lead to leakage of sensitive information if the traffic is redirected to an attacker-controlled system, (Wang *et al.,* 2022).
2. For Teardrop attack a faster network transmission technique called fragmentation is used in which IP packets are divided into smaller parts with each fragment containing the original IP packet's header which is useful to reassemble at the destination host. However, if the TCP/IP stack is superimposed with IP fragments the reassembling becomes difficult and sometimes quickly fails. In this attack, the attacker sends flawed or overlapping fragments to the target system which contains overlapping or incorrect offset values, leading the target system's IP stack to handle the reassembly process inappropriately. Thus, when the target system tries to reassemble the fragmented packets, it encounters errors or crashes due to these anomalous fragments which leads to resource exhaustion and system

instability. Whereas SYN-flood attack harnesses the TCP handshake process to disable a targeted server, (Tan *et al.,* 2020).

3. A TCP handshake is a 3-step process that establishes a TCP/IP connection between a client and a server which involves synchronize (SYN), synchronize-acknowledge (SYN-ACK), and acknowledge (ACK) packets. In this attack, first, the attacker sends a flood of TCP/SYN packets usually from a fake IP address to the target server's port and every packet appears to start a new connection. The server then mistakenly allocates resources to each of these back packets and sends a SYN-ACK packet as a signal to the so-called client's IP address and waits for a final ACK packet. However, the attacker never sends the ACK packet to complete the connection which keeps the half-open connection alive while consuming server resources. Since the attacker continues to send these SYN packets the server's resources continue to get tied up with these half-open connections eventually leading to denial of service to authorized users, (Girma *et al.,* 2015).
4. A PING of death attack is a type of malicious PING attack that sends a malicious PING to a computer. These PING packets exceeded the maximum IP packet size allowed by the IP protocol which is 65535 bytes and due to the actual data link layer often imposing a much smaller limit, packets larger need to be fragmented. In this attack, the attacker first sends a PING request that exceeds the acceptable size and when the targeted system tries to reassemble such fragmented packets into their original size, it leads to buffer overflows and reduces the capacity of the system, causing it to freeze or crash. A buffer overflow attack occurs if a program writes data to a buffer more than its capacity. Since the buffer is a temporary data storage area, designed to hold a fixed amount of data, the extra information spills to the adjacent buffers thus manipulating or overwriting the valid data already held in there. This can result in unstable program behavior leading to system crashes. First, a software program is identified that is sensitive to buffer overflow due to poor coding practices. Then the attacker creates such input data that is purposefully designed to exceed the buffer capacity, by doing this the attacker can easily overwrite the specific areas of the program's memory and divert the program execution flow to the injected malicious code. In some cases, the attacker can also gain illegitimate access to the system's resources thus taking control of the affected system, (Sahi *et al.,* 2017a).

To easily mitigate these DDoS attacks, we need to identify them first. The most common symptom of a DDoS attack is a website, or a service becomes slow or unavailable suddenly. Still, this information is not merely enough since an authorized spike in traffic can also create similar performance issues. Some of the signs of a DDoS attack include suspicious large amounts of traffic originating from a sole IP address, an unwanted or unexplained rise in requests to a single page, a flood of traffic from users who share similar behavioral profiles, and odd traffic patterns that appear to be unnatural, (Iyengar *et al.,* 2014).

3. PROPOSED STUDY

Detecting and mitigating Distributed Denial of Service (DDoS) attacks involves employing various tools and approaches due to the diverse forms these attacks can take. A pivotal tool in this realm is Snort, an open-source Intrusion Prevention System (IPS). Snort operates using a predefined set of rules, allowing it to identify malicious traffic effectively. MATLAB stands out as another widely used tool, while Wireshark examines packet headers to uncover potential malicious content, (Tehaam *et al.,* 2022). These tools rely on specific features, to assess and combat DDoS threats. Recognition of data shifts and network abnormalities precedes proposing any countermeasure for DDoS attacks. Notably, various research papers emphasize certain features, with 'duration,' 'source byte,' and 'destination byte' consistently identified as critical parameters. It's worth highlighting the importance of striking a balance in the number of features and detection logic employed. Therefore, careful consideration of the number and relevance of features is essential for effective DDoS detection solutions, (Girma *et al.,* 2015). DDoS attacks manifest across multiple layers, featuring various types that are often categorized hierarchically, as depicted. While it is impractical to detail every DDoS attack type, a classification is established, focusing on common ones prevalent in cyber-attacks. TCP-SYN flood and ICMP flood emerge as the most frequently encountered DDoS attack types, underscoring their prominence in cyber threats. Although a great deal of research has been done on many different areas of DDoS attacks, there is a notable void in the analysis of particular attacks, most notably the Smurf and SYN attacks, (Sahi *et al.,* 2017).

These two kinds of attacks provide difficulties and require in-depth research to improve our comprehension and develop defenses. This proposed review aims to mitigate networks' susceptibility to DDoS attacks, emphasizing Smurfing and SYN attacks. The problem formulation process includes determining the gaps in the existing mitigation and detection measures. Our goal is to provide a comparative study for choosing more efficient ways to reduce the impact of Smurfing and SYN attacks on network infrastructure by comprehending their complexities, (Mohapatra, 2021). A suitable environment setup is essential for thoroughly investigating Smurf and SYN attacks. Replicating actual conditions involves deploying network simulation tools like GNS3 or NS-3. Strong algorithms like Snort are helpful to detect and stop these attacks. The feasibility, and dependability of the recommended solutions will be thorough examination of the results obtained from the study of detection and mitigation strategies. Comparative studies evaluate the effectiveness of the developed strategies among all the methodologies, (Iyengar *et al.,* 2014). In Figure 4 the flow chart shows the different types of DDoS attacks and smurfing, TCP SYN, and ICMP attacks.

Figure 4. Types of DDoS attacks

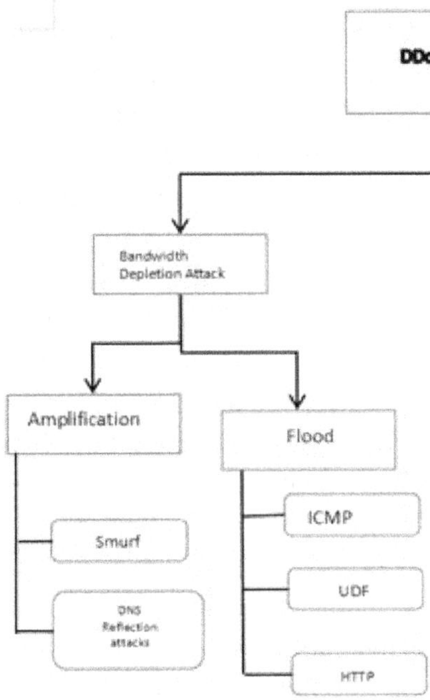

A DDoS attack assault known as a TCP SYN DDoS attack aims to overwhelm the target server's capacity with unsolicited requests, making it very difficult for authorized users to receive a response from the server. It may cause a sharp decline in performance, which may cause a sharp decline in business and frustration, (Tehaam *et al.,* 2022). SYN packets that are suspicious or malicious can be identified and eliminated before they overwhelm server resources and create interruption, which might help lessen the impact of these assaults. However, because the attackers focus more on making these malicious packets appear to be originating from a legitimate source, it can occasionally be challenging to identify the packets at early stages, (Harshita, 2017). Employing different techniques like SYN cookies, rate limiting, and firewalls can prove to be useful to defend against TCP-SYN attacks, (Mohapatra, 2021). SYN cookies use a technique that aims to avoid the half-open connections between the client and the server to prevent the server from allocating resources to the illegitimate requests made by the attacker and getting exhausted. In this technique, the server will not allocate the resource to the client based on the initial SYN request. Instead, it generates a unique SYN cookie containing some information from the client's SYN packet and some information from the server's side. This SYN cookie is then sent along with the SYN-ACK packet. The server considers a request to be valid when it receives an ACK packet with the right SYN cookie, (Zargar, Joshi, & Tipper, 2013). If not, it simply discards the packets, viewing them as originating from an unauthorized source, such as an attacker. The OS level is where this strategy is put into practice. In normal load scenarios, this strategy can be helpful in preventing TCP SYN attacks; however, in other scenarios, it may negatively affect performance because it requires the server to generate a SYN cookie per request that comes in. Rate limitation is another method used to lessen the effect of these attacks. This method caps the number of connections or requests coming from a single source for a predetermined amount of time.

This method seeks to avoid service misuse or overloading by placing a restriction on the number of requests that can be made in a specified amount of time. Administrators first set a limit on the total amount of requests that are permitted for a specific IP address, user, the source, and API key. Then, the system records the frequency and source of all incoming requests and connections while continuously monitoring them. A program uses the IP address as its primary means of identifying what or who is requesting anything, (Harshita, 2017). Every time a client request is received, the system determines whether it falls within the specified threshold or not. This method can assist in identifying excessive requests from one IP address, which could be interpreted as an attack. By identifying anomalous traffic patterns, network flow analysis seeks to stop TCP-SYN flooding DDoS attacks. In the case of valid TCP SYN traffic, it first creates a baseline for typical behavior of network flow by monitoring network traffic over time and recognizing patterns. A sudden increase in SYN packets may be an indication of a possible syn flood assault if it deviates from this baseline, (Mohapatra & Mishra, 2024). Additionally, it can be helpful in identifying abnormalities in the traffic, such as a sudden spike in requests generated by one IP address or plenty of half-open connections. Additionally, because the administrators can select a threshold according to baseline traffic analysis, it can aid in the implementation of the rate-limiting strategy. As a result, this method can improve an organization's ability to recognize, detect and stop these threats, (Zargar, Joshi, & Tipper, 2013).

ICMP flood attacks exploit the Internet Control Message Protocol (ICMP) to burden a targeted network by flooding it with a huge volume of ICMP packets. ICMP is mainly used for network devices like routers and is crucial in error reporting and testing. During an ICMP flood attack, attackers exploit the target network with self-generated ICMP packets, using legitimate source IP addresses to hinder their origin, (Mohapatra & Mishra, 2024). This flush of incoming ICMP traffic can exhaust available bandwidth and saturate network resources, leading to average performance and degraded service availability. Some mitigation strategies include ICMP rate limiting, anomaly detection, traffic analysis, and ICMP echo request filtering. ICMP rate limiting deals with controlling the rate of incoming ICMP packets to stop flooding and effectively manage network resources, (Darwish *et al.,* 2013). Anomaly detection recognizes deviations from regular network traffic patterns, while traffic analysis inspects packet attributes to identify signs of illicit activity. Anomaly detection with traffic analysis can increase the detection and prevention of ICMP flood attacks. ICMP echo request filtering controls ICMP echo request packets exceeding a specific limit based on predetermined policies, selectively allowing or blocking requests based on attributes like source and destination IP addresses. However, these techniques require regular monitoring and updating to adjust to changing network needs, security policies, and other considerations, (Sahi *et al.,* 2017b).

Table 1. Comparative study of the critical attacks

Attacks	How it acts	How it can be identified	Mitigation Strategies
TCP-SYN	The attacker sends massive numbers of packets to the server overwhelming it and hindering its ability to handle real requests.	● Spike in SYN packets ● Huge numbers of half-open connections ● Anomaly Detection	● SYN cookies ● Rate limiting ● Firewalls and IPS (Intrusion Prevention System)
Smurfing	Exploits the Internet Control Message Protocol (ICMP) and IP address spoofing to flood a target network with a large volume of traffic.	● High ping response time ● Source IP Address spoofing ● Broadcast access traffic	● Ingress Filtering ● Traffic scrubbing ● Rate limiting
ICMP	ICMP floods involve overwhelming the target server or network with a large number of ICMP packets. These attacks exploit its vulnerabilities using Ping Flood, Smurf Attack, and Ping of Death.	● Spike in ICMP Traffic ● High ping ● Network Anomaly	● Firewalls and ACLs (Access Control Lists) ● Ingress Filtering ● ICMP Hardening

A software-defined network is a type of network architecture that allows for centralized management by separating the control plane from the data plane. SDN promptly implements fixes and adjusts to shifting traffic patterns. Traffic can be real-time diverted by SDN according to pre- established regulations. The most often used tools are MATLAB, Wireshark, and Snort. An open-source intrusion prevention and identification system (IPS) is what Snort does. To find and stop threats, it makes use of detection using signatures, protocol analysis, and inconsistency analysis. It is possible to alter Snort rules to incorporate identification linked to well-known DDoS assault patterns. A network traffic analyzer called Wireshark makes it possible to encapsulate and analyze network load. Wireshark facilitates defense mechanism adaptation and post-incident analysis. MATLAB is a commonly utilized numerical computing environment, often employed for various purposes such as signal processing and data analysis. MATLAB analyzes traffic patterns and recognizes inconsistencies in DDoS attacks. It may involve the construction of custom algorithms or models for identification. The integration of SDN for flexible network adjustment methods enhances intelligent detection using tools such as Snort, MATLAB, and Wireshark. These work together comprehensively to identify, interpret, and mitigate DDoS attacks, (Douligeris & Mitrokotsa, 2003).

In summary, the mitigation strategy for SYN, ICMP, and smurfing attacks often involves a combination of techniques, including SYN cookies, rate limiting, ingress filtering, and traffic scrubbing services. Organizations should assess their specific needs and environments to determine the most effective combination of mitigation strategies for their situation. Additionally, proactive monitoring and response procedures are crucial for quickly identifying and mitigating DDoS attacks as they occur, (Kumar, Trivedi, & Mehtre, 2014). The main outcome was the creation of sophisticated detection and mitigation methods tailored specifically for Smurfing and SYN attacks. This involved the development of strong algorithms, possibly leveraging tools like Snort, an open-source Intrusion Prevention System (IPS), which operates using predefined rules to identify malicious traffic effectively. Wireshark and MATLAB could be utilized for analyzing network traffic patterns and identifying anomalies indicative of DDoS attacks, (Velliangiri, Karthikeyan, & Kumar, 2021). Results obtained from the proposed detection and mitigation strategies were thoroughly examined, and comparative studies were conducted to evaluate their effectiveness against existing methodologies (Table. 1 shows a comparative study of the critical attacks).

4.CONCLUSION

Load Balancers efficiently distribute the traffic among different servers. However, if not secured properly they can become a vulnerable target for the attackers. This study addresses different security challenges associated with load balancers and deals with implementing access control mechanisms. Denial of service attacks is becoming a challenge for the emerging technology, and it can affect the availability of services for legitimate users. This paper focused on studying different types of DDoS attacks and their respective mitigation techniques. The study classifies the different types of attacks based on characteristics and the process followed by the attacker to restrict authorized users from accessing services. After classifying the

DDoS attacks this research paper aims to explore smurfing, TCP-SYN, and ICMP attacks. Firstly, the nature of the attacks is examined and then the relevant mitigation strategy is suggested for each of them. This study concludes that the identification of a DDoS attack is crucial before implementing any particular mitigation strategy. For example, if the attack is targeting the network bandwidth like an ICMP attack, then network-based mitigation solutions like ICMP rate-limiting techniques and anomaly detection can be implemented. If the attack aims to flood the server's resources as in the case of a TCP-SYN attack, then proper mitigation solutions like load balancing, SYN-cookie, rate limiting, and network flow analysis can be implemented. This paper provides some basic knowledge on how to identify different types of DDoS attacks and suggests some mitigation strategies accordingly. Research in the future might include protecting the servers using zero-trust security principles. After identifying the type of DDoS attack, zero trust security principles might be useful to mitigate the attack. It can be deployed by adopting a strict access control model and implementing layered defenses. It follows the principle of "never trust". It always suggests verifying the client demanding the resource by following strict authentication and authorization, regardless of their location. SDN controllers can dynamically redirect traffic away from targeted servers under attack whereas zero trust uses the micro-segmentation technique to divide the network into smaller segments which can prevent the spread of the attack to every part of the network.

REFERENCES

AlHuwaishel, N., & Zaghloul, S. S. (2013, September). A technique for load-balanced management of security tasks load in grids. In 2013 Africon (pp. 1-5). IEEE.

Belyaev, M., & Gaivoronski, S. (2014, October). Towards load balancing in SDN-networks during DDoS-attacks. In 2014 international science and technology conference (modern networking technologies)(MoNeTeC) (pp. 1-6). IEEE.

Buvaneswari, M., Loganathan, M. P., & Sangeetha, S. (2017, February). Cloud challenges of load balancing and security issues using ICLoS algorithm. In 2017 2nd International Conference on Computing and Communications Technologies (ICCCT) (pp. 103-105). IEEE.

Darwish, M., Ouda, A., & Capretz, L. F. (2013, June). Cloud-based DDoS attacks and defenses. In International Conference on Information Society (i-Society 2013) (pp. 67-71). IEEE.

Douligeris, C., & Mitrokotsa, A. (2003, December). DDoS attacks and defense mechanisms: a classification. In Proceedings of the 3rd IEEE International Symposium on Signal Processing and Information Technology (IEEE Cat. No. 03EX795) (pp. 190-193). IEEE.

Girma, A., Garuba, M., Li, J., & Liu, C. (2015, April). Analysis of DDoS attacks and an introduction of a hybrid statistical model to detect DDoS attacks on cloud computing environment. In 2015 12th International Conference on Information Technology-New Generations (pp. 212-217). IEEE.

Guirguis, M., Bestavros, A., Matta, I., & Zhang, Y. (2007, May). Reduction of quality (RoQ) attacks on dynamic load balancers: Vulnerability assessment and design tradeoffs. In IEEE INFOCOM 2007-26th IEEE International Conference on Computer Communications (pp. 857-865). IEEE.

Harshita, H. (2017). Detection and prevention of icmp flood ddos attack. *International Journal of New Technology and Research*, 3(3), 263333.

He, J. (2022). [Retracted] Cloud Computing Load Balancing Mechanism Taking into Account Load Balancing Ant Colony Optimization Algorithm. *Computational Intelligence and Neuroscience*, 2022(1), 3120883.

Iyengar, N. C. S. N., Ganapathy, G., Mogan Kumar, P., & Abraham, A. (2014). A multilevel thrust filtration defending mechanism against ddos attacks in cloud computing environment. *International Journal of Grid and Utility Computing*, 5(4), 236–248. DOI: 10.1504/IJGUC.2014.065384

Kaviarasan, R., Balamurugan, G., & Kalaiyarasan, R. (2023). *Venkata Ravindra Reddy Effective load balancing approach in cloud computing using Inspired Lion Optimization Algorithm-Prime - Advances in Electrical Engineering* (Vol. 6). Electronics and Energy.

Mi, W., Qiu, X., & Zhang, C. (2011, December). The analysis of security threats in structured P2P load balancing schemes. In 2011 International Conference on Cloud and Service Computing (pp. 296-301). IEEE.

Mohapatra, H. (2021, September). Socio-technical challenges in the implementation of smart city. In 2021 international conference on innovation and intelligence for informatics, computing, and technologies (3ICT) (pp. 57-62). IEEE.

Mohapatra, H., & Mishra, S. R. (2024). Unlocking Insights: Exploring Data Analytics and AI Tool Performance Across Industries. In Singh, P., Mishra, A. R., & Garg, P. (Eds.), *Data Analytics and Machine Learning. Studies in Big Data* (Vol. 145). Springer., DOI: 10.1007/978-981-97-0448-4_13

Musa, N. S., Mirza, N. M., Rafique, S. H., Abdallah, A. M., & Murugan, T. (2024). Machine Learning and Deep Learning Techniques for Distributed Denial of Service Anomaly Detection in Software Defined Networks—Current Research Solutions. *IEEE Access : Practical Innovations, Open Solutions*, 12, 17982–18011. DOI: 10.1109/ACCESS.2024.3360868

Ramprasath, J., Krishnaraj, N., & Seethalakshmi, V. (2022). Mitigation services on SDN for distributed denial of service and denial of service attacks using machine learning techniques. *Journal of the Institution of Electronics and Telecommunication Engineers*, (Nov), 1–12.

Sahi, A., Lai, D., Li, Y., & Diykh, M. (2017). An efficient ddos tcp flood attack detection and prevention system in a cloud environment. *IEEE Access : Practical Innovations, Open Solutions*, 5, 6036–6048. DOI: 10.1109/ACCESS.2017.2688460

Sahi, A., Lai, D., Li, Y., & Diykh, M. (2017). An efficient ddos tcp flood attack detection and prevention system in a cloud environment. *IEEE Access : Practical Innovations, Open Solutions*, 5, 6036–6048. DOI: 10.1109/ACCESS.2017.2688460

Sebbar, A., & Zkik, K. (2023). "Enhancing Resilience against DDoS Attacks in SDN -based Supply Chain Networks Using Machine Learning," 2023 9th International Conference on Control, Decision and Information Technologies (CoDIT), Rome, Italy. DOI: 10.1109/CoDIT58514.2023.10284387

Tan, L., Pan, Y., Wu, J., Zhou, J., Jiang, H., & Deng, Y. (2020). A new framework for DDoS attack detection and defense in SDN environment. *IEEE Access : Practical Innovations, Open Solutions*, 8, 161908–161919. DOI: 10.1109/ACCESS.2020.3021435

Tayfour, O., & Marsono, M. N. (2020). Collaborative Detection and Mitigation of Distributed Denial-of-Service Attacks on Software-Defined Network. *Mobile Networks and Applications*, 25(4), 1338–1347. Advance online publication. DOI: 10.1007/s11036-020-01552-0

Tehaam, M., Ahmad, S., Shahid, H., Saboor, M. S., Aziz, A., & Munir, K. (2022, October). A Review of DDoS Attack Detection and Prevention Mechanisms in Clouds. In 2022 24th International Multitopic Conference (INMIC) (pp. 1-6). IEEE.

Velliangiri, S., Karthikeyan, P., & Kumar, V. V. (2021). Detection of distributed denial of service attack in cloud computing using the optimization-based deep networks. *Journal of Experimental & Theoretical Artificial Intelligence*, 33(3), 405–424. DOI: 10.1080/0952813X.2020.1744196

Wang, S., Balarezo, J. F., Chavez, K. G., Al-Hourani, A., Kandeepan, S., Asghar, M. R., & Russello, G. (2022). Detecting flooding DDoS attacks in software defined networks using supervised learning techniques. Engineering science and technology, an international journal, 35, 101176.

Yadav, V. K., Trivedi, M. C., & Mehtre, B. M. (2016). DDA: an approach to handle DDoS (Ping Flood) attack. In Proceedings of International Conference on ICT for Sustainable Development: ICT4SD 2015 Volume 1 (pp. 11-23). Springer Singapore.

Zargar, S. T., Joshi, J., & Tipper, D. (2013). A survey of defense mechanisms against distributed denial of service (ddos) flooding attacks. *IEEE Communications Surveys and Tutorials*, 15(4), 2046–2069. DOI: 10.1109/SURV.2013.031413.00127

Chapter 8

Exploring Effective Strategies for Combatting Cybercrime and Intersection of IoT, Deep Learning:

Legal Standpoints on Progressive Data Analytics

Bhupinder Singh
https://orcid.org/0009-0006-4779-2553
Sharda University, India

Christian Kaunert
https://orcid.org/0000-0002-4493-2235
Dublin City University, Ireland & University of South Wales, UK

ABSTRACT

The Internet of Things (IoT) represents a network of interconnected devices that collect and exchange data, while deep learning, a subset of artificial intelligence involves algorithms that model high-level abstractions in data through neural networks. The fusion of these technologies has transformed various sectors, from healthcare and agriculture to smart cities and autonomous vehicles. However, this convergence has also created new avenues for cybercrime, posing significant challenges to data security and privacy. The combination of deep learning and the Internet of Things has resulted in new vulnerabilities that hackers may take advantage of in addition to creative uses. This chapter looks at legal approaches to

DOI: 10.4018/979-8-3693-9235-5.ch008

enhanced data analysis as well as practical methods for fighting cybercrime in the context of new technologies. With a focus on deep learning, legal frameworks and forward-thinking solutions, this study attempts to convey a thorough knowledge of the confluence of deep learning, cybercrime, and IoT.

1. INTRODUCTION AND BACKGROUND

The vast network of devices with sensors or actuators that are linked by wired or wireless networks is referred to as the Internet of Things (IoT) (Ziwei et al., 2024; Kumar, 2024). This technology has a significant influence on daily life since it integrates easily with a number of industries, such as healthcare, smart homes, and smart cities (Thapaliya & Sharma, 2023). Internet of Things (IoT) security encompasses the tools and strategies used to safeguard cloud-connected devices and the networks they utilize for communication (Djenna et al., 2023). Its primary objectives are to protect user data, prevent cyber-attacks, and ensure the seamless operation of devices (Awajan, 2023). The recent data breaches have highlighted the importance of prioritizing IoT security for manufacturers and developers (Attaran & Deb, 2018). The quick growth of IoT applications and devices brings substantial security and privacy issues, notwithstanding its advantages (Brotcke, 2022). Major problems now include node spoofing, illegal data access, and cyberattacks such as denial of service (DoS), eavesdropping, and intrusion detection (Abebe et al., 2020). Lately, significant developments in deep learning (DL) and machine learning (ML) have offered reliable ways to improve IoT device security (Elluri et al., 2023; Hagendorff, 2019; Singh & Kaunert, 2024). The term "Internet of Things" (IoT) describes a network in which different intelligent gadgets and things exchange data via the Internet (Thapaliya & Sharma, 2023; Dash et al., 2022). Globally, there are already 17 billion linked devices; of them, 7 billion are Internet of Things (IoT) devices not including computers, smartphones, or tablets. By 2025, it is predicted that there will be 75.44 billion IoT devices globally (Barocas et al., 2023; Narayana & Sreedevi, 2023; Mhlanga, 2021).

There are many applications in industries including healthcare, home automation, agriculture, transportation, and education that are greatly advanced by IoT technology (Pocher et al., 2023; Chen et al., 2018). As a result of ongoing technical developments and the expansion of application fields, IoT has grown into a suite of specialized solutions made to meet particular requirements (Tyagi et al., 2020; Cao et al., 2021). Within artificial intelligence, deep learning is a subfield of machine learning (Alazab et al., 2023). Artificial Neural Networks, which are intended to mimic the connection and functioning of neurons in the human brain, are used in it (Zhang et al., 2022; Singh, 2023; Lee & Shin, 2020). So, compared to other AI techniques like machine learning, deep learning is called for the usage of deeper networks (AJ & Kaythry, 2023; Li et al., 2020). The number of layers in an ANN determines the depth of the network. For instance, Convolutional Neural Networks a popular kind of ANN are frequently employed in computer vision applications (Cheng et al., 2021). An input that travels through several network levels reaches the initial layer in a deep learning network design (Bhuvaneshwari & Kaythry, 2023). Every layer possesses distinct functions and scales that modify the input in a specified order, ultimately yielding an output or forecast (Mühlhoff, 2021; Saltz et al., 2019; Hoijtink & Planqué-van Hardeveld, 2022).

Figure 1. Diverse aspects of introduction split sections (Original)

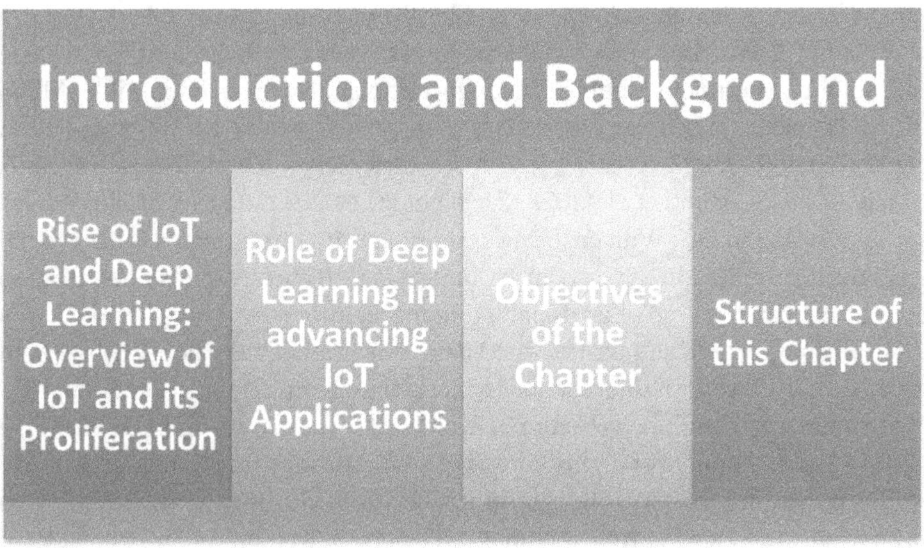

1.1 Rise of IoT and Deep Learning: Overview of IoT and its Proliferation

IoT devices are any electronics, including locks, garage door openers, refrigerators, security cameras, ovens, televisions, and contemporary warehouse gear, that are connected to the cloud and gather data (Utami et al., 2022; Zhang et al., 2022). Examples of these gadgets are Google Nest temperature monitors and refrigerators. These gadgets are not like mobile devices, which have pre-established cybersecurity mechanisms and common operating systems (Baker & Robinson, 2020). Usually running Linux, customized versions of operating systems are used by IoT devices

(Aziz & Andriansyah, 2023; Bao et al., 2022). IoT devices need special cybersecurity protections because of the way they operate; unlike mobile operating systems like iOS and Android, they don't have built-in security capabilities (McKendrick, 2019; Rai & Sahu, 2020; Sharma et al., 2023). IoT security is still a major concern for developers and manufacturers, as seen by the numerous data breaches and assaults that occurred throughout the IoT's growth (Sharma et al., 2023).

1.2 Role of Deep Learning in advancing IoT Applications

It is anticipated that new strategies, such the application of artificial intelligence (AI) technologies for cybersecurity, would provide answers to this problem (Varma et al., 2022; Tippins et al., 2021). These methods, however, usually ask for a large volume of training data that closely resembles the patterns identified in the test data (Lui & Lamb, 2018). Since new threats are found every day in the world of cybersecurity, obtaining pertinent training data might be difficult or even impossible (Mijwil et al., 2023). The classification tasks are then carried out by learning algorithms using these taught characteristics, leading to extremely accurate danger detection (Schmitt, 2020; Siwakoti et al., 2023; Zhang et al., 2020). The lack of labeled data is not a constraint in DL. With ensuring system security throughout its lifespan, DL algorithms are applied in cybersecurity, improving efficiency and safety. Because deep learning (DL), a kind of artificial intelligence, allows networks and devices to learn from complicated and unstructured data, it is dramatically boosting the high-tech sector. Systems with intelligent deep learning are able to learn continually to adapt to changing conditions (Nassar & Kamal, 2021; Alruwaili, 2023; Grimm et al., 2021). Large amounts of unprocessed network data may be automatically mined using deep learning to extract insightful information, eliminating the need for human specialists and saving time and money (Dhoni & Kumar, 2023; Kordzadeh & Ghasemaghaei, 2022; Mijwil et al., 2023).

1.3 Objectives of the Chapter

This chapter has the following objectives to:

- study the expanding roles of deep learning and the Internet of Things (IoT) in cybercrime will be looked at in this section. It examine the new assault avenues and difficulties that these developments present, as well as how the current legislative frameworks might need to change to deal with these new dangers (Sambasivan et al., 2021).
- explore the legal issues surrounding the application of deep learning to data analytics in Internet of Things systems will be examined in this section. It

will cover topics including ownership, data privacy, possible biases in deep learning algorithms, and how the law can guarantee ethical data gathering, processing, and use in the Internet of Things (Singh, 2023).

- concentrate on the fine line that must be drawn between protecting fundamental human rights and enabling law enforcement to work together effectively to combat cybercrime. It observes possible issues with cybercrime treaties' too general language as well as the significance of protecting digital rights in the digital age (Zang et al., 2023).
- examine current international treaties and agreements, such the Budapest Convention, that lay the groundwork for international collaboration in the fight against cybercrime. It looks at how these frameworks help with information exchange, cybercrime investigations, and cybercriminal prosecution (Singh, 2023; Katyal, 2019).
- proposals for enhancing the legal framework to combat cybercrime will be made in this section. It looks at how to maintain the efficacy of global collaboration while respecting human rights and encouraging creativity in the digital sphere.

Figure 2. Objectives of the chapter (Original)

1.4 Structure of this Chapter

This chapter deeply dives into the diverse arena of Exploring Effective Strategies for Combatting Cybercrime and Intersection of IoT, Deep Learning: Legal Standpoints on Progressive Data Analytics. Section 2 elaborates the Emergence of Cybercrime: Definition and Scope. Section 3 explores the IoT and Deep Learning. Section 4 discusses the Cybercrime Landscape. Section 5 specifies the Legal Frameworks: Progressive Data Analytics. Section 6 conveys the Intersection of IoT, Deep Learning, and Cybercrime. Section 7 Conclude the Chapter with Future Scope.

Figure 3. Flow of this chapter (Original)

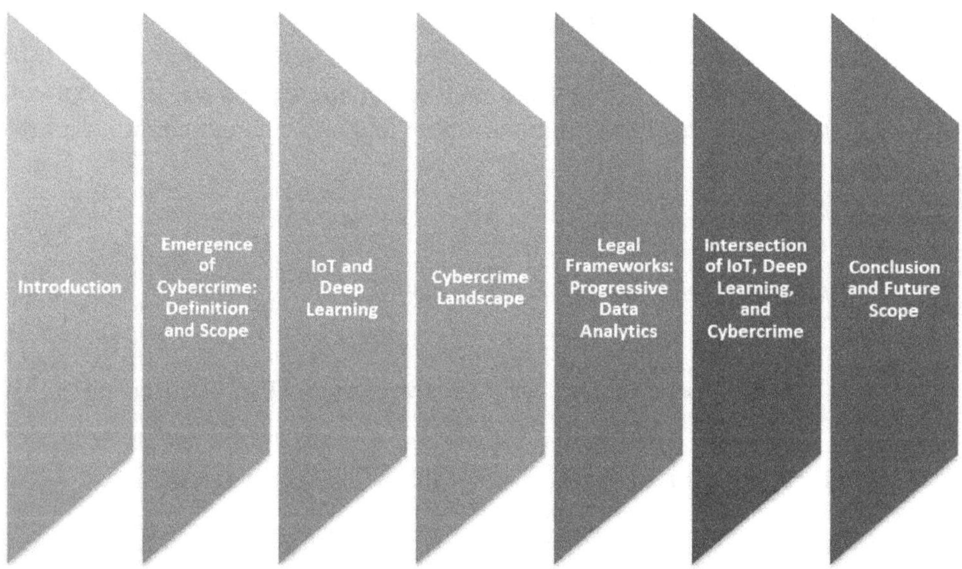

2. EMERGENCE OF CYBERCRIME: DEFINITION AND SCOPE

As information and communication technology permeate every part of daily lives in the digital era, the surge in cybercrimes has become a serious problem (Irfan et al., 2023; Selbst & Barocas, 2018; Chohan et al., 2023). A new type of criminal activity has emerged that is immune to traditional investigation techniques and geographical constraints, the unmatched connection provided by the digital world (Singh et al., 2023; Sowmya et al., 2023; Daugherty & Wilson, 2018). So, fighting these constantly changing dangers requires making the most of artificial intelligence (AI) technologies (Swiątkowska, 2020). The potential for averting cybercrimes through the deployment of AI techniques like machine learning, data analytics, and pattern recognition is enormous (Berk et al., 2021; Abbas et al., 2024). With the help of AI-driven solutions, users can quickly evaluate enormous volumes of data to spot abnormalities and possible threats that could go missed using more conventional techniques (Sudhakar & Kumar, 2023; Kochhar et al., 2023; Kaushik, 2024). With continually adapting to new approaches and learning from past attack patterns, AI systems may proactively forecast and repel cyber-attacks, turning cybersecurity from a reactive to a proactive profession (Liu et al., 2024; Rajkumar et al., 2023). Also, integrating AI methods into risk assessment and policy execution might improve decision-making procedures and maximize resource distribution to stop and lessen cybercrimes (Nisha & Muthurajkumar, 2023; Shukla & Tiwari, 2024; Paddalwar et al., 2023).

The significant amount of data produced by Internet of Things devices poses difficulties for processing, storing, and analyzing. Effective data management techniques are crucial to extracting valuable insights from the massive volumes of data produced by IoT devices while maintaining privacy and safeguarding sensitive data (Itani et al., 2023; Odeh & Abu Taleb, 2023; Ortiz-Ruiz et al., 2024). These techniques include secure storage and efficient processing methods. The other crucial component in the IoT space is trust management (Ali et al., 2024). Building trust between different entities devices, apps, and users is essential to ensuring safe communication and sharing of data (Hamad, 2023). The ensuring the integrity and security of Internet of Things systems requires the development of strong trust models for entity authentication and authorization (Latif et al., 2024; Anis et al., 2023; Abdalrdha et al., 2023).

2.1 Impact of IoT and Deep Learning on Cybercrime Trends

The number of Internet of Things (IoT) devices on the market has greatly increased the number of possible targets that hackers may attack (AL-Dosari et al., 2024). The strong security features are frequently absent from these networked gadgets, which range from industrial sensors to smart household appliances (Ambika, 2024). The attackers can use these vulnerabilities to execute a variety of attacks. These devices may be taken over by hostile actors to create botnets, which are strong networks that are used to distribute malware or conduct denial-of-service attacks (Aljuhani et al., 2023). Also, there is a security concern due to the massive volume of data that

IoT devices gather. This information might be exploited for identity theft, targeted scams, or even physical violence if it ends up in the wrong hands (Lone et al., 2023)

Cybercriminals as well as cybersecurity experts are increasingly using deep learning, a potent subset of artificial intelligence. Deep learning algorithms are perfect for threat identification and prevention because they can examine enormous volumes of data to find patterns and abnormalities. Attackers, however, can utilize these same skills to create more advanced malware and hacking methods (Messai & Seba, 2023). For example, deepfakes employ deep learning to produce audio or video recordings that are artificially realistic but nevertheless realistic. These recordings may be used in misinformation campaigns or social engineering assaults. The potential for deep learning technology to be abused in cybercrime will grow as it develops (Manimaran et al., 2023).

3. IOT AND DEEP LEARNING

IoT devices are growing and integrating at a quick pace, which has greatly increased the attack surface and created risks to connected devices as well as the network infrastructure as a whole (Nehinbe et al., 2023). DoS assaults, spoofing, jamming, eavesdropping, data manipulation, and other malevolent actions are examples of common IoT attacks. Cybercriminals take advantage of weaknesses in Internet of Things systems to get unapproved entry, alter information, interfere with services, or jeopardize privacy (Ali & Farooq, 2023). Although standardized protocols and interfaces are required to provide smooth communication and interoperability across IoT platforms and devices, they can cause incompatibilities, fragmentation of data, and difficulties in administering and protecting various IoT settings (Escorcia-Gutierrez et al., 2023; Kongsorot et al., 2023; Costa & Sofikitis, 2024). A number of deep learning frameworks like TensorFlow and PyTorch, let users build their own models and carry out deep learning experiments (Ali et al., 2024). Both frameworks offer a wealth of first guidelines for novices and aficionados (Tok & Chattopadhyay, 2023). You may choose which framework to utilize with the aid of this tutorial. But before you start developing models, you should be aware that deep learning model training requires a lot of work, especially when it comes to Graphics Processing Units (GPUs) (Wu et al., 2023). The development of the technology was first hampered by the high cost of GPUs. However, deep learning gained enormous traction as these processors got more potent and reasonably priced (Segovia-Vargas, 2024).

Figure 4. Key aspects of IoT and deep learning (Original)

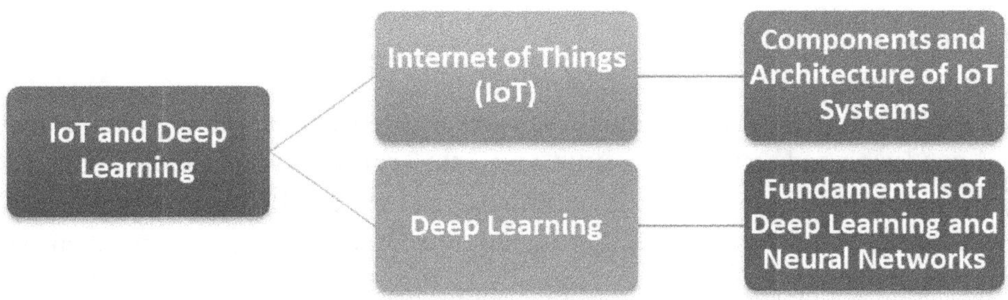

3.1 Internet of Things (IoT)

In the context of the Internet of Things, data and service availability, confidentiality, and integrity are critical considerations (Lipsa & Dash, 2023; Virmani et al., 2023). The robust security measures, including as encryption, access control mechanisms, intrusion detection systems, and redundancy planning, are necessary to protect confidentiality, ensure the integrity of transmitted and stored information, and ensure the availability of important services (Messai & Seba, 2023). A basic value that needs to be upheld in the IoT ecosystem is privacy, in addition to security. Massive volumes of personal data are being collected and processed by IoT devices, which might result in privacy violations and put people at danger. Protecting people's privacy within the context of the Internet of Things requires putting privacy-by-design principles into practice, getting user agreement, and using technologies that enhance privacy (Venkatasubramanian et al., 2023; Vatambeti & Mamidisetti, 2023).

3.1.1 Components and Architecture of IoT Systems

The network layer, the application layer, and the terminal perception layer make up the three levels of the Internet of Things architecture (Singh et al., 2024). IoT systems are susceptible to a wide range of dynamic threats and security issues due to their complexity and resource constraints. The challenge of securing these systems is incredibly difficult and complex (Das et al., 2023). Numerous issues, including as standardization, interoperability, data storage, processing, trust management, identification, and privacy, are brought about by the expansion of the Internet of Things. Developing a dependable and safe Internet of Things environment requires addressing these issues (Kumar et al., 2023).

3.2 Deep Learning

Deep learning (DL) is a technique that uses a variety of methodologies that need rigorous design and testing to execute computational tasks intelligently and independently (Alabdulkreem et al., 2023; Nandan & Dey, 2023). Massive volumes of data must be computed and stored efficiently for DL to work. DL is an expensive and computationally demanding subset of DL (Priyadarshini et al., 2023). Since it automatically pulls high-level information from unprocessed data, it is the perfect answer to IoT security issues (Moustafa et al., 2023). Also, deep learning (DL) has advanced significantly in training intricate deep neural network designs, improving decision-making skills for a variety of tasks such as detection, classification, and prediction (Afrifa et al., 2023).

3.2.1 Fundamentals of Deep Learning and Neural Networks

Artificial intelligence in the form of deep learning is causing waves in cybercrime on both sides of the border (Soliman et al., 2023; Cao et al., 2024). Deep learning uses artificial neural networks, which are intricately linked systems that imitate the structure and functionality of neurons and are inspired by the structure of the human brain. Because these networks have been trained on vast volumes of data, they are remarkably accurate at identifying patterns and making predictions (Abbas et al., 2024). The professionals in cybersecurity may excel in anomaly detection with deep learning. These networks can identify the characteristics of typical activity and highlight any differences that can point to a cyberattack by examining network traffic or user behavior (Saha, 2024). Cybercriminals, however, are also making use of this ability. With creating realistic deepfakes, deep learning may be used to automate operations such as creating malware and customizing phishing emails, as well as social engineering attempts (Al-Quayed et al., 2024). The struggle in cyberspace between good and bad actors is only going to get more intense as deep learning keeps developing (Kumar et al., 2024).

4. CYBERCRIME LANDSCAPE

The main goals of Internet of Things security are preventing device compromise and securing data as it travels from the device to the cloud. Because consumers never alter their default passwords, a lot of IoT devices are still open to viruses like Mirai (Vasan et al., 2024). Mirai uses default passwords on Internet of Things devices to infiltrate them into a botnet and perform distributed denial-of-service (DDoS) assaults (Rathee et al., 2024). These hazards may be reduced with easy actions like changing default passwords and disabling Telnet services. The security measures must safeguard the transmitted data and its storage as IoT devices interface with the cloud. Cloud data compromises may result in identity theft or privacy violations (Sharma & Annaboina, 2024). Even though SSL/TLS is widely used on websites, some IoT manufacturers continue to send data in an unencrypted manner. The other major worry in IoT security is authentication, particularly with children's toys where personal information can be exposed via compromised or absent authentication. To stop these breaches, enhanced authentication procedures and defenses against brute-force assaults are crucial (Gangula et al., 2024) .

The development of complete solutions and the resolution of these complex issues are essential for the safe and secure implementation of IoT systems as well as their long-term growth (Niu et al., 2024; Shaikh et al., 2024). Working together, industry players, legislators, and researchers may help create standards, guidelines, and best practices that advance the security, privacy, and dependability of the Internet of Things. The dynamic arena of cybercrime, propelled by IoT and deep learning, demands a reassessment of the existing legal frameworks and security protocols (Plageras et al., 2024). Laws must change to handle concerns such as data ownership and responsibility in Internet of Things networks and to provide unambiguous standards for the appropriate application of deep learning technology (Demir & Serkan, 2024; Rakha et al., 2024). For IoT devices, cybersecurity safeguards also need to be greatly improved, with an emphasis on strong authentication procedures and secure communication protocols (Nkoro et al., 2024) We can only effectively reduce the increasing risks that IoT and deep learning offer to the world of cybercrime by taking a holistic strategy that takes into account both the legal and security issues (Alrubayyi et al., 2024).

5. LEGAL FRAMEWORKS: PROGRESSIVE DATA ANALYTICS

In order to use threat intelligence sources for AI-driven threat detection and prediction, it starts with data collection and preparation. AI is used by the security analytics platform to track and examine security-related data. AI-assisted incident response planning is used in the event of an occurrence (Samsudeen & Thomas, 2024). AI also helps in the creation and application of governance frameworks and policies to combat cyberthreats. Collectively, these interrelated phases present a thorough strategy for using AI tools to tackle cybercrimes (Sakthibalan et al., 2024). Based on the particular technology and tactics being used, this diagram can be further elaborated to provide a higher level depiction. These resources include historical and current data on emerging risks, weak points, and assault strategies (Din et al., 2024). From threat intelligence streams, they gather information on malicious IP addresses, domains, malware samples, and hacking strategies. This data is processed and analyzed using AI algorithms, which find connections and patterns that may point to possible hazards. On the basis of certain security problems, appropriate security measures are suggested (Hemamalini et al., 2024). The utilization of ML/DL techniques which successfully solve security concerns and have applications in a variety of fields, including voice recognition and image processing is the specific emphasis (Tejasvi et al., 2024). They are useful instruments for enhancing security and advancing numerous areas due to their adaptability and efficacy (Devan et al., 2024).

The security analytics platform, to put it briefly, is a central repository for security data gathered from many sources, such as firewalls and antivirus software (Reddy et al., 2024). This data is analyzed by AI to look for unusual activity that might be an indication of a cyberattack. However, incident response planning is a methodical strategy that businesses employ to address cyber security events like malware attacks and data breaches (Pritee et al., 2024). Reduced damage, a speedy return to regular operations, and the ability to draw lessons from the event to avoid it happening again are the main objectives. International collaboration in the form of treaties and accords has been sparked by the increase of cybercrime (Zhang et al., 2024). These legal frameworks have a significant impact on how nations respond to cyberthreats (Li & Dong, 2024). The Convention on Cybercrime or Budapest Convention is the most notable example (Nyarko et al., 2024). This convention, which was drafted by the Council of Europe, is the first global accord that addresses cybercrime alone (Ababneh & Aljarrah, 2024). It provides a framework for member governments to cooperate together on matters such as obtaining electronic evidence, punishing cybercriminals, and investigating cyberattacks (Montasari, 2024: Mishra et al., 2024).

The Budapest Convention acts as a cornerstone for the worldwide fight against cybercrime by promoting international cooperation and harmonizing state legislation (Mittal, 2024; Behiry & Aly, 2024). The Budapest Convention is not the only piece of international cybercrime legislation, though. Currently, negotiations are underway at the UN to draft a comprehensive convention that expressly addresses cybercrime (Gunavathi & Bharathi, 2024). With more measures for avoiding cyberattacks, looking into crimes, and prosecuting hackers, this possible treaty might give an even stronger foundation for international collaboration (Saiyed & Al-Anbagi, 2024). Although this has the potential to improve international cybersecurity efforts, questions have been raised over the possibility of unduly vague language or inadequate protections for human rights (Dasari & Kaluri, 2024). Critics caution that totalitarian countries would abuse such a convention to violate digital rights and suppress online protest (Ganji & Afshan, 2024).

Figure 5. Legal frameworks: progressive data analytics (Original)

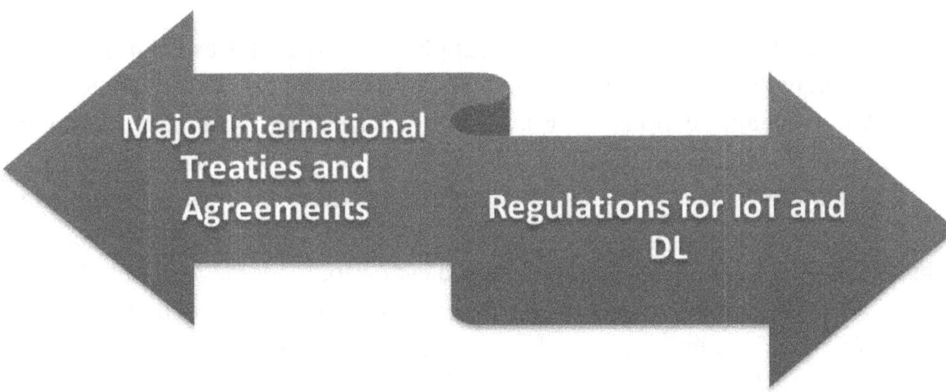

5.1 International Cybercrime Laws: Major International Treaties and Agreements

The UN is drafting a global accord to combat cybercrime and this would be the first significant UN law pertaining to internet matters. It may be an effective weapon for coordinating efforts across borders to combat hackers. Some fear, meanwhile, that the pact may be overly expansive and grant government's excessive authority (Roshanaei, 2024). This may restrict free expression online and facilitate their ability to eavesdrop on individuals. The internet is a global community, and international collaboration is necessary to make it secure and equitable (Lightbody et al., 2024). For this reason, nations collaborate to develop robust cyber laws. These rules guarantee that everyone's rights are upheld online, combat cybercrime, and safeguard privacy (Nguyen et al., 2024). Cyber law addresses topics like data protection, online crime, and even our behavior when using digital platforms (Bui et al., 2024). It is essentially the rulebook for our digital age. This framework is further strengthened by international agreements that enable nations to work together to combat cyber threats and enforce these rules (Sahingoz et al., 2024). The process of creating worldwide legislation against cybercrime is ongoing. These legal frameworks must change as cyber threats grow more complex and technology advances. Ensuring a safe and secure digital environment for everyone requires striking a balance between efficient law enforcement cooperation and safeguarding basic rights (Abdulhussein, 2024; Costa & Sofikitis, 2024).

5.2 Regulations for IoT and DL

The IoT systems brain is located at the application layer. It uses the unprocessed data that is gathered from devices (AL-Dosari & Kucukvar, 2024; Singh & Kaunert, 2024). All of the applications, programs, and services that examine this data and provide insightful analysis are included in this layer (Singh et al., 2024; Singh, 2024). This analysis shows that chores can be automated and actions may be triggered by the application layer, improving our quality of life. The application layer enables tasks like improving industrial operations in a factory or managing smart lighting in a house. But this layer also has to be protected from assaults like denial-of-service (DoS) efforts, which aim to overload the system with data in an attempt to interfere with its functionality (Singh & Kaunert, 2024).

6. INTERSECTION OF IOT, DEEP LEARNING, AND CYBERCRIME

The information technology cybersecurity seeks to shield systems against cyberattacks, reduce the likelihood of such assaults, and stop illegal access to technology, data, and network and internet devices. Protecting fundamental principles like equity, tolerance, liberty, and the privacy of individuals and organizations, as well as upholding the dependability and trustworthiness of digital infrastructure, has become imperative (Singh, 2023). Cybersecurity encompasses a variety of tactics and technologies aimed at preventing unwanted access and assaults on data records, end-to-end systems, and communication networks. Almost every tier of the Internet network model has cyber-defense mechanisms in place (Singh, 2023). There are numerous network security concerns, such as malware, phishing, denial of service, and routing attacks, have been discussed by experts. The main focus is on creating techniques and technologies such as online application security, firewalls, antivirus software, and detecting systems. However, attackers are always coming up with new, more advanced strategies to get beyond suggested safeguards, which puts the efficacy of the security measures in place to the test. The continued growth of end-user devices and networks is the primary driver of the continual need to enhance cybersecurity (Singh, 2024).

7. CONCLUSION AND FUTURE SCOPE

IoT security cannot be solved in a single way, but cybersecurity experts work to improve cloud security and teach developers and manufacturers safe coding techniques. Encrypting cloud data, putting strong password protections in place, and building IoT features that can withstand attack tools are all necessary for effective IoT security. IoT security duty rests on device users as well as the makers and developers that release these devices onto the market in the absence of established protocols. The increasing digitalization of every aspect of life has made it possible to store a huge amount of data. Because digitally stored data is sensitive, it is more important than ever to ensure security. While the internet and other digital technologies have made life easier and more simplified many everyday activities, they also pose serious risks to data security and can result in cyber assaults. Insecure data is the root cause of data loss caused by hackers or software breaches, which can have dire repercussions. Threats are changing quickly; they can occasionally be serious and persistent, but they can also be fleeting and cyber-attacks are very hard to identify and anticipate.

REFERENCES

Ababneh, M., & Aljarrah, A. (2024). cybersecurity: malware multi-attack detector on android-based devices using deep learning methods. *Journal of Theoretical and Applied Information Technology*, 102(1).

Abbas, S., Bouazzi, I., Ojo, S., Al Hejaili, A., Sampedro, G. A., Almadhor, A., & Gregus, M. (2024). Evaluating deep learning variants for cyber-attacks detection and multi-class classification in IoT networks. *PeerJ. Computer Science*, 10, e1793. DOI: 10.7717/peerj-cs.1793 PMID: 38259893

Abbas, S., Bouazzi, I., Ojo, S., Al Hejaili, A., Sampedro, G. A., Almadhor, A., & Gregus, M. (2024). Evaluating deep learning variants for cyber-attacks detection and multi-class classification in IoT networks. *PeerJ. Computer Science*, 10, e1793. DOI: 10.7717/peerj-cs.1793 PMID: 38259893

Abdalrdha, Z. K., Al-Bakry, A. M., & Farhan, A. K. (2023). A Survey on Cybercrime Using Social Media. *Iraqi Journal for Computers and Informatics*, 49(1), 52–65. DOI: 10.25195/ijci.v49i1.404

Abdulhussein, M. (2024). The Impact of Artificial Intelligence and Machine Learning on Organizations Cybersecurity.

Abebe, R., Barocas, S., Kleinberg, J., Levy, K., Raghavan, M., & Robinson, D. G. (2020, January). Roles for computing in social change. In *Proceedings of the 2020 conference on fairness, accountability, and transparency* (pp. 252-260). DOI: 10.1145/3351095.3372871

Afrifa, S., Varadarajan, V., Appiahene, P., & Zhang, T. (2023). Using Machine Learning to Classify Network Abnormalities into Legitimate or Assault in IoT-based Cyber Physical System. *Sensors and Electronic Instrumentation Advances*, 150.

AL-Dosari, K., Fetais, N., & Kucukvar, M. (2024). Artificial intelligence and cyber defense system for banking industry: A qualitative study of AI applications and challenges. *Cybernetics and Systems*, 55(2), 302–330. DOI: 10.1080/01969722.2022.2112539

AL-Dosari, K., Fetais, N., & Kucukvar, M.. (2024). Artificial intelligence and cyber defense system for banking industry: A qualitative study of AI applications and challenges. *Cybernetics and Systems*, 55(2), 302–330. DOI: 10.1080/01969722.2022.2112539

Al-Quayed, F., Ahmad, Z., & Humayun, M. (2024). A situation based predictive approach for cybersecurity intrusion detection and prevention using machine learning and deep learning algorithms in wireless sensor networks of industry 4.0. *IEEE Access : Practical Innovations, Open Solutions*, 12, 34800–34819. DOI: 10.1109/ACCESS.2024.3372187

Alabdulkreem, E., Alotaibi, S. S., Alamgeer, M., Marzouk, R., Hilal, A. M., Motwakel, A., & Rizwanullah, M. (2023). Intelligent Cybersecurity Classification Using Chaos Game Optimization with Deep Learning Model. *Computer Systems Science and Engineering*, 45(1), 971–983. DOI: 10.32604/csse.2023.030362

Alazab, M., Soman, K. P., Srinivasan, S., Venkatraman, S., & Pham, V. Q. (2023). Deep learning for cyber security applications: A comprehensive survey. *Authorea Preprints*.

Ali, B., & Farooq, A. (2023, May). Ensemble Based AI Detector for Cyber Crimes. In *2023 6th International Conference on Electronics Technology (ICET)* (pp. 619-623). IEEE. DOI: 10.1109/ICET58434.2023.10211904

Ali, H. H., Naif, J. R., & Humood, W. R. (2024, March). Deep learning algorithms for IoT security (survey). In *AIP Conference Proceedings* (Vol. 2885, No. 1). AIP Publishing.

Ali, M., Shahroz, M., Mushtaq, M. F., Alfarhood, S., Safran, M., & Ashraf, I. (2024). Hybrid Machine Learning Model for Efficient Botnet Attack Detection in IoT Environment. *IEEE Access : Practical Innovations, Open Solutions*, 12, 40682–40699. DOI: 10.1109/ACCESS.2024.3376400

Aljuhani, A., Kumar, P., Alanazi, R., Albalawi, T., Taouali, O., Islam, A. N., & Alazab, M. (2023). A deep learning integrated blockchain framework for securing industrial iot. *IEEE Internet of Things Journal*.

Alrubayyi, H., Alshareef, M. S., Nadeem, Z., Abdelmoniem, A. M., & Jaber, M. (2024). Security Threats and Promising Solutions Arising from the Intersection of AI and IoT: A Study of IoMT and IoET Applications. *Future Internet*, 16(3), 85. DOI: 10.3390/fi16030085

Alruwaili, F. F. (2023). Optimal hybrid deep learning enabled attack detection and classification in IoT environment. *Computers, Materials & Continua*, 75(1), 99–115. DOI: 10.32604/cmc.2023.034752

Ambika, N. (2024). Early Detection of Darknet Traffic in Internet of Things Applications. *Automated Secure Computing for Next-Generation Systems*, 139-153.

Anis, G. M., Aboutabl, A. E., & Galal, A. (2023). MACHINE LEARNING FOR DETECTING CYBERCRIME IN THE BANKING SECTOR. *Journal of Southwest Jiaotong University*, 58(5).

Attaran, M., & Deb, P. (2018). Machine learning: The new'big thing'for competitive advantage. *International Journal of Knowledge Engineering and Data Mining*, 5(4), 277–305. DOI: 10.1504/IJKEDM.2018.095523

Awajan, A. (2023). A novel deep learning-based intrusion detection system for IOT networks. *Computers*, 12(2), 34. DOI: 10.3390/computers12020034

Aziz, L. A. R., & Andriansyah, Y. (2023). The Role Artificial Intelligence in Modern Banking: An Exploration of AI-Driven Approaches for Enhanced Fraud Prevention, Risk Management, and Regulatory Compliance. *Reviews of Contemporary Business Analytics*, 6(1), 110–132.

Baker, D. J., & Robinson, P. H. (Eds.). (2020). *Artificial Intelligence and the Law: Cybercrime and Criminal Liability*. Routledge. DOI: 10.4324/9780429344015

Bao, Y., Hilary, G., & Ke, B. (2022). Artificial intelligence and fraud detection. *Innovative Technology at the Interface of Finance and Operations*, I, 223–247. DOI: 10.1007/978-3-030-75729-8_8

Barocas, S., Hardt, M., & Narayanan, A. (2023). *Fairness and machine learning: Limitations and opportunities*. MIT Press.

Behiry, M. H., & Aly, M. (2024). Cyberattack detection in wireless sensor networks using a hybrid feature reduction technique with AI and machine learning methods. *Journal of Big Data*, 11(1), 16. DOI: 10.1186/s40537-023-00870-w

Berk, R., Heidari, H., Jabbari, S., Kearns, M., & Roth, A. (2021). Fairness in criminal justice risk assessments: The state of the art. *Sociological Methods & Research*, 50(1), 3–44. DOI: 10.1177/0049124118782533

Bhuvaneshwari, A. J., & Kaythry, P. (2023). A review of deep learning strategies for enhancing cybersecurity in networks: Deep learning strategies for enhancing cybersecurity. [JSIR]. *Journal of Scientific and Industrial Research*, 82(12), 1316–1330.

Bhuvaneshwari, A. J., & Kaythry, P. (2023). A Review of Deep Learning Strategies for Enhancing Cybersecurity in Networks: DEEP LEARNING STRATEGIES FOR ENHANCING CYBERSECURITY. [JSIR]. *Journal of Scientific and Industrial Research*, 82(12), 1316–1330.

Brotcke, L. (2022). Time to assess bias in machine learning models for credit decisions. *Journal of Risk and Financial Management*, 15(4), 165. DOI: 10.3390/jrfm15040165

Bui, H. T., Aboutorab, H., Mahboubi, A., Gao, Y., Sultan, N. H., Chauhan, A., Parvez, M. Z., Bewong, M., Islam, R., Islam, Z., Camtepe, S. A., Gauravaram, P., Singh, D., Ali Babar, M., & Yan, S. (2024). Agriculture 4.0 and Beyond: Evaluating Cyber Threat Intelligence Sources and Techniques in Smart Farming Ecosystems. *Computers & Security*, 140, 103754. DOI: 10.1016/j.cose.2024.103754

Cao, D. M., Sayed, M. A., Islam, M. T., Mia, M. T., Ayon, E. H., Ghosh, B. P., & Raihan, A. (2024). Advanced Cybercrime Detection: A Comprehensive Study on Supervised and Unsupervised Machine Learning Approaches Using Real-world Datasets. *Journal of Computer Science and Technology Studies*, 6(1), 40–48. DOI: 10.32996/jcsts.2024.6.1.5

Cao, L., Yang, Q., & Yu, P. S. (2021). Data science and AI in FinTech: An overview. *International Journal of Data Science and Analytics*, 12(2), 81–99. DOI: 10.1007/s41060-021-00278-w

Chen, Z., Van Khoa, L. D., Teoh, E. N., Nazir, A., Karuppiah, E. K., & Lam, K. S. (2018). Machine learning techniques for anti-money laundering (AML) solutions in suspicious transaction detection: A review. *Knowledge and Information Systems*, 57(2), 245–285. DOI: 10.1007/s10115-017-1144-z

Cheng, X., Liu, S., Sun, X., Wang, Z., Zhou, H., Shao, Y., & Shen, H. (2021). Combating emerging financial risks in the big data era: A perspective review. *Fundamental Research (Beijing)*, 1(5), 595–606. DOI: 10.1016/j.fmre.2021.08.017

Chohan, M. N., Haider, U., Ayub, M. Y., Shoukat, H., Bhatia, T. K., & Hassan, M. F. U. (2023). Detection of Cyber Attacks using Machine Learning based Intrusion Detection System for IoT Based Smart Cities. *EAI Endorsed Transactions on Smart Cities*, 7(2), e4–e4.

Costa, M. B., & Sofikitis, D. (2024). Applying Deep Learning and Data Analytics to identify Malware Attacks.

Costa, M. B., & Sofikitis, D. (2024). Applying Deep Learning and Data Analytics to identify Malware Attacks.

Das, S., Balmiki, A. K., Mazumdar, K., & Bhowmick, P. (2023). Cyber-Physical Security Issues and Challenges Using Machine Learning and Deep Learning Technologies. In *Artificial Intelligence in Cyber-Physical Systems* (pp. 105–123). CRC Press. DOI: 10.1201/9781003248750-7

Dasari, S., & Kaluri, R. (2024). An Effective Classification of DDoS Attacks in a Distributed Network by Adopting Hierarchical Machine Learning and Hyperparameters Optimization Techniques. *IEEE Access : Practical Innovations, Open Solutions*, 12, 10834–10845. DOI: 10.1109/ACCESS.2024.3352281

Dash, B., Sharma, P., & Ali, A. (2022). Federated learning for privacy-preserving: A review of PII data analysis in Fintech. [IJSEA]. *International Journal of Software Engineering and Its Applications*, 13(4).

Daugherty, P. R., & Wilson, H. J. (2018). *Human+ machine: Reimagining work in the age of AI*. Harvard Business Press.

Demir, B., & Serkan, A. (2024). Cyber Vigilantes: A Deep Dive into the Art and Science of Digital Defense. *Integrated Journal of Science and Technology, 1*(2).

Devan, A. M., Raghul, V., Dhasmana, U., Rath, A., & Jacob, L. (2024). 6 Deep Support Learning Model Decision for Police Investigation. *Artificial Intelligence for Cyber Defense and Smart Policing*, 76.

Dhoni, P., & Kumar, R. (2023). Synergizing generative ai and cybersecurity: Roles of generative ai entities, companies, agencies, and government in enhancing cybersecurity. *Authorea Preprints*.

Din, S. M. U., Sharma, R., Rizvi, F., & Sharma, N. (2024). Detection of botnet in IoT network through machine learning based optimized feature importance via ensemble models. *International Journal of Information Technology : an Official Journal of Bharati Vidyapeeth's Institute of Computer Applications and Management*, 16(2), 1203–1211.

Djenna, A., Barka, E., Benchikh, A., & Khadir, K. (2023). Unmasking Cybercrime with Artificial-Intelligence-Driven Cybersecurity Analytics. *Sensors (Basel)*, 23(14), 6302. DOI: 10.3390/s23146302 PMID: 37514596

Elluri, L., Mandalapu, V., Vyas, P., & Roy, N. (2023). Recent Advancements in Machine Learning for Cybercrime Prediction. *Journal of Computer Information Systems*, •••, 1–15. DOI: 10.1080/08874417.2023.2270457

Escorcia-Gutierrez, J., Gamarra, M., Leal, E., Madera, N., Soto, C., Mansour, R. F., Alharbi, M., Alkhayyat, A., & Gupta, D. (2023). Sea turtle foraging algorithm with hybrid deep learning-based intrusion detection for the internet of drones environment. *Computers & Electrical Engineering*, 108, 108704. DOI: 10.1016/j.compeleceng.2023.108704

Gangula, R., Vutukuru, M. M., & Kumar, R. (2024). Hybridization of Bottlenose Dolphin Optimization and Artificial Fish Swarm Algorithm with Efficient Classifier for Detecting the Network Intrusion in Internet of Things (IoT). *International Journal of Intelligent Systems and Applications in Engineering*, 12(6s), 220–232.

Ganji, K., & Afshan, N. (2024). A bibliometric review of Internet of Things (IoT) on cybersecurity issues. *Journal of Science and Technology Policy Management*.

Grimm, P. W., Grossman, M. R., & Cormack, G. V. (2021). Artificial intelligence as evidence. *Nw. J. Tech. & Intell. Prop.*, 19, 9.

Gunavathi, R., & Bharathi, K. M. (2024). 2 Cybercrimes in the. *Artificial Intelligence for Cyber Defense and Smart Policing*, 21.

Hagendorff, T. (2019). From privacy to anti-discrimination in times of machine learning. *Ethics and Information Technology*, 21(4), 331–343. DOI: 10.1007/s10676-019-09510-5

Hamad, S. I. (2023). A review of deep learning applied to cyber security. *Texas Journal of Engineering and Technology*, 22, 49–57.

Hemamalini, V., Mishra, A. K., Tyagi, A. K., & Kakulapati, V. (2024). Artificial Intelligence–Blockchain-Enabled–Internet of Things-Based Cloud Applications for Next-Generation Society. *Automated Secure Computing for Next-Generation Systems*, 65-82.

Hoijtink, M., & Planqué-van Hardeveld, A. (2022). Machine learning and the platformization of the military: A study of google's machine learning platform TensorFlow. *International Political Sociology*, 16(2), olab036. DOI: 10.1093/ips/olab036

Irfan, M., Elmogy, M., & El-Sappagh, S. (Eds.). (2023). *The impact of AI innovation on financial sectors in the era of industry 5.0*. IGI Global.

Itani, M., Basheer, H., & Eddine, F. (2023, July). Attack Detection in IoT-Based Healthcare Networks Using Hybrid Federated Learning. In *2023 International Conference on Smart Applications, Communications and Networking (SmartNets)* (pp. 1-7). IEEE. DOI: 10.1109/SmartNets58706.2023.10216144

Katyal, S. K. (2019). Private accountability in the age of artificial intelligence. *UCLA Law Review. University of California, Los Angeles. School of Law*, 66, 54.

Kaushik, K. (2024). Leveraging Deep Learning Techniques for Securing the Internet of Things in the Age of Big Data. *Applying Artificial Intelligence in Cybersecurity Analytics and Cyber Threat Detection*, 309.

Kochhar, S. K., Bhatia, A., & Tomer, N. (2023). Using Deep Learning and Big Data Analytics for Managing Cyber-Attacks. In *New Approaches to Data Analytics and Internet of Things Through Digital Twin* (pp. 146–178). IGI Global.

Kongsorot, Y., Musikawan, P., Aimtongkham, P., You, I., Benslimane, A., & So-In, C. (2023). An Intrusion Detection and Identification System for Internet of Things Networks Using a Hybrid Ensemble Deep Learning Framework. *IEEE Transactions on Sustainable Computing*, 8(4), 596–613. DOI: 10.1109/TSUSC.2023.3303422

Kordzadeh, N., & Ghasemaghaei, M. (2022). Algorithmic bias: Review, synthesis, and future research directions. *European Journal of Information Systems*, 31(3), 388–409. DOI: 10.1080/0960085X.2021.1927212

Kumar, A. (2024). Cybersecurity Threat Detection using Machine Learning and Network Analysis. *Journal of Artificial Intelligence General science (JAIGS) ISSN: 3006-4023, 1*(1), 38-46.

Kumar, A. K., Vadivukkarasi, K., & Dayana, R. (2023, February). A Novel Hybrid Deep Learning Model for Botnet Attacks Detection in a Secure IoMT Environment. In *2023 International Conference on Intelligent Systems for Communication, IoT and Security (ICISCoIS)* (pp. 44-49). IEEE. DOI: 10.1109/ICISCoIS56541.2023.10100396

Kumar, P., Gowda, D. Y., & Prakash, A. M. (2024). Machine Learning in Cybersecurity: A Comprehensive Survey of Data Breach Detection, Cyber-Attack Prevention, and Fraud Detection. *Pioneering Smart Healthcare 5.0 with IoT, Federated Learning, and Cloud Security*, 175-197.

Latif, S., Boulila, W., Koubaa, A., Zou, Z., & Ahmad, J. (2024). DTL-IDS: An optimized Intrusion Detection Framework using Deep Transfer Learning and Genetic Algorithm. *Journal of Network and Computer Applications*, 221, 103784. DOI: 10.1016/j.jnca.2023.103784

Lee, I., & Shin, Y. J. (2020). Machine learning for enterprises: Applications, algorithm selection, and challenges. *Business Horizons*, 63(2), 157–170. DOI: 10.1016/j.bushor.2019.10.005

Li, H., & Dong, S. (2024). Image steganalysis algorithm based on deep learning and attention mechanism for computer communication. *Journal of Electronic Imaging*, 33(1), 013015–013015. DOI: 10.1117/1.JEI.33.1.013015

Li, L., Zhao, T., Xie, Y., & Feng, Y. (2020). Interpretable machine learning based on integration of nlp and psychology in peer-to-peer lending risk evaluation. In *Natural Language Processing and Chinese Computing: 9th CCF International Conference, NLPCC 2020, Zhengzhou, China, October 14–18, 2020* [Springer International Publishing.]. *Proceedings*, 9(Part II), 429–441.

Lightbody, D., Ngo, D. M., Temko, A., Murphy, C. C., & Popovici, E. (2024). Dragon_Pi: IoT Side-Channel Power Data Intrusion Detection Dataset and Unsupervised Convolutional Autoencoder for Intrusion Detection. *Future Internet*, 16(3), 88. DOI: 10.3390/fi16030088

Lipsa, S., & Dash, R. K. (2023). A novel intrusion detection system based on deep learning and random forest for digital twin on IOT platform. *Int. J. Sch. Res. Eng. Technol*, 2, 51–64.

Liu, C., Chen, B., Shao, W., Zhang, C., Wong, K., & Zhang, Y. (2024). Unraveling Attacks in Machine Learning-based IoT Ecosystems: A Survey and the Open Libraries Behind Them. arXiv preprint arXiv:2401.11723.

Lone, A. N., Mustajab, S., & Alam, M. (2023). A comprehensive study on cybersecurity challenges and opportunities in the IoT world. *Security and Privacy*, 6(6), e318. DOI: 10.1002/spy2.318

Lui, A., & Lamb, G. W. (2018). Artificial intelligence and augmented intelligence collaboration: Regaining trust and confidence in the financial sector. *Information & Communications Technology Law*, 27(3), 267–283. DOI: 10.1080/13600834.2018.1488659

Manimaran, M., Dhar, M., Norabuena-Figueroa, R., Mahaveerakannan, R., Saraswathi, S., & Selvakumarasamy, K. (2023). Implementing Machine Learning-based Autonomic Cyber Defense for IoT-enabled Healthcare Devices. *Journal of Artificial Intelligence and Technology*, 3(4), 162–172. DOI: 10.37965/jait.2023.0209

McKendrick, K. (2019). Artificial intelligence prediction and counterterrorism. *London: The Royal Institute of International Affairs-Chatham House, 9.*

Messai, M. L., & Seba, H. (2023, August). IoT Network Attack Detection: Leveraging Graph Learning for Enhanced Security. In *Proceedings of the 18th International Conference on Availability, Reliability and Security* (pp. 1-7). DOI: 10.1145/3600160.3605053

Messai, M. L., & Seba, H. (2023, June). POSTER: Activity Graph Learning for Attack Detection in IoT Networks. In *2023 IEEE 24th International Symposium on a World of Wireless, Mobile and Multimedia Networks (WoWMoM)* (pp. 320-322). IEEE.

Mhlanga, D. (2021). Financial inclusion in emerging economies: The application of machine learning and artificial intelligence in credit risk assessment. *International journal of financial studies, 9*(3), 39.

Mijwil, M., & Aljanabi, M. (2023). Towards artificial intelligence-based cybersecurity: The practices and ChatGPT generated ways to combat cybercrime. *Iraqi Journal For Computer Science and Mathematics*, 4(1), 65–70.

Mijwil, M., Salem, I. E., & Ismaeel, M. M. (2023). The significance of machine learning and deep learning techniques in cybersecurity: A comprehensive review. *Iraqi Journal For Computer Science and Mathematics*, 4(1), 87–101.

Mishra, A. K., Hemamalini, V., & Tyagi, A. K. (2024). Digital Forensics with Emerging Technologies: Vision and Research Potential for Future. *Conversational Artificial Intelligence*, 675-697.

Mittal, H. (2024). Software security: Threats, solutions and challenges. *Computer Software and Media Applications*, 6(1), 3769. DOI: 10.24294/csma.v6i1.3769

Montasari, R. (2024). Machine Learning and Deep Learning Techniques in Countering Cyberterrorism. In *Cyberspace, Cyberterrorism and the International Security in the Fourth Industrial Revolution: Threats, Assessment and Responses* (pp. 135–158). Springer International Publishing. DOI: 10.1007/978-3-031-50454-9_8

Moustafa, N., Koroniotis, N., Keshk, M., Zomaya, A. Y., & Tari, Z. (2023). Explainable intrusion detection for cyber defences in the internet of things: Opportunities and solutions. *IEEE Communications Surveys and Tutorials*, 25(3), 1775–1807. DOI: 10.1109/COMST.2023.3280465

Mühlhoff, R. (2021). Predictive privacy: Towards an applied ethics of data analytics. *Ethics and Information Technology*, 23(4), 675–690. DOI: 10.1007/s10676-021-09606-x

Nandan, M., & Dey, S. (2023). Cybersecurity: Techniques and Applications to Combat Vicious Threats in Modern-Era Indices. In *AI-Aided IoT Technologies and Applications for Smart Business and Production* (pp. 248-270). CRC Press.

Narayana, Y. V., & Sreedevi, M. (2023, October). DDCATF: Deep Learning Approach for Detection of Cybercrime Activities Based on Temporal Features. In *2023 International Conference on Self Sustainable Artificial Intelligence Systems (ICSSAS)* (pp. 462-469). IEEE. DOI: 10.1109/ICSSAS57918.2023.10331644

Nassar, A., & Kamal, M. (2021). Ethical Dilemmas in AI-Powered Decision-Making: A Deep Dive into Big Data-Driven Ethical Considerations. *International Journal of Responsible Artificial Intelligence*, 11(8), 1–11.

Nehinbe, J. O., Benson, J. A., & Chibuzor, L. (2023). The classification of the investigations and punishment for crime syndicates that relate to intrusions against IoT-based healthcare systems. In *Blockchain Technology Solutions for the Security of IoT-Based Healthcare Systems* (pp. 113–131). Academic Press. DOI: 10.1016/B978-0-323-99199-5.00010-0

Nguyen, H., Nawara, D., & Kashef, R. (2024). Connecting the Indispensable Roles of IoT and Artificial Intelligence in Smart Cities: A Survey. *Journal of Information and Intelligence*.

Nisha, S. R., & Muthurajkumar, S. (2023). Semantic Graph Based Convolutional Neural Network for Spam e-mail Classification in Cybercrime Applications. *International Journal of Computers, Communications & Control*, 18(1).

Niu, T., Li, W., & Liu, Y. (2024). DarkGuardNet: A deep learning framework for imbalanced dark web traffic identification and application classification.

Nkoro, E. C., Njoku, J. N., Nwakanma, C. I., Lee, J. M., & Kim, D. S. (2024). Zero-Trust Marine Cyberdefense for IoT-Based Communications: An Explainable Approach. *Electronics (Basel)*, 13(2), 276. DOI: 10.3390/electronics13020276

Nyarko, B. N. E., Bin, W., Zhou, J., Odoom, J., Danso, S. A., & Addai, G. E. S. (2024). Forensic detection of heterogeneous activity in data using deep learning methods. *Intelligent Systems with Applications*, 21, 200303. DOI: 10.1016/j.iswa.2023.200303

Odeh, A., & Abu Taleb, A. (2023). Ensemble-Based Deep Learning Models for Enhancing IoT Intrusion Detection. *Applied Sciences (Basel, Switzerland)*, 13(21), 11985. DOI: 10.3390/app132111985

Ortiz-Ruiz, E., Bermejo, J. R., Sicilia, J. A., & Bermejo, J. (2024). Machine Learning Techniques for Cyberattack Prevention in IoT Systems: A Comparative Perspective of Cybersecurity and Cyberdefense in Colombia. *Electronics (Basel)*, 13(5), 824. DOI: 10.3390/electronics13050824

Paddalwar, S., Ragha, L., & Mane, V. (2023). Cyber threat mitigation using machine learning, deep learning, artificial intelligence, and blockchain. In *Intelligent Approaches to Cyber Security* (pp. 163–179). Chapman and Hall/CRC. DOI: 10.1201/9781003408307-14

Plageras, A., Stergiou, C. L., & Psannis, K. (2024). Secure Edge Communications Over the IoT.

Pocher, N., Zichichi, M., Merizzi, F., Shafiq, M. Z., & Ferretti, S. (2023). Detecting anomalous cryptocurrency transactions: An AML/CFT application of machine learning-based forensics. *Electronic Markets*, 33(1), 37. DOI: 10.1007/s12525-023-00654-3

Pritee, Z. T., Anik, M. H., Alam, S. B., Jim, J. R., Kabir, M. M., & Mridha, M. F. (2024). Machine learning and deep learning for user authentication and authorization in cybersecurity: A state-of-the-art review. *Computers & Security*, 140, 103747. DOI: 10.1016/j.cose.2024.103747

Priyadarshini, I., Mohanty, P., Alkhayyat, A., Sharma, R., & Kumar, S. (2023). SDN and application layer DDoS attacks detection in IoT devices by attention-based Bi-LSTM-CNN. *Transactions on Emerging Telecommunications Technologies*, 34(11), e4758. DOI: 10.1002/ett.4758

Rai, R., & Sahu, C. K. (2020). Driven by data or derived through physics? a review of hybrid physics guided machine learning techniques with cyber-physical system (cps) focus. *IEEE Access : Practical Innovations, Open Solutions*, 8, 71050–71073. DOI: 10.1109/ACCESS.2020.2987324

Rajkumar, S., Sheeba, S. L., Sivakami, R., Prabu, S., & Selvarani, A. (2023). An IoT-Based Deep Learning Approach for Online Fault Detection Against Cyber-Attacks. *SN Computer Science*, 4(4), 393. DOI: 10.1007/s42979-023-01808-y

Rakha, M. A., Khan, I. U., Ouaissa, M., Ouaissa, M., & Ayub, M. Y. (2024). Hybrid Model for IoT-Enabled Intelligent Towns Using the MQTT-IoT-IDS2020 Dataset. In *Cyber Security for Next-Generation Computing Technologies* (pp. 159-176). CRC Press.

Rathee, G., Iqbal, R., Kerrache, C. A., & Song, H. (2024). TrustNextGen: Security Aspects of Trustworthy Next Generation Industrial Internet of Things (IIoT). *IEEE Internet of Things Journal*, 11(15), 25568–25576. DOI: 10.1109/JIOT.2024.3361801

Reddy, B. B., Pasha, S. G., Kameswari, M., Chinkera, R., Fatima, S., Bhargava, R., & Shrivastava, A. (2024). Classification Approach for Face Spoof Detection in Artificial Neural Network Based on IoT Concepts. *International Journal of Intelligent Systems and Applications in Engineering*, 12(13s), 79–91.

Roshanaei, M. (2024). Enhancing Mobile Security through Comprehensive Penetration Testing. *Journal of Information Security*, 15(2), 63–86. DOI: 10.4236/jis.2024.152006

. Saha, S. (2024). SECURITY IN IOT USING ARTIFICIAL INTELLIGENCE. *The Fusion of Artificial Intelligence and Soft Computing Techniques for Cybersecurity.*

Sahingoz, O. K., Buber, E., & Kugu, E. (2024). DEPHIDES: Deep Learning Based Phishing Detection System. *IEEE Access : Practical Innovations, Open Solutions*, 12, 8052–8070. DOI: 10.1109/ACCESS.2024.3352629

Saiyed, M. F., & Al-Anbagi, I. (2024). A Genetic Algorithm-and t-Test-Based System for DDoS Attack Detection in IoT Networks. *IEEE Access : Practical Innovations, Open Solutions*, 12, 25623–25641. DOI: 10.1109/ACCESS.2024.3367357

Sakthibalan, P., Saravanan, M., Ansal, V., Rajakannu, A., Vijayalakshmi, K., & Vani, K. D. (2024). A Federated Learning Approach for ResourceConstrained IoT Security Monitoring. In *Handbook on Federated Learning* (pp. 131–154). CRC Press.

Saltz, J., Skirpan, M., Fiesler, C., Gorelick, M., Yeh, T., Heckman, R., & Beard, N. (2019). Integrating ethics within machine learning courses. [TOCE]. *ACM Transactions on Computing Education*, 19(4), 1–26. DOI: 10.1145/3341164

Sambasivan, N., Arnesen, E., Hutchinson, B., Doshi, T., & Prabhakaran, V. (2021, March). Re-imagining algorithmic fairness in india and beyond. In *Proceedings of the 2021 ACM conference on fairness, accountability, and transparency* (pp. 315-328). DOI: 10.1145/3442188.3445896

Samsudeen, S., & Thomas, L. (2024). Cybersecurity Warning System Using Diluted Convolutional Neural Network Framework for IOT Attack Prevention. *International Journal of Intelligent Engineering & Systems*, 17(1).

Schmitt, M. (2020). Artificial intelligence in business analytics, capturing value with machine learning applications in financial services.

Segovia-Vargas, M. J. (2024). Money Laundering in the Age of Cybercrime and Emerging Technologies.

Selbst, A. D., & Barocas, S. (2018). The intuitive appeal of explainable machines. *Fordham Law Review*, 87, 1085.

Shaikh, J., Butt, Y. A., & Naqvi, H. F. (2024). Effective Intrusion Detection System Using Deep Learning for DDoS Attacks. *The Asian Bulletin of Big Data Management*, 4(1). Advance online publication. DOI: 10.62019/abbdm.v4i1.113

Sharma, A., Mansotra, V., & Singh, K. (2023). Detection of Mirai Botnet Attacks on IoT devices Using Deep Learning. *Journal of Scientific Research and Technology*, 174-187.

Sharma, N., & Annaboina, K. (2024). Analytical Study On Prevention And Detection Of Financial Cybercrime And Frauds Using Transaction Pattern Generation Tool. *Journal of Scientific Research and Technology*, 9-31.

Shukla, R. K., & Tiwari, A. K. (2024). Security Analysis of the Cyber Crime. In *The Ethical Frontier of AI and Data Analysis* (pp. 257–271). IGI Global. DOI: 10.4018/979-8-3693-2964-1.ch016

Singh, B. (2023). Federated Learning for Envision Future Trajectory Smart Transport System for Climate Preservation and Smart Green Planet: Insights into Global Governance and SDG-9 (Industry, Innovation and Infrastructure). *National Journal of Environmental Law*, 6(2), 6–17.

Singh, B. (2023). Tele-Health Monitoring Lensing Deep Neural Learning Structure: Ambient Patient Wellness via Wearable Devices for Real-Time Alerts and Interventions. *Indian Journal of Health and Medical Law*, 6(2), 12–16.

Singh, B. (2023). Blockchain Technology in Renovating Healthcare: Legal and Future Perspectives. In *Revolutionizing Healthcare Through Artificial Intelligence and Internet of Things Applications* (pp. 177-186). IGI Global.

Singh, B. (2023). Unleashing Alternative Dispute Resolution (ADR) in Resolving Complex Legal-Technical Issues Arising in Cyberspace Lensing E-Commerce and Intellectual Property: Proliferation of E-Commerce Digital Economy. *Revista Brasileira de Alternative Dispute Resolution-Brazilian Journal of Alternative Dispute Resolution-RBADR*, 5(10), 81–105. DOI: 10.52028/rbadr.v5i10.ART04.Ind

Singh, B. (2023). Blockchain Technology in Renovating Healthcare: Legal and Future Perspectives. In *Revolutionizing Healthcare Through Artificial Intelligence and Internet of Things Applications* (pp. 177-186). IGI Global.

Singh, B. (2023). Unleashing Alternative Dispute Resolution (ADR) in Resolving Complex Legal-Technical Issues Arising in Cyberspace Lensing E-Commerce and Intellectual Property: Proliferation of E-Commerce Digital Economy. *Revista Brasileira de Alternative Dispute Resolution-Brazilian Journal of Alternative Dispute Resolution-RBADR*, 5(10), 81–105. DOI: 10.52028/rbadr.v5i10.ART04.Ind

Singh, B. (2024). Social Cognition of Incarcerated Women and Children: Addressing Exposure to Infectious Diseases and Legal Outcomes. In Reddy, K. (Ed.), *Principles and Clinical Interventions in Social Cognition* (pp. 236–251). IGI Global., DOI: 10.4018/979-8-3693-1265-0.ch014

Singh, B. (2024). Lensing Legal Dynamics for Examining Responsibility and Deliberation of Generative AI-Tethered Technological Privacy Concerns: Infringements and Use of Personal Data by Nefarious Actors. In Ara, A., & Ara, A. (Eds.), *Exploring the Ethical Implications of Generative AI* (pp. 146–167). IGI Global., DOI: 10.4018/979-8-3693-1565-1.ch009

Singh, B., & Kaunert, C. (2024). Integration of Cutting-Edge Technologies such as Internet of Things (IoT) and 5G in Health Monitoring Systems: A Comprehensive Legal Analysis and Futuristic Outcomes. *GLS Law Journal*, 6(1), 13–20. DOI: 10.69974/glslawjournal.v6i1.123

Singh, B., & Kaunert, C. (2024). Future of Digital Marketing: Hyper-Personalized Customer Dynamic Experience with AI-Based Predictive Models. *Revolutionizing the AI-Digital Landscape: A Guide to Sustainable Emerging Technologies for Marketing Professionals*, 189.

Singh, B., & Kaunert, C. (2024). Harnessing Sustainable Agriculture Through Climate-Smart Technologies: Artificial Intelligence for Climate Preservation and Futuristic Trends. In *Exploring Ethical Dimensions of Environmental Sustainability and Use of AI* (pp. 214-239). IGI Global.

Singh, B., Kaunert, C., & Vig, K. (2024). Reinventing Influence of Artificial Intelligence (AI) on Digital Consumer Lensing Transforming Consumer Recommendation Model: Exploring Stimulus Artificial Intelligence on Consumer Shopping Decisions. In Musiolik, T., Rodriguez, R., & Kannan, H. (Eds.), *AI Impacts in Digital Consumer Behavior* (pp. 141–169). IGI Global., DOI: 10.4018/979-8-3693-1918-5.ch006

Singh, C., Singh, R., Tiwari, M., & Hazela, B. (2024). Analyse and Predict the Detection of the Cyber-Attack Process by Using a Machine-Learning Approach. *EAI Endorsed Transactions on Internet of Things, 10.*

Singh, N. J., Hoque, N., Singh, K. R., & Bhattacharyya, D. K. (2023). Botnet-based IoT network traffic analysis using deep learning. *Security and Privacy*, •••, 355.

Siwakoti, Y. R., Bhurtel, M., Rawat, D. B., Oest, A., & Johnson, R. C. (2023). Advances in IOT security: Vulnerabilities, enabled Criminal Services, attacks and countermeasures. *IEEE Internet of Things Journal*, 10(13), 11224–11239. DOI: 10.1109/JIOT.2023.3252594

Soliman, S., Oudah, W., & Aljuhani, A. (2023). Deep learning-based intrusion detection approach for securing industrial Internet of Things. *Alexandria Engineering Journal*, 81, 371–383. DOI: 10.1016/j.aej.2023.09.023

Sowmya, B. J., Hanumantharaju, R., Kumar, D. P., & Srinivasa, K. G. (2023). Identification of authorship and prevention of fraudulent transactions/cybercrime using efficient high performance machine learning techniques. *International Journal of Business Intelligence and Data Mining*, 22(1-2), 144–169. DOI: 10.1504/IJBIDM.2023.127312

Sudhakar, & Kumar, S. (2023, April). ABBDIoT: Anomaly-based botnet detection using machine learning model in the Internet of Things network. In *International Conference on IoT, Intelligent Computing and Security: Select Proceedings of IICS 2021* (pp. 235-245). Singapore: Springer Nature Singapore.

Swiątkowska, J. (2020). Tackling cybercrime to unleash developing countries' digital potential. *Pathways for Prosperity Commission Background Paper Series*, 33, 2020–01.

TEJASVI, K., BEGUM, R., & JABBAR, M. (2024). SECURITY IN IOT: SYSTEMATIC REVIEW. *The Fusion of Artificial Intelligence and Soft Computing Techniques for Cybersecurity*, 217.

Thapaliya, S., & Sharma, P. K. (2023). Cyber Forensic Investigation in IoT Using Deep Learning Based Feature Fusion in Big Data. *International Journal of Wireless Information Networks*, 30(1), 16–29.

Thapaliya, S., & Sharma, P. K. (2023). Optimized deep neuro fuzzy network for cyber forensic investigation in big data-based IoT infrastructures. [IJISP]. *International Journal of Information Security and Privacy*, 17(1), 1–22. DOI: 10.4018/IJISP.315819

Tippins, N. T., Oswald, F. L., & McPhail, S. M. (2021). Scientific, legal, and ethical concerns about AI-based personnel selection tools: A call to action. *Personnel Assessment and Decisions*, 7(2), 1. DOI: 10.25035/pad.2021.02.001

Tok, Y. C., & Chattopadhyay, S. (2023). Identifying threats, cybercrime and digital forensic opportunities in Smart City Infrastructure via threat modeling. *Forensic Science International Digital Investigation*, 45, 301540. DOI: 10.1016/j.fsidi.2023.301540

Tyagi, A. K., Aswathy, S. U., & Abraham, A. (2020). Integrating blockchain technology and artificial intelligence: Synergies perspectives challenges and research directions. *Journal of Information Assurance and Security*, 15(5), 1554.

Utami, S. H., Purnama, A. A., Hidayanto, A. N., Utami, S. H., Purnama, A. A., & Hidayanto, A. N. (2022). Fintech Lending in Indonesia: A Sentiment Analysis, Topic Modelling, and Social Network Analysis using Twitter Data. *International Journal of Applied Engineering & Technology*, 4(1), 50–56.

Varma, P., Nijjer, S., Sood, K., Grima, S., & Rupeika-Apoga, R. (2022). Thematic Analysis of Financial Technology (Fintech) Influence on the Banking Industry. *Risks*, 10(10), 186. DOI: 10.3390/risks10100186

Vasan, D., Hammoudeh, M., & Alazab, M. (2024). Broad Learning: A GPU-Free Image-based Malware Classification. *Applied Soft Computing*, 154, 111401. DOI: 10.1016/j.asoc.2024.111401

Vatambeti, R., & Mamidisetti, G. (2023). Routing attack detection using ensemble deep learning model for IIoT. *Inf. Dyn. Appl*, 2(1), 31–41. DOI: 10.56578/ida020104

Venkatasubramanian, M., Lashkari, A. H., & Hakak, S. (2023). Iot malware analysis using federated learning: A comprehensive survey. *IEEE Access : Practical Innovations, Open Solutions*, 11, 5004–5018. DOI: 10.1109/ACCESS.2023.3235389

Virmani, D., Ravishankar, T. N., & Tesfayohanis, M. (2023). 6 IoT attack detection using quantum deep learning in large-scale networks. *Quantum-Safe Cryptography Algorithms and Approaches: Impacts of Quantum Computing on Cybersecurity*, 67.

Wu, L., Peng, Q., & Lembke, M. (2023). Research trends in cybercrime and cybersecurity: A review based on web of science core collection database. *International Journal of Cybersecurity Intelligence & Cybercrime*, 6(1), 5–28. DOI: 10.52306/2578-3289.1154

Zhang, A., Lipton, Z. C., Li, M., & Smola, A. J. (2023). *Dive into deep learning*. Cambridge University Press.

Zhang, X., Liu, L., Lan, M., Song, G., Xiao, L., & Chen, J. (2022). Interpretable machine learning models for crime prediction. *Computers, Environment and Urban Systems*, 94, 101789. DOI: 10.1016/j.compenvurbsys.2022.101789

Zhang, Y., Suleiman, B., Alibasa, M. J., & Farid, F. (2024). Privacy-Aware Anomaly Detection in IoT Environments using FedGroup: A Group-Based Federated Learning Approach. *Journal of Network and Systems Management*, 32(1), 20. DOI: 10.1007/s10922-023-09782-9

Zhang, Y., Xiong, F., Xie, Y., Fan, X., & Gu, H. (2020). The impact of artificial intelligence and blockchain on the accounting profession. *IEEE Access : Practical Innovations, Open Solutions*, 8, 110461–110477. DOI: 10.1109/ACCESS.2020.3000505

Zhang, Z., Al Hamadi, H., Damiani, E., Yeun, C. Y., & Taher, F. (2022). Explainable artificial intelligence applications in cyber security: State-of-the-art in research. *IEEE Access : Practical Innovations, Open Solutions*, 10, 93104–93139. DOI: 10.1109/ACCESS.2022.3204051

Ziwei, H., Dongni, Z., Man, Z., Yixin, D., Shuanghui, Z., Chao, Y., & Chunfeng, C. (2024). The applications of internet of things in smart healthcare sectors: A bibliometric and deep study. *Heliyon*, 10(3), e25392. DOI: 10.1016/j.heliyon.2024.e25392 PMID: 38356528

Chapter 9
A Security and Privacy Validation Methodology for E-Health Systems Using Cloud Storage

Aparna Datta
https://orcid.org/0009-0006-2552-9017
Meghnad Saha Institute of Technology, India

Sanchayan Sen
Meghnad Saha Institute of Technology, India

ABSTRACT

E-Health applications enable one to acquire, process, and share patient medical data to improve diagnosis, treatment, and patient monitoring. Despite the undeniable benefits brought by the digitization of health systems, the transmission of and access to medical information raises critical issues, mainly related to security and privacy. This paper describes a safe e-health data management system that employs the MERN stack (MongoDB, Express, React, and Node.js) and strong encryption algorithms. The solution improves security by using client-side encryption with the AES-256-CBC technique to encrypt e-health files before uploading them to MongoDB. To improve security, encrypted files and keys are stored separately. User authentication employs bcryptjs for password hashing and JSON Web Tokens (JWT) for permission, ensuring that only authorized users can access and decrypt data. The study demonstrates the efficiency of coupling MERN stack development with encryption in protecting sensitive patient information, establishing confidence, and boosting the adoption of e-health solutions.

DOI: 10.4018/979-8-3693-9235-5.ch009

INTRODUCTION

E-Health Data, also known as Electronic Health Data, is any digital information relating to a person's overall health. These data include but are not limited to records or imaging relating to the person's health. Such data range from:

- Medical records that may consist of a person's past medical history, diagnoses, procedures, prescribed medications, allergies or side effects of the medication, immunizations, as well as a variety of laboratory tests such as blood tests, urine tests, and many others.
- Patient monitoring data mainly include data or vital signs of a person such as heart rate, blood pressure, oxygen saturation, and others. These data can be measured or obtained through different means and devices, as hospitals and clinics have monitoring devices, and nowadays many people can acquire, through which vital signs, through daily life at home, can be measured and recorded in real time through monitoring devices or nowadays through wearable devices that measure it all day. It is also used in some measurement devices that measure sugar through the body without the need for a blood test.
- Imaging data or radiological examinations include X-rays, CTs, and MRIs stored in digital forms.
- Genomics data, which include data related to DNA sequencing in the field of personalized medicine.
- Lifestyle data, such as data related to the person's amount of activity, amount and quality of sleep or weight, all of which can be obtained through the use of wearable technology such as different watches and bands as Fitbit.
- Self-reported outcomes from patients, which include data that the patient self-reports regarding their health such as the extent of the disease, symptoms, and health effects on them.

Historical Incidents of E-Health Data Breaches

The use of e-health data is increasing, and that makes it a target for cybercriminals. Here are some of the historical incidents that show the need for better security and why we should not make the same mistake:

- ***Anthem (2015):*** The attack has leaked personal information of around 78 million health insurance customers associated with Anthem. The affected data has touched upon such points as names of the clients, their social security, addresses, information about birth, and the place of work for these users. It was one of the most devastating data breaches that have occurred, which made the U.S. insurance company aware of the danger of storing all the information in a centralised way.

- ***DHHS (2019):*** The particular incident has disclosed 25 million individuals' personal health-related data as the root of it for being hackers that could get access to a server that stores records for HHS's program. The affected data included information that concerned financial costs, which had to be covered by the healthcare program that helps low-income families. At this point, the event can help to realize the potential dangers of government's holding of such e-health data.
- ***Singapore Health Ministry (2021***): Medical records, identification numbers more that 1.4 million Singapora residents It had left almost every critically sensitive health data public and put a question mark of the national healthcare systems.
- ***AmeriHealth Caritas (2023):*** This healthcare provider reported a ransomware attack that exposed the data of roughly 4 million patients. In addition to the names and addresses, lists of patients included Social Security numbers along with small amounts of medical data. This latest attack serves as a reminder of the Amnesty International report on ransomware attacks against e-health data.

People can use stolen data for things like identity theft and medical fraud, or sell it on the black market. The above-mentioned are the events that signal to us.

- ***Better encryption:*** It is critical to encrypt your at rest and in transit data using strong encryption methods (client-side with AES-256-CBC just as you have done).
- ***Multi-factor Authentication:*** By enabling multi factor authentication (MFA) to users' logins is very helpful way of securing that the person logging in would be right user accessing it and reduces vulnerability towards unauthorized access.

But there are resistance which some have eluded to that even with regular security audits and penetration testing done would only find out vulnerabilities in e-health systems sooner or later they will be compromised by attackers of the under-world. The benefits of having the data shared through e-health to provide better care should be balanced with improvements in patient awareness about information security and protecting their own health records.

Importance of E-Health Data

E-health data security and privacy extend far beyond protecting individual patient information. Here's a look at the broader significance:

- ***Better Health Care Delivery:***
  - ***Fast and Accurate Diagnosis & Treatment***: The urge to compile thorough e-health data as patient profile will result in the ability of healthcare professionals to access all crucial information when making decisions, improving diagnoses accurateness with personalized treatment plans.
  - ***Increased Coordination of Care:*** Shared and secure data between healthcare providers, helps in achieving a comprehensive care coordination which leads to enhanced patient outcomes little or no medication errors.
  - ***Remote Monitoring and Telehealth:*** Strong security supports safe remote patient monitoring and telehealth consultations, bringing healthcare services to people in rural areas or with limited mobility
- ***Public Health Benefits:***
  - ***Disease Outbreak Detection:*** Anonymized, and securely collection of e-health data can help in assessing the likelihood of a disease outbreak to control it as soon as possible.
  - ***Research and Development:*** It can spice up timely R&D for advanced therapies, medications as well preventative measures with safe access to anonymized e-health data.
  - ***Personalized Medicine:*** Using secure e-health data to pursue the dream of personalized medicine, informed by individual genetic and medical history.
- ***Economic Impact:***
  - ***Lower Healthcare Costs:*** Safe and efficient management of e-health data contributes to the simplification of healthcare administration, reduces human error in medicine and as a result can lead into treatments that are proactively adjusted by quality-correctness decision support massively improving cost-benefit ratios.
  - ***Enhanced Innovation:*** Safer E-health Data Environments encourage Healthcare Technology Advancements and AI solutions for a Smarter Health-care System.
  - ***Patient Empowerment:*** With the ability to securely access their own e-health data, patients can become more active participants in healthcare decisions and better manage health.

- ***Social and ethical considerations***
  - ***Building Trust:*** Strong data security, and privacy enabling the e-health applications to protect patient data from unauthorized breaches maintaining a trust among patients that his/her information is secure in this environment promote him more willingly share their health conditions for further treatment as well without fear of revealing their vulnerability under investigation.
  - ***Addressing Discrimination:*** Strong data protection rules avoid unjust discrimination against individuals, stemming from their intimate health information by insurance companies or employers.
  - ***Ensuring Equity:*** Equal e-health data access for rich or poor anywhere leads in health equity and public advancement of the entire population.

The Future of E-Health Data

E-health data indicates holds promise to revolutionize healthcare delivery and research public health initiatives. Below is a peek into the e-health data future that gets me excited, as well as some things we need to work on:

- ***Emerging Technologies and Applications:***
  - ***Artificial Intelligence (AI) and Machine Learning (ML):*** AI/MLS will be used to analyze large volumes of e-health data to recognize patterns, forecast disease risks, personalize medication regimens or even assist in diagnosing medical conditions.
  - ***Internet of Things (IoT) & Wearable Devices:*** With IoT and wearables integrating healthcare, you can expect to have a continuous inflow real-time health data that in turn will allow patient monitoring 24×7 and possibly early diagnosis.
  - ***Blockchain Technology:*** Blockchain has the capability to focus on security and transparency, could revolutionize e-health data management by providing a secure and tamper-proof platform for data storage and sharing.
- ***Emphasize Interoperability and Standardization:***
  - ***Standardized Data Formats:*** Seamless E-health Data Exchange with standardised data formats healthcare systems, and improving care coordination from the different home-based health aides doing this work, increased research capacity.
  - ***OpenAPIs:*** Open with the help of APIs (Application Programming Interfaces developers can build a cost-cutting, e-health powered data

streams and innovative e-health applications of it will actually foster a more open, collaborative health system.

- ***Ethical Concerns and Patient Empowerment:***
  - ***Privacy-Enhancing Technologies:*** Progress in Privacy-enhanced technologies such as federated learning and homomorphic encryption can make data analytics whilst keeping individual privacy intact.
  - ***Focus on Explainable AI:*** As AI plays a larger role in healthcare decisions, ensuring explainable AI will be crucial for building trust and transparency with patients.
- ***Security and Privacy Issues on E-health Data:***
  - ***Data Breaches***: There is explicit risk involved as e-health data — being information of a personal nature about all kinds printed on the internet cloud space where money circulating cybercriminal sharks swim. Health hackers may infiltrate healthcare systems and make off with private medical records, which can be used for both identity theft and to commit insurance fraud - peddling the records in back alley markets.
  - ***Unauthorized Access:*** Someone with access to e-health data may share it inappropriately, even accidentally as we have seen a number of times. In addition, human error and a lack of access control keep imperfect data flow open.
  - ***Malware Attacks:*** A malicious actor may use malware to interfere with healthcare delivery, corrupt or encrypt e-health data and blackmail its release.
  - ***Ethical Frameworks:*** There is a need to develop an appropriate set of ethical frameworks that guide how e-health data use in conducting research while being useful for society and at the same time ensuring individual rights.
  - ***Digital Divide:*** Closing the digital divide will be critical to achieving equitable access to e-health technologies and data-driven healthcare services.
- ***E-health Data privacy Issues:***
  - ***Loss of Control:*** Patients may feel like they lose control over their health information if it is digitalized and stored electronically. But as such data are about individuals, concerns inevitably arise over who has access to this data and how they can use it.
  - ***Misuse of Data:*** E-health data may be misused by insurance companies, employers or even third-party vendors without due patient consent. People might be discriminated in insurance coverage, employment opportunities or even societal stigmatic.

- *Secondary Data Usage:* E-health information collected by others for one purpose, but repurposed without appropriate anonymization or patient consent.

Solutions and Best Practices

Additional and Broader Key Solutions, Best Practices

- *Technical Solutions*
    - *Robust Encryption:* Use strong encryption algorithms (AES-256) to secure data at rest and in transit for unreadable decryption upon breach.
    - *Multi-Factor Authentication (MFA):* Use MFA to ensure all user logins can only be initiated by providing an additional verification factor beyond just username and password, such as a code from a phone app or using their security key.
    - *Data Access Control (DAC):* Granular DAC to be realised for restricting access to e- health data with no permission sharing based on Least Privilege. This means that they should have limited access to only the data need for their specific work.
    - *Activity Monitoring and Logging:* Keep track of user activity, log activities to detect suspicious actions which may lead to security breaches.
    - *Routine Security Audits and Wireless Penetration Testing:* Perform routine security audits, wireless penetration testing to detect vulnerabilities in e-health systems before malicious users turn them into weapons.
    - *Data Backup and Disaster Recovery:* Implementing a robust data backup and disaster recovery plan to ensure data availability and minimize downtime in case of a cyberattack or other disruptions.
- *Regulatory Compliance*
    - *HIPAA compliance standards (US)*: Be compliant with specific regulations such as HIPAA through which US based healthcare organizations are required to implement national security and privacy laws regarding health information including PHI.
    - *GDPR (EU):* Comply with the General Data Protection Regulation of the EU that gives each individual more power over their personal data and enforces tough measures for protecting privacy.
- *Organizational Practices*
    - *Security Awareness Training:* Regular security awareness training should be provided to healthcare professionals for the safe handling

e-health data, recognizing phishing attempts and reporting suspicious activity.

- *Incident Response Plan:* Develop an incident response plan detailing how your organisation would detect, contain and recover from a security breach.
- *Risk Management Framework:* Organisational entities should have a risk management framework in place to determine, measure and control e-health data security and privacy.
- *Patient education:* Patients should be educated and informed about their rights concerning there e-health records, otherwise they are gravely confused on when such data can be accessed or shared.

- *Transparency and Accountability*
  - *Clear Privacy Policies:* Create clear privacy policies that detail the gathering, usage and dissemination of e-health data with patient approval.
  - *Data Subject Access Requests (DSARs):* Enable patients to execute, free of charge and at any time, a DSAR for the right access their e-health data and correct it or erase it.
  - *Regular Communication with Patients:* Be open in your communication to patients about how you are making sure their data is stored and processed ranks among the top 10 health IT concerns.

Our MERN stack application with encryption directly addresses some of these security and privacy concerns. Here's how:

- *Client-side encryption:* Encrypts e-health data before uploading, ensuring it's unreadable even if intercepted during transfer.
- *Separate storage of files and keys:* Further minimizes the risk of unauthorized access by storing the encryption key separately from the encrypted file.
- *Secure authentication:* Using bcryptjs for password hashing and JWTs for authorization protects user credentials and controls access to data.

Cloud-based Healthcare Computing is widely used that has facilitated further data storage scalability, AI collaboration and enhanced access. This shift requires effective security and privacy so that sensitive patient information can be protected. Consequently, this research identifies the issues with a possible solution using MERN stack technologies (MongoDB/ NoSQL dbm, Express js framework for backend web application development and Node.JS on runtime environment) to develop an e-health data management system secure enough based on global standards of ACM. js) application, deployed into a cloud forest. To protect the privacy of its user data, it uses client-side encryption on e-health records using AES-256-CBC before uploading them to cloud storage. Encryption of the data at rest in combination with separate storage for encrypted files and encryption keys within the cloud adds an additional security layer.

By leveraging cloud computing and MERN stack technologies, this project contributes to e-health data security by:

- ***Enhanced Data Privacy in the Cloud:*** Encryption protects e-health data at rest and in transit, mitigating unauthorized access risks even within a cloud environment.
- ***Scalable and Secure Storage:*** Cloud storage provides scalability to accommodate growing e-health data volumes while maintaining security through encryption techniques.
- ***Strengthened User Authentication:*** Secure password hashing and JSON Web Tokens are used for authorization which ensures only authorized users can access and decrypt their e-health data within the cloud.

This project offers a secure solution for e-health data management in the cloud, fostering trust and promoting wider adoption of cloud-based healthcare services.

Related Works

Table 1. Literature review

REFRENCE	SCHEME	ADVANTAGES	DISADVANTAGES
L. Zhu, C. Zhang, C. Xu, X. Liu and C. Huang, "An efficient and privacy-preserving biometric identification scheme in cloud computing"(Zhu et al., 2018)	Privacy-Preserving Biometric Identification scheme.	Ensuring data privacy is important to prevent collusion attacks	It's crucial to rely on the cloud service provider. Centralized data storage can be costly, in terms of computing power, for large scale issues
R. Charanya and M. Aramudhan, "Survey on access control issues in cloud computing" (Charanya et al., 2016)	Identity based encryption	Simplifies encryption procedures	A secure connection must be established between the user and the key generator
R. Charanya and M. Aramudhan, "Survey on access control issues in cloud computing" (Charanya et al., 2016)	Attribute based encryption	Precise control, over access resistant to collusion and minimal need, for communication	The data owner needs the key of each authorized user to encrypt the data

continued on following page

Table 1. Continued

REFRENCE	SCHEME	ADVANTAGES	DISADVANTAGES
Hupperich, T, Löhr, H, Sadeghi, A, Winandy, M. "Flexible Patient-Controlled Security for Electronic Health records."(Hupperich et al., 2012)	Modern cryptographic security approach	Access is not limited by time and place	Key management involves complexity
P.-W. Chi and C.-L. Lei, "Audit-free cloud storage via deniable attribute-based encryption"(Chi et al., 2018)	Audit-free cloud storage via Deniable ABE	A detailed access control system guarantees data privacy	Chances of decryption issues and the additional workload of creating keys
W. Li, B. M. Liu, D. Liu, R. P. Liu, P. Wang, S. Luo, et al, "Unified fine-grained access control for personal health records in cloud computing"(Li et al., 2019)	Unified fine-grained access control for PHR in cloud computing	Flexible and detailed access control, for Personal Health Records (PHR) leading to costs for encryption and decryption	The process involves generation and relies on trusting the Authorization Agent (AA) and policy manager, it does not allow for user revocation. Is only accessible, to a number of users
J. Wei, W. Liu and X. Hu, "Secure data sharing in cloud computing using revocable-storage identity-based encryption"(Wei et al., 2018)	Secure data sharing in cloud computing using revocable storage IBE	Keeping information secure and ensuring privacy both in the present and retroactively	The current system has limitations in terms of scalability as there is a risk of the authority being compromised
C. Huang, K. Yan, S. Wei, G. Zhang and D. H. Lee, "Efficient anonymous attribute-based encryption with access policy hidden for cloud computing"(Huang et al., 2017)	Efficient anonymous ABE with access policy hidden for cloud computing	Anonymity, safeguarding data and precise access control are essential	A trusted authentication authority is needed, along, with the challenges of complexity and increased storage demands resulting from adding attributes to the access framework
Kim S, Sung M, Chung Y. "A framework to preserve the privacy of electronic health data streams."(Kim et al., 2014)	Delay-free anonymization	This method avoids any delays, in processing as data streams are promptly anonymized with values	It does not delve into the timing aspect of validation.
Simplicio M, Iwaya L, Barros B, Carvalho T, Naslund M. "SecourHealth: a delaytolerant security framework for mobile health data collection."(Simplicio et al., 2015)	Transport Layer Security/Secure Sockets Layer (TLS/SSL)	It stops outsiders from gaining entry	It relies on the platform. Isn't easily expanded
Rezaeibagha F, Mu Y. "Distributed clinical data sharing via dynamic access control policy transformation."(Rezaeibagha et al., 2016)	Hybrid clouds as well as access control policy transformation and cryptographic building blocks	Users of health records (EHR) have varying levels of access and permissions	It hinders the scalability

METHODOLOGY

In this paper we have described the details of our Secure E-Health Data Management with MERN Stack (MongoDB, Express, React/frontend framework, Node.js) and Encryption. It prioritizes user privacy by employing robust encryption techniques for uploaded files.

User Authentication

- Registration: Users create accounts by providing credentials. The system validates email format and utilizes bcryptjs to securely hash passwords before storing them in the MongoDB database.
- Login: Users authenticate with their username and password. The client-side hashes the password before sending it. The server retrieves the user record from MongoDB, compares the hashed passwords, and generates a JWT (JSON Web Token) upon successful login. This JWT serves as an authorization token for subsequent requests.

Encrypted Uploads and Secure Storage

- File Selection and Encryption: From the dashboard, users can select files for upload. The client-side generates a random 256-bit encryption key using the Node.js crypto library. The chosen file content is then encrypted using the AES-256-CBC (Cipher Block Chaining) mode with this generated key.
- Server-Side Processing: The client sends the encrypted file content, original filename, and the separate encryption key to the server. The server validates the user's JWT for authorization. It retrieves the user's secret key (stored securely in the environment) and uses it to decrypt the encryption key received from the client.
- Storage and Key Management: The server decrypts the file content using the decrypted key. It then stores the decrypted file content and filename in MongoDB (consider cloud storage services for larger files). Importantly, the encryption key is stored separately in the database, but it's also encrypted with a user-specific secret for an additional layer of security.

Secure File Access and Decryption

- File Listing: Users can view a list of uploaded files on the dashboard. The client sends a request to the server with the JWT to retrieve this list. The server retrieves filenames associated with the user from MongoDB and sends them back.

- Retrieving Keys and Downloading Files: For each file, the client requests the decryption key from the server, including the JWT and filename. The server retrieves the corresponding encryption key from the database and decrypts it using the user's secret key. This decrypted key is then sent to the client.
- Client-Side Decryption and Display: The client receives the decrypted key and uses it to request the download of the encrypted file content from the server (using the filename). The server retrieves and sends the encrypted file content. Finally, the client decrypts the downloaded file content using the previously retrieved decryption key and displays the decrypted content to the user.

Security Considerations

- This implementation prioritizes user privacy by encrypting files at rest (stored in the database) and in transit (during upload and download).
- Using separate storage locations for encrypted files and encryption keys strengthens security.
- Employing strong password hashing (bcryptjs) and JWT authentication protects user credentials.

Figure 1. Representaion of our proposed system

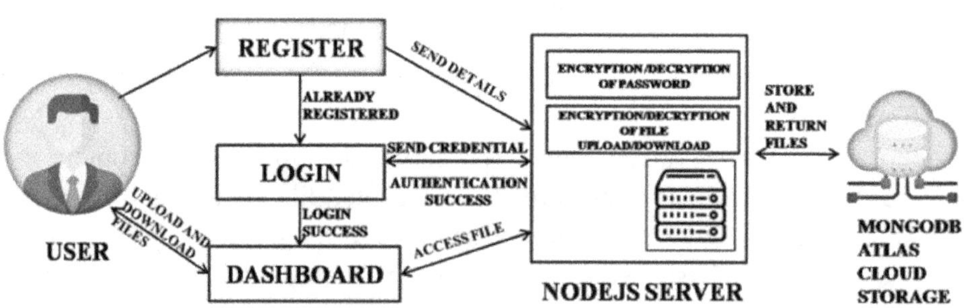

The above figure represents how our proposed system works. When the user enters our website they first landed to our register page, if they are new they register to the website by giving their name, email and password after that they will get a registration successful message. If they are registered user then they will go to the login page where it will ask for email and password. When the users are registered their password are encrypted and then stored in the database cloud by the nodejs server. After successful login the login page will give a login successful message and redirects to the dashboard of that user. In the dashboard the user can upload their ehealth data or download their ehealth data. The server encrypts the uploaded files and metadata using the encryptData function. The secretKey and algorithm are hardcoded as 'secret-key' and 'aes-256-cbc', respectively.The encrypted metadata and files are then saved to a MongoDB database using the File model. When it is downloaded, the server decrypts the file data using the decryptData function. The secretKey and algorithm are hardcoded as 'secret-key' and 'aes-256-cbc', respectively. The decrypted file data is then sent as a download response using the res.sendFile method. The res.sendFile method sends the file data along with the appropriate headers, including the Content-Type header, which is set to the file's original content type.

Result

Figure 2. Signup page

Figure 3. Login page

Figure 4. Dashboard page

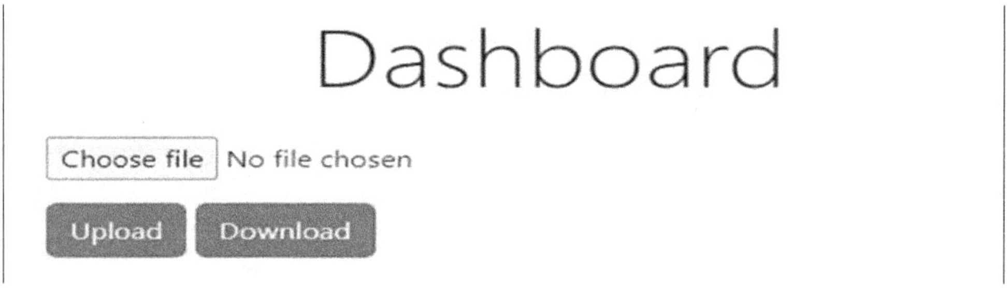

Figure 5. Database screenshot

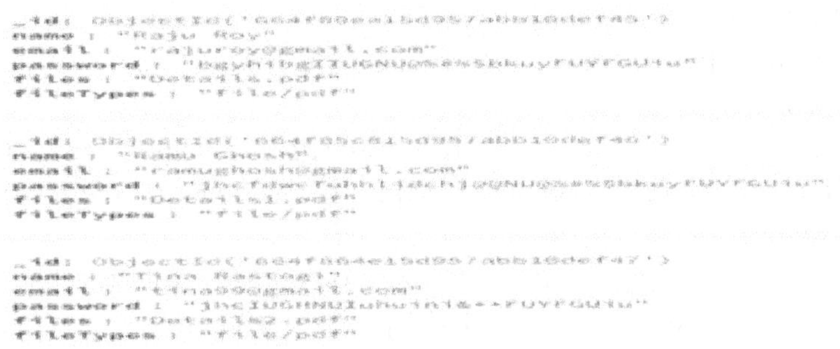

CONCLUSION

Use of electronic and digital technologies for health & social care are called e-Health Solutions that benefit global healthcare systems. Despite the benefits of Apify its security and privacy have to be in place so that no breaches or vulnerabilities come into play. The study of security and privacy research publications on e-Health solutions is important to ensure the effectiveness in this field. Through the review of literature on this topic, answers that are either missing or inadequate in these solutions can be identified. Adopting recommended empirical solutions to e-Health systems modeling is among the most robust means of improving their efficiency and safety. This will include the formulation of holistic models or policies for e-health implementation and act as a model to be adopted at governmental level so that health care can greatly benefit from this. Furthermore, governments ought to create research organizations or hubs where experts on security coordinate for more advanced e-Health implicable solution which are sextacular in terms of cyber threats and vulnerabilities. Such institutes could fuel the dialogue for new e-Health security and possibly even act as breeding grounds of innovation. Besides, to apply e-Health privacy regulations should be clear and descriptive. Rules governing the distribution, storage and security of patient information should specify mechanisms to ensure confidentiality and trust. When patients feel assured that their health-related data is secure, they're more likely to engage with e-Health services confidently.

Future Works

There are some possible future work ideas that we thought of for our Secure E-Health Data Management with MERN Stack and Encryption:

Enhanced Security Features

- *Two-Factor Authentication (2FA):* Enhance login security with 2FA, where users need to provide a code from a phone app or email along, with their password.
- *Client-Side Encryption Key Management:* Manage Encryption Keys Investigate methods of storing encryption keys generated by clients, on the user's device.
- *Automatic Key Rotation:* Implement automatic key rotation for encryption keys to further strengthen security by periodically changing them.

Advanced Functionality

- *File Access Control:* Introduce access control mechanisms to allow users to share uploaded files with others and define permission levels (read-only, read/write).
- *File Versioning:* Implement file versioning to track changes made to uploaded files and allow users to revert to previous versions if needed.
- *File Preview:* Incorporate a feature, for file preview that enables users to view the contents of encrypted files without having to download and decrypt them fully.

Scalability and Performance

- *Cloud Storage Integration:* Letting our system connect with a storage platform such, as Amazon S3, Google Cloud Storage or Microsoft Azure Blob Storage. This will help to store files effectively and expand your storage capabilities as needed.
- *Background Processing:* Implement background processing for tasks like file uploads and decryptions to improve responsiveness for users, especially when dealing with large files.
- *Database Sharding:* If your project experiences significant user growth and data volume, consider database sharding to distribute the load across multiple database servers.

Usability Enhancements

- *Drag-and-Drop Upload:* Enhance the file upload experience by adding drag and drop functionality, for an user approach.

- *File Organization:* Allow users to create folders and subfolders to organize their uploaded files within the dashboard.
- *Search Functionality:* Implement a search bar to allow users to easily find specific files based on keywords.

REFERENCES

Charanya, R., & Aramudhan, M. (2016). Survey on access control issues in cloud computing. *1st International Conference on Emerging Trends in Engineering, Technology and Science, ICETETS 2016 - Proceedings*. DOI: 10.1109/ICETETS.2016.7603014

Chi, P. W., & Lei, C. L. (2018). Audit-Free Cloud Storage via Deniable Attribute-Based Encryption. *IEEE Transactions on Cloud Computing*, 6(2), 414–427. DOI: 10.1109/TCC.2015.2424882

Huang, C., Yan, K., Wei, S., Zhang, G., & Lee, D. H. (2017). Efficient anonymous attribute-based encryption with access policy hidden for cloud computing. *Proceedings of 2017 International Conference on Progress in Informatics and Computing, PIC 2017*, 266–270. DOI: 10.1109/PIC.2017.8359555

Hupperich, T., Löhr, H., Sadeghi, A. R., & Winandy, M. (2012). Flexible patient-controlled security for electronic health records. *IHI'12 - Proceedings of the 2nd ACM SIGHIT International Health Informatics Symposium*, 727–731. DOI: 10.1145/2110363.2110448

Kim, S., Sung, M. K., & Chung, Y. D. (2014). A framework to preserve the privacy of electronic health data streams. *Journal of Biomedical Informatics*, 50, 95–106. DOI: 10.1016/j.jbi.2014.03.015 PMID: 24704716

Li, W., Liu, B. M., Liu, D., Liu, R. P., Wang, P., Luo, S., & Ni, W. (2019). Unified fine-grained access control for personal health records in cloud computing. *IEEE Journal of Biomedical and Health Informatics*, 23(3), 1278–1289. DOI: 10.1109/JBHI.2018.2850304 PMID: 29994490

Rezaeibagha, F., & Mu, Y. (2016). Distributed clinical data sharing via dynamic access-control policy transformation. *International Journal of Medical Informatics*, 89, 25–31. DOI: 10.1016/j.ijmedinf.2016.02.002 PMID: 26980356

Simplicio, M. A., Iwaya, L. H., Barros, B. M., Carvalho, T. C. M. B., & Naslund, M. (2015). Secour health: A delay-tolerant security framework for mobile health data collection. *IEEE Journal of Biomedical and Health Informatics*, 19(2), 761–772. DOI: 10.1109/JBHI.2014.2320444 PMID: 24801629

Wei, J., Liu, W., & Hu, X. (2018). Secure data sharing in cloud computing using revocable-storage identity-based encryption. *IEEE Transactions on Cloud Computing*, 6(4), 1136–1148. DOI: 10.1109/TCC.2016.2545668

Zhu, L., Zhang, C., Xu, C., Liu, X., & Huang, C. (2018). An Efficient and Privacy-Preserving Biometric Identification Scheme in Cloud Computing. *IEEE Access : Practical Innovations, Open Solutions*, 6(c), 19025–19033. DOI: 10.1109/ACCESS.2018.2819166

Chapter 10
Improving the Quality of the Face Recognition Using LBPH in Machine Learning

Ratnesh Kumar Shukla
https://orcid.org/0000-0002-8279-7011
Dr. APJ Abdul Kalam Technical University

Arvind Kumar Tiwari
KNIT Sultanpur, India

Vinay Kumar Mishra
https://orcid.org/0000-0002-5301-3599
Babu Banarasi Das University, Lucknow, India

ABSTRACT

The objective of this article is to recognize facial features from images using face recognition approaches. For preprocessed face images with equalized histograms, the suggested solution employs a local binary pattern histogram (LBPH). One of the long-standing issues with computer vision is accurate face detection and recognition. The Local Binary Pattern (LBP) is a better facial descriptor in face recognition, in recent study. A person's identity, sentiments, and ideas may be more easily discernible from their face. Everyone wants to feel safe from unauthorized authentication in the current world. To improve security, face detection and recognition have joined the scene and are tackling the most challenging challenge of effectively recognizing faces without creating any false identities. The histogram values are extracted and joined into a single vector. After applying these methods, the training loss decreases

DOI: 10.4018/979-8-3693-9235-5.ch010

and the validation of accuracy rise by over 96.5%. This vector compares the facial likenesses and produces the most advantageous outcome.

1 INTRODUCTION

Artificial intelligence (AI) is solving the problem of faces in computer vision including large datasets. These include subjects such as machine learning (ML) and the deep learning (DL). These are used artificial intelligence technologies for developing expert systems that classify data and predict outcomes based on input datasets. They are commonly cited in discussions concerning artificial intelligence. The digital revolution has already altered to ways in which people communicate, work and live. It's also just getting started. However, the same breakthroughs that have the potential to improve billions of people's happiness, health, and productivity also pose new concerns for individuals and governments around the world. It is critical to understand distinction between the DL and ML. These are frequently used interchangeably throughout the procedure. DL and ML are used well established branches of the artificial intelligence for communication. DL is actually combination of the neural networks. Neural network are classified in DL with three layers, including input layers, fully connected layers and output layers. Deep learning and machine learning have different learning algorithms. Deep learning enables the usage of larger datasets by significantly lowering amount of the manual human. That is necessary during interaction of the feature extraction stage in the process. Machine learning is non-deep and traditionally relies on human input. Human specialists create a hierarchy of attributes to better grasp the distinctions between the various data inputs. These are derived from more organized datasets. Labeled datasets are found in the supervised learning. That can be used direct deep features in the machine learning algorithms, but they are not essential. It can take unstructured raw data forms, such as text and photos. It can automatically find hierarchy in features that distinguish different types of data from one to another's. It has required humans intervention to the handles data and scale ML in the new and intriguing ways of data. AI systems process vast volumes of tagged training data, looking for connections and patterns. The recorded data is then used to forecast future analyses. Similar to chatbots, image recognition algorithm may learn and verify identity and explains item in photos by examining the millions of instances. Chatbots are taught examples of the text that can learn and engage in realistic discussions from humans. AI approaches can produce realistic images, text, graphics, music and other multimedia supports. Banks are successfully using chatbots to manage duties. Customers can learn about various services and opportunities without having to engage with a human. AI virtual machine are assistants to utilized and simplify banking regulations and updation.

Banking institutions employ AI to the improve loan choices, modify credit limits and identify the investment opportunities. These technologies are used to increase transportation efficiency by managing traffic, anticipating airline delays, and increasing maritime shipping safety. AI is playing an important part in the functioning of self-driving cars. AI is replacing traditional approaches for anticipating demand and detecting supply chain disruptions. COVID19 accelerated this trend, surprising many corporations with its impact on global commodity supply and demand.

AI programming prioritizes the following cognitive qualities:

Learning: The purpose of AI programming tools is to collect data and generate the rules necessary to convert it into knowledge. These rules are known as algorithms to use computing devices and detailed instructions on how to do specific tasks.

Reasoning: AI programming is an optimum algorithm for the given result from datasets.

Self-Correction: These algorithms are always being self-improved and also ensure. So they are produces most accurate result.

Creativity: Artificial intelligence is built on the neural network, rule-based system, statistical approaches and another AI technology. AI creates original visuals, texts, melodies and concepts.

AI can automate self-grading, allowing instructor to devote more time to education. The student studies at their own pace so that their needs can be identified and met. AI technology can help pupils increase their knowledge. AI is used may also affect where and how students learn. Such as ChatGPT, Bard and other big languages model, Artificial Intelligence can help teachers create teaching plans and other educational materials to engage students in novel technologies. Instructors are forced to reevaluate student assignments, exams, and plagiarism policies as a result of the advent of these technologies. New generative AI tools are based on natural language prompts and used to generate application code. These tools are still in their early stages, and they are unlikely to replace software professionals anytime soon. AI is automating a wide range of IT operations. These include data entry, customer service, fraud detection, predictive maintenance and security. Some of the ethical difficulties that AI encounters are as follows: Human prejudice and badly trained algorithms both contribute to bias; DeepFakes and phishing both contribute to misuse and legal concerns. .

History of Artificial Intelligence: AI concepts are imbuing inanimate object with intelligence has existed past since to beginning of time. The Greek god Hephaestus has created robot to work like servants out of myths in the gold. Egypt engineers have made big god statues. Those priests can pray to animate that god. René Descartes, Thomas Bayes and Ramon Llull are introducing 13th-century Spanish cleric and Aristotle all described human mental processes as symbols. The foundation ideas are found in AI such as general knowledge of the representation. 19th and the beginning of 20th centuries laid foundation of the modern digital computers. Augusta Ada King, Countess of the Lovelace and mathematician Charles Babbage from Cambridge University are developed a programming machine in 1836.

1940s: John Von Neumann and Princeton mathematician created and design stored program in the computer. That stores both programs and data are processes in memory. Additionally, Walter Pitts and Warren McCulloch are provided foundation in neural networks.

1950s: Scientists are able to verify predictions by using artificial intelligence thanks to modern technology. British mathematician breaker Alan Turing is breaker Alan Turing in World War II with code x. These tests have evaluated and performed a computer's ability to questioner obtain and created the answers.

1960s: After the symposium at Dartmouth College, pioneers in emerging field of the artificial intelligence predicted the creation of machine intelligence on par with the human brain, resulting in major government and business support. AI performs better solutions and well-funded research in the previous 20 years. McCarthy has developed a programming language called Lisp. Lisp is basically useful for AI performance. Newell and Simon are published a general problem solver (GPS) algorithm late 1950s century. Despite the GPS algorithm's inability to handle complicated issues, it helped set the stage for the development of more sophisticated cognitive architectures.

1970s & 1980s: The complexity issues are limitations of computer memory and computer processing made the development of artificial general intelligence challenging but not imminent. The first "AI Winter," which lasted from 1974 to 1980, was sparked by the cessation of financing for AI research from the government and business. Deep learning is a very attractive and well performs result given by researcher and industrial. Edward Feigenbaum's expert systems are helping second wave to enthusiasm for AI in the 1980s. However, this time, government funding and corporate support collapsed. There was a 2nd artificial intelligence winter up until middle of the 1990s.

1990s: AI saw a resurgence in late 1990s that paved stage for the incredible advancements we see today. Increases in computer power and a data boom propelled this renaissance. Advancements in computer vision, robotics, ML, NLP and DL were made possible by the use of big data and more potent computers. The world chess champion was defeated by the IBM's Deep Blue in 1997, marking first time computer program has ever done it. Research on AI was expanding at the time.

2000s: Additional advancements in speech recognition, computer vision, deep learning and machine learning resulted in the development of products and services. It has impacted how we live today. It has included and launches of the Amazon recommendation engine in 2001 and Google search engine in 2000. Microsoft introduced its speech recognition system, Netflix has developed movie recommendation system and Facebook unveiled facial recognition technology. Watson was announced by IBM, while Google's self-driving initiative, Waymo, and was presented.

2010s: AI has made steady progress during the last ten years, from 2010 to 2020. Apple's Siri and Amazon's Alexa have both introduced speech assistant. IBM Watson's success on the Jeopardy in self-driving car led to creation of first generative adversarial network. Google published TensorFlow, an open-source DL platform, to launch its own research department, OpenAI. The developers created GPT-3 language models and Dall-E picture generators. They beat world Go champion Lee Sedol thanks to Google DeepMind Alpha.

2020s: AI generation is a subfield of the artificial intelligence. That can produces creative content. AI begins to process the user's input data. Such as text, image, video, design, musical notation or input data. Then, as a response to the proposal, various AI systems return brand-new information. Content options include essays, problem-solving strategies, and lifelike impersonations created using a person's photos or speech. Language models are using ChatGPT-3, Google Bard and Microsoft's Megatron-Turing NLG have impressed globe with abilities. These technologies are still used infancy, indicated by its tendency to the produce incorrect and warped responses. AI model develops cutting-edge AI models in addition to these cloud services. For conversation, NLP, image generation, and code generation, a large number of language models. That performs OpenAI and made available in Azure. In Nvidia has taken more cloud-agnostic strategy, developing AI infrastructures and core models. They are designed to work with text, images, and medical data from any cloud provider. A significant number of additional businesses also provide models. That is designed for specific sectors and use circumstances.

AI tools and Services: Artificial Intelligence related models and systems are progressively swiftly improved. Recent advancements in AI tools and applications are attributed to AlexNet neural network from the 2012, which heralded new era of high performance to AI. These are made from GPUs and enormous datasets. Primary advancement ability was to train the neural networks across several GPU cores on the massive amounts simultaneously. AI is one of many diverse type of technology with numerous examples.

Machine Learning: This paper describes machine learning for controlling computer programs. DL is sub part of ML to put it simply, automation of predictive analytics. We have generally known as three types in ML algorithms.

Supervised Learning: Dataset is classified in the order to trends and utilize them to the label new datasets.

Unsupervised Learning: Without assigning labels, datasets are sorted to base on their similar values or different values.

Reinforcement Learning: AI technology receives feedback after performing one action or more actions on datasets that are not tagged.

Speech Recognition: It is a concept to converts spoken sounds and words in written ones via NLP. These procedures are known as the speech-to-text, computer speech recognition and automatic speech recognition (ASR). Mobile devices and operating systems have speech recognition as a feature to enable voice search and increase messaging accessibility.

Computer Vision: Artificial intelligence is employed in the computers to organize other systems to manipulate data from videos, digital photos and other visual inputs to respond appropriately. They are recommended to differ from occupations involving image recognition systems to collect images from the radiological imaging in healthcare, social media and self-driving cars. They are used automotive industry using computer vision with CNN.

Automate Stock-Trading: We are working on order to optimized stock portfolios. AI driven is working high frequency trading platform. That carries out hundreds and millions of transactions per day.

Recommended Engines: AI algorithms are helping to identify data trends. It is used to develop cross selling techniques. It is more successful in data identification. They are using such as online retailers to recommend relevant add-ons to the material of clients during the checkout process.

Robotics: The development and design of robots is the focus of this branch of engineering. Jobs that are difficult for humans to do or are inconsistently completed by humans are typically completed by robots. For instance, NASA uses robots to handle large objects in orbit or along auto production lines. Researchers are developing socially engaging robots by utilising machine learning.

Text, Images and Audio Generation: Businesses are heavily utilising generative AI techniques to generate an almost limitless range of the content types from stunning paintings to E-mail messages and scripts, all from text inputs.

Self-driving Cars: The autonomous vehicles have made use of the image recognition, computer vision and DL. These are learned automated system and skills for driving car. They are following designated lane and ignored unanticipated obstacles, like pedestrians.

Security Issues: Artificial intelligence and model intelligence are at top of list of buzzwords used by security providers to sell their solutions; however, purchasers should proceed with caution. However, a range of cyber security-related tasks, such as anomaly detection, false positive resolution, and behavioral threat analytics, are already being done effectively with AI programming. Organizations utilize machine learning in the fields of security information and event management (SIEM) models and related disciplines detect irregularities and the suspicious behavior suggests dangers. In examining the data are using logic tips to the identify similarities in current harmful codes. AI may detect new and the emerging attacks considerably earlier human personnel and past technology versions. DL is working computer based modeling techniques. That are uses many processing layers to the comprehend data represented at different levels of the abstraction.

Face Recognition Systems: Face detection and recognition has a hot topic in current years for security and identity reasons. It is prevalent problem, because it has wide range of the applications. It can aid to develop of the advanced algorithms that use CNN and deep learning techniques. Face recognition has grabbed academics' interest for many years due to the increasing number of applications. Face recognition research has also piqued the interest of many people, owing to theoretical problems and a wide range of applications. Researchers created algorithms for the face identification, age variation, features based on the human faces and facial emotion detection that work best with well illuminated, face aligned and frontal posture images. First focuses on essential face recognition and the facial characteristics needed for face identification. At the time, the most prevalent strategy was to use the face's geometric structure to examine feature points and their homogenous relationships. Face recognition technology advanced significantly in the 1990s, enabling rapid computer development and continuous increases in calculation accuracy in face identification and recognition. Faces with different facial emotions, ages and lighting conditions can be identified, as well as those in frontal, well-lit and clear faces. Machine learning methodologies have advanced in the twenty-first century, allowing facial recognition technology to evolve into many ways such as support vector machines (SVM), kernel methods, and so on. Face recognition are moving away controlled situations and toward uncontrolled the scenes. A deep learning strategy has been used with good success rate, however these method have substantial costs and require enormous amounts of data. The major goal is to create a facial recognition system that is lightweight, accurate, and efficient. Hash's purpose was to the extract most robust and valuable facial feature from a image data set. CNN and SVM have high level feature facial recognition model, (Shukla, Tiwari, & Mishra, 2024). The CNN model is using several images to diverse hand signals for different people in order to group the letters for this application, which seeks to learn motions and reliably detect and find them, (Mahammad & Kumar, 2023). They are reduced model computational cost while also establishing required connections between the magnetoencephalogram (MEG) signal and facial detection, (Shukla & Tiwari, 2020). After applying central mechanism to failures in mutual monitoring, a transfer learning strategy was applied. Mobilenet is an upgraded CNN model that combines consistency with speedup for offline and natural time environments, resulting in rapid and accurate real-time output, (Hariri, 2022). Combined method improves real-time responses time and retrieval accuracy with lowering computational complexity, (Tiwari & Shukla, 2019). This outperforms current cutting edge techniques works with same data. These preliminary results are despite the aging process with suggested system in personal identification potential,

(Gosain, Aggarwal,. & Kumar, 2023). In Face presentation attack detection (FPAD) demonstrated great overall the performance and significant improvement of cross database. Their computational complexity is appropriate for real time applications, (Shukla & Tiwari, 2023). Face detection and recognition are commonly employed in biometric security and safety applications. Facial recognition system works like biometric model that maps facial characteristics into mathematics for face image. These models employ DL approaches to compare real time and digital photos with saved faces to verify identity. The face recognition has also been used on some mobile phones, (Teke, Manjare, & Jamdar, 2021). The LBP is a high performance technique for the face detection and recognitions. This approach is particularly useful for identifying unknown and unauthorized individuals. DL based malware detectors are under consideration viable solution. These detectors are subject in hostile attacks. Harmful files created as result of adversarial attacks cannot be discovered, (Shukla & Tiwari, 2021). Majority of these cyber security risk strategies are focused on fraud, intrusion, spam, and virus detection, (Wang *et al.,* 2023). This research is to analyze the most prominent ML algorithms for detecting some of most dangerous cyber-attacks in cyberspace, (Jaiwal & Kumar, 2023).

2 RELATED WORKS

Face detection and recognition technique employ adaptive lighting and normalizing under changing illuminations caused by variations in the light projection angle. Normalization and Illumination have been applied to subset in low frequency discrete cosine transform coefficients (CT) and generated adaptively in magnitude as they change. Floating numbers of the low frequency discrete cosine transform (DCT) coefficients are calculated based on light in the images. These are modified non-linear modifiers selected from illumination based on face photos, (Sharma, Chakraborty, & Kumar, 2023). Some benchmark datasets like Caltech-face, labeled faces in the wild (LFW), color-FERET (facial Recognition Technology) and CASIA-face-v5, suggested descriptors retrieval and recognition accuracies compared to the state-of-the-art hand-crafted descriptor, (Shukla, Das, & Aggarwal, 2016). The proposed techniques are very modular, making them easily integrated into existing deep CNN. Extensive experiments large scale items, like classification, acceptable grained visual recognition, scene categorization and the texture classification, shows algorithms outperform competitors and produce state-of-the-art results, (Kumar & Kumar, 2022). DL techniques are used to improve accuracy of face detection and identification methods. Face recognition technology has advanced with the training of massive datasets, (Singh & Srivastava, 2018). Optimum evolutionary 3D deep CNN works deep networks for medical segmentation. Then it converts to

2D, and 3D network, (Shukla, Prakash, & Pandey, 2020). It considers source of the knowledge, represented and fits into ML pipeline. They represent a variety of sorts, including mathematical equations, number system and simulation rules for learning system, (Tomás *et al.,* 2021). According to systemic effectiveness research are profound features to analyze and construct deep network that preserves inter cluster variations in group. These classic representations are learning frameworks for resolving unequal class outcomes, (Din *et al.*, 2020). Deep learning beats LPBH in terms of multiple video views, any distance of footage obtained for moving, immobile objects from a mobile video camera, and a CCTV camera, (Misra, Kumar, & Jain, 2021). The disentangled identity representations were learned using a neural network technique. Proposed network neutralizes facial expression IN input-expressive 3D face while providing important face identifying components, (Kumar *et al.,* 2021). LFW and MegaFace demonstrates cutting edge performance. They perform substantially better on severe benchmarks like TinyFace and IJB-S, (Anwar & Raychowdhury, 2020). These algorithms use projected linear subspace face to capture and detect facial changes. In this strategies are effective in the ideal situations. These are totally reversed with the majority of current face detection and face recognition algorithms focused on the local features usage robustness storing in important local features, (Chowdary *et al.*, 2020). Vector quantized local pixels are employed to harness local information, whereas other methods for face detection employ battery of the spatially localized Gabor filters in a multilayer framework. The most common approaches based on LBP use a local binary pattern histogram, (Agarwal & Jain, 2019).

3 FACE RECOGNITION METHODS

Face detection and recognition techniques are recognizing person's faces to store database of their photos. Face recognition has long been an important fields of research, even though other identification technique. They can more accurate in nature and the fact most practical way for people to the identify themselves.

3.1 Face Recognition using Deep Learning

In machine learning, algorithms are employed to help computer systems learn from examples rather than being manually programmed to perform tasks. Deep learning techniques have been developed as computational power and access to big datasets have increased, resulting in advances in a variety of domains speech recognition, NLP and computer vision. DL is used to solve difficult tasks by training computer models composed of many layers to learn data in multiple levels of abstractions,

(Qin & Li, 2020). Deep convolutional neural networks are employed in image and video processing method for human facial identification and fine-grained recognition to many faces and they are particularly efficient way in computer vision, exceeding humans for speed and accuracy, (Sethi, Kathuria, & Kaushik, 2021).

3.2 Geometrical Face Recognition

Geometry based algorithms are using to identify and recognize faces. Geometry based algorithm can developed using statistical tool such as LDA, SVM, PCA and Kernel methods. Local face traits and the geometric correlations are investigated utilizing geometric feature-based methods and commonly referred feature-based approach, (Eikenberry *et al.,* 2020).

3.3 Faces Recognition using Eigenfaces

Eigen faces in face recognizers treat all training photographs of all complex characters and try to the decrease components. Components are crucial or advantageous since they catch the majority of variance or change while discarding the remainders of images. This technique extracts important aspects from the trained data while collect memory from eliminating in critical portions, (Vu, Ngguyen, & Pham, 2022)

3.4 Fisher Faces Recognition

Instead of gathering usable qualities that reflect all faces of people, the Fisher faces method eliminates the valuable features to identify person to person. These attributes do not take precedence over others, but they do distinguish one person from another, (Li *et al.,* 2021).

3.5 Euclidean Distance

Centralized binary patterns integrated with image Euclidean Distance (ED) in the face emotion detection (ED) as technique for calculating straight line between points. This situation, it entails measuring histogram. These algorithm returns computed relation between histograms of the nearest photos. Distance values can assess degree of confidence in accuracy to facial recognition values using ED technique, (Mliki, Dammak, & Fendri, 2020).

3.6 Face Recognition using Local Pattern-Based

LBP works on simple, efficient and extracts each feature effectively. Academics began working LBP in a variety of domains, particularly face recognition, leveraging these properties. The LBP is an effective way to express local characteristics in texture. LBP, grey level images are converted to binary and setting a threshold for the center pixel and comparing its values to nearest neighbors. The binary valued images serve as local descriptors, (Xia, Chen, & Ren, 2022).

LBP works on 3x3 neighborhoods from photos. It are operated several different values of the (x,y) where x represents number in neighbor pixels and y represents radius. Generally LBP operates to expresses (x,y) and the codes values from 0 to 255, between 8-bit binary representation and 8-neighboring pixels values in 3×3 resolution neighbourhood to (x,y). As shown in equation 1, the LBP operator has the following form.

LBP(x,y)=

$$\sum_{0}^{7}(X_c - X_n)\, 2^n \qquad (1)$$

Where 'n' describes across center pixel C's eight neighbors (0 to 7), X_c and X_n are the grey level intensities of c and n and LBP (x,y) is 1 if n > 0 and otherwise 0. Figure 1 shows LBP encoding method on 3×3 neighbourhood (x,y).

Figure 1. Conversation of the RGB image using LBP threshold value into LBP

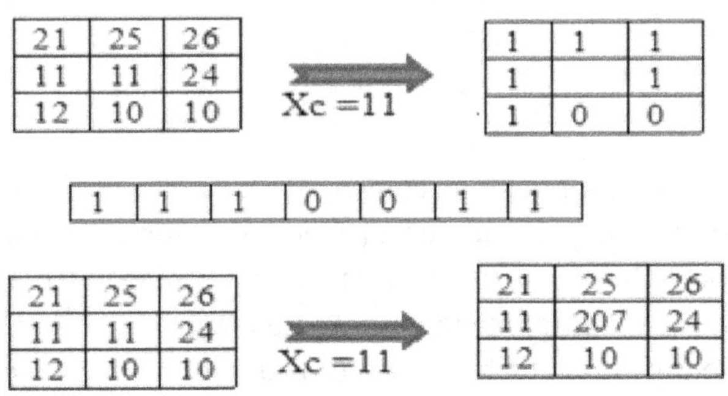

Figure 1 depicts the conversion of an RGB image (red, green, and blue) to gray images. Then we converted to 0 and 1 using threshold value 11. Following that, we convert it to binary and finally to decimal numbers. Then we position the values in the middle, ensuring that all values are in the same place. It is known as a Low Binary Pattern picture. Consider a grayscale face. A 3×3 matrix with intensity values ranging from 0 to 255 can also be used. Next step is utilizing threshold as matrix center values. New values from the eight neighbors are operated each neighbor of threshold value and generate new binary value. Define the 1 for the values that exceed or equal to threshold otherwise 0. Middle value will not be regarded to matrix but only included binary values. The matrix binary values must be concatenated line to line and generates new binary value (like 11110011). There is no matter to concatenate clockwise binary values. Result will be generated binary values from pixel values in images. Then assigned center values matrix translated after a decimal integer. To utilizing this procedure are produces current image to closely properties of captured original image obtained using threshold LBP method and make different variety of grids using image from the previous stage.

Figure 2. (A) original image and (B) LBP converted original image

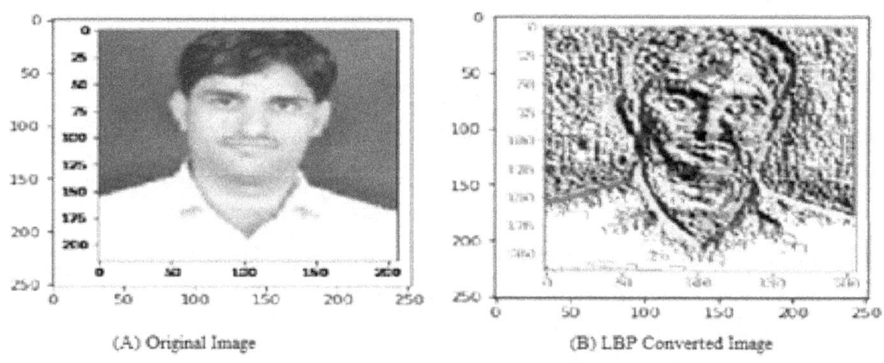

Figure 2 depicts original image and converted LBP images using the python. Each image data is processed LBP technique and generate histograms indicating intensity of pixels. Conventional histogram is constantly transforming into new histogram that displays properties of training image data. In this study, LBPH methods are used to calculate different picture attributes. Face recognition determines the closest or lowest value between the histogram values of two pictures. The ED was used as a similarity metric for comparing two attributes. There is a commitment to addressing object tracking problem to deformation to other disturbances and evident errors are optimizing effectiveness circumstances using object tracking algorithm. Positive aspects of effective models are compensating for each other's flaws, (Shukla, Tiwari, & Jha, 2023). The integration of many features with discriminative correlation filters and enhanced tracking representation demonstrated significant potential for the object tracking. Preset weights are used by existing trackers to combine features or a response map, which renders them incapable of taking object drift into account, (Li & Chen, 2022). Current image inpainting methods often display fuzzy texture properties and structural disarray. During the reconstruction phase image, it is difficult to inpainting network to effectively use information in e non-damaged surface in order to appropriately infer the content of the damaged area, (Zhang *et al.*, 2022). The most crucial pieces of the information in automobiles utilizes to navigate and existence of the traffic signs like intelligent transportation systems and autonomous driving greatly depend on detection of these indicators. Traffic sign detection will be advance creation of traffic sign dataset that has large sample size and enough attribute categories, (Shukla *et al.*, 2021).

4 LOCAL BINARY PATTERN HISTOGRAM

Grayscale changes that are monotonic can be accommodated using the LBP operator. The LBP values are counted number of LBP values in surface area of the region's LBP value histogram created. Once each section is constructed, the histograms are combined to create the feature vector of the image. Next, we retrieve the image with the most similar histogram by comparing the test image's histogram to that of photos in the database. By comparing the characteristics of the test image with the dataset, Euclidean distances may be calculated. The matching rate is shortest time interval between test and original image. Consequently, we derive an identifier for the picture within the database, (Shukla *et al.*, 2022)

Figure 3. Above figure shows a grey image, LBP image and LBPH

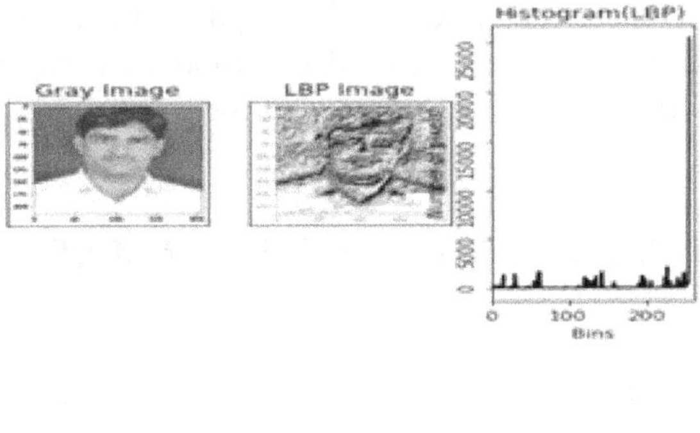

Figure 3 illustrates executing the following actions on image above and extracting histogram of each region: Because image is grayscale, histogram (each grid) will included 256 (0 to 255) represents occurrences in pixel intensity. The next stages are combining each histogram form a single, larger histogram. The generated histogram captures properties of original image. Given that face image analysis is the most widespread and important use of LBP, it serves as an excellent example of its use, development, and performance. Local and oriented component of LBP representations are useful to facial image analysis because local structural provides patterns while also encoding information about facial arrangement. Feature selections are critical variety of facial image analysis application since local and oriented component LBP face representations significantly extend feature.

5 FACE RECOGNITION USING LOW BINARY PATTERN HISTOGRAM

Current approach demonstrates LBP based descriptor picture. LBP is focusing on this model to working with the pattern concept. Pattern is the fundamental component of categorization for the identification. A threshold value can be used to automatically evaluate algorithm's ability to accurately recognize image. The confidence level falls below predetermined threshold, we can believe algorithm correctly identified the item.

To construct the dataset, photographs from a camera or previously saved the photos can be used. There will be multiple samples of same individual. Figure 4 depicts data flow in specific feature and faces given to individual LBPH images in the database. ML is a crucial component project in areas like as finance, security, marketing and more. The LBHP algorithms are widely utilized in the face recognition. Histogram equalization method uses cumulative distribution function of histogram to equalize the gray degree values in the image data. Then draws straight diagonal lines of the graph between sums of pictures that ranges from 0 to 255 that are flattened. LBPH face recognizer is a development to correct problem. Finding images local features is not purpose. LBPH method are compared every pixels to their neighbors to determine images in local structure.

6 EXPERIMENTAL ANALYSIS OF THE ARTICLE

These algorithms generate representation of the each histogram from training datasets. To create a histogram that accurately portrays the original images and repeat process after receiving input image database. These pictures resemble given image, simply compare two histograms and return closest histogram. There are numerous approaches for comparing two histograms, Euclidean distance and chi-square. Identification (ID) algorithm finds image with closest histogram value from output. Program should return with computed distance and used confidence metric.

The advantages of the particularly are used computational simplicity and tolerance for monotonic illumination fluctuations. LBP approach has gone through multiple modifications to improve its robustness, efficacy, and applicability in one or more areas. Getting a modest number of LBP-based features yields the most accurate results. LBP representations are combined with standard features selection methods.

In this process, tested data are recognize from local video files and real time recordings in different time interval examined to using face recognition method. Time interval is number of seconds it takes for program's facial recognition function to respond. Camera are used in real time video stream for same quality webcam of local video and modified to improve webcam's video capture quality. Face recognition method are using tested data and repeated continuously participant to determine average accuracy level.

Table 1. Different algorithms accuracy with subjects and errors

Methods	Subject	Errors	Accuracy
Eigenfaces	15	5	75%
Fisherfaces	17	3	85%
LBP	19	1	95%
LBPH	0-255	1	96.5%

7 DISCUSSIONS

The proposed method's performance could be improved using the most recent deep learning or machine learning methods. Nonetheless, multiple studies address disadvantages of the ML and DL based face recognition. Face recognition system are using lighting fluctuation, facial expression changes, age, position variation, scaling factors, presence and absence of spectacles, mustache or beard and the occlusion caused by a scarf, mask, or items in the front. Massive data sets that are inclusive, unbiased, and of high quality are required for training. Furthermore, there will be the times and wait fresh data generate. Furthermore, ML requires enough time to train the order and reach goal with a high level accuracy. Furthermore, it requires a large amount of resources function. This may result in the need for additional computational power. Face recognition algorithms based on deep learning have been effectively deployed to a wide range of real-time applications. Applications for widespread recognition remain ambitious ambition. It is difficult to the collect and identifies enough samples in many real world situations. As training loss diminishes, accuracy validation improves by more than 96.5%. This graph depicts how, as the epochs go, study of a feature produces increasingly exact results. LBP is most effective descriptors for structure description. LBP image are analysis the tasks included facial image analysis, aerial image analysis, biological image analysis, motion analysis and video retrieval. The study's face recognition prototype accurately identified four different facial objects at the same time. During testing, LBPH approach produced equivalent results with local data and real time stream video data. Study's scientific contribution is the recommended approach for detecting faces in still pictures, video streams, and low-resolution images using LBPH. The proposed approach can be used in real time multi-face recognition from still photos and video streams, lowering computation time when compared sequential recognition of the numerous single faces.

8 COMPARATIVE ANALYSES OF FACE RECOGNITION

This article evaluates the performance of facial recognition algorithms Eigenfaces, Fisherfaces, and LBPH, using OpenCV classifiers and Haar Cascades to detecting human faces. History of facial recognition technology was given first, describing the major milestones in its development. Examining related works focuses on their methods and results. The technologies are used and described in accordance with the technique employed, (Kumar & Jain, 2021).

Figure 4. Representing accuracy with the different algorithm and their subjects

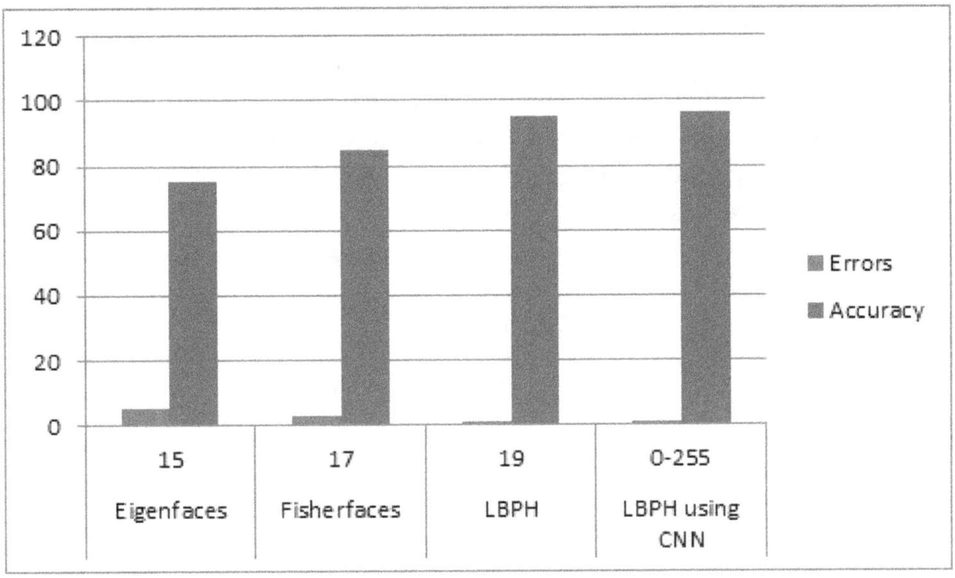

In this trial, the HP integrated the true vision of high definition (HD) camera was used record participants, and the speed was satisfactory with no perceptible lag. The Haar cascades were used distinguish human face and they worked fairly work. Furthermore, faces could found even if user was wearing glasses. Table 1 and Figure 4 show how combining LBPH with CNN results in a cost-effective and beneficial face detection and identification application that outperforms all three tested algorithms. With LBPH algorithm and CNNs excellent accuracy, less dependable training set can used with satisfactory results.

Following techniques are providing best results in the terms of goal accuracy and speed. While Eigenface and Fisherface's accuracy fell as number of training images increased non-normalized training data, LBPH accuracy improved with same training. No model demonstrated a delay felt by people. Eigenface's accuracy declined again on normalized data, but this time LBPH joined in. Fisherface first performed well on one trained image before underperforming on the next five training images.

9 CONCLUSION OF THE ARTICLE

According to the findings of their experiments, LBP, like all texture based algorithms, appears sensitive to major variations in illumination, as well as noisy and fuzzy images. When training loss is reduced, validation accuracy rises above

96.5%. This graph shows how study of a feature leads to more accurate conclusions as epoch's progress. They are 3D volume structures created from flat texture pictures, whereas human faces reflect non-monotonic light fluctuations. As a result, non-monotonic changes such as shadows and bright spots are widespread, and they can move depending on the illumination angle. The latter is usually the result of insufficient user interaction, unsuitable capture conditions, and poor camera sensor quality. The preprocessing images are applying LBP is both necessary and advantageous in these cases.

REFERENCES

Agarwal, A. K., & Jain, A. (2019). Synthesis of 2D and 3D NoC mesh router architecture in HDL environment. *Journal of Advanced Research in Dynamical and Control Systems*, 11(4), 2573–2581.

Anwar, A., & Raychowdhury, A. (2020). Masked face recognition for secure authentication. *arXiv preprint arXiv:2008.11104*.

Din, N. U., Javed, K., Bae, S., & Yi, J. (2020). A novel GAN-based network for unmasking of masked face. *IEEE Access : Practical Innovations, Open Solutions*, 8, 44276–44287. DOI: 10.1109/ACCESS.2020.2977386

Eikenberry, S. E., Mancuso, M., Iboi, E., Phan, T., Eikenberry, K., Kuang, Y., & Gumel, A. B. (2020). To mask or not to mask: Modeling the potential for face mask use by the general public to curtail the COVID-19 pandemic. *Infectious Disease Modelling*, 5, 293–308. DOI: 10.1016/j.idm.2020.04.001 PMID: 32355904

Gosain, M. S., Aggarwal, N., & Kumar, R. (2023, April). A study of 5G and edge computing integration with IoT-A Review. In *2023 International Conference on Computational Intelligence and Sustainable Engineering Solutions (CISES)* (pp. 705-710). IEEE. DOI: 10.1109/CISES58720.2023.10183438

Hariri, W. (2022). Efficient masked face recognition method during the covid-19 pandemic. *Signal, Image and Video Processing*, 16(3), 605–612. DOI: 10.1007/s11760-021-02050-w PMID: 34804243

Jaiswal, A., & Kumar, R. (2023). Breast cancer diagnosis using stochastic self-organizing map and enlarge C4. 5. *Multimedia Tools and Applications*, 82(12), 18059–18076. DOI: 10.1007/s11042-022-14265-1

Jignesh Chowdary, G., Punn, N. S., Sonbhadra, S. K., & Agarwal, S. (2020). Face mask detection using transfer learning of inceptionv3. In *Big Data Analytics: 8th International Conference, BDA 2020, Sonepat, India, December 15–18, 2020* [Springer International Publishing.]. *Proceedings*, 8, 81–90.

Kumar, A., & Jain, A. (2021). Image smog restoration using oblique gradient profile prior and energy minimization. *Frontiers of Computer Science*, 15(6), 156706. DOI: 10.1007/s11704-020-9305-8 PMID: 34221535

Kumar, S., Jain, A., Kumar Agarwal, A., Rani, S., & Ghimire, A. (2021). [Retracted] Object-Based Image Retrieval Using the U-Net-Based Neural Network. *Computational Intelligence and Neuroscience*, 2021(1), 4395646. DOI: 10.1155/2021/4395646 PMID: 34804141

Kumar, S., & Kumar, R. (2022). Intelligent model to image enrichment for strong night-vision surveillance cameras in future generation. *Multimedia Tools and Applications*, 81(12), 16335–16351. DOI: 10.1007/s11042-022-12496-w

Kumar Shukla, R., & Kumar Tiwari, A. (2021). Comparative analysis of machine learning based approaches for face detection and recognition. *Journal of Information Technology Management*, 13(1), 1–21.

Kumar Shukla, R., Das, D., & Agarwal, A. (2016, March). A novel method for identification and performance improvement of Blurred and Noisy Images using modified facial deblur inference (FADEIN) algorithms. In *2016 IEEE Students' Conference on Electrical, Electronics and Computer Science (SCEECS)* (pp. 1-7). IEEE.

Li, P., & Chen, Y. (2022). Research into an image inpainting algorithm via multilevel attention progression mechanism. *Mathematical Problems in Engineering*, 2022(1), 8508702. DOI: 10.1155/2022/8508702

Li, Y., Guo, K., Lu, Y., & Liu, L. (2021). Cropping and attention based approach for masked face recognition. *Applied Intelligence*, 51(5), 3012–3025. DOI: 10.1007/s10489-020-02100-9 PMID: 34764581

Mahammad, A. B., & Kumar, R. (2023, April). Scalable and security framework to secure and maintain healthcare data using blockchain technology. In *2023 International Conference on Computational Intelligence and Sustainable Engineering Solutions (CISES)* (pp. 417-423). IEEE. DOI: 10.1109/CISES58720.2023.10183494

Misra, N. R., Kumar, S., & Jain, A. (2021, February). A review on E-waste: Fostering the need for green electronics. In *2021 international conference on computing, communication, and intelligent systems (ICCCIS)* (pp. 1032-1036). IEEE.

Mliki, H., Dammak, S., & Fendri, E. (2020). An improved multi-scale face detection using convolutional neural network. *Signal, Image and Video Processing*, 14(7), 1345–1353. DOI: 10.1007/s11760-020-01680-w

Qin, B., & Li, D. (2020). Identifying facemask-wearing condition using image super-resolution with classification network to prevent COVID-19. *Sensors (Basel)*, 20(18), 5236. DOI: 10.3390/s20185236 PMID: 32937867

Sethi, S., Kathuria, M., & Kaushik, T. (2021). Face mask detection using deep learning: An approach to reduce risk of Coronavirus spread. *Journal of Biomedical Informatics*, 120, 103848. DOI: 10.1016/j.jbi.2021.103848 PMID: 34171485

Sharma, N., Chakraborty, C., & Kumar, R. (2023). Optimized multimedia data through computationally intelligent algorithms. *Multimedia Systems*, 29(5), 2961–2977. DOI: 10.1007/s00530-022-00918-6

Shukla, R. K., Prakash, V., & Pandey, S. (2020, December). A perspective on Internet of Things: Challenges & applications. In *2020 9th International Conference System Modeling and Advancement in Research Trends (SMART)* (pp. 184-189). IEEE.

Shukla, R. K., Sengar, A. S., Gupta, A., & Chauhan, N. R. (2022, December). Deep Learning Model to Identify Hide Images using CNN Algorithm. In *2022 11th International Conference on System Modeling & Advancement in Research Trends (SMART)* (pp. 44-51). IEEE. DOI: 10.1109/SMART55829.2022.10047661

Shukla, R. K., Sengar, A. S., Gupta, A., Jain, A., Kumar, A., & Vishnoi, N. K. (2021, December). Face recognition using convolutional neural network in machine learning. In *2021 10th International Conference on System Modeling & Advancement in Research Trends (SMART)* (pp. 456-461). IEEE. DOI: 10.1109/SMART52563.2021.9676308

Shukla, R. K., & Tiwari, A. K. (2020). A Machine Learning Approaches on Face Detection and Recognition. *Solid State Technology*, 63(5), 7619–7627.

Shukla, R. K., & Tiwari, A. K. (2023). Masked face recognition using mobilenet v2 with transfer learning. *Computer Systems Science and Engineering*, 45(1).

Shukla, R. K., Tiwari, A. K., & Jha, A. K. (2023). An Efficient Approach of Face Detection and Prediction of Drowsiness Using SVM. *Mathematical Problems in Engineering*, 2023(1), 2168361. DOI: 10.1155/2023/2168361

Shukla, R. K., Tiwari, A. K., & Ranjan Mishra, A. (2024). Face Recognition Using LBPH and CNN. *Recent Advances in Computer Science and Communications (Formerly: Recent Patents on Computer Science), 17*(5), 48-58.

Singh, V. P., & Srivastava, R. (2018). Automated and effective content-based mammogram retrieval using wavelet based CS-LBP feature and self-organizing map. *Biocybernetics and Biomedical Engineering*, 38(1), 90–105. DOI: 10.1016/j.bbe.2017.09.003

Teke, K., Manjare, A., & Jamdar, S. (2021). Survey on face mask detection using deep learning. *International Journal on Data Science and Machine Learning with Applications*, 1(1), 1–9.

Tiwari, A. K., & Shukla, R. K. (2019, March). Machine learning approaches for face identification feed forward algorithms. In *Proceedings of 2nd International Conference on Advanced Computing and Software Engineering (ICACSE)*. DOI: 10.2139/ssrn.3350264

Tomás, J., Rego, A., Viciano-Tudela, S., & Lloret, J. (2021, August). Incorrect facemask-wearing detection using convolutional neural networks with transfer learning. [). MDPI.]. *Health Care*, 9(8), 1050. PMID: 34442187

Vu, H. N., Nguyen, M. H., & Pham, C. (2022). Masked face recognition with convolutional neural networks and local binary patterns. *Applied Intelligence*, 52(5), 5497–5512. DOI: 10.1007/s10489-021-02728-1 PMID: 34764616

Wang, Z., Huang, B., Wang, G., Yi, P., & Jiang, K. (2023). Masked face recognition dataset and application. *IEEE Transactions on Biometrics, Behavior, and Identity Science*, 5(2), 298–304. DOI: 10.1109/TBIOM.2023.3242085

Xia, R., Chen, Y., & Ren, B. (2022). Improved anti-occlusion object tracking algorithm using Unscented Rauch-Tung-Striebel smoother and kernel correlation filter. *Journal of King Saud University. Computer and Information Sciences*, 34(8), 6008–6018. DOI: 10.1016/j.jksuci.2022.02.004

Zhang, J., Zou, X., Kuang, L. D., Wang, J., Sherratt, R. S., & Yu, X. (2022). CCTSDB 2021: a more comprehensive traffic sign detection benchmark. *Human-centric Computing and Information Sciences, 12*.

Chapter 11

Kinship Verification by Analysing Facial Images to Ensure Human Security

Arkadyuti Mahato
Dr. B.C. Roy Engineering College, India

Sourav Das
Dr. B.C. Roy Engineering College, India

Sumana Kundu
https://orcid.org/0000-0003-0731-8284
Dr. B.C. Roy Engineering College, India

Anandaprova Majumder
https://orcid.org/0000-0003-1676-6206
Dr. B.C. Roy Engineering College, India

ABSTRACT

Kinship verification involves determining the relatedness between individuals by analysing their genetic or phenotypic characteristics or traits. The realm of kinship research has garnered substantial attention particularly in computer vision, with broad applications spanning forensic analysis, genealogy exploration, immigration law and more. This chapter introduces a five-stage methodology for kinship verification through facial images, employing Convolutional Neural Networks (CNNs). The process involves dataset acquisition, preprocessing with FaceNet and Res-Net-50, feature extraction, and CNN model development utilizing Inception Resnet V1 and ResNet-50. The proposed model attains a remarkable accuracy exceeding 85% on a substantial dataset, showcasing its efficacy in identifying kinship relations. Thus,

DOI: 10.4018/979-8-3693-9235-5.ch011

the proposed work contributes to reshaping the methodology for kin verification, enhancing human surveillance through the development of facial image analysis techniques with immense potential for practical applications.

INTRODUCTION

Kinship verification is the procedure of establishing whether two individuals share a biological relationship and, if confirmed, assessing the degree of closeness in their genetic connection. In forensic science, paternity testing, and genealogy research are very common tasks. The methods that can be used to verify the kinship are genetic testing, facial recognition, and anthropological analysis.

One of the most common methods used for kinship verification is genetic testing. This method involves analysing the DNA of both individuals to determine if they share common genetic traits. The degree of relatedness can be estimated based on the number of traits they have in common.

Another method used for kinship verification is facial recognition. This method uses the facial features of two individuals are compared to determine if they share any common traits. It is a method in which photographs or other images of individuals are used for analysis.

The third method used for kinship verification is anthropological analysis. In this method, the physical characteristics of two individuals are used to determine if they share any common traits. This is a method which is used for skeletal remains, as it can provide valuable information about the age, gender, and ancestry of the individuals being studied.

Overall, kinship verification is a complex process that requires a combination of scientific methods and expert analysis to determine the degree of relatedness between two individuals. The selection of a method for kinship verification is contingent upon the particular circumstances of the case, along with the resources and expertise accessible to the researchers engaged in the process.

Significance and Applications of Kinship Verification

Kinship Verification finds diverse applications across crucial domains. Firstly, in immigration, it serves as a pivotal tool to authenticate relationships between sponsors and beneficiaries, thwarting fraudulent entry attempts into a country. Secondly, it aids in cases like locating missing children, resolving child adoption queries, custody disputes, and validating inheritance claims, ensuring clarity on biological or legal ties. Thirdly, its role in medical research is significant, delving into genetic diseases and curbing their transmission across generations. Moreover, within counter-terrorism efforts, it assists in identifying individuals through their kin connections. Additionally, genealogists benefit from Kinship Verification, leveraging it to validate family relationships and bridge gaps within family trees. Overall, Kinship Verification stands as a paramount instrument across various sectors, essential for establishing the veracity of biological or legal connections between individuals.

LITERATURE SURVEY

Kinship Verification is an important aspect to verify family relationships, as siblings inherit similar facial feature to their parents. There have been many works done in kinship verification. Some of the works are discussed below:

One of the initial kinship verification approaches was put forward by Fang et al. (2010). This approach showcased 22 hand crafted (facial) features to find the genetic similarity betwixt parents and their offsprings. Using some of the low-level features namely facial geometry, color, and texture, the K-Nearest Neighbors and SVMs were trained. The peak 14 features were chosen based on the accuracy of classification. From this most of the descriptive portions were found to be around the eyes. Global features were also incorporated in it as the attributes resemble to some of the local parts of the face. The dense SIFT (dSIFT) descriptor was used later by Fang et al. (2013) to verify the kinship.

A two-stream adversarial convolutional network (AdvKin) model was presented by Zhang et al. (2020) in accordance with family ID information. In this method, a self-adversarial strategy was utilized to scale down the divergency in feature distribution.

With the kinship relation information and opposite-gender pairs, Hörmann et al. (2020) proposed a comparator framework.

Neighborhood Repulsed Metric Learning (NRML) is a metric learning framework introduced by Lu et al. (2012), with a subsequent enhancement published by Lu et al. (2013). NRML aims to position samples from the same class (intra-class samples) closely within the feature space while ensuring that samples from different classes (inter-class samples) are spaced as far apart as possible. This strategy is intended to boost the discriminative ability of the learned metric. Unlike earlier metric learning techniques that treat all samples uniformly, NRML incorporates a method to identify and prioritize more informative samples. By concentrating on these crucial samples, NRML seeks to enhance the efficiency and effectiveness of the metric learning process. This targeted focus on informative samples aids in better capturing the intrinsic structure of the data, thereby improving the overall performance of the learned metric.

Liang et al. (2017) used genetic information, which may be less effective when dealing with test pairs that have significant age differences, resulting in a decrease in the accuracy of kinship verification.

Yan et al. (2014) proposed a technique known as discriminative multi-metric learning (DMML). This method aims to harness different features by simultaneously learning multiple distance metrics, thereby utilizing additional complementary information. Unlike NRML, which focuses on directly minimizing intra-class distances and maximizing inter-class distances, DMML aims to maximize the likelihood that each pair of positive samples will have a shorter distance than the most similar negative sample. Moreover, DMML also maximizes the correlation between different features.

Deeper non-linear representations are preferred over linear transformations because the latter tend to be overly simplistic and lack the necessary complexity. In the context of Deep Metric Learning (DML), Discriminative Deep Metric Learning (DDML) utilizes a deep neural network to learn hierarchical, non-linear transformations, which project pairs into a more effective feature space. Lu et al. (2017) describes a deep neural network designed to generate representations of sample pairs, which are processed through the network via non-linear methods.

Another method known as the Kin Mix method was put forward by Song and Yan (2020) to generate positive samples which have a kin relationship in the feature space. The assumption that was made was the linearly combined kinship features yielded an indistinguishable clustering. After this step, auto-encoders were used for kinship verification.

According to Xia et al. (2012), individuals who are placed together in an image are more likely to be related. For example, in a standard family photo, older members typically occupy the central spot, with relatives positioned around them. This research uses spatial information to improve kinship verification by considering factors such as age difference, gender relationships, kinship scores, and relative distance.

Guo et al. (2014) proposed transforming the potential relationships depicted among individuals in a photograph into a set of candidate graphs that represent all conceivable connections. They then evaluated and aggregated the scores for each candidate graph, determining that the graph with the highest score indicates the most probable kinship relationships.

Cai et al. (2012) show some advancement in face recognition, specifically concentrating on face verification and addressing challenges posed by varying conditions like illumination and pose. Traditional methods may be insufficient for handling such diversities. A nonlinear metric learning method is proposed in this paper which utilizes an Independent Subspace Analysis network (ISA). ISA is employed to transform features into a discriminative subspace, mitigating the limitations associated with linear metrics. This method combines metric learning constraints with ISA within a deep architecture. The paper articulates the approach as an optimization problem, incorporating discriminative pre-training and fine-tuning. The evaluation on Labeled Faces in the Wild benchmark illustrates superior performance in contrast to state-of-the-art techniques. The paper was structured to introduce traditional metric learning, elaborate on the suggested process, present experimental results, and conclude.

Li et al. (2020) introduced a graph-based kinship reasoning (GKR) network designed to perform relational reasoning using extracted features. These features are obtained through a convolutional neural network and then constructed into a Kinship Relational Graph. The network utilizes a recursive message passing approach, with the final outcomes being determined by a predefined multilayer perceptron (MLP).

Meta-learning with deep learning techniques has shown promise in tackling extrinsic challenges, such as the inherent imbalance in kinship verification datasets. Typically, a dataset with N pairs of positive samples can generate N(N-1) potential negative pairs, leading to a significant imbalance. Conventional methods often utilize only N negative pairs. To overcome this issue, Li et al. (2021) proposed a Discriminative Sample Meta-Mining (DSMM) approach that uses all possible pairs to extract discriminative information. This method employs a meta-miner that adjusts sample ratios within the training batch using a meta-gradient. The framework involves sampling two training batches with different ratios and conducting sample mining on the training batch, guided by a balanced meta-train batch. The work proposed by Huang et al. (2012) addresses recent progress in face verification, focusing on pairs of images for training, distinguishing matched and mismatched pairs. Unlike traditional setups, it allows recognition of new faces with no identity overlap between training and test sets. Unconstrained face verification poses challenges due to dissimilarity in background, lighting, posture, and occlusions. The Labeled Faces in the Wild (LFW) dataset serves as the benchmark. While existing methods rely on handcrafted descriptors like SIFT and LBP, the paper suggests using deep learning for unsupervised feature learning, capturing higher-order statistics, and adapting to new domains. Novel contributions include local convolutional RBMs and applying deep learning to Local Binary Pattern representation. The findings show comparable accuracy with state-of-the-art techniques, indicating the complementarity of deep learning and handcrafted descriptors for more and improved face verification on LFW.

The study presented by Sun et al. (2014) delivers a comprehensive survey of recent progress in unconstrained face verification, with a particular emphasis on practical applications and the significance of the Labeled Faces in the Wild (LFW) dataset. Commonly employed in notable face verification algorithms are over-complete low-level features and shallow models. The research introduces the utilization of deep Convolutional Neural Networks (ConvNets) for effective feature learning, proposing a distinctive approach that concurrently classifies all identities. This approach yields highly discriminative and compact features, achieving an impressive 97.45% face verification accuracy on LFW, which is nearly on par with human performance. A comparative analysis with existing methods underscores improvements with an increasing number of training identities. The survey also reviews related work, encompassing methods utilizing high-dimensional descriptors and shallow models, as well as exploring deep models like Siamese networks and ConvNets for face verification and identification.

For the first time, Zhang et al. (2015) used a deep learning model. He proposed a convolutional neural network that includes three convolutional layers and one fully connected layer. Based on facial landmarks, the images were trimmed into non-identical patches to utilize the local information. The next step consisted of previously aligned patches which were given as input to the matched sub-models. The sub-models then calculated whether the images have a kin relation or not.

From the above papers, we can see that K-Nearest Neighbor, SVMs, dSIFT(denseSIFT), ConvNets, and Siamese networks were used to find the kin relationship among human beings.

METHODOLOGY

To study the existence of kin relation between human face image pairs, here the kinship system falls into five stages. The five stages are dataset collection, preprocessing, feature extraction, CNN model, and kinship verification.

Dataset Collection

The dataset utilized in this paper, titled "Recognizing Faces in the Wild" and available on Kaggle (https://www.kaggle.com/competitions/recognizing-faces-in-the-wild), is derived from the Families in the Wild (FIW) dataset. The FIW dataset comprises approximately 11,932 natural family photos featuring 1,000 families. Within this dataset, there are 656,954 image pairs representing 11 distinct relationships, such as Father-Son (FS), Father-Daughter (FD), Mother-Son (MS), and Mother-Daughter (MD). This dataset significantly surpasses the size of the second-largest Kin-Wild II, which contains only 2,000 pairs for four kinship types. Notably, FIW stands as the largest and most comprehensive image database for automatic kinship recognition. Importantly, FIW's data is sourced from publicly available images of celebrities.

Preprocessing

In this stage, the images are split into training and testing data. The number of images for training is 12,379 and for testing is 6282. The dataset has a CSV file that shows the actual relationships in the training dataset. The training dataset is split into training and validation datasets. We are using FaceNet and ResNet50.

As FaceNet uses the GoogLeNet which uses the Inception module, it is also called the Inception network. For the inception module, the images are preprocessed using a function that resizes the image to a size of 160x160. The pixel values of images are converted to an array of floats.

The pre-whitening technique plays a crucial role in image processing and computer vision. In this approach, the input data is normalized by subtracting the mean and dividing by the standard deviation. The method intelligently adapts to the dimensions of the input. Specifically, when the dimension is 4, implying a batch of 3D images, the algorithm calculates the mean and standard deviation along axes (1, 2, 3). In cases where the dimension is 3, indicating a single 3D image, the mean, and standard deviation are computed along axes (0, 1, 2). However, if the dimension is neither 3 nor 4, the function raises a Value Error.

Upon determining the appropriate axes for mean and standard deviation calculations, the code proceeds to compute these values. The standard deviation is then obtained by taking the element-wise maximum of the calculated standard deviation and a small value($1.0/np.sqrt(size)$) to prevent division by zero. Here, 'size' represents the totalnumber of elements in one image or one image within a batch. Finally, the prewhiteneddata is derivedby subtracting the mean and dividing by the adjusted standard deviation. Figure 1 provides a visual representation of the process.

Figure 1. An example of preprocessing image using pre-whiten function

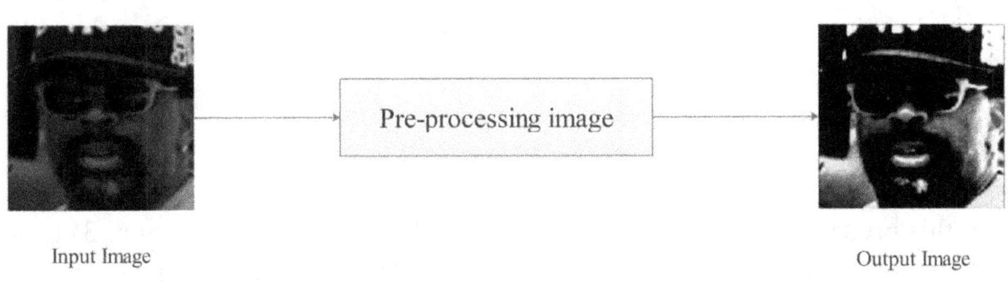

For the ResNet-50 preprocess_input function is used for preprocessing the images. The images are resized to a size of 224x224. The pixel values of images are converted to an array of floats.

In this, the function starts to subtract channel-wise mean values from the input image data. Here we used version 2 so, for the first channel, the function reverses the order of color channels and then subtracts specific mean values from each channel. For the last channel, it reverses the order of color channels and then subtracts mean values from each channel. An example is shown in Figure 2.

Figure 2. An example of preprocessing an image using preprocess_input

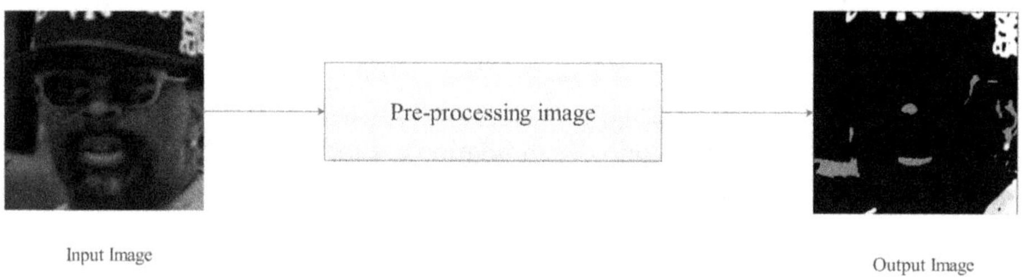

Feature Extraction

In this procedure, FaceNet, a deep convolutional neural network, is employed to generate a mapping or embedding from pairs of facial images to a 128-dimensional Euclidean space. Subsequently, the similarity between two facial images is determined by calculating the square of the Euclidean distance between the corresponding normalized vectors within the 128-dimensional space. The FaceNet system adopts a triplet loss function as its cost function and introduces a novel method for online triplet mining.

CNN Model

In this process a Convolution Neural Network model (Refer to Figure 3) is prepared to perform the kinship verification. We used transfer learning using FaceNet.

The Triplet Loss function employed in FaceNet serves to minimize the separation between an anchor and a positive, representing images of the same individual, while concurrently maximizing the distance between the anchor and a negative sample from a distinct identity.

Two models are Inception Resnet V1 and ResNet-50.

The model (inception_resnet_v1) has two input layers (input_2, input_3) each of 160x160 with 3 colored channels.

The two outputs are taken input in two Reshape layers (reshape_2, reshape_1) respectively. The output of Reshape layers is 1,1,128. Then, max pooling layer (global_max_pooling2d_2) and average pooling layer (global_average_pooling2d_2) are added which does max pooling and average pooling for output of reshape layer (reshape_2). Again, max pooling layer (global_max_pooling2d_1) and average pooling layer (global_average_pooling2d_1) are added which does max pooling and average pooling for the other output of reshape layer (reshape_1). The max pooling layer selects the highest values, while the average pooling layer computes the average of the values.

Then after this step two concatenate layers (concatenate_2 is added for global_max_pooling2d_2 and global_average_pooling2d_2) and (concatenate_1 is added for global_max_pooling2d_1 and global_average_pooling2d_1) are used to concatenate the average pooling and max pooling layers.

A subtract layer (subtract_3) is added which subtracts the output values of concatenated layers (concatenate_2, concatenate_1). A multiply layer (multiply_1) is added multiplies the outputs of the two concatenated layers (concatenate_2, concatenate_1). An add layer (add_17) performs addition of the outputs of the two concatenated layers (concatenate_2, concatenate_1). A lambda layer (lambda_2) is added which takes input as one of outputs of concatenate layers (concatenate_2), and here a function is used which makes sure the square root is positive and accounts for small numerical issues when small values are found. Another subtract layer (subtract_1) is added which subtracts the output values of concatenate layers (concatenate_2, concatenate_1). Another lambda layer (lambda_1) is added which takes input as the other output of concatenate layer (concatenate_1), and the same function is used which was used in the first lambda layer.

Figure 3. CNN model architecture of the developed system

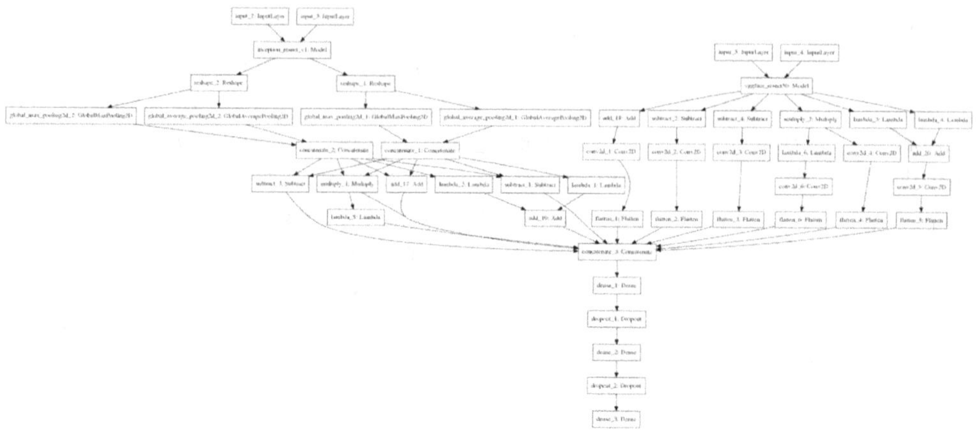

Next a lambda layer (lambda_5) is added which takes input as the output of the multiply layer(multiply_1), and the same function is used which was used in the first lambda layer to make sure the square root is positive. An add layer (add_19) per-forms addition of the outputs of the two lambda layers (lambda_2, lambda_1).

The ResNet-50 model was modified by excluding the fully connected layer at the end, and additional layers were incorporated instead.

The ResNet-50 takes two input layers (input_5, input_4) each of 224x224 pixels with 3 colored channels. An add layer (add_18) takes the outputs of the ResNet-50 model(vggface_resnet50) and performs addition. A subtract layer (subtract_2) takes the outputs of the ResNet-50 model (vggface_resnet50) and performs subtraction operation. Another, subtract layer (subtract_4) is included which takes the outputs of theResNet-50 model (vggface_resnet50) and performs subtraction. A multiply layer(multiply_2) is added which multiplies the output of the ResNet-50 model (vggface_resnet50). Two lambda layers are included (lambda_3, lambda_4) which takes input each of the output of the ResNet-50 model (vggface_resnet50), and a function is used which is used so as to make sure the square root is positive and accounts for small numerical issues when small values are found.

Three Conv2D layers (conv2d_1, conv2d_2, conv2d_3) are added to the neural network which takes the output of add layer (add_18), subtract layer (subtract_2) and subtract layer (subtract_4) respectively and applies a convolution operation with 128filters and a 1x1 kernel to the input. The purpose of this layer might be to perform channel-wise transformations or reduce/increase the number of channels in the data. A lambda layer (lambda_6) is added which takes the output of the multiply layer(multiply_2) as input and the same function is used which was used in previous lambda layer makes sure the square root is positive and accounts for small numerical issues when small values are found. Another Conv2D layer (conv2d_4) is added which takes the output of the multiply layer (multiply_2) as input and applies a convolution operation with 128 filters and a 1x1 kernel to the input. An add layer (add_20) is added which performs addition using the two lambda layers (lambda_3, lambda_4).

An additional Conv2D layer, named conv2d_6, has been introduced in the architecture. This layer processes the output from the lambda layer (lambda_6) by applying a convolution operation with 128 filters and a 1x1 kernel to the input. Furthermore, another Conv2D layer, denoted as conv2d_5, has been incorporated, which takes the output from the add layer (add_20) and performs a convolution operation with 128filters and a 1x1 kernel on the input.

In the subsequent stage, six flatten layers, namely flatten_1, flatten_2, flatten_3, flatten_4, flatten_5, and flatten_6, are incorporated into the architecture. Each of these flatten layers is designed to process the output of the corresponding Conv2D layers (conv2d_1, conv2d_2, conv2d_3, conv2d_4, conv2d_5, conv2d_6). This operation serves to compress the spatial dimensions of the input data, collapsing them into the channel dimension.

In the subsequent stage, a concatenate layer, denoted as concatenate_3, is introduced. This layer performs the concatenation operation on the six distinct outputs: subtract layer (subtract_3), lambda layer (lambda_5), multiply layer (multiply_1), add layer(add_17), add layer (add_19), and subtract layer (subtract_1) originating from the left segment as illustrated in the figure. Additionally, concatenate_3 incorporates the outputs from the six flatten layers, namely flatten_1, flatten_2, flatten_3, flatten_4, flatten_5, and flatten_6, portrayed in the diagram. This strategic concatenation ensures that the model captures and combines relevant information from both the subtract, lambda, multiply, add, and subtract operations, as well as the flattened representations, contributing to the overall learning process.

Incorporated within the neural network architecture is a dense layer denoted as"dense_1." This layer operates as a fully connected layer, accepting the output from the preceding concatenate layer, identified as "concatenate_3," as its input. With a configuration of 100 neurons, each node within the dense layer establishes connections with every node in the layer preceding it. The activation function employed in this dense layer is the Rectified Linear Unit (ReLU), a widely utilized non-linear activation function in neural networks. Specifically, ReLU applies the mathematical function $f(x) = max(0, x)$ elementwise to the output of the dense layer. This activationfunction proves effective in introducing non-linearity to the network, facilitating the acquisition of intricate patterns and relationships within the dataset.

A dropout layer, denoted as dropout_1, has been incorporated into the neural network. This layer accepts the output from the dense layer (dense_1) as its input and serves the purpose of mitigating overfitting. During training, the dropout layer selectively zeros out certain input units in a random manner, acting as a preventative measure against the co-adaptation of hidden units. This strategy contributes to enhancing the generalization capability of the neural network.

Another dense layer (dense_2) is added which takes the output of the dropout layer(dropout_1) as input. This dense layer has 25 neurons and each neuron in the layer is connected to every neuron in the previous layer. The activation function is the Rectified Linear Unit (ReLU) activation function.

Another dropout layer (dropout_2) is added in the neural network, which takes the output of the dense layer (dense_2) as input and the dropout layer is used to prevent overfitting. This layer randomly sets some of the input units to zero during training, which helps prevent the co-adaptation of hidden units.

The final step in the kinship verification process involves adding an output layer, which takes the output of the dropout layer (drop-out_2) as its input. This output layer, denoted asdense_3, is configured with a single output unit and utilizes the sigmoid activation function. It is employed to squash the output values between 0 and 1, rendering it well-suited for binary decision-making. Figure 4 visually represents the outlined steps in kinship verification.

Figure 4. Block diagram of the proposed kinship verification system

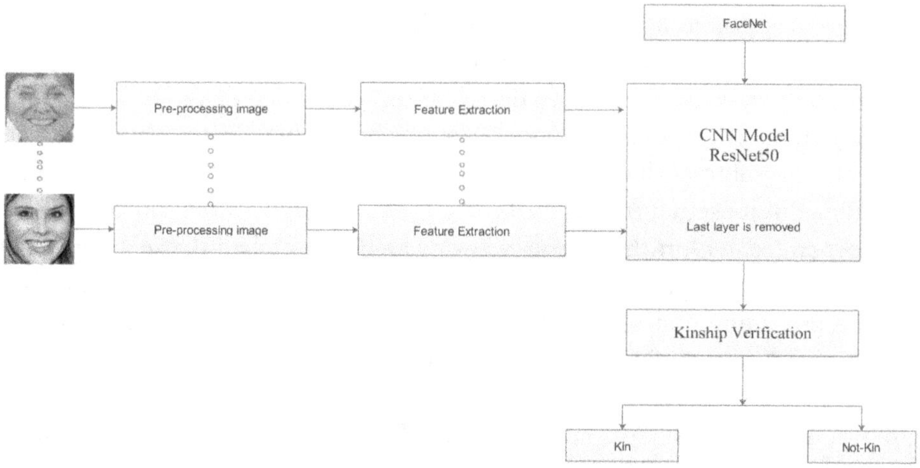

Kinship Verification

During this stage, the model is presented with test images to discern kinship relations between pairs of face images. It outputs a percentage indicating the degree of relatedness between each image and others in the dataset. Higher percentage values suggest a kinship relationship, such as father-son, father-daughter, mother-son, mother-daughter, and so forth. Conversely, lower percentage values indicate the absence of a kinship connection between the images. The threshold value is taken as 0.8.

RESULTS AND ANALYSIS

The dataset is split into training and testing data. For about, 12,379 images are kept for training and 6282 images are kept for testing.

The model accuracy is analysed through a graph given in Figure 5:

As we can see around epoch 35-50 the model achieved its highest accuracy. The accuracy shows how good a model can predict for a particular example.

Figure 5. Accuracy of the model

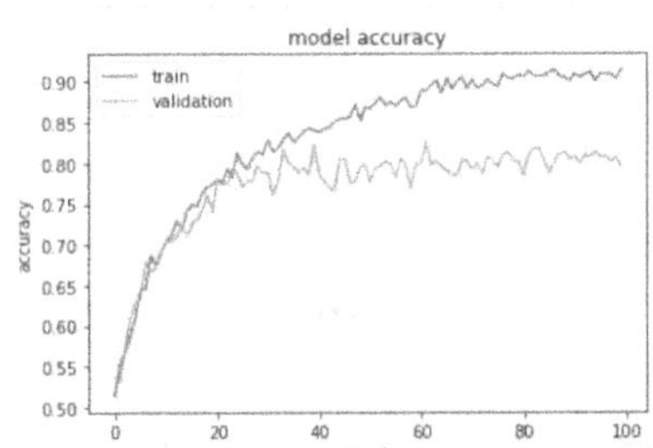

The loss of model in analysed through the graph of Figure 6, shows how bad a model can perform for a particular example. It can be clearly seen that around epoch 35 the model achieved its lowest loss.

Figure 6. Loss of the model

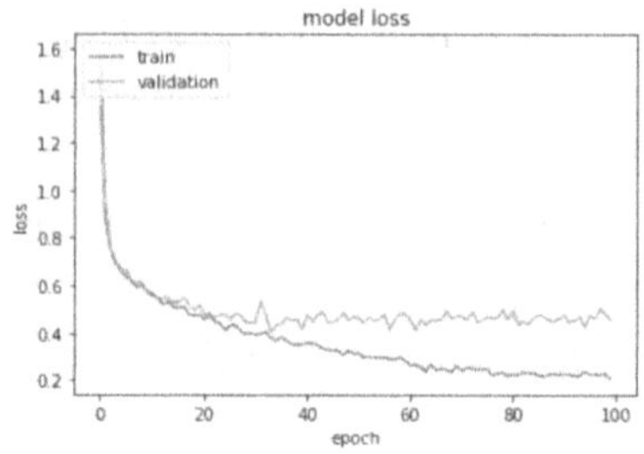

Some of the metrics which were used to evaluate our model is given below:

$$\text{Accuracy} = \frac{\text{TP} + \text{TN}}{\text{TP} + \text{TN} + \text{FP} + \text{FN}} \tag{1}$$

$$\text{Precision} = \frac{\text{TP}}{\text{TP} + \text{FP}} \tag{2}$$

$$\text{Recall} = \frac{\text{TP}}{\text{TP} + \text{FN}} \tag{3}$$

$$\text{F1 Score} = \frac{2 * \text{Precision} * \text{Recall}}{\text{Precision} + \text{Recall}} \tag{4}$$

where TP, TN, FP, and FN denote the true positive, true negative, false positive, and false negative, respectively.

In the realm of predictive analysis, a positive prediction aligning with a positive actual value signifies a True Positive (TP) scenario. Conversely, when a positive prediction is juxtaposed with a negative actual value, it results in a False Positive (FP). True Negative (TN) occurrences arise when both the prediction and actual value are negative. On the other hand, instances of False Negative (FN) occur when the prediction is negative, but the actual value is positive.

The accuracy, precision, recall, and F1-score on the test data are shown in Table1:

Table 1. Accuracy, precision, recall, and f1-score

Accuracy	**Precision**	**Recall**	**F1 Score**
0.854	0.903	0.892	0.897

Figure 7 shows the comparison of the accuracy of the method used to some of the other related works done in this field.

Figure 7. Comparison of few other models to our model

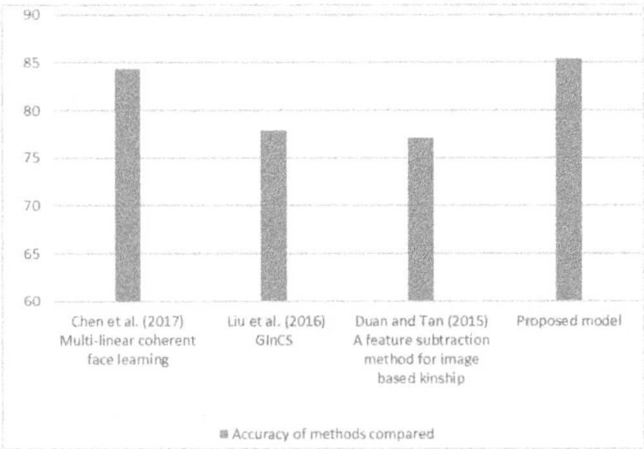

In the proposed model the output is given in a CSV file which shows how much every image is related to the other images which is shown by the similarity values. The similarity values are a very important aspect of determining a kinship relation between two image pairs in this model. The threshold value is taken as 0.80, the image pairs with values above 0.80 are considered to have kinship relation, and the image pairs with values below 0.80 are considered as no kinship relation.

Some of the images with the highest facial similarity are as follows (Refer to Figure 8 and Figure 9):

Figure 8. Example of father-daughter relation with highest kinship score

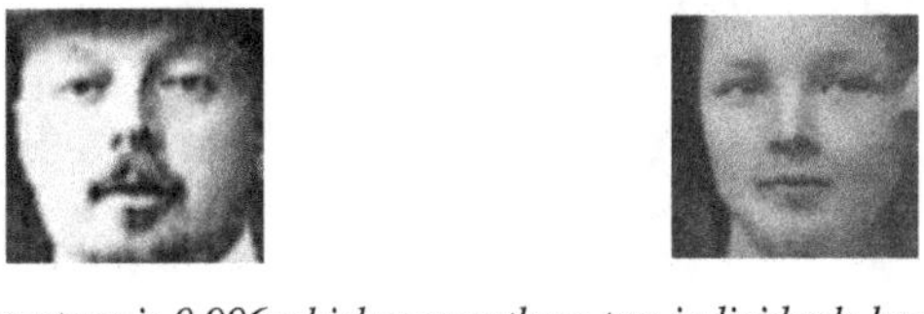

Note: The similarity percentage is 0.996 which means these two individuals have kinship relations.

Figure 9. Example of siblings with the highest kinship score

Note: Similarity percentage: 0.997 which means these two individuals have kinship relation

CONCLUSION AND FUTURE SCOPE

The field of kinship verification is a captivating area of research, marked by various challenges that pose significant threats to its accuracy. Factors like illumination and pose limitations can profoundly impact the verification process. This developed system has three main concepts such as preprocessing of the images, and feature extraction process in the model we used FaceNet which is a neural network-based system that uses deep learning algorithms to recognize faces. Here convolutional neural network (CNN) is used to find the facial features in the Euclidean distances which corresponds to measuring the facial similarity. With these two models, Inception Resnet V1 and ResNet-50, the fully connected layer is not included in ResNet-50, instead we add some more layers to it. Overall, kinship verification is a complex process that requires a combination of scientific methods and expert analysis to determine the degree of relatedness between two individuals. The selection of a method for kinship verification is contingent upon the particular circumstances of the case, along with the resources and expertise accessible to the researchers engaged in the process.

REFERENCES

Cai, X., Wang, C., Xiao, B., Chen, X., & Zhou, J. (2012). Deep nonlinear metric learning within dependentsubspace analysis for face verification. *Proceedings of the20th ACM International Conference on Multimedia, ACM*, 749–752. DOI: 10.1145/2393347.2396303

Chen, X., An, L., Yang, S., & Wu, W. (2017). Kinship verification in multi-linear coherent spaces. *Multimedia Tools and Applications*, 76(3), 4105–4122. DOI: 10.1007/s11042-015-2930-9

Duan, X., Tan -H. Z. (2015). A feature subtraction method for image-based kinship verificationunder uncontrolled environments.*2015 IEEE International Conference on Image Processing (ICIP)*,1573–1577. DOI: 10.1109/ICIP.2015.7351065

Fang, R., Gallagher, C. A., Chen, T., & Loui, A. (2013), Kinship classification by modeling facialfeature heredity.*IEEE International Conference on Image Processing*, 2983–2987. DOI: 10.1109/ICIP.2013.6738614

Fang, R., Tang, D. K., Snavely, N., & Chen, T. (2010). Towards computational models of kinshipVerification.*IEEE International Conference on Image Processing*,1577–1580. DOI: 10.1109/ICIP.2010.5652590

Guo, Y., Dibeklioglu, H., & Van der Maaten, L. (2014). Graph-based kinship recognition. *2014 22nd International Conference on Pattern Recognition, IEEE*.DOI: 10.1109/ICPR.2014.735

Hörmann, S., Knoche, M., & Rigoll, G. (2020). A multi-task comparator framework for kinship verification.*15th IEEE International Conference on Automatic Face and GestureRecognition(FG 2020)*, 863–867. DOI: 10.1109/FG47880.2020.00106

Huang, G. B., Lee, H., & Learned-Miller, E. (2012, June). Learning hierarchical representations for face verification with convolutional deep belief networks. In 2012 IEEE conference on computer vision and pattern recognition (pp. 2518-2525). IEEE.

Li, W., Wang, S., Lu, J., Feng, J., & Zhou, J. (2021). Meta-mining discriminative samples for kinship verification. *2021 IEEE/CVF Conference on Computer Vision and Pattern Recognition (CVPR)*.DOI: 10.1109/CVPR46437.2021.01587

Li, W., Zhang, Y., Lv, K., Lu, J., Feng, J., & Zhou, J. (2020). Graph-based kinship reasoning network. *(2020)IEEE International Conference on Multimedia and Expo (ICME)*. DOI: 10.1109/ICME46284.2020.9102823

Liang, J., Guo, J., Lao, S., & Li, J. (2017). Using deep relational features to verify kinship.*CCF Chinese Conference on Computer Vision*.DOI: 10.1007/978-981-10-7299-4_47

Liu, Q., Puthenputhussery, A., & Liu, C. (2016). A novel inheritable color space with application tokinship verification.*2016 IEEE Winter Conference on Applications of Computer Vision (WACV)*, 1–9. DOI: 10.1109/WACV.2016.7477667

Lu, J., Hu, J., & Tan, Y.-P. (2017). Discriminative deep metric learning for face and kinship verification. *IEEE Transactions on Image Processing*, 26(9), 4269–4282. Advance online publication. DOI: 10.1109/TIP.2017.2717505 PMID: 28644806

Lu, J., Hu, J., Zhou, X., Shang, Y., Tan, Y.-P., & Wang, G. (2012). Neighborhood repulsed metric learning for kinship verification.*IEEE Conference on Computer Vision and Pattern Recognition*. DOI: 10.1109/CVPR.2012.6247978

Lu, J., Zhou, X., Tan, Y.-P., Shang, Y., & Zhou, J. (2013). Neighborhood repulsed metric learning for kinship verification. *IEEE Transactions on Pattern Analysis and Machine Intelligence*, 36(2), 331–345. Advance online publication. DOI: 10.1109/TPAMI.2013.134 PMID: 24356353

Song, C., & Yan, H. (2020).Kinmix: A data augmentation approach for kinship verification. *IEEE International Conference on Multimedia and Expo (ICME)*, 1–6. DOI: 10.1109/ICME46284.2020.9102891

Sun, Y., Wang, X., & Tang, X. (2014). Deep learning face representation from predicting10,000 classes.*Proceedings of the IEEE Conference on Computer Vision and Pattern Recognition*, 1891–1898.DOI: 10.1109/CVPR.2014.244

Xia, S., Shao, M., Luo, J., & Fu, Y. (2012). Understanding kin relationships in a photo. *IEEE Transactions on Multimedia*, 14(4), 1046–1056. Advance online publication. DOI: 10.1109/TMM.2012.2187436

Yan, H., Lu, J., Deng, W., & Zhou, X. (2014). Discriminative multimetric learning for kinship verification. *IEEE Transactions on Information Forensics and Security*, 9(7), 1169–1178. Advance online publication. DOI: 10.1109/TIFS.2014.2327757

Zhang, K., Huang, Y., & Song, C., WuH., WangL. (2015). Kinship verification with deep convolutionalneural networks.*British Machine Vision Conference 2015*. DOI: 10.5244/C.29.148

Zhang, L., Duan, Q., Zhang, D., Jia, W., & Wang, X. (2020). Advkin: Adversarial convolutionalnetworkfor kinship verification. *IEEE Transactions on Cybernetics*. Advance online publication. DOI: 10.1109/TCYB.2019.2959403 PMID: 31945005

Chapter 12
Exploring the Social Model of Smart Home Devices:
An In-Depth Analysis of Social Impact and Security Issues

Adyan Rauf
School of Computer Engineering, KIIT (Deemed to Be) University, Bhubaneswar, India

Abhishek Guru
https://orcid.org/0000-0002-2479-6424
Koneru Lakshmaiah Education Foundation, India

Hitesh Mohapatra
https://orcid.org/0000-0001-8100-4860
School of Computer Engineering, KIIT (Deemed to Be) University, Bhubaneswar, India

ABSTRACT

The field of exploring social models of smart home appliances aims to understand how these technologies interact with mobility and security issues, highlighting their broader social implications. This research has emerged due to the ubiquity of smart home devices and the need to comprehend their social impact. It focuses on the interplay between technology and its effects on equity and privacy concerns, aiming to develop policies that prioritize users over technology providers, while ensuring the protection of both smart home technologies and user privacy. The main challenge is understanding the integrated social safety functionality of these

DOI: 10.4018/979-8-3693-9235-5.ch012

appliances. By examining the relationships between different countries, the research seeks to address differences through an approach that includes cultural norms, technological infrastructure, legal expertise, and user education. This anticipates a shift in smart home research towards a holistic approach, considering complex interactions. The goal is to provide insights for developing flexible and socially responsive smart home technologies.

1. INTRODUCTION

The integration of Smart Home Devices (SHDs) has permeated throughout the modern household, prompting an era transformation that has irrevocably altered the framework of domestic living, (Khan, Salah, & Al-Fuqaha, 2018). Figure 1 represents a smart home environment. With smart thermostats, security devices, and lighting systems now commonplace in residences throughout the country, the complex implications that these technologies have for societal dynamics have increasingly attracted the public's interest. This paper is designed to investigate the complex interplay of the social impact of SHDs and the resultant rise in security concerns. It is undeniable that SHDs promise a vastly improved quality of life, increased accessibility and environmental sustainability, (Jin *et al.,* 2014). However, the unprecedented level of connectivity they bring directly contradicts this infinite improvement in that it raises crucial questions about user privacy and data security .For example, consider recent studies that specifically highlight instances of privacy invasion unauthorized access and potential vulnerabilities within the specific IoT ecosystem – all of which demand a detailed analysis of the double-edged sword that is SHDs, (Atami & Al-Namanny, 2021). When we talk about changes, not just simple ones, they bring more than just ease. Getting SHDs into our homes can change the way families work. They bring new ways to talk to each other and get along. Helpful tech tools also aim to welcome everyone. They help make home a place for people with many needs. But it goes beyond that. Smart home upgrades save resources. This means less energy use and a smaller footprint on our Earth, (Dillahunt, Mankoff, & Paulos, 2019). As these devices steadily work their way into the fabric of everyday lives — for both individual users and families — it's critical to understand both the broader societal implications and the potential risks. Drawing insights from recent literature, as well as from conducting a case study or two, and synthesizing user perceptions, this research is intended to offer a comprehensive and timely snapshot of the rapidly shifting landscape for these devices.

In addressing the convergence of their social impact and security implications, the findings have significant relevance for both end-user constituencies and a broader ecosystem of policymakers and industry stakeholders. As smart home technologies continue a trajectory of rapid evolution, the study aims to contribute to contemporary dialogue about responsible innovation, suggesting the need for careful consideration and informed decision-making as the marketplace for smart home technologies continues to morph and expand. As these devices continue to work their way into the fabric of everyday life — for individual users and families — it is important to understand the broader social implications and potential risks Insights from recent literature, developing one or two cases and consolidating user perspectives aimed to providing a timely picture of the convergence of their social impact and identified safety outcomes is increasingly important for companies both end-users and the broader ecosystem of policy makers and business stakeholders ñ It also illustrates the importance of critical thinking and decision-making with a continuously expanding knowledge age. To look at the complexities of the social model of smart home devices, this paper will examine the multiple ways in which those technologies influence social interactions across families and communities. At the same time, it will scrutinize the capacity vulnerabilities and security challenges of smart home systems, highlighting those that are critical to a robust cybersecurity strategy.

Figure 1. A smart home environment and its services

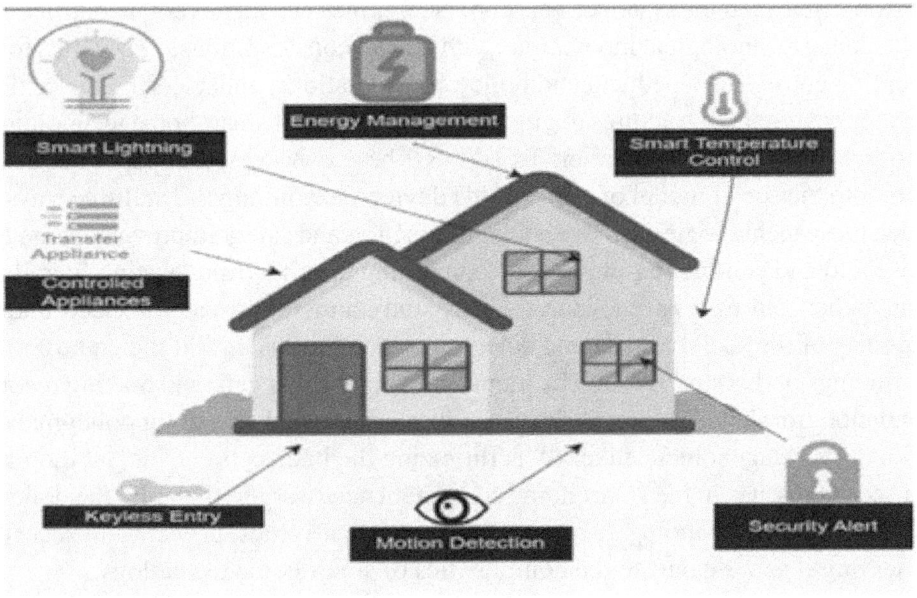

To navigate the complexities of the Social Model of Smart Home Devices, this paper will delve into the multifaceted methods in which those technologies affect social interactions inside families and broader communities. Simultaneously, it's going to scrutinize the capability vulnerabilities and safety challenges inherent in clever home systems, emphasizing the vital for robust cybersecurity measures. The overarching aim is to contribute to an extra informed and responsible integration of clever home devices into our daily lives. To support this analysis, a comprehensive review of existing literature on smart home technologies, social implications, and cybersecurity will be conducted. By synthesizing insights from scholarly works, industry experts, and policy documents, this paper aims to present a thorough overview of the current landscape, identify knowledge gaps, and propose recommendations for a secure and socially responsible evolution of smart home ecosystems. As we embark on this exploration, it is essential to recognize the delicate balance between technological innovation and the preservation of societal values, privacy, and security in the ever-expanding realm of smart homes, (Lee *et al.,* 2019). While security vulnerabilities are well-documented there is limited research on the social dimensions of security issues. A study highlighted that perceived security risks can lead to distrust among users, affecting their willingness to adopt and integrate smart home devices into their daily lives. Ethical decision-making and policy have become an important part of the discussion regarding smart home technology. The European Union Cybersecurity Agency provides important guidance on smart buildings and network security, emphasizing the importance of developing and implementing responsible management systems. This underscores the need for governance structures that balance technological innovations with ethical considerations. This points to an emerging consensus on ethical and policy considerations, underscoring the critical need for governance structures to guide the deployment of smart home technologies in a socially responsible manner. To address these concerns, this paper begins to delve into the social model of smart home devices, examining the multiple ways in which these technologies achieve social interaction and safety improvements in the household and community impact. By combining insights from existing literature, case studies and user psychoanalysis, this study aims to provide nuanced understandings of the social impact and safety of a SHD brings with it the end users of the findings of this study as well by identifying knowledge gaps and making recommendations for shared responsibility in terms of important benefits for policymakers and industry stakeholders alike. By scrutinizing the intersection of social mobility and security issues in the smart home ecosystem necessary to maintain the delicate balance between technological innovation and social values, privacy and security, preserving it as we navigate the complexities of smart home technology.

2. LITERATURE REVIEW

The growth of smart home devices in recent years has changed the way people interact with their living spaces. From voice assistants to connected devices, these devices deliver convenience, productivity, and connectivity. However, their widespread adoption has raised concerns about their social and security impacts. This literature review aims to provide a better understanding of social patterns in smart home devices, focusing on their impact on personal relationships, privacy, and security. The integration of smart home devices has a great impact on social life at home. Research shows that these tools can impact family and communication patterns. Traditionally, families operate within established roles and hierarchies, assigning specific responsibilities to each member. However, the introduction of technology can affect these changes by dividing labor and changing the power structure. Smith's qualitative research explores the impact of smart home devices on family life, showing changes in interactions and discussions of new roles. The findings show that while smart devices provide convenience and functionality, they can lead to conflicts between management and decision-making processes in the home. For example, disputes may arise over who has the right to adjust the temperature or control smart equipment, affecting the design process and operation, (Smith, 2019). Also, some studies shed light on users' perceptions of privacy and social interaction in smart homes. This study investigates how people deal with privacy issues and establish boundaries in the smart home environment. Participants expressed concerns about the potential privacy implications of constant monitoring and data collection with smart devices. Research continues to explore how smart home technology affects relationships at home. Although some participants reported increased convenience and connection, others expressed concerns about the impact of face-to-face communication and reliance on communication through the use of technology. These findings highlight the need to understand user behavior and attitudes to address issues of privacy violations and foster better relationships within households, (Johnson *et al.*, 2020). The widespread use of smart home devices has created significant security problems as well as social impacts. Various studies provide a comprehensive review of security issues on the Internet of Things (IoT), focusing on smart home devices. Studies have revealed vulnerabilities in authentication tools and data encryption and highlighted risks associated with unsecured IoT deployments. One of the main security issues in the smart home environment is the risk of unauthorized access and data leakage. Smart devices often collect sensitive information about users' behavior, preferences and routines, making them an attractive target for criminals. Without adequate security measures, these devices can become entry points for cyber-attacks, cause privacy breaches, and harm users. That day, Zhang conducted a systematic review of vulnerability assessment in smart home devices. The research identified a number of security vulnerabilities, including weak authentication systems, insecure communication systems and lack of timely software updates. These vulnerabilities pose a significant risk to the security and privacy of the smart home ecosystem, revealing the need for security measures and business models, (Zhang *et al.*, 2021). Figure 2 shows smart devices that may possess harm.

Figure 2. Smart devices that may pose harm

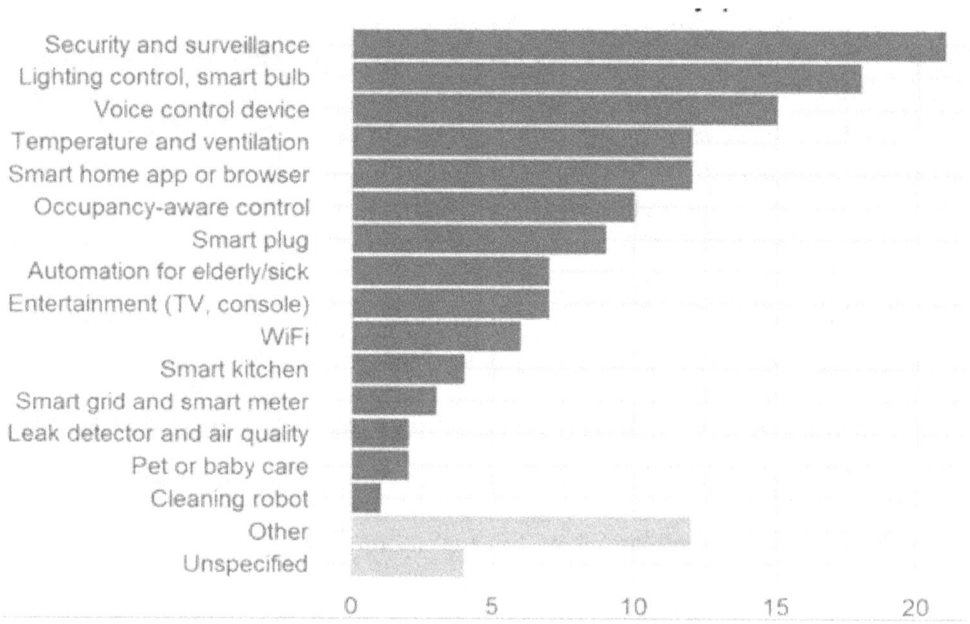

Regarding security issues associated with smart home devices, the National Institute of Standards and Technology (NIST) has issued a Special Notice 800-213 (2020) providing guidance. The document provides security guidance for IoT manufacturers and highlights best practices for improving the security of smart devices and protecting user data. NIST recommendations include using strong authentication tools, encrypting sensitive data at rest and in transit, and regularly updating device firmware to fix bad situations. Additionally, the guide emphasizes the importance of integrating security into the smart home design and development process, rather than treating it as an afterthought. Manufacturers can improve the overall security of smart home devices by following these best practices. building materials and mitigating risks associated with inaccessibility and data leakage. Additionally, it is crucial that collaboration between industry stakeholders, policymakers, and cybersecurity experts continues to combat emerging threats and actions to ensure the long-term security and privacy of the smart home ecosystem. AS smart home technology continues to develop, balancing the social benefits provided by this device and using security measures becomes important. Although smart devices offer convenience, efficiency and connectivity at home, they also pose risks to privacy and security. An effective risk management plan should consider both social and technological aspects of the smart home environment. This requires a collaborative effort between researchers, designers, policy makers, and end users to identify risks, develop mitigation strategies, and promote the use of responsibility. Additionally, building digital awareness and raising awareness of privacy and security issues is important to help users make informed decisions about using home technology. Individuals can improve the complexity of the digital environment and reduce risk by providing education and resources on best practices for protecting smart devices and personal data. Figure 3 tells us various security risks and mitigation approaches. Understanding these cultural nuances is essential for designing inclusive smart home IoT technologies that account for diverse societal values and preferences. While existing research has identified security vulnerabilities in smart home IoT devices, there is a research gap concerning the dynamic nature of emerging security challenges and the adaptive responses required. As technology evolves, new threats may emerge, requiring constant vigilance and proactive strategies to safeguard user data and privacy. Future research should focus on anticipating and addressing emerging security challenges in the rapidly evolving landscape of smart home IoT technology. This includes studying novel cyber threats, evaluating the effectiveness of existing security measures, and proposing adaptive strategies to mitigate evolving risks. By staying ahead of potential security threats, researchers can contribute to the ongoing development of secure smart home IoT ecosystems, (Zhang *et al.,* 2021). Existing research often addresses various aspects of social structure without comprehensive research. For example, while research discusses privacy concerns, not all social impacts, such as changes in relationships, family relationships, or social cohesion, are still adequate. Understanding the entire social structure requires comprehensive research, including the transformation of culture through technology and smart home devices.

Figure 3. Security risks and mitigation approaches are pointed to an actual smart home environment

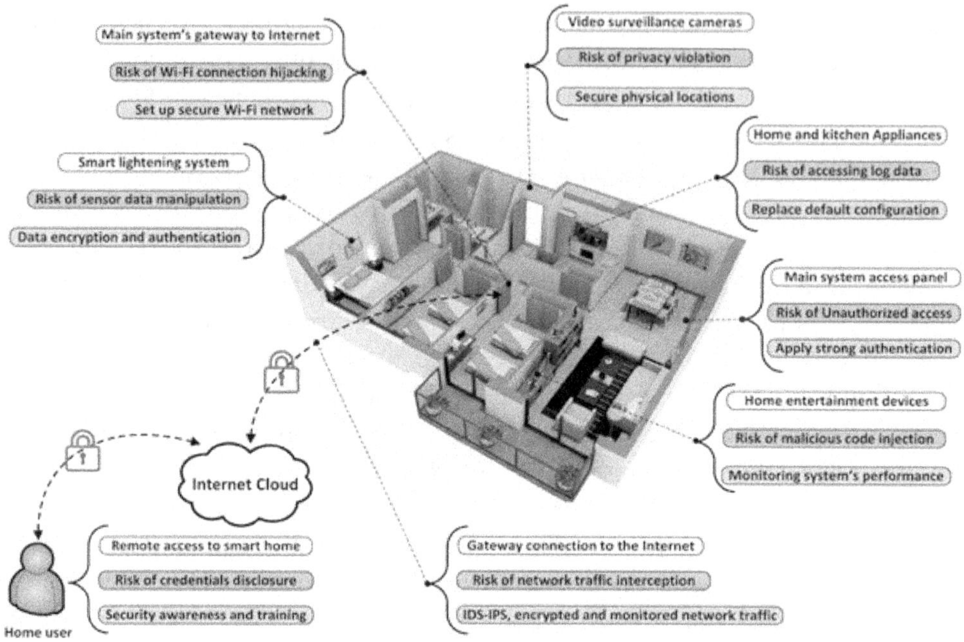

Ethical decision-making and policy have become an important part of the discussion regarding smart home technology. The European Union Cybersecurity Agency provides important guidance on smart buildings and network security, emphasizing the importance of developing and implementing responsible management systems. This underscores the need for governance structures that balance technological innovations with ethical considerations. This points to an emerging consensus on ethical and policy considerations, underscoring the critical need for governance structures to guide the deployment of smart home technologies in a socially responsible manner. In summary, this literature review provides insight into various examples of social models in smart home devices, highlighting their advantages and disadvantages. Understanding user perceptions, addressing vulnerabilities, and following helpful guidelines are important steps to creating a safer and more responsible environment in the smart home. In synthesizing these different strands of writing, it becomes apparent that the investigation of the social demonstration of keen domestic gadgets requires an intrigue approach. The interconnecting of societal, innovative, and approach measurements requires an all-encompassing understanding to educate the continuous improvement, arrangement, and utilize of savvy domestic gadgets. As we set out on our investigate travel, we look for to construct upon this existing establishment, contributing to a nuanced comprehension of the all-encompassing effect of savvy domestic innovations on clients and society at huge. Table 1 shows various research papers and their focus and missing aspects.

Table 1. Research paper focus and missing aspects

Research Paper	Focus	Methodology	Missing Aspects
Acquisti et al. (2014)	Privacy concerns	Qualitative analysis	Limited exploration of the broader societal implications.
Pitt & Sassatelli (2002)	Domestication of media and technology	Ethnographic research	Insufficient attention to the technological security aspects.
Checkoway et al. (2011)	Cybersecurity Challenges in smart home devices	Security analysis	Limited integration of social perspectives with security.
McLaughlin et al. (2013)	Security analysis of emerging smart home apps	Security assessment	Insufficient consideration of diverse user demographics.
Lazar et al. (2017)	User centered design in smart Homes	Human -computer interaction methods	Inadequate consideration of cultural dimensions.
Gubbi et al. (2013)	IoT and Social Implications	Review and analysis	Limited exploration of the impact on user behaviors.
Lee et al. (2015)	Smart Home ecosystems	Holistic approach	Lack of explicit focus on ethical implications

To address the identified research gap, future studies should adopt a more holistic approach that seamlessly integrates social dynamics and security considerations within the context of smart home devices. This involves exploring not only the immediate impact on user behaviors and social interactions but also understanding how these dynamics evolve over time with advancements in technology. The Need for Reconciliation when considering the overall integration of social and security issues in the social model of smart home devices. Existing literature tends to operate in interdisciplinary silos, with social scientists focusing on the humanities and practitioners investigating the complexities of sustainability. This slied approach has led to contradictory understandings, leaving the interconnectedness of these dimensions largely unexplored. The first dimension of the research gap lies in the limited relationship between health and safety considerations. Moreover, there is a need for research that actively seeks to include diverse demographics, ensuring that the social model is representative of the broader population. In our pursuit of exploring the social model of smart home devices, this research aims to contribute to closing this gap by providing a more comprehensive understanding of the interconnected relationship between societal dynamics and security challenges within smart home ecosystems, (Lee, Lee, & Kim, 2015). By conducting an in-depth analysis that bridges disciplinary boundaries, we aspire to offer insights that can inform the development of user-centered design, robust security measures, and policies that navigate the evolving landscape of smart home technologies. IN conclusion, the research gap identified in exploring the social model of smart home devices underscores the need for a more holistic and integrated approach. As smart home technologies become an integral part of our daily lives, understanding their impact requires a comprehensive examination that spans both social and security dimensions. Bridging this gap is essential not only for academic rigor but also for the practical development of inclusive and secure smart home solutions. Through interdisciplinary research that incorporates insights from sociology, technology, and policy, we can navigate the uncharted territories of the social model. By doing so, we contribute to an informed understanding of smart home technologies, paving the way for advancements that prioritize both user experience and security in the rapidly evolving landscape of the digital home.

As we navigate the unexplored territories of the social model of smart home devices, a more nuanced examination of the research gap reveals additional layers that warrant attention. One pivotal dimension of this gap lies in the limited consideration of the ethical implications associated with smart home technologies. While scholars have extensively addressed privacy concerns, the broader ethical landscape, encompassing issues such as data ownership, algorithmic biases, and the potential societal repercussions of smart home adoption, remains conspicuously underexplored. Bridging this gap is essential for developing ethically sound smart home technologies that prioritize the well-being of users and mitigate unintended consequences, (Floridi *et al.,* 2018). Moreover, the temporal dimension of the research gap demands further scrutiny. Smart home technologies, marked by their rapid evolution, necessitate ongoing research efforts to keep pace with the latest advancements. A continuous, dynamic understanding of the smart home landscape is essential for identifying emerging societal patterns, user behaviors, and security challenges associated with novel technological developments. Addressing this temporal aspect of the gap ensures that research remains relevant, providing timely insights into the ever-changing dynamics of smart home ecosystems, (Poler, Molina, & Giret, 2012). The exploration of the social impact of smart home IoT devices is a multifaceted endeavor that requires a nuanced understanding of the evolving dynamics between technology and society. The identified research gaps highlight the need for a more comprehensive, interdisciplinary, and culturally sensitive approach to studying smart home IoT ecosystems. Addressing these gaps will not only contribute to academic knowledge but will also inform practical strategies for developing smart home IoT technologies that are socially responsible, secure, and widely accepted.

3. RESEARCH GAP

Although there has been a plethora of research on smart home devices and their social implications as well as safety, there still exists significant lacunae in research concerning social integration, quality and security. Previous literature largely fails to consider these variables and thereby limits our understanding about their intersection point and how they affect each other under the context of smart home ecosystems. Ethics research is not enough-Primary research tends to focus on reducing personal risk and ensuring data protection within the building but there is a gap in exploring deeper ethical considerations beyond privacy. Issues such as the role of data, the ethical implications of algorithms, and the social impact of smart home technologies have yet to be addressed in the existing literature. Ignoring algorithm bias-Often, the privacy conversation is about data protection but fails to deal with fair competition. Algorithmic bias in smart home devices. What is lacking in the literature is a clear assessment of how the algorithms governing smart buildings exhibit bias and the social benefits of bias for different users. Ignoring social consequences-Although confidentiality is an important ethical consideration, existing research tends to overlook the impact of domestic adoption. What is lacking is an understanding of how these technologies influence social processes, social change, and long-term individual behavior. Examining these relationships is important for the development of ethical and social aspects of smart home technology, (Friedman & Kahn, 2003).

- Telling social apart from security: Existing studies are more into looking into the issues of social impacts and security thus leading to an absence of knowledge on the concurrence between these two values' interaction. Not completely linked-up data which lead out the connections amid user behavior or society form, as well as security gadgets around a smart household.
- Ignoring the social aspect of safety: Research focuses on methods like encryption and authentication for securing systems but neglects any possible impact they may have on the general wellbeing of users or communities. Failure to relate to this will result in poor adaptation of security measures for consumers' requirements, desires and actions hence undermining entire security structure intended for smart homes.
- User perception study: The integration of social and security requires the investigation of user opinion and nature. The present research does not provide a clear understanding of users' cultural backgrounds, social orientations, and safety attitudes that shape their acceptance and application of smart home appliances, (Patil & Javali, 2018). Addressing this gap in research is important to improve our understanding of smart home devices, ensuring that security measures are not only voice-based but also based on the social context in

which they are used. This combination will help increase the efficiency and usage of security solutions for smart homes. Although the existing literature on the social design of smart home devices provides valuable insights into security and privacy issues, conduct-based research is yet to be conducted on considerations of goodness One important limitation is that the importance of privacy often overshadows the ethical assessment of smart home appliances. This research gap is important because it ignores important factors such as responsible data use, algorithmic bias, and the overall impact of smart home IoT environment. The few existing studies indicate an opportunity and a need for detailed cross-national analyses to fill the existing research gap.

4. PROPOSED STUDY

Cross-national comparative research on the integration of social and safety aspects in researching social models of smart home appliances is needed to address existing research gaps and a broader understanding of the global situation. By examining how these aspects are used and emphasized in different cultural, technological, legal, socio-economic and educational contexts, researchers can identify common challenges, best practices and unique insights a specific to each country Provides visibility. Moreover, it facilitates the development of tailored solutions that reflect country-specific nuances and preferences, ultimately improving the effectiveness and global acceptance of smart home appliances Overall a, the comparative analysis is an important tool to advance knowledge, inform policy decisions, and drive innovation in smart home technologies.

4.1 Basis: As this is small-scale research, we compare 3 countries based on 4 parameters.

The parameters are:

1. Cultural norms: Cultural norms include shared values, customs, and traditions within a society that govern the behavior and interactions of individuals. These standards affect technology acceptance and usability, as well as the desirability of specific technology features or functionality. Understanding cultural values is critical in designing technology that is user-friendly and in line with societal expectations.\
2. Technological Infrastructure: Technology infrastructure refers to the physical and organizational elements that support the development, implementation, and operation of technology in a region or country. This includes telecommunications

systems, Internet connections, hardware components, software platforms, and related services. Strong technical infrastructure enables access to technologies, drives innovation and drives economic growth.

3. Legal Framework: The regulatory framework includes rules, regulations, and policies that govern the use, development, and distribution of technologies. This framework establishes guidelines for data privacy, cybersecurity, intellectual property rights, consumer protection, and industry standards. An effective regulatory framework encourages innovation by ensuring that technology is used in a safe, secure, and ethical manner.
4. User Education: It consists of activities aimed at increasing individual knowledge, skills and awareness of technology and its implications. This includes educating users on digital literacy, privacy protection, cybersecurity best practices and responsible use of technology. Effective user education programs enable individuals to make informed decisions, reduce risks, and maximize the value of technology in their daily lives.

4.2 Comparison

4.2.1 India

In India, the adoption of smart home devices is influenced by deep-rooted cultural values that prioritize family ties and communal living. These values drive the desire to enhance social interactions within households, leading to the adoption of technologies that facilitate remote communication and promote family-oriented applications. According to recent studies, (Chaurasia & Gupta, 2020), features such as remote communication and family-oriented applications are particularly valued among Indian consumers, reflecting the importance placed on maintaining connections within familial networks.

However, India's technological infrastructure presents a significant disparity between urban and rural areas, impacting the accessibility and efficiency of smart home devices. While urban centers typically benefit from adequate infrastructure to support advanced functionalities, rural areas often face challenges related to internet connectivity and power supply, (Kishore, Kumar, & Krishna, 2020) This discrepancy underscores the need for tailored solutions that address the unique infrastructure constraints in different regions of the country.

In response to the evolving landscape of technology adoption, India is in the process of developing a regulatory framework to govern data privacy and cybersecurity. The proposed Personal Data Protection Law aims to safeguard the security and privacy of smart home devices and user data, (Paliwal & Sultania, 2021). Compliance with these regulations is essential to build consumer trust and ensure responsible use of smart home technology, highlighting the government's commitment to protecting individual privacy rights in the digital age.

Furthermore, practical education initiatives in India are focused on increasing digital literacy, privacy protection, and cybersecurity awareness among consumers, (Swami & Gupta, 2019). These efforts aim to empower users with the knowledge and skills needed to navigate the risks and benefits of smart home technology effectively. By educating consumers about privacy risks and best practices for secure usage, these initiatives contribute to building a more informed and responsible user base, thereby fostering a safer and more trustworthy smart home ecosystem in India.

4.2.2 China

In China, the adoption of smart home devices is deeply influenced by cultural values that prioritize communal living and family harmony. These values drive households to embrace technology that enhances social interaction and promotes family cohesion. As a result, desirable features such as remote communication and family-oriented applications are highly valued among Chinese consumers, (Du & Fan, 2020). This cultural emphasis on interconnectedness and harmony has a significant impact on the development and adoption of smart home technology in the country.

China's technological infrastructure is characterized by its robustness and widespread accessibility. With extensive internet access and advanced telecommunications connectivity, China's infrastructure facilitates the seamless integration of smart home devices into daily life, (Li & Hu, 2019). This infrastructure supports a range of features, including remote monitoring, housekeeping automation, and easy communication between family members. The availability of such advanced functionalities contributes to the widespread adoption of smart home technology across various segments of the population.

In response to the growing importance of data privacy and cybersecurity, China has implemented legislative frameworks to regulate these aspects. The Cybersecurity Law and the anticipated Personal Information Protection Law aim to safeguard the security and privacy of smart home devices and user data, (Xue & Yuan, 2021). Compliance with these regulations is crucial to ensuring consumer trust and confidence in smart home technology. By establishing clear guidelines and standards, China's regulatory frameworks contribute to a more secure and transparent ecosystem for smart home devices.

Furthermore, practical education initiatives in China focus on increasing consumer awareness of digital literacy, privacy protection, and cybersecurity. Efforts are underway to educate users about the risks and benefits of smart home technology, empowering them to make informed decisions, (Zhou, Yang, & Cheng, 2019). By promoting digital literacy and cybersecurity awareness, these initiatives help users navigate the complexities of smart home technology and protect themselves from potential threats or vulnerabilities.

4.2.3 USA

In the United States, cultural values emphasizing individuality and privacy significantly influence attitudes toward smart home technology. Consumers prioritize products that not only offer convenience and interactivity but also prioritize personal privacy. This reflects a societal preference for maintaining control over personal data and digital security. The country's robust technological infrastructure, characterized by high-speed internet and advanced telecommunications networks, further facilitates the integration of smart home devices into daily life. This infrastructure supports seamless connectivity and enables a wide range of functionalities, from remote monitoring to home automation, (Junglas, Watson, & Robinson, 2020).

Moreover, the legal landscape in the US includes comprehensive laws and regulations aimed at protecting data privacy and security. Notable examples include the California Consumer Privacy Act (CCPA) and the Health Insurance Portability and Accountability Act (HIPAA), which establish stringent requirements for the collection, storage, and use of personal data. Compliance with these regulations is essential for companies operating in the smart home technology sector to ensure the security and privacy of user information.

In addition to regulatory measures, education plays a crucial role in empowering US users to navigate the complexities of smart home technology. Education initiatives focus on increasing consumer awareness of digital literacy, privacy protection, and cybersecurity. Through educational materials, programs, and online resources, users are equipped with the knowledge and skills needed to make informed decisions about smart home technology, (Williams et al., 2022). By promoting awareness of potential risks and best practices for safeguarding personal information, these initiatives contribute to building a more knowledgeable and proactive user base in the USA.

4.3 Critical Analysis

In this we read the above study and do a critical analysis by creating a table and gives conclusion on how various countries handle these situations for improving security in integrating smart home devices. Table 2. summarizes the above points in the research.

Table 2. Study and conclusion

Aspect	India	China	USA	Conclusion
Cultural Norm	Basic family relationships and civic life; the desire to increase social cohesion within households; experimentation with such things as distance communication and family services. Deep cultural values driving adoption; The importance of maintaining communication within family networks is emphasized. Family-oriented long-distance communication is considered valuable.	Emphasis on community life and family unity; willingness to embrace technology for social interaction and family interaction; Assessment of factors such as distance communication and family-centered interventions. Cultural emphasis on communication and cooperation in driving adoption; Key impacts on the development and adoption of smart home technologies.	Emphasis on individuality and privacy; preferred personal privacy priorities; society wants to maintain control over personal data and digital security. Cultural emphasis on personal privacy and acceptance of driving; Social desirability for factors that prioritize individuality and privacy.	Comparisons across India, China, and the United States reveal distinct cultural norms that influence the adoption of smart home devices. India emphasizes family ties and civic life, while China emphasizes civic solidarity, and the US. emphasize individuality and privacy These cultural differences lead to a preference for smart home devices.
Technological Infrastructure	Significant disparity between urban and rural areas affecting accessibility and efficiency.	Robust and widespread infrastructure with extensive internet access and advanced telecommunications.	High-speed internet and advanced telecommunications networks facilitating seamless integration of devices.	India faces a significant urban-rural infrastructure gap, impacting the accessibility of smart home devices, while China boasts robust and widespread infrastructure, supporting seamless integration. The USA also has advanced infrastructure, further facilitating the adoption and integration of smart home technology.

continued on following page

Table 2. Continued

Aspect	India	China	USA	Conclusion
Legal Framework	Developing regulatory framework for data privacy and cybersecurity; Proposed Personal Data Protection Law aimed at safeguarding security and privacy	Implementation of legislative frameworks such as Cybersecurity Law and anticipated Personal Information Protection Law for safeguarding security and privacy, (Xue & Yuan, 2021). Compliance crucial for consumer trust.	Presence of comprehensive laws and regulations including CCPA and HIPAA aimed at protecting data privacy and security; Compliance essential for ensuring security and privacy of user information.	India is in the process of developing regulations with the proposed Personal Data Protection Law, China has implemented laws like the Cybersecurity Law, and the USA has established comprehensive laws like CCPA and HIPAA.
User Education	Focus on increasing digital literacy, privacy protection, and cybersecurity awareness among consumers.	Efforts underway to educate users about the risks and benefits of smart home technology.	Promotion of awareness of potential risks and best practices for safeguarding personal information.	While all three countries emphasize practical education initiatives to increase consumer awareness of digital literacy, privacy protection, and cybersecurity. India and China both focus on empowering users with knowledge and skills to navigate risks effectively, while the USA emphasizes promoting awareness of potential risks and best practices.

4.4 Findings

The research provides valuable information on how different factors across 3 different countries affect security and social aspects in Integration of smart home devices. The findings from the provided paragraphs highlight several key aspects that are crucial for the security and social aspects of smart home IoT integration across India, China, and the USA. This research paper can be valuable for several reasons, some of which have been listed below: -

1. Helps in developing enhanced security measures: By reading this the development of regulatory frameworks and compliance mechanisms can be made that ensures smart home IoT devices adhere to stringent security standards. This protects users' personal data and privacy and reduces the risk of cyber-attacks and unauthorized access to smart devices.
2. Improvement in technological Infrastructure: Addressing differences in technology infrastructure across various countries ensures that smart home IoT technology is accessible to all segments of society, regardless of geographic or socioeconomic status. By strengthening internet connectivity and electrification in rural areas, marginalized communities can also benefit from the convenience and security provided by smart home devices.
3. Improves Social connectivity: Cultural considerations in smart home IoT design, such as the prioritization of family relationships and communal living, enhance social connectivity and interaction in homes and by reading this the people can make up for what they are missing. Smart devices that facilitate remote communication, family-oriented applications allow people to stay connected with their loved ones even when they are physically separated from them This strengthens family bonds and develops a sense of community and enhances social the aspect of smart home integration is huge.
4. Privacy Enhancement: Regulatory frameworks aimed at protecting data privacy ensure that users are in control of their personal information and how it is collected, stored and used in smart home devices. By empowering users with privacy rights and educating them about privacy risks, people can make informed decisions about their data and maintain their privacy in an interconnected environment This forces individualization strengthen autonomy and control over their own affairs and contribute to a smart home highly privacy-respecting ecosystem.

Figure 4. Mitigation options for customers across different countries

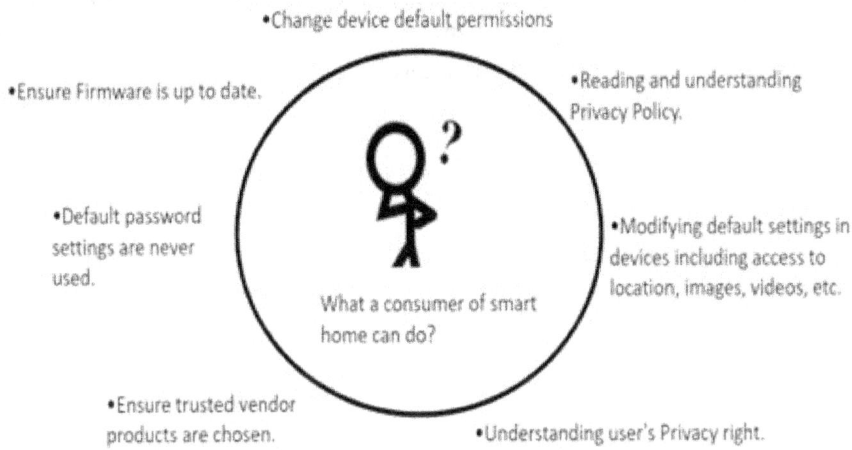

5. CONCLUSION

A comparative study in India, China and the US. all shed light on the various factors affecting the integration of smart home appliances and highlight important measures to enhance security in this area. First, the study highlights the significant impact of cultural norms on smart home adoption. Understanding these cultural nuances can help tailor security measures and device functionality to lifestyle preferences, increasing user acceptance and trust. Second, the disparity in technology infrastructure, which is particularly evident in India's urban-rural divide, highlights the importance of addressing infrastructure barriers to care recognizing that smart home appliances will move everywhere and accentuate the task. Bridging these gaps is important to enhance security by ensuring consistent connectivity and trust, thereby reducing the vulnerabilities associated with insufficient infrastructure. Third developed or existing regulatory frameworks in these countries play an important role in creating security and privacy among smart-home users. User confidence in testing and it is important that they are reinforced. Finally, practical educational programs that focus on digital literacy, privacy protection, and cybersecurity skills help enable users to make informed and acceptable security decisions best practices by educating users about potential hazards and guiding them on how to use them safely, these systems contribute significantly to enhance overall safety as a smart home creature the living being stands Figure 4 show various mitigation approaches. In conclusion, this comparative study is a valuable resource for policymakers, industry stakeholders, and consumers alike, providing insights into several aspects of smart home security and suggesting strategies for risk reduction types to improve security standards in the integration of smart home appliances.

REFERENCES

Acquisti, A., Gross, R., & Stutzman, F. (2014). Privacy in the Age of Augmented Reality. *IEEE Security and Privacy*.

Anderson, T. (2018). Security Challenges in the Internet of Things: A Case Study of Smart Home Devices. *IEEE Security and Privacy*, 16(5), 26–35.

Atami, A., & Al-Namanny, A. (2021). Security and Privacy Concerns of IoT in Smart Home Environments: A Comprehensive Survey. *IEEE Access : Practical Innovations, Open Solutions*, 9, 36627–36646.

Chaurasia, V., & Gupta, M. (2020). Analyzing Smart Home Adoption through the Lens of Indian Culture: An Empirical Investigation.

Dillahunt, T., Mankoff, J., & Paulos, E. (2019). Understanding conflict in the smart home through role-play. *Proceedings of the 2019 CHI Conference on Human Factors in Computing Systems*, 1-13.

Du, Y., & Fan, H. (2020). Exploring the impact of cultural dimensions on smart home technology adoption.

Floridi, L., Cowls, J., Beltrametti, M., Chatila, R., Chazerand, P., Dignum, V., & Luetge, C. (2018). AI4People—An ethical framework for a good. *AI & Society*. PMID: 30930541

Friedman, B., & Kahn, P. H., Jr. (2003). Human values, ethics, and design. Handbook of human-computer interaction, 1177-1201.

Hasan, M. A.. (2019). Smart Homes for Elderly Healthcare—Recent Advances and Research Challenges. *Sensors (Basel)*.

Jin, X., Lin, X., Vasilakos, A. V., Hou, Y. T., & Liu, L. (2014). The architecture of the internet of things (IoT) for enabling ubiquitous healthcare monitoring and management. *IEEE Network*, 28(6), 6–14.

Johnson, B.. (2020). Privacy Perceptions in Smart Home Environments: A Survey of User Attitudes and Behaviors. *Proceedings of the ACM Conference on Human Factors in Computing Systems*, 112-125.

Junglas, I., Watson, R. T., & Robinson, S. (2020). An analysis of smart home development: Evidence from the USA.

Khan, F., Salah, K., & Al-Fuqaha, A. (2018). Toward efficient data collection in smart cities using edge and fog computing. *IEEE Internet of Things Journal*, 5(3), 1596–1605.

Kishore, K., Kumar, N., & Krishna, V. (2020). Smart Home Systems: Opportunities and Challenges in India.

Lee, J. H.. (2019). The Internet of Things (IoT): Applications, investments, and challenges for enterprises. *Business Horizons*.

Lee, K., Lee, Y., & Kim, Y. (2015). Smart home ecosystems: A holistic approach. *IEEE Access : Practical Innovations, Open Solutions*.

. Li, Y., & Hu, R. (2019). The development of smart homes in China: An analysis of recent trends, drivers and challenges.

McLaughlin, N., Weir, D., & Argyros, A. (2013). Security Analysis of Emerging Smart Home Applications. *IEEE Security and Privacy*.

National Institute of Standards and Technology. (2020). NIST Special Publication 800-213: Security Guidance for IoT Device Manufacturers.

Norman, D. A. (2013). *The Design of Everyday Things*. Basic Books.

Paliwal, R., & Sultania, S. (2021). Data Protection and Privacy in Smart Homes: Challenges and Solutions.

Patil, S., & Javali, P. (2018). A review on smart home present and future. *Materials Today: Proceedings*, 5(1), 1518–1523.

Poler, R., Molina, A., & Giret, A. (2012). A survey of models for the Internet of Things. *Journal of Systems and Software*.

Smith, A. (2019). The Impact of Smart Home Devices on Family Dynamics: A Qualitative Study. *Journal of Human-Computer Interaction*, 25(3), 345–362.

Swami, D., & Gupta, P. (2019). Internet of Things (IoT) and Smart Home Technology: Awareness and Perception among Indian Consumers.

Williams, P., Dutta, I. K., Daoud, H., & Bayoumi, M. (2022). A survey on security in internet of things with a focus on the impact of emerging technologies. *Internet of Things : Engineering Cyber Physical Human Systems*, 19, 100564. DOI: 10.1016/j.iot.2022.100564

Xue, K., & Yuan, D. (2021). Review of the development of intelligent home and intelligent hardware industry in China under the background of "New Infrastructure".

Zhang, L.. (2021). Vulnerability Analysis of Smart Home Devices: A Systematic Review. *Computers & Security*, 90, 102038.

Zhou, T., Yang, L., & Cheng, Y. (2019). Understanding Smart Home Acceptance in Urban China: An Empirical Study.

Chapter 13
Social Media Revolution:
Unravelling the Threads of Connectivity and Influence

Syed Adnan Afaq
Integral University, India

Shweta Dwivedi
Integral University, India

Saurabh Srivastava
MIT Moradabad, India

Syed Khalida Izhar
Integral University, India

Mohammad Faisal
Integral University, India

Gausiya Yasmeen
https://orcid.org/0000-0002-7853-1376
Integral University, India

Qudsia Shahab
Integral University, India

ABSTRACT

The chapter explores the transformative journey of social media and its impact on contemporary society, highlighting both challenges and opportunities. From its origins to its global ubiquity, social media has redefined communication, transcending geographical and cultural barriers. While it empowers global sharing and creativity, it also raises issues like privacy breaches, data security, and misinformation. Despite these challenges, social media drives social movements, political engagement, and revolutionizes marketing. It influences agriculture by spreading innovative techniques and bioinformatics by enhancing research collaboration. Emerging technologies like AR, VR, and AI will further shape its future. Integrating bioinformatics and agricultural analytics into social media can address global challenges, fostering positive societal change and connectivity.

DOI: 10.4018/979-8-3693-9235-5.ch013

1. INTRODUCTION

Social media has become an essential component of our digital environment, transforming how individuals, businesses, and communities interact and communicate. Social media refers to internet platforms and programs that enable people to create, share, and swap material. It comprises a variety of services such as social networking sites (e.g., Facebook and Twitter), photo-sharing platforms (e.g., Instagram), professional networks (e.g., LinkedIn), and multimedia platforms (e.g., YouTube and TikTok).

Social media lets people connect and communicate across ideological, cultural, and geographic divides in today's globally interconnected globe. Social media has completely changed the way we engage with like-minded communities, network with colleagues, and maintain relationships with friends and family. Moreover, the ubiquity of social media in our daily lives has reshaped various aspects of society, from how we consume news and information to how we conduct business and participate in civic discourse. As we delve deeper into the complexities and nuances of social media, it becomes increasingly clear that its impact extends far beyond individual interactions, influencing everything from political mobilization and cultural trends to economic dynamics and social norms (Varghese 2024) (Farooq et al. 2021).

1.1. Innovations in Social Media

Social media may trace its roots back to the early days of the internet, when message boards and online communities were in their infancy. However, the contemporary form of social media did not materialize until the late 1990s and early 2000s, at which point websites like Six Degrees became popular, allowing users to create profiles and engage with one other.

Figure 1. Evolution of social media

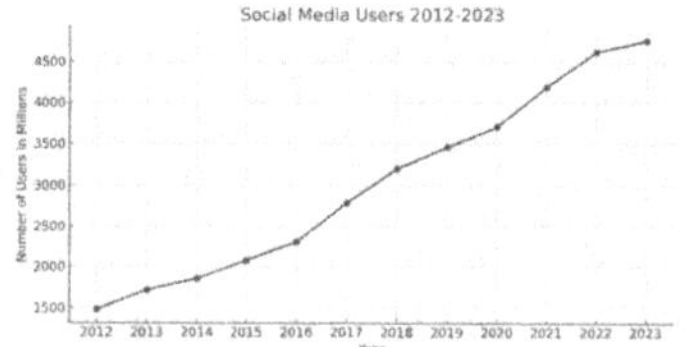

Midway through the 2000s, social media underwent a dramatic shift with the adoption of Web 2.0 technology, which ushered in an era of interactive communication and user-generated content. The emergence of Facebook, Twitter, YouTube, and other industry giants, which transformed the way people communicate and share content online, was made possible by platforms like Friendster, MySpace, and LinkedIn.

Since then, social media has kept up its rapid evolution, with fresh functions & platforms emerging on a regular basis to cater to users' shifting demands and tastes. From the launch of photo-sharing apps like Instagram and Snapchat to the rise of video-sharing platforms like TikTok and Twitch, the landscape of social media is continuously changing, driven by technological advancements or variations in user behavior, (Asuamah Yeboah, 2023)

This section delves into the key stages and milestones that have defined this evolutionary journey:

- **Early Beginnings**

Social media's beginnings can be found in the early years of the internet, when rudimentary online communication platforms created the foundation for the modern digital world we live in. Bulletin board systems (BBS) were one of the first social media platforms in the decades between the years 1970 and 1980, allowing users to publish messages and share information within specialized groups. Despite their limited reach and the scope, these early platforms hinted at the social connection that would characterize later social media iterations, (August, 2022).

- **Rise of Social Networking**

The true dawn of social media occurred with the introduction of social networking platforms in the late 1990s and early 2000s. Virtual social networking services such as Six Degrees, which debuted in 1997, invented the idea of user profiles and online friend connections. Even while Six Degrees eventually perished in the dot-com crisis, it opened the door for other platforms to profit from the growing need for online socialising.

The early 2000s saw the rise of iconic platforms like Friendster and MySpace, which introduced features such as friend networks, profile customization, and photo sharing. MySpace, in particular, achieved unprecedented popularity, boasting millions of users and revolutionizing the way people interacted online (Appel et al. 2020).

- **The Facebook Era**

When Facebook was founded in 2004 by Mark Zuckerberg and his undergraduate roommates, it became the most popular social networking site at the time. Before becoming available to the general public in 2006, Facebook was first restricted to students at Harvard University. However, it quickly spread to other schools. With its clear and simple user interface, features, and emphasis on real identity, Facebook struck a chord with users worldwide and rapidly amassed a massive user base.

Facebook's success solidified its position as a dominant force in social media and catalyzed a paradigm shift in online interaction. The platform's emphasis on sharing personal updates, photos, and status updates fostered a culture of transparency and connectedness, redefining the way people communicated and shared information (Dhillon 2014).

- **Birth of Microblogging**

In the late 2000s, microblogging services developed as a new frontier in social media, allowing users to exchange short-form information in real time. With its 2006 inception, Twitter helped popularise the idea of microblogging by enabling users to exchange links, updates, and opinions in 280-character entries called “tweets.” Twitter became a worldwide forum for breaking news, cultural commentary, and viral trends because of its simplicity and immediacy, which attracted a lot of users.

- **Visual Revolution**

The growth of smartphones and high-speed internet cleared the way for a new wave of social media sites based on visual material. Instagram, which debuted in 2010, capitalised on the growing popularity of smartphone photography by providing an environment for users to share filtered photographs and short videos with their followers. The platform's emphasis on aesthetics, creativity, and visual storytelling drove it to mainstream success, drawing millions of users and establishing its place as a cultural phenomenon.

Following in Instagram's footsteps, Snapchat introduced the concept of ephemeral messaging, allowing users to share disappearing photos and videos with their friends. This unique feature appealed to younger audiences seeking more private and spontaneous forms of communication, catapulting Snapchat to prominence among millennials and Generation (Dhingra and Mudgal 2019).

- **The Era of Video**

Video-sharing websites have become the next big thing in social media, transforming the way people produce and watch content online in recent years. YouTube, which debuted in 2005, democratised video production by allowing anybody with a camera and an internet connection to share their creation with the world. YouTube's extensive content library, which includes anything from music films and clips to tutorials and vlogs, appeals to a wide range of interests and users, making it one of the most popular websites on the internet, (Dhingra & Mudgal, 2019).

In the realm of short-form video, TikTok has emerged as a cultural juggernaut, captivating audiences with its endless stream of bite-sized content. Launched in 2016, TikTok revolutionized social media with its algorithm-driven feed, which serves up an endless stream of videos tailored to each user's interests and preferences. Its emphasis on creativity, humor, and authenticity has made it a favorite among younger audiences, propelling it to meteoric success and cultural relevance (Appel et al. 2020).

- **Current Landscape**

Today, the social media landscape is more diverse and dynamic than ever before, encompassing a wide range of platforms catering to various niches and demographics. From messaging apps like WhatsApp and Facebook Messenger to professional networks like LinkedIn and niche communities like Reddit, there's a social media platform for virtually every interest and inclination.

As social media continues to expand, new technologies and trends will surely affect its future path. With the emergence of augmented and virtual reality, as well as the expanding influence of artificial intelligence and machine learning, the opportunities for innovation and disruption are endless. But despite all of the change and instability, one thing is certain: social media will keep revolutionizing the ways in which we interact, connect, and correspond with the world around us, (Dixit & Rajaura, 2023).

2. THE IMPACT OF SOCIAL MEDIA

Virtually every element of our life is impacted by social media's significant and pervasive influence on society. One of digital media's most important achievements is its capacity to facilitate communication and develop ties between people, regardless of geographical distance or cultural differences. Users may keep in real-time communication with friends, family, and co-workers by using social media sites like Facebook, Twitter, and WhatsApp. With few clicks, they may share updates, images, and messages. Social media has also given common people the ability to produce and distribute content, making the data flow and upending the gatekeepers that regulate conventional media.

Platforms like YouTube, TikTok, and Twitch have provided aspiring artists, influencers, and activists with a global stage to showcase their talents, share their perspectives, and mobilize communities around shared interests and causes (Scharlach, Hallinan, and Shifman 2023). However, increased social media use has created worries about privacy, misrepresentation, and the transmission of hazardous content. Data breaches, online harassment, and the dissemination of fake news have become more common, prompting requests for increased regulation and accountability from social media businesses and governments.

This section digs into the enormous impact of social media on numerous aspects of society:

Figure 2. Impact of social media

1. *Redefining Communication and Connectivity:*
    - The internet has brought through geographical barriers, enabling real-time communication among people from varied backgrounds. Whether it's reconnecting long-lost acquaintances, building global communities, or promoting cross-cultural interchange, social media has democratized communication in new ways.
    - Changing Communication Paradigms: As social media platforms have grown in popularity, face-to-face interactions have given way to digital dialogues conducted through screens. The aforementioned shift has profoundly changed the complexities of interpersonal relationships, resulting in an amalgamation of the online and tangible worlds and establishing new expectations for behavior and communicating on the World Wide Web, (Funk & Owen-Smith, 2017).
2. *Influencing Consumer Behavior and Trends:*
    - The Power of Influence: Purchase behavior is significantly influenced by social media influencers, who set trends and direct purchases made by customers. Influencers, ranging from lifestyle bloggers and beauty gurus to gaming streamers and fitness enthusiasts, use their online

platforms to endorse items, give advice, and build brand loyalty among their followers, (Goh, Al-Tabbaa, & Khan, 2023).

The emergence of user-generated content has given individuals the ability to freely share their thoughts, experiences, and tales with a worldwide audience thanks to networking platforms. User-generated content not only increases engagement and authenticity, but it also provides vital feedback and insights for brands and organisations looking to understand customer preferences and trends, (Jabbour *et al.*, 2023).

3. *Transforming News and Information Consumption*:
    - Citizen Journalism: social media has made it easier for individuals to report and share news in real-time. From citizen journalists chronicling unfolding disasters to smartphone-captured viral moments, social media has transformed the media environment, upset established gatekeepers and promoting new voices and opinions.
    - Navigating the Misinformation Minefield: The rise of social networks has raised concerns about misinformation, fake news, and echo chambers. The viral nature of social media algorithms, as well as the ease with which content may be shared, make it difficult to distinguish between reality and fiction, creating substantial challenges to media literacy and public discourse, (Kridera & Kanavos, 2024).
4. *Influencing Sociopolitical Dynamics:*
    - The Weaponization of social media: Social media platforms have evolved into arenas for political activism, conversation, and propaganda, hence impacting sociopolitical dynamics. Political actors and interest groups use social media to spread propaganda, sway public opinion, and rally followers, blurring the distinction between genuine grassroots movements and organized campaigns.
    - Social media fueled social movements like the Arab Spring, Occupy Wall Street, and Black Lives Matter. These movements used social media to organize protests, promote awareness, and hold authorities responsible, proving the transformative effects of digital activism, (Olan *et al.*, 2024).
5. Effect on Well-Being and Behavioral Health:
    - The Double-Edged Sword of Social Connectivity: Social networking offers incredible opportunities for friendship and community building, but it also poses risks to one's mental health and general wellbeing. Excessive internet use has been related to feelings of loneliness, melancholy, and anxiety, as users compare themselves to curated images of others and seek validation through likes and comments.

- Dealing with Social Media's Negative Aspects: Platforms are under increasing pressure to address social media's harmful influence on mental health by introducing features such as screen time management tools, content moderation regulations, and mental health services. But the intricate relationship between using social media and and mental health remains an ongoing area of research and concern (Rone 2022).

6. Navigating Privacy and Data Security:
   - The Privacy Paradox: Social media sites collect large amounts of user data to tailor content, target adverts, and improve user experiences. However, worries about data privacy, spying, and algorithmic manipulation have called into question the ethical implications of internet corporations' data gathering and usage.
   - Balancing innovation with privacy protection is a challenge for governments and politicians in the digital era. Initiatives such as the European Union's General Data Protection Regulation (GDPR) seek to increase user control over personal data and make tech corporations accountable for data practices, indicating a rising recognition of the importance of privacy rights in the digital age, (Pokharel *et al.,* 2023).

3. THE ROLE OF SOCIAL MEDIA IN SOCIETY

Social media plays a multifaceted role in shaping society, influencing everything from political discourse and cultural trends to economic dynamics and social norms. In the realm of politics, social media has emerged as a powerful tool for political mobilization and advocacy, enabling activists to organize campaigns, raise awareness, and galvanize support for social change (Stellefson et al. 2020). From the Arab Spring to the Black Lives Matter movement, social media has played a pivotal role in amplifying marginalized voices and challenging entrenched power structures. Moreover, social media has transformed the way businesses engage with consumers, offering new opportunities for marketing, advertising, and customer feedback. Platforms like Instagram, Pinterest, and Snapchat have become indispensable tools for brands looking to connect with their target audiences, leveraging influencers and sponsored content to drive sales and build brand loyalty (August 2022).

This section delves into the multifaceted role of social media in shaping societal dynamics and cultural norms:

Figure 3. Role of social media in the society

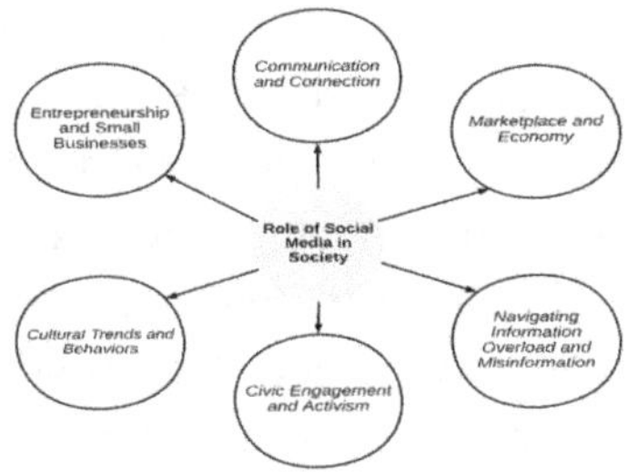

1. *Facilitating Communication and Connection:*
    - A Global Village: Social media has transformed the world into a global village, breaking down geographical barriers and facilitating instant communication between individuals across continents. Whether it's staying in touch with friends and family, forging new connections, or participating in virtual communities, social media has revolutionized the way we interact and build relationships, (Kridera and Kanavos 2024).
    - Fostering Diversity and Inclusivity: Social media platforms serve as inclusive spaces where individuals from diverse backgrounds can connect, share their stories, and celebrate their identities. From LGBTQ+ communities to cultural affinity groups, social media provides a platform for marginalized voices to be heard, fostering empathy, understanding, and solidarity among users, (Ansari and Khan 2020).
2. *Empowering Civic Engagement and Activism:*
    - The Digital Public Square: Social media platforms have become digital public squares where citizens gather to discuss, debate, and mobilize around social and political issues. From hashtag campaigns and online petitions to viral movements and digital protests, social media has empowered individuals to advocate for change, hold authorities accountable, and amplify marginalized voices.
    - Amplifying Grassroots Movements: Social media played a pivotal role in catalyzing grassroots movements such as the Arab Spring, Occupy Wall Street, and the #BlackLivesMatter movement, (Olan et al. 2024). These movements leveraged the power of social media to organize protests, raise awareness, and mobilize supporters, demonstrating the transformative potential of digital activism in effecting social change, (Bae and Zamrudi 2018).

3. *Influencing Cultural Trends and Behaviors:*
    - Shaping Popular Culture: Social media platforms serve as influential hubs for cultural expression, shaping trends, memes, and viral phenomena that permeate popular culture. From dance challenges and meme culture to viral marketing campaigns and influencer endorsements, social media has become a driving force behind the dissemination and adoption of cultural trends and behaviors, (Pokharel et al. 2023).
    - Redefining Beauty Standards and Body Image: Social media has played a significant role in reshaping beauty standards and body image perceptions, as users are bombarded with curated images and idealized representations of beauty. Platforms like Instagram have been criticized for promoting unrealistic beauty standards and fueling body dissatisfaction among users, raising important questions about the impact of social media on self-esteem and mental health, (Funk and Owen-Smith 2017).
4. *Transforming the Marketplace and Economy:*
    - The Rise of Social Commerce: Social media platforms have become powerful tools for e-commerce, enabling businesses to reach customers, showcase products, and drive sales directly through social channels. From sponsored posts and influencer marketing to shoppable tags and live streaming, social media has transformed the way brands engage with consumers and monetize their online presence, (Vandenbosch, Fardouly, and Tiggemann 2022).
    - Empowering Entrepreneurship and Small Businesses: Social media has leveled the playing field for entrepreneurs and small businesses, providing affordable and accessible platforms to market their products and services, build brand awareness, and cultivate loyal customer communities. Platforms like Facebook, Instagram, and Etsy have democratized entrepreneurship, enabling individuals to turn their passions into profitable ventures and connect with customers on a global scale, (Pieterse 2021).
5. *Navigating Information Overload and Misinformation:*
    - The Age of Information Abundance: Social media has democratized access to information, providing users with instant access to news, entertainment, and educational content from around the world. However, the abundance of information also poses challenges, as users navigate through a sea of content to discern credible sources from misinformation, fake news, and propaganda, (Dixit and Rajaura 2023).
    - • Social media platforms are implementing fact-checking, content moderation, and algorithmic modifications to battle misinformation and disinformation. However, the fight against misinformation continues,

underscoring the importance of media literacy education as coordinated efforts to ensure the accuracy of information published on social media.

The role of social media in society is multifaceted and dynamic, shaping cultural norms, facilitating civic engagement, and transforming the way we communicate and consume information. As social media continues to evolve, it's essential to critically examine its impact on societal dynamics and strive to harness its potential for positive social change and collective empowerment, (Jabbour et al. 2023).

6. *Agriculture and Social Media*

A. Knowledge Sharing and Community Building:

Social media platforms allow farmers and agricultural professionals to share knowledge, discuss challenges, and disseminate innovative farming techniques. This community-building aspect helps in spreading sustainable and efficient farming practices, crucial for addressing global food security, (Balkrishna and Deshmukh 2017).

B. Marketing and Direct Sales:

Farmers use platforms like Instagram and Facebook to market their produce directly to consumers, bypassing traditional supply chains. This can increase profits and provide fresher options to consumers, fostering a closer farmer-consumer relationship.

C. Real-time Monitoring and Crowdsourced Solutions:

Farmers and agricultural researchers can use social media to monitor crops and livestock through shared images and videos, receiving real-time advice and solutions from peers worldwide, (Suhaimin et al. 2023).

7. *Microbiology and Social Media*

A. Public Health Awareness and Education:

Microbiologists and health organizations use social media to educate the public on important health issues, from hygiene practices to updates on pandemics. This plays a crucial role in public health campaigns and disease prevention, (Asuamah Yeboah 2023).

B. Research Collaboration and Information Dissemination:

Social media serves as a platform for microbiologists to collaborate across borders, share research findings rapidly, and discuss new theories and discoveries. It accelerates the pace of scientific discovery and broadens the reach of advanced microbiological research, (Sandeep et al. 2020).

C. Combating Misinformation:

During health crises, social media allows experts to combat misinformation swiftly, providing accurate, science-based information to counteract myths and unfounded rumors about diseases and treatments, (Goh, Al-Tabbaa, and Khan 2023).

4. FUTURE TRENDS IN SOCIAL MEDIA

As technology advances, so will the landscape of social media, providing new opportunities and problems to consumers, corporations, and politicians alike. The incorporation of cutting-edge technology like machine learning (AI), virtual worlds (VR), and the use of augmented reality (AR) is one of the most intriguing topics in social media. By providing individualized and immersive experiences that conflate the real and virtual worlds, these technologies have the power to completely transform the way people interact and use social media platforms.

Furthermore, the growing influence of social media influencers and content creators is likely to continue, as brands and advertisers increasingly recognize the value of authentic, user-generated content in driving engagement and building brand loyalty. From sponsored posts and product placements to brand partnerships and influencer marketing campaigns, influencers have become key players in the social media ecosystem, shaping consumer preferences and driving trends across a wide range of industries, (Suhaimin et al. 2023).

However, as social media continues to evolve, it is essential to address the challenges and risks associated with its use. From safeguarding user privacy and combating online harassment to addressing the spread of misinformation and harmful content, stakeholders must work together to ensure that social media remains a safe, inclusive, and empowering space for all users.

5. CONCLUSION

The exploration of the social media revolution has uncovered a tapestry of interconnected threads, weaving together the transformative power of connectivity and influence in our digital age. As we conclude our journey through the evolution, impact, and role of social media in society, several key insights emerge:

First and foremost, social media demonstrates our modern world's unmatched connection. It has spanned physical borders and united individuals and groups in ways that were unthinkable a short time ago. People can connect, exchange stories, and develop relationships across continents via social media sites like Facebook, Instagram, and Twitter, which promotes a sense of global interconnectedness that cuts beyond national boundaries.

Secondly, social media wields significant influence over various aspects of our lives, from consumer behavior and cultural trends to civic engagement and political discourse. It has redefined the way we consume information, shaping public opinion, and mobilizing collective action on issues of societal importance. However, its influence is not without challenges, as we grapple with issues of misinformation, privacy concerns, and the commodification of attention in the digital marketplace.

Despite these challenges, the social media revolution holds immense potential for positive change and collective empowerment. It has democratized communication, amplifying marginalized voices and providing a platform for civic engagement and grassroots activism. Moreover, it has democratized entrepreneurship, enabling individuals to pursue creative passions and build communities around shared interests.

REFERENCES

Ansari, J. A. N., & Khan, N. A. (2020). Exploring the Role of Social Media in Collaborative Learning the New Domain of Learning. *Smart Learning Environments*, 7(1), 9. DOI: 10.1186/s40561-020-00118-7

Appel, G., Grewal, L., Hadi, R., & Stephen, A. T. (2020). The Future of Social Media in Marketing. *Journal of the Academy of Marketing Science*, 48(1), 79–95. DOI: 10.1007/s11747-019-00695-1 PMID: 32431463

Asuamah Yeboah, S. (2023). Sustaining Change: Unravelling the Socio-cultural Threads of Sustainable Consumption.

August, V. (2022). Network Concepts in Social Theory: Foucault and Cybernetics. *European Journal of Social Theory*, 25(2), 271–291. DOI: 10.1177/1368431021991046

Bae, I.-H., & Muhammad, F. Y. Z. (2018). CHALLENGE OF SOCIAL MEDIA MARKETING & EFFECTIVE STRATEGIES TO ENGAGE MORE CUSTOMERS: SELECTED RETAILER CASE STUDY. *International Journal of Business & Society*, 19(3).

Balkrishna, B. B., & Deshmukh, A. A. (2017). A study on role of social media in agriculture marketing and its scope. International Journal of Management. *IT and Engineering*, 7(4), 416–423.

Dhillon, A. (2014). Social Media & Revolution: The Importance of the Internet in Tunisia's Uprising.

Dhingra, M., & Mudgal, R. K. (2019, March). Historical evolution of social media: An overview. In *International Conference on Advances in Engineering Science Management & Technology (ICAESMT)*-2019, Uttaranchal University, Dehradun, India.

Dixit, R., & Rajaura, S. (2023). The Impact of Social Media on Mental Health: Understanding the Effects and Finding Balance. *Research in Multidisciplinary Subjects*, 12, 50.

Farooq, K.. (2021). The Study on the Role of Social Media in Social Change in Society. *International Journal of Innovation, Creativity and Change.*, 15(2), 1298. www.ijicc.net

Funk, R. J., & Owen-Smith, J. (2017). A Dynamic Network Measure of Technological Change. *Management Science*, 63(3), 791–817. DOI: 10.1287/mnsc.2015.2366

Goh, E., Al-Tabbaa, O., & Khan, Z. (2023). Unravelling the Complexity of the Video Game Industry: An Integrative Framework and Future Research Directions. *Telematics and Informatics Reports*, 12(August), 100100. DOI: 10.1016/j.teler.2023.100100

Jabbour, D., Masri, J. E., Nawfal, R., Malaeb, D., & Salameh, P. (2023). Social media medical misinformation: impact on mental health and vaccination decision among university students. Irish Journal of Medical Science (1971-), 192(1), 291-301.

Kridera, S., & Kanavos, A. (2024). Exploring Trust Dynamics in Online Social Networks: A Social Network Analysis Perspective. *Mathematical & Computational Applications*, 29(3), 37.

Olan, F., Jayawickrama, U., Arakpogun, E. O., Suklan, J., & Liu, S. (2024). Fake News on Social Media: The Impact on Society. *Information Systems Frontiers*, 26(2), 443–458. DOI: 10.1007/s10796-022-10242-z PMID: 35068999

Pieterse, J. N. (2021). *Connectivity and Global Studies*. Springer Nature. DOI: 10.1007/978-3-030-59598-2

Pokharel, M., Lillie, H. M., Nagatsuka, K., Barbour, J. B., Ratcliff, C. L., & Jensen, J. D. (2023). Social Media Narratives Can Influence Vaccine Intentions: The Impact of Depicting Regret and Character Death. *Computers in Human Behavior*, 141, 107612. DOI: 10.1016/j.chb.2022.107612

Rone, J. (2022). Fake Profiles, Trolls, and Digital Paranoia: Digital Media Practices in Breaking the Indignados Movement. *Social Movement Studies*, 21(1–2), 25–41. DOI: 10.1080/14742837.2019.1679108

Sandeep, G. P., Prashanth, P., Sreenivasulu, M., & Madhavilata, A. (2020). Social Media in Agriculture–A Profile Analysis. *International Journal of Current Microbiology and Applied Sciences*, 9(7), 2727–2736. DOI: 10.20546/ijcmas.2020.907.322

Scharlach, R., Hallinan, B., & Shifman, L. (2023). Governing principles: Articulating values in social media platform policies. new media & society, 14614448231156580.

Stellefson, M., Paige, S. R., Chaney, B. H., & Chaney, J. D. (2020). Evolving Role of Social Media in Health Promotion: Updated Responsibilities for Health Education Specialists. *International Journal of Environmental Research and Public Health*, 17(4), 1153. DOI: 10.3390/ijerph17041153 PMID: 32059561

Suhaimin, M. S. M.. (2023). Social Media Sentiment Analysis and Opinion Mining in Public Security: Taxonomy, Trend Analysis, Issues and Future Directions. *Journal of King Saud University. Computer and Information Sciences*, 35(9), 101776. DOI: 10.1016/j.jksuci.2023.101776

Vandenbosch, L., Fardouly, J., & Tiggemann, M. (2022). Social Media and Body Image: Recent Trends and Future Directions. *Current Opinion in Psychology*, 45, 101289. DOI: 10.1016/j.copsyc.2021.12.002 PMID: 35030460

Varghese, S. (2024). Dynamics of Social Media Networks in the Post-Truth Era. In *Handbook of Digital Journalism: Perspectives from South Asia* (pp. 419–429). Springer. DOI: 10.1007/978-981-99-6675-2_36

Chapter 14
Cyber Security Concerns in Social Media and Online Interactions

Rohit Kumar Singh
https://orcid.org/0009-0001-3104-0350
Moradabad Institute of Technology, India

Vinay Pant
Moradabad Institute of Technology, India

ABSTRACT

Along with human evolution, communication has continued to change. Social media has surfaced as yet another revolution in the vast spheres of mass media and communication in general in the modern day. Social media has completely changed how people connect and communicate with each other. It has brought the diversity of the world onto one platform, transcending time, national boundaries, racial and cultural divides, and more. Nevertheless, the other aspect of this information society's development—its insatiable thirst for knowledge—cannot be ignored. The risk of social engineering is one of the main weaknesses of social media. The practice of influencing someone's thoughts through deft communication techniques are known as social engineering or social manipulation, and it has existed for as long as communication itself. It combines creativity and science. The primary issue with social media is that people tend to overshare. This, however, simply makes it easier for a social engineer to prepare an assault.

DOI: 10.4018/979-8-3693-9235-5.ch014

1. INTRODUCTION

Social media platforms give users the opportunity to make friends online with an array of people who might have similar interests, backgrounds, or are open to pursue a long-term relationship. There has never been a simpler way to increase your social network and find new acquaintances. Thanks to internet interactions, friendship can now flourish beyond national boundaries. The convenience and accessibility offered by electronic handheld devices have revolutionized the way we communicate and access information. Whether you're at work, relaxing at home, or even on the go, these devices empower you to stay connected and informed with just a few taps or clicks. From instant messaging and video calls to file transfers and browsing the internet, the capabilities of modern handheld devices make it easier than ever to stay productive and connected from virtually anywhere. The Internet of Things as a whole would make it easier for Social media platforms to grow much more widely. Social networking refers to the act of broadening connections with others, primarily through online platforms such as Facebook, Twitter, Instagram, LinkedIn, and others Brain, J. (2021). It serves both personal and professional purposes, facilitating communication, idea sharing, and friendship formation. Essentially, it enables individuals from diverse locations to interact and collaborate. Social networking sites are generally known for their user-friendly interfaces. As depicted in Figure 1, social networks encompass fundamental components and have significant impact across various domains. The illustration highlights their versatility, illustrating their utility in entertainment, fostering business prospects, career advancement, enhancing social aptitude, and cultivating interpersonal connections with others Bright, L et al. (2021). With a considerable portion of the online populace engaging with social media platforms, these channels have emerged as vital mediums for promoting businesses and conducting awareness campaigns. As individuals tend to perceive social media primarily as a tool for personal communication, the significance of safeguarding the information stored on these platforms is frequently underestimated.

Figure 1. Social networks

Over time, there's been a notable increase in the volume and variety of information shared on social networks, which can result in unprecedented access to both personal and business data. The abundance of data stored within these networks presents a tempting target for adversaries seeking to cause harm to individuals or businesses. The vast amount of information at their disposal empowers adversaries to potentially wreak havoc on a global scale. Additionally, given that social media has evolved into a prominent advertising platform for marketers, neglecting to address social media security concerns leaves them susceptible to an array of threats, jeopardizing the confidentiality of their data. The Facebook exploit involved several vulnerabilities: a Logout CSRF bug forcing users to log out, a Login CSRF bug enabling login to the attacker's account, a Checkpoint tool flaw leaking visited URLs, and an XSS vulnerability allowing execution of JavaScript in the Sandbox Domain Di Minin et al. (2021). These flaws compromised user accounts and privacy, underscoring the need for robust security measures and continuous patching. The Internet Security Threat Report highlights a concerning trend: the growing number of hackers worldwide who target social networking sites to obtain information illegally. These hackers employ various tactics such as malware, spam emails, and deceptive advertisements to monetize their activities through SNSs. Notable figures and prominent organizations, including Mark Zuckerberg, CEO of Facebook, have fallen victim to hacking incidents. For instance, Zuckerberg's Twitter and Pinterest accounts were compromised, with the hacker exploiting his LinkedIn password, which was reportedly 'dadada'. Similarly, hackers have successfully breached the accounts of Newsweek and Delta Air Lines Inc., disseminating false messages. These instances underscore the prevalent method of choice for cybercriminals today: exploiting vulnerabilities within Social media websites.

In response to the increasing array of security threats, both conventional and emerging, particularly those exploiting multimedia content on social networks, numerous innovative solutions have been developed by security firms and researchers. These solutions, such as Steganalysis, digital oblivion, and watermarking, aim to safeguard individuals from cybercriminal activities and provide a secure environment for sharing multimedia content W. Luo et al. (2009). Additionally, traditional online threats like phishing and spam can be mitigated through the use of specialized detection tools. Furthermore, implementing robust privacy settings, authentication mechanisms, and utilizing social protection applications like Monitor Minor can actively combat security threats on social networking sites. The paper is structured as follows: Section 2 delves into notable previous works. Section 3 outlines the primary threats and security issues in Social Networking websites. Section 4 classifies security solutions. Finally, Section 5 concludes the paper.

2. LITERATURE REVIEW

Gao *et al.* (2011) categorize security concerns in Social media sites into four primary groups: (a) Malware attacks, (b) Viral marketing, (c) Network structural-based attacks, and (d) Privacy issues. They offer a comprehensive examination of defence mechanisms tailored to mitigate these challenges.

Novak and Li (n.d.) conducted a survey highlighting privacy concerns and major security challenges within SNS. Their work introduces users to existing techniques aimed at ensuring security from various entities online, such as Social media providers, advertisers, and third-party application developers. They also provide an overview and discuss how factors like location hubs, users' attributes, and link prediction contribute to interference. Jin *et al.* (2013) focus on studying user behaviours in social media from four perspectives: (a) traffic activity, (b) interaction and connection, (c) malicious behaviour, and (d) mobile social behaviour. Their review examines existing security schemes necessary for users' motivations, and the primary challenges faced by users in maintaining security. Fire, Goldschmidt, and Elovici (2014) conducted a comprehensive survey focusing on various security and privacy threats within Social Networking Sites. They grouped these dangers into four categories: (a) threats aimed at children, (b) contemporary risks, (c) amalgamated hazards, and (d) traditional perils. Their work includes a high-standard taxonomy aimed at aiding users in protecting themselves from these threats. Building upon this taxonomy, Kayes and Iamnitchi (2015) further elaborate on how stakeholders in social networks can prevent traditional privacy and security attacks. They delve into the specifics of the taxonomy, offering insights into preventive measures against these threats. Deliri et al. (2015) discuss prevalent attacks encountered in Social

Networking Sites, such as phishing, malware, identity theft, Sybil attacks, and others. They also propose various counter measures aimed at mitigating these threats. While previous studies have addressed conventional security risks confronting social media users, they have not extensively covered challenges related to multimedia sharing. Rathore *et al* (2017) systematically examined issues, challenges, threats, and solutions in this domain.

3. PRIMARY PERILS AND SECURITY CONCERNS IN SOCIAL MEDIA & ONLINE INTERACTIONS

In the era predating social media, interacting with friends often required stepping outdoors—an intimidating prospect for some. Nowadays, virtually everyone, including the older generation, maintains a presence on social media platforms. These platforms serve as avenues for expressing creativity, sharing life updates with friends, and meticulously organizing our various interests and activities. Regardless of the specific platform you prefer, it's evident that many individuals underestimate the importance of social media safety Jain et al.(2021). They freely post, share, and re tweet content without adequately considering their privacy. We're exploring 11 significant threats and scams prevalent on social media that require your attention.

3.1 Likejacking, or clickjacking

Likejacking, or clickjacking, operates by deceiving users into interacting with elements on a webpage without their knowledge, often resulting in unintentional likes on social media. The technique involves two layers: a concealed "Like" button that follows the user's cursor and a visually appealing post displayed on the forefront. This post could be anything enticing, such as a captivating video or a remarkable body transformation story.

While Facebook has introduced measures to mitigate likejacking through features like a bookmarklet, it remains a concern in 2017 due to the buying and selling of previously liked pages. Pages once considered safe may now harbor malware or suspicious links. Therefore, it's crucial to exercise caution when interacting with any content to avoid potential security threats.

3.2. Fake giveaways

In recent years, major brands have increasingly turned to competitions on social media as a cost-effective method to garner likes, clicks, and traffic. These competitions are ubiquitous across various platforms. For instance, Mondolez International, a chocolate conglomerate, organized a Snapchat contest inviting users to submit hand-drawn photos of their TimeOut bar for a chance to win €10,000. Similarly, designer Marc Jacobs utilized Instagram for a social media casting call under the hashtag #castmemarc, seeking new models.

While social media competitions generate significant engagement, they also pose a risk in the form of fake giveaways designed to deceive users into divulging personal information. An infamous instance involved several pages falsely claiming to represent renowned car brands, offering new cars as prizes. Many of these pages were established for "like farming," gathering likes before being sold to third parties.

3.3 Unbelievable news stories

Unbelievable news stories, often disguised as sensational videos, are a common tactic used to spread malware. These stories feature outrageous titles and cover a wide range of topics, from reports about recently deceased celebrities to shocking global events or explicit content.

Driven by morbid curiosity, many individuals click on these links in large numbers, unwittingly compromising their accounts or computers. In some cases, these clicks result in monetary gains for scammers through affiliate scams. This highlights the importance of staying vigilant and cautious while consuming online content.

3.4 Affiliate scams

The primary goal of any scam is financial gain. When scammers fail to make money from one method, they quickly pivot to new ideas or technologies to deceive people. In the realm of social media scams, affiliate programs often serve as a lucrative source of income M. Raggo (2019).

Affiliate scams operate through incentive programs where companies compensate affiliates for directing traffic or acquiring new subscribers for their website. For instance, you might come across an advertisement on Twitter offering a gift card for an upscale department store to the first 20 individuals who provide their email addresses.

Upon entering your email address and submitting it, the scammer earns a referral fee, while you never receive the promised gift card. Subsequently, you may find your inbox flooded with spam emails, promising various incentives. This underscores the importance of exercising caution and skepticism when encountering such offers online.

3.5 Fake Followers

Purchasing followers has become a widespread practice, with countless services offering thousands of followers for a nominal fee, applicable across various social media platforms.

Why would someone resort to buying fake followers? Often, it's to inflate their perceived popularity and bolster their ego.

However, the implications of fake followers extend beyond vanity. Some fake accounts may add or follow you with the intention of sending dangerous phishing messages. While having a large following can be appealing, it's crucial to ensure that your followers are genuine and not potential threats.

3.6 Phishing

Phishing involves fraudulent attempts where individuals receive messages disguised as legitimate correspondence from reputable companies or contacts, aiming to extract personal information such as passwords or credit card details K. Thakur et al. (2018). One of the reasons phishing is so effective is because the emails or messages often appear genuine. Some phishing emails even include links to spoofed versions of familiar websites, like banks or online stores, prompting users to enter their sensitive information. Unbeknownst to the user, this information could then be exploited by hackers for credit card fraud or identity theft.

While phishing is commonly associated with email, it's important to note that private messages on social media platforms can also contain phishing links. It's crucial never to click on a link in an unsolicited email unless you explicitly requested it and are certain of its destination. Vigilance is key to protecting yourself against phishing attempts.

3.7 Catfishing

The link between phishing and catfishing lies in the deceptive nature of both practices. Phishing involves tricking individuals into revealing personal information by masquerading as a trustworthy entity, while catfishing entails creating fake personas to deceive others online, often for personal gain or emotional manipulation. The term "catfishing" originated from the 2010 documentary "Catfish," directed by Nev Schulman, which explores the phenomenon of creating fake online personas. In the documentary, one of the characters uses an analogy involving catfish and cod to describe people who misrepresent themselves online to keep others on their toes. This analogy led to the coining of the term "catfishing" to describe the act of creating fake identities online. While catfishing can sometimes be harmless or even entertaining, it can also have serious consequences. In some cases, catfishes may be bots created by spammers to distribute malicious links on social platforms. Additionally, there have been instances where catfishing has led to dangerous situations, such as

the case where a woman discovered her niece's murderous intentions after befriending her through a fake Facebook account.

3.8 Cyberbullying and abuse

The internet's inherent anonymity often facilitates negative behaviour, particularly on social media platforms where there are few regulations or enforcement measures. This lack of accountability can lead to a surge in harmful conduct. Celebrities, in particular, are vulnerable to receiving an onslaught of hurtful comments and derogatory remarks on their accounts. Over the past few years, cyber bullying has become a prevalent issue in social media usage, prompting numerous organizations and networks to take proactive measures against this form of abuse.

3.9 Identity theft

Identity theft affects millions of individuals annually, driven by a combination of factors including a lack of awareness, growing trust in social media, and insufficient data standards regarding personal information collected online. The rise of social advertising also contributes, as individuals often unwittingly disclose vast amounts of personal data A.-S.K. Pathan (2018).

Criminals exploit social media platforms to gather information, such as ticket stubs for duplicating barcodes, holiday posts for planning burglaries, and personal details for cracking passwords or stealing identities.

To mitigate the risk, it's crucial to refrain from publicly posting sensitive information such as full names, birthdates, hometowns, relationship statuses, or pet names on social accounts. Every interaction on social media, including likes, shares, and comments, provides insights into one's identity, so it's essential to carefully consider before sharing personal information online.

3.10 Fake apps

Quizzes and social apps can be deceptively enticing, often drawing users in with catchy titles such as "What Harry Potter character are you?" or "What's your personality type?" or "What color is your personality?"

These quizzes are ubiquitous on social media platforms. Many users, and perhaps you've been among them, have engaged with these quizzes. However, it's essential to be aware of the risks involved. In 2015, for instance, a Facebook quiz titled "Most Used Words" came with terms and conditions that allowed developers to sell user data to third parties. This included not only basic information like names and profile pictures but also more extensive data such as friends lists, entire Facebook histories, IP addresses, and device information.

While these quizzes may seem harmless or entertaining on the surface, they often come with significant privacy implications. It's crucial for users to exercise caution and carefully review the terms and conditions before participating in such activities on social media platforms.

3.11 Private messages with dodgy links

Worms are a particularly sneaky form of malware that replicate themselves to spread across multiple computers or devices. They often exploit human curiosity or trust by masquerading as enticing files, messages, or links. For example, a worm might appear as a video file, a compromising photo, or a message from a friend urging you to click on a shortened link out of curiosity.

The danger lies in the fact that clicking on these malicious links or files can unleash the worm onto your device, potentially compromising your data, spreading further to your contacts, or even hijacking your device for nefarious purposes. Shortened links, in particular, pose a significant risk as they obscure the destination URL, making it difficult to discern whether the link leads to a legitimate website or a malicious one. While curiosity may tempt you to click on such links, it's essential to exercise caution and refrain from putting your device at risk for the sake of curiosity. Always verify the source of the message or link before clicking, and be wary of unsolicited messages or suspicious content, even if it appears to come from someone you know.

4. SOME SECURITY SOLUTIONS FOR SOCIAL MEDIA

4.1 Fake Profile Detection

There are several techniques and strategies used to detect fake profiles, Profile Analysis, Behavioural Analysis, Machine Learning Algorithms, Image Recognition, Network Analysis, Verification Processes, and Community Reporting. Overall, detecting fake profiles requires a combination of technological solutions, human oversight, and user participation to effectively identify and mitigate the risks associated with fraudulent or deceptive behaviour online.

4.2 Watermarking

Watermarking is a technique used to add identifying information or a mark onto digital content, such as images, videos, or documents. The purpose of watermarking is to claim ownership, deter unauthorized use, or provide additional information about the content. Watermarking is commonly used by photographers, artists, and content creators to protect their work from unauthorized use or distribution. It is also employed by organizations to track the usage of sensitive documents or to verify the authenticity of digital assets.

4.3 Cyber grooming

Cyber grooming is a serious form of online child exploitation and abuse that can have lasting psychological, emotional, and physical consequences for victims K. Ignatiev (2019). It is essential for parents, caregivers, educators, and young people themselves to be aware of the signs of grooming and take steps to protect against it, including monitoring online activities, setting appropriate boundaries, and encouraging open communication about internet safety. Additionally, reporting any suspected instances of cyber grooming to the relevant authorities or online platforms can help prevent further harm to children and hold perpetrators accountable for their actions.

4.4 Integrated security measures

Integrated security measures refer to the security features and functionalities that are integrated directly into software, hardware, or digital platforms to help protect against various threats and vulnerabilities. These solutions are designed to provide baseline security measures and may include:

4.4.1Firewalls:

Built-in firewalls serve as either software or hardware setups designed to oversee and regulate both inbound and outbound network traffic. They function as a protective shield, segregating a trusted internal network from external ones, notably the internet. Firewalls are adept at thwarting unauthorized entry, intercepting malicious data transmissions, and identifying and notifying users of potentially suspicious behaviours.

4.4.2Antivirus/Antimalware Software:

Many operating systems come with built-in antivirus or antimalware capabilities that help detect and remove malicious software, such as viruses, worms, trojans, and spyware. These security solutions often include real-time scanning, automated updates, and quarantine features to protect against known and emerging threats.

4.4.3 Encryption:

Encryption entails transforming data into a secure format that's only accessible or decipherable with the correct encryption key. Numerous software applications and digital platforms incorporate encryption functionalities to safeguard sensitive data, like passwords, financial transactions, and communication channels, from unauthorized access or interception.

4.4.4User Authentication:

Incorporated user authentication mechanisms, such as passwords, biometric identification (like fingerprints or facial recognition), and multi-factor authentication (MFA), play a vital role in confirming users' identities and managing access to digital assets. These security measures help prevent unauthorized access to accounts, devices, and data.

4.4.5Security Updates and Patches:

Operating systems, software applications, and digital platforms regularly release security updates and patches to address known vulnerabilities and weaknesses. Built-in update mechanisms automate the process of downloading and installing these updates to ensure that systems and devices are protected against the latest security threats.

4.4.6 Secure Boot

Secure boot is a security measure that guarantees the integrity of the boot process by authenticating the digital signatures of firmware and operating system components before they are loaded into memory. This serves to thwart unauthorized or malicious software from running during the boot sequence, thus safeguarding system security.

4.4.7 Data Backup and Recovery

Integrated backup and recovery solutions empower users to generate duplicates of their data and reinstate it should data loss, corruption, or unauthorized access occur. These capabilities are instrumental in upholding the availability and integrity of vital data while mitigating the repercussions of security breaches.

4.4.8 Privacy Settings and Controls:

Numerous digital platforms and online services incorporate built-in privacy settings and controls, enabling users to tailor their privacy preferences, regulate data sharing permissions, and determine who can access their personal information. These functionalities empower users to safeguard their privacy and curtail exposure to potential risks

5 PHISHING DETECTION

Phishing detection refers to the process of identifying and thwarting phishing attempts, which are fraudulent schemes aimed at tricking individuals into divulging sensitive information such as passwords, usernames, credit card numbers, or other personal data. Here are several common methods used for phishing detection Email Filters and Spam Detection, URL Inspection, Sender Authentication, Anti-Phishing Tools and Software, Multi-Factor Authentication.

6. CONCLUSIONS

Billions of internet users have embraced Social media as a crucial means of communication. The allure of freely sharing personal photos, opinions, accomplishments, and more has captivated many, encouraging daily engagement with these platforms to connect with friends and family. The beauty of Social media lies in their ability to transcend geographical boundaries, allowing users to connect without worrying about additional costs beyond their monthly internet fees. Life has undoubtedly become more convenient, but with this convenience comes heightened risks. Sensitive and personal information can easily be compromised and leaked through social networks, posing significant privacy and security concerns for users. While academia has developed innovative solutions to address security concerns in social media, there remains a significant gap between theoretical advancements and practical implementation. Many proposed solutions struggle to transition from the academic realm to real-world applications due to various challenges, such as feasibility, scalability, and compatibility with existing platforms. Therefore, there is an urgent need for ongoing and iterative review of security issues in social networks to keep pace with technological advancements. By continuously evaluating and adapting security measures, researchers and practitioners can better address evolving threats and enhance the overall security posture of social media platforms. This iterative approach is essential to effectively safeguarding user data and privacy in an ever-changing digital landscape.

This paper delves into various privacy and security concerns that affect users of Social media. The primary objective of this study is to enlighten users about these issues and provide guidance on how to safeguard themselves when engaging with social media platforms. By elucidating the potential risks and vulnerabilities associated with Social media, the paper aims to empower users to take proactive measures to protect their privacy and security while navigating the online social landscape.

REFERENCES

Brain, J. (2021). Social Media in the Workplace: What Every Executive Should Know. Retrieved from https://everyonesocial.com/blog/social-media-in-the-workplace

Bright, L. F., Lim, H. S., & Logan, K. (2021). "Should I Post or Ghost?": Examining how privacy concerns impact social media engagement in US consumers. *Psychology and Marketing*, 38(10), 1712–1722. DOI: 10.1002/mar.21499

Deliri, S., & Albanese, M. (2015). *Security and privacy issues in social networks.* Data Management in Pervasive Systems. DOI: 10.1007/978-3-319-20062-0_10

Di Minin, E., Fink, C., Hausmann, A., Kremer, J., & Kulkarni, R. (2021). How to address data privacy concerns when using social media data in conservation science. *Conservation Biology*, 35(2), 437–446. DOI: 10.1111/cobi.13708 PMID: 33749044

Fire, M., Goldschmidt, R., & Elovici, Y. (2014). Online social networks: Threats and solutions. *IEEE Communications Surveys and Tutorials*, 16(4), 2019–2036. DOI: 10.1109/COMST.2014.2321628

Gao, H., Hu, J., Huang, T., Wang, J., & Chen, Y. (2011, July-August). Security issues in online social networks. *IEEE Internet Computing*, 15(4), 56–63. DOI: 10.1109/MIC.2011.50

Ignatiev, K. (2019) "Statistics on Parental Control Alerts for Various Countries," https://securelist.com/page/107/?calendar=2010-12&chapter=8 (last accessed: 16 December 2019)

Jain, A. K., Sahoo, S. R., & Jyoti, K. (2021). Online social networks security and privacy: Comprehensive review and analysis. *Complex & Intelligent Systems*, 7(5), 2157–2177. DOI: 10.1007/s40747-021-00409-7

Jin, L., Chen, Y., Wang, T., Hui, P., & Vasilakos, A. V. (2013, September). Understanding user behavior in online social networks: A survey. *IEEE Communications Magazine*, 51(9), 144–150. DOI: 10.1109/MCOM.2013.6588663

Kayes, I., & Iamnitchi, A. (2015). A survey on privacy and security in online social networks. arXiv preprint arXiv:1504.03342.

Luo, W., Liu, J., Liu, J., & Fan, C. "An Analysis of Security in Social Networks," *2009 Eighth IEEE International Conference on Dependable, Autonomic and Secure Computing (DASC'09)*, 12-14 Dec. 2009, Chengdu, China. DOI: 10.1109/DASC.2009.100

Novak, E., & Li, Q. "A Survey of Security and Privacy in Online Social Networks," available at: https://pdfs.semanticscholar.org/f602/caa6f711f57369246fefa0d608d10bc7e35e.pdf (last accessed: 16 December 2019)

"Number of social network users worldwide from 2010 to 2021 (in billions)," Statista Inc., available at: https://www.statista.com/statistics/278414/number-of-worldwide-social-network-users/ (last accessed: 16 December 2019)

Pathan, A. S. K. (Ed.). (2014). *The state of the art in intrusion prevention and detection* (Vol. 44). CRC press.

Raggo, M. "Anatomy of a Social Media Attack," available at: https://www.darkreading.com/analytics/anatomy-of-a-social-media-attack/a/d-id/1326680 (last accessed: 16 December 2019).

Rathore, S., Shamra, P. K., Loia, V., Jeong, Y.-S., & Park, J. H. (2017, December). Social network security: Issues, challenges, threats, and solutions. *Information Sciences*, 421, 43–69. DOI: 10.1016/j.ins.2017.08.063

Thakur, K., Shan, J., & Pathan, A.-S. K. (2018, April). Innovations of Phishing Defense: The Mechanism, Measurement and Defense Strategies. *International Journal of Communication Networks and Information Security*, 10(1), 19–27.

"The Top 20 Valuable Facebook Statistics," Zephoria Digital Marketing, available at: https://zephoria.com/top-15-valuable-facebook-statistics/ (last accessed: 16 December 2019). "2019 Top 5 Facebook Video Statistics Infographics," available at: https://www.everincreasingcircles.com/2019-top-5-facebook-video-statistics-infographics/ (last accessed: 16 December 2019).

Chapter 15

Theoretical Insights Into User Security and Privacy in Social Media Environments

Koppala Venugopal
https://orcid.org/0000-0002-3472-1477
Aditya Institute of Technology and Management, India

Bellala Jagadeesh
Aditya Institute of Technology and Management, India

ABSTRACT

This study offers theoretical insights into user security and privacy within social media environments, addressing the complex interplay of socio-cultural, psychological, and technological factors shaping users' experiences. Employing an exploratory design and qualitative approach, the research delves into user perceptions, behaviors, and coping mechanisms regarding security and privacy threats on social media platforms. Secondary data collection, including literature reviews and empirical studies, informs the analysis within a theoretical framework drawn from sociology, psychology, communication studies, and computer science. Findings highlight diverse user concerns, including data privacy, cyber threats, misinformation, and platform accountability, underscoring the need for proactive measures to mitigate risks and protect user rights. Recommendations include enhancing user education, promoting platform accountability, advocating for regulatory frameworks, fostering interdisciplinary collaboration, and supporting continuous research and evaluation efforts.

DOI: 10.4018/979-8-3693-9235-5.ch015

1. INTRODUCTION

The proliferation of social media platforms has revolutionized the way individuals interact, communicate, and share information online. With billions of users worldwide engaging in various social media activities daily, concerns regarding user security and privacy have become paramount. Social media environments serve as virtual spaces where users disclose personal information, interact with others, and engage in various online activities, raising significant questions about the protection of their data and privacy.

Theoretical insights into user security and privacy in social media environments are essential for understanding the complex dynamics at play within these digital spaces. Such insights delve into the underlying principles, mechanisms, and factors influencing user security and privacy in social media interactions. By employing theoretical frameworks, researchers can elucidate the multifaceted nature of these phenomena and identify potential strategies for mitigating risks and enhancing user protection (Gopalakrishna Vakamullu et al. 2023).

At the core of this study is the recognition that social media platforms serve as rich ecosystems where users navigate a delicate balance between social interaction and personal privacy. Theoretical perspectives draw from diverse disciplines such as sociology, psychology, communication studies, and computer science to provide a holistic understanding of user behaviors, platform dynamics, and socio-technical factors shaping security and privacy outcomes (Koppala Venugopal and Saumendra Das, 2022).

Sociological theories offer valuable insights into the social dynamics of online interactions, highlighting the role of norms, trust, and social capital in shaping user behavior and attitudes towards privacy. Psychological theories shed light on individual motivations, cognitive biases, and privacy preferences, informing our understanding of why users may engage in risky behaviors or disclose sensitive information online.

Communication theories contribute to the examination of information flow, disclosure patterns, and privacy management strategies within social media environments (Koppala Venugopal et al. 2023). They explore how users negotiate privacy boundaries, engage in self-presentation, and manage their online identities amidst evolving communication norms and platform affordances.

From a technical standpoint, theoretical frameworks rooted in computer science and information security provide insights into the technological infrastructure, algorithmic processes, and security mechanisms underpinning social media platforms. These theories elucidate the vulnerabilities, threats, and privacy risks inherent in the design and operation of these platforms, guiding efforts to develop robust security solutions and privacy-enhancing technologies.

Moreover, interdisciplinary approaches that integrate insights from various theoretical perspectives enable a comprehensive understanding of user security and privacy in social media environments. By synthesizing sociocultural, psychological, communicative, and technical dimensions, researchers can unravel the complexities of online privacy and security, paving the way for more effective interventions, policies, and design guidelines (Gopalakrishna, V. et al. 2021).

In summary, theoretical insights into user security and privacy in social media environments provide a nuanced understanding of the underlying dynamics shaping user experiences and outcomes in these digital spaces. By drawing upon diverse disciplinary perspectives and interdisciplinary frameworks, researchers can address the multifaceted challenges and opportunities inherent in safeguarding user security and privacy online.

The increasing ubiquity of social media platforms has brought forth complex challenges concerning user security and privacy. While these platforms offer unprecedented opportunities for social interaction, content sharing, and information dissemination, they also expose users to various risks, ranging from data breaches and identity theft to surveillance and exploitation. Despite the proliferation of privacy settings and security features, users continue to grapple with maintaining control over their personal information and safeguarding their online privacy (Murlikrishna, P.N. et al. 2020)

One of the primary issues revolves around the collection, storage, and utilization of user data by social media companies and third-party entities. Social media platforms often collect vast amounts of user information, including demographic data, browsing history, location data, and content preferences, to fuel targeted advertising, algorithmic recommendations, and personalized services. However, the opacity surrounding data collection practices, the lack of user consent mechanisms, and the potential for data misuse raise concerns about privacy infringement and user autonomy.

Furthermore, the inherent architecture and functionality of social media platforms introduce vulnerabilities that can be exploited by malicious actors to compromise user security. Cyberattacks, phishing scams, malware distribution, and account hijacking are just a few examples of the threats facing social media users. Moreover, the interconnected nature of social networks amplifies the spread of misinformation, fake accounts, and malicious content, undermining trust and exacerbating security risks.

Another critical issue pertains to the erosion of privacy boundaries and the blurring of public and private spheres in online environments. Social media users often grapple with the tension between sharing personal information to connect with others and maintaining privacy to protect sensitive data. The fluidity of privacy settings, the persistence of digital footprints, and the lack of control over shared content contribute to a sense of vulnerability and exposure among users.

Moreover, social media platforms' business models, which rely heavily on advertising revenue and user engagement metrics, incentivize the commodification of user data and the prioritization of profit over privacy (Koppala Venugopal et al. 2022). This commercialization of user information creates conflicts of interest between platform operators, advertisers, and users, undermining efforts to prioritize user security and privacy.

Additionally, cultural and contextual factors shape users' perceptions, attitudes, and behaviors regarding security and privacy in social media environments. Cultural norms, societal expectations, and regulatory frameworks vary across regions and demographics, influencing how users navigate privacy settings, interact with others, and perceive online risks (Koppala Venugopal, 2020). Understanding these cultural nuances is crucial for developing tailored interventions and policies that address the diverse needs and preferences of social media users worldwide.

In light of these challenges, there is a pressing need for theoretical insights into user security and privacy in social media environments. Such insights can inform the development of comprehensive frameworks, strategies, and interventions aimed at promoting user empowerment, enhancing platform accountability, and fostering a safer and more privacy-respecting online ecosystem. By addressing the multifaceted dimensions of user security and privacy, researchers can contribute to the advancement of knowledge in this critical area and support efforts to mitigate risks and protect user rights in the digital age.

2. OBJECTIVES OF THE STUDY

Objectives of the study are to

- Investigate how social media users perceive and experience security and privacy concerns within online environments, shedding light on their attitudes, behaviors, and coping mechanisms.
- Examine the role of social media platform features, policies, and algorithms in shaping user security and privacy outcomes, providing insights into the socio-technical factors influencing online interactions.
- Identify and analyze emerging threats, vulnerabilities, and risks to user security and privacy in social media environments, including the impact of evolving cyber threats, misinformation campaigns, and data breaches.

3. LITERATURE REVIEW

Various social media platforms and services are accessible in the contemporary landscape, including but not limited to Facebook, YouTube, Twitter, Instagram, LinkedIn, and Snapchat, as noted by A. Smith and M. Anderson in 2018.

In today's world, the Internet stands out as the ubiquitous technology used by nearly everyone on a daily basis. With Internet technology, individuals worldwide, regardless of their level of experience with information technology, can easily engage in communication, share information, participate in various activities, and utilize the Internet for a multitude of purposes, as highlighted by D. Chaffey in 2019.

Social media serves the purpose of facilitating personal and business-oriented interactions among individuals globally, as outlined by Edosomwan et al. in 2011. It is a platform that enables users to share content.

Despite the positive aspects and various constructive impacts, there are also negative effects associated with wasting time. This can lead to academic failures in schools and universities, as well as adverse impacts on social aspects such as marriage, employment, and various other destructive issues. Researchers worldwide urgently need to investigate these issues, finding solutions to mitigate or eliminate the destructive consequences, as emphasized by Abbas et al. in 2019.

The growing prevalence of social media usage has turned it into a breeding ground for cybercriminals and cybercrime. Previous research indicates numerous threats and security risks confronting users of social media, with organizations also falling victim. Those particularly susceptible to attacks and threats are individuals or entities lacking a culture of safe Internet usage, as highlighted by Alguliyev et al. in 2018. This implies that virtually all social media platforms carry security risks

The risks posed by these issues can extend to governments, impacting national security and economic stability. Consequently, it is imperative for everyone to cultivate a baseline level of Internet literacy, enabling awareness of illegal activities, potential threats, and the importance of protective measures. This involves using Internet applications efficiently and avoiding misuse, as emphasized by Kumar and Somani in 2018.

Social media serves as a platform enabling users to share diverse content, encompassing various forms of information such as messages, documents, and videos covering a wide array of topics. Additionally, this service provides users the opportunity to disseminate new ideas, express opinions, and share thoughts with a broad audience, as highlighted by McCarroll and Curran in 2013

Over the past decade, social media platforms like Facebook, Twitter, Snapchat, YouTube, and Instagram have experienced significant expansion in user numbers, as noted by E. Ortiz-Ospina in 2019. This surge in popularity is attributed to widespread adoption, particularly through smartphone usage, as a means of communication, knowledge-sharing, expressing thoughts, and sharing various forms of media. The diverse features offered by these platforms continue to attract an ever-growing global audience.

It is crucial to disseminate this information within communities, organizations, and universities through knowledgeable individuals who can actively educate others on these matters. These advocates should strive to establish and promote best practices that can be standardized and regularly updated, akin to applications, as emphasized by Oxley in 2011

Civilized regions encompass countries and cities that possess a comprehensive range of services, including the internet and other technologies, as defined by Chan and Virkki in 2014. It is widely acknowledged that there exist distinct variations in cyberculture among users in different countries or cities.

Research indicates that numerous organizations can effectively revise their security policies to encompass social media without necessitating the creation of separate and specific guidelines for it. The findings also emphasize the importance of implementing a robust overall security awareness program, coupled with technical and administrative safeguards, for organizations and government officials to consider, as highlighted by Hogben in 2007 and Hiatt & Choi in 2016.

In broad terms, the threats can be categorized into two forms. The first is the input form, where users share their personal information, reflecting their cultural background. Much of this personal information provides attackers with a comprehensive understanding of an individual, including details necessary for various attacks such as credit card fraud or identity theft. Sharing routine activities like vacations and current locations amplifies the attacker's level of control, as noted by Adu Michael & Adewale Olumide in 2014.

This constitutes a significant aspect of the problem, and a potential solution to address this will be suggested later. Occasionally, this behavior stems from a desire for popularity, while at other times, it is simply a manifestation of pure disregard (Barnes, S. 2006).

He further emphasizes that although Facebook incorporates privacy settings that users can manage, the default setting upon creating an account is set to public. Therefore, a new user who does not adjust these settings to make them more stringent is essentially sharing information that is visible to the public and non-friends (Verma, A. et al. 2013).

Facebook has undergone several updates to its security framework with the aim of enhancing user-friendliness in customizing settings and granting users greater control over the visibility of individual posts. Although this doesn't offer foolproof security, it proves beneficial as long as users are aware of the features and use them judiciously. Nevertheless, relying solely on these settings is not a substitute for exercising prudence in online content sharing. The speaker continues to highlight that many educational institutions are taking proactive measures to educate students on the significance of online privacy, aiming to bolster overall security in the digital realm (Verma, A. et al. 2013)

This strategy encompasses a feature allowing a user to either accept or decline another user's request for information, irrespective of their friendship status. Furthermore, users have the flexibility to establish two distinct databases for information based on their level of trust in the requester. By doing so, they gain the ability to safeguard their most sensitive information, creating a nuanced approach to data sharing that reflects the user's varying levels of trust in different individuals. This not only provides users with a more tailored and secure experience but also underscores the importance of user control in managing the flow of personal information within online platforms (Barnes, S. 2006).

Implementing such a system would significantly contribute to preventing a potential adversary from fully recovering a user's profile. An example of a social network that employs this approach is Diaspora. Furthermore, as highlighted, it is imperative to conduct thorough risk management. This involves assessing and mitigating potential risks, ultimately aiding in the establishment of a robust security policy within the organization in question. By prioritizing risk management, organizations can proactively address vulnerabilities, enhance resilience, and fortify their security measures, thereby creating a safer digital environment for users. This underscores the importance of a holistic approach to security that combines user-level controls with overarching organizational strategies (Kim, H. J. 2012).

An assailant has the potential to embed malicious scripts into URLs, and when users click on these URLs, the injected script may execute on their systems. This execution poses a significant threat as it can enable the collection of sensitive information from the compromised system (Zhang Z, Gupta BB (2018). This form of cyber-attack is known as URL-based script injection, where the attacker exploits vulnerabilities in web security to introduce harmful scripts. These scripts can execute unauthorized actions on the user's system, such as data theft, and pose a considerable risk to the security and privacy of the affected individuals. Implementing robust security measures, including secure coding practices and regular system updates, is essential to mitigate the risks associated with URL-based script injections.

Cyber espionage represents a specific category within targeted attacks. In the exploration of this domain, Sahoo et al. presented a comprehensive ATA (Advanced Persistent Threat) detection framework. This framework is meticulously crafted to identify and counteract targeted attacks, as elaborated in their work (Sahoo SR, Gupta BB (2020). Additionally, the authors introduced a system design checklist, specifically tailored to enhance the capability of detecting and mitigating the impact of such sophisticated and focused cyber threats. This framework and checklist collectively contribute to strengthening the defense mechanisms against cyber espionage, providing a valuable resource for organizations aiming to fortify their cybersecurity posture

It is advisable to revoke access to an application if it remains unused for an extended period. Numerous third-party applications utilize social media accounts for authentication. To address security and privacy apprehensions, it is prudent to grant access exclusively to applications that are deemed trustworthy, as emphasized in Michael and Olumide (2014). This precautionary measure ensures a more secure and privacy-conscious approach to managing third-party application access tied to social media accounts (Bailey, Michael. et al 2009).

The implementation of an Intrusion Detection and Prevention System (IDSS) effectively addresses the challenges associated with low accuracy and prolonged response times. Leveraging machine learning classifiers within the IDSS framework not only mitigates these issues but also facilitates swift response times, a critical factor in the timely detection of spam on Facebook, as discussed in reference (Rathore S et al. 2018). This integration of machine learning enhances the system's efficiency, enabling it to rapidly identify and combat spam, thereby contributing to an improved overall security posture on the platform. The utilization of advanced technologies within IDSS underscores its pivotal role in proactively safeguarding against spam-related threats.

In their work, Al-Qurishi et al. (2018) introduced an innovative Sybil detection system leveraging a deep learning model designed for precise prediction of Sybil attacks. The proposed model is composed of three integral modules: a data harvesting module, a feature extracting module, and a deep regression model. These modules operate in a cohesive manner to systematically analyze user profiles on Twitter, enhancing the accuracy of Sybil attack detection. Similarly, Rahman et al. put forth a model named SybilTrap, presenting a graph-based semi-supervised learning system. This model incorporates a comprehensive approach, utilizing both content-based and structure-based techniques for the detection of Sybil attacks. By integrating information from the content of user interactions and the underlying network structure, SybilTrap aims to provide a robust defence mechanism against Sybil attacks. These advancements in Sybil detection models highlight the significance of integrating sophisticated techniques, such as deep learning and graph-based semi-supervised learning, to bolster the efficacy and accuracy of identifying and mitigating Sybil attacks in online social networks.

Just as the medical study used algorithms like SVM, DT, RF, XGBoosting, and ANN to achieve high accuracy and efficiency in diagnosis (A. B. Mahammad and R. Kumar, 2023), similar approaches can enhance security and privacy in social media also. By evaluating algorithms on metrics like accuracy, precision, recall, and F1 score, and identifying critical features, social media security can be significantly improved. Implementing these models in robust environments and continuously refining them for larger datasets can ensure better detection and mitigation of security threats and privacy breaches, demonstrating the cross-disciplinary potential of machine learning applications.

As like as Human Computer Interaction research employs diverse data sources like EEG, EOG, and EMG for accurate action identification (Kumar, Amit et al. 2019), social media security can benefit from using varied data types to improve threat detection. Additionally, the focus on inclusive communication methods in HCI can inspire more accessible security measures for all user demographics in social media. Future advancements with deep learning in HCI also suggest potential improvements in social media security, offering more precise and adaptive protection against evolving threats.

The image enhancement study addresses the challenge of poor-quality night images by refining contrast and reducing noise (Kumar, Sandeep & Kumar, Dr Rajeev 2022) and in the same way, social media security research can benefit from using advanced data processing techniques to enhance the detection and mitigation of security threats. By applying sophisticated algorithms to analyze and improve data quality, both fields aim to achieve clearer, more accurate results—whether in visual clarity for surveillance or in identifying security breaches and preserving user privacy on social media platforms.

Advanced security measures in social media can similarly use these techniques to enhance threat detection and privacy protection just as SNA leverages soft computing methodologies like neuro-fuzzy hybridization to efficiently analyze and derive meaningful insights from complex social data (Kumar, Dr Rajeev & Sharma, M.K.. (2016). By employing fuzzy sets, neural networks, and genetic algorithms, researchers can develop more accurate, cost-effective, and adaptive solutions for maintaining security and privacy amidst the growing and dynamic landscape of social media. This approach ensures that social media platforms can better handle imprecise data and model complex user interactions to prevent the spread of harmful opinions and protect user information.

Just as the algorithm enhances the clarity and accuracy of images in hazy conditions by effectively processing color and illuminance-reflectance data (Meenu et al. 2019), analogous advanced data processing techniques can be applied to enhance the detection and analysis of security threats on social media platforms. By improving the descriptive power and robustness of data analysis methods, researchers can more accurately identify and mitigate privacy and security issues, thereby providing clearer and more reliable protection for users in the complex environment of social media.

The ANN and big data techniques improve the prediction of complex, non-linear phenomena like climate and traffic (M. H. F. Siddiqui and R. Kumar, 2020) and related advanced computational models can enhance the detection and mitigation of security and privacy threats on social media platforms. By leveraging data from diverse sources and utilizing state-of-the-art computing technologies, researchers can develop more accurate and efficient methods to protect user privacy and secure social media environments against evolving threats.

Lesser-known social media platforms, which cater to niche communities with specific interests, often foster different privacy expectations among users. Nissenbaum (2010) suggests that privacy norms vary contextually, leading users on smaller platforms to share more personal information under the assumption of greater privacy within tightly-knit communities. However, these platforms frequently lack robust privacy policies and security measures, leaving users vulnerable to data breaches and privacy violations (Boyd, 2014). Moreover, limited resources hinder smaller platforms' ability to implement advanced security infrastructure, as highlighted by Kontaxis et al. (2011), making them attractive targets for cyberattacks. Smaller platforms may also lack scrutiny in data handling practices, potentially exploiting user data without transparency (Zuboff, 2019). Compliance with data protection regulations like GDPR and CCPA poses additional challenges, with smaller platforms often lacking the resources for full compliance and facing legal risks (Bennet & Raab, 2017). Despite these challenges, the communal nature of niche platforms can be leveraged for enhanced security through community-driven moderation and user education (Kraut & Resnick, 2012).

Mahammad and Kumar (2023) propose a blockchain-based framework for securing healthcare data in Greater Noida, India, highlighting scalability and security amidst the country's ongoing healthcare digitization efforts. This research is significant given India's unique healthcare landscape and diverse challenges in data security and privacy. By leveraging blockchain technology for decentralized and tamper-proof data management, the framework addresses critical trust and protection issues in digital healthcare systems. Its insights are globally relevant, providing valuable perspectives on user security and privacy across varied cultural and geographical contexts, and offering potential strategies to enhance data protection globally.

Siddiqui and Kumar (2020) explore AI and big data models to interpret rainfall patterns, focusing on London, UK. This study underscores the global applicability of advanced computational models in understanding complex environmental phenomena, reflecting the broader implications of data-driven approaches for enhancing decision-making and resource management across different geographic regions.

4. METHODOLOGY

This study employs a multi-faceted approach to gain theoretical insights into user security and privacy in social media environments. The methodology encompasses exploratory design, qualitative methods, secondary data collection, and theoretical frameworks.

The research adopted an exploratory design to comprehensively investigate the intricate dynamics of user security and privacy on social media platforms. This approach was chosen to delve deeply into diverse perspectives, experiences, and factors that influence security and privacy outcomes in online environments. A qualitative methodology was employed to capture rich, nuanced data that elucidates the subjective experiences, perceptions, and behaviors of social media users regarding security and privacy. Techniques such as interviews, focus groups, and participant observations facilitated thorough exploration and interpretation of user perspectives. Additionally, the study incorporated secondary data collection by reviewing existing literature, research studies, reports, and empirical findings related to user security and privacy in social media contexts. This comprehensive review of secondary sources provided a foundational understanding of key concepts, theories, and empirical evidence informing the study. The research utilized theoretical frameworks from sociology, psychology, communication studies, and computer science to guide the analysis and interpretation of findings. These frameworks provided conceptual lenses through which to examine the socio-cultural, psychological, technological, and institutional dimensions influencing user security and privacy in social media environments, thereby enriching the study's theoretical grounding and analytical depth.

By integrating exploratory design, qualitative methods, secondary data collection, and theoretical frameworks, this methodology enables a holistic and nuanced exploration of user security and privacy in social media environments, ultimately contributing to theoretical insights and knowledge advancement in this critical area.

5. ANALYSIS AND INTERPRETATION

5.1. User Perceptions on Social Media Security and Privacy

Social media platforms have become integral parts of daily life, facilitating communication, networking, and information sharing. However, concerns regarding user security and privacy persist, stemming from various factors such as data breaches, cyber threats, and the proliferation of misinformation. This report aims to analyze different user perceptions regarding these security and privacy concerns related to social media.

5.1.1. Concerns About Data Privacy

Many users expressed concerns about the privacy of their personal data on social media platforms. They were worried about how their information was being collected, stored, and used by platform providers and third-party entities for targeted advertising and data analytics purposes. Users expressed a desire for more transparency and control over their data.

5.1.2. Fear of Cyber Threats

Users highlighted fears of cyber threats such as hacking, identity theft, and phishing scams while using social media. They were concerned about the security of their accounts and the potential for unauthorized access to their personal information. Some users reported experiencing security incidents firsthand, which heightened their awareness of online risks.

5.1.3. Impact of Misinformation

Many users were concerned about the proliferation of misinformation and fake news on social media platforms. They expressed worries about the spread of false information, conspiracy theories, and propaganda, which could manipulate public opinion and undermine trust in reliable sources of information. Users emphasized the need for platforms to address these issues and promote media literacy.

5.1.4. Privacy Settings and Control

Users highlighted the importance of privacy settings and control features offered by social media platforms. They appreciated the ability to customize their privacy preferences, manage visibility settings, and control who can access their content and personal information. However, some users found these settings confusing or difficult to navigate, leading to concerns about inadvertent exposure of private data.

5.1.5. Trust in Platform Providers

Many users expressed skepticism about the trustworthiness of social media platform providers in safeguarding their security and privacy. They were concerned about past incidents of data breaches, privacy violations, and controversies surrounding platform policies and practices. Users called for greater accountability, transparency, and ethical standards from platform operators.

User perceptions on security and privacy concerns in social media reflect a range of anxieties, fears, and expectations regarding data privacy, cyber threats, misinformation, and platform accountability. Addressing these concerns requires collaborative efforts from platform providers, policymakers, and users themselves to enhance transparency, promote security best practices, and foster a culture of responsible digital citizenship in the online ecosystem.

5.2. Social Media Platform Features, Policies, and Algorithms in Shaping User Security and Privacy Outcomes

Social media platforms play a pivotal role in shaping user security and privacy outcomes through their features, policies, and algorithms. Understanding how these elements interact can provide valuable insights into the mechanisms that influence user experiences and perceptions of security and privacy. This analysis explores the impact of platform features, policies, and algorithms on user security and privacy outcomes.

5.2.1. Platform Features

Social media platforms offer a wide array of features that have implications for user security and privacy. These features include privacy settings, content moderation tools, encryption protocols, and authentication mechanisms. Privacy settings allow users to control who can access their content and personal information, providing a level of autonomy over their privacy preferences. Content moderation tools enable platforms to identify and remove harmful or inappropriate content, enhancing user safety. Encryption protocols ensure the confidentiality of user communications, mitigating the risk of unauthorized access to sensitive information. Authentication mechanisms verify the identity of users, preventing account hijacking and unauthorized access. By leveraging these features, social media platforms can empower users to manage their security and privacy effectively.

5.2.2. Platform Policies

The policies implemented by social media platforms play a crucial role in shaping user security and privacy outcomes. These policies encompass terms of service, community guidelines, data handling practices, and transparency measures. Terms of service outline the contractual agreements between platforms and users, establishing the rules and responsibilities governing their interactions. Community guidelines define acceptable behavior and content standards, guiding users on appropriate conduct within the platform. Data handling practices dictate how user data is collected, stored, and used by platforms, influencing user trust and confidence in their privacy protection measures. Transparency measures provide users with insight into platform policies and practices, fostering accountability and trust. By enforcing clear and consistent policies, social media platforms can promote user security and privacy while maintaining a conducive online environment.

5.2.3. Platform Algorithms

Algorithms deployed by social media platforms play a significant role in shaping user experiences and security outcomes. These algorithms govern content curation, recommendation systems, and advertising targeting, influencing the visibility and dissemination of user-generated content. Content curation algorithms determine the content displayed on users' feeds based on relevance, engagement, and user preferences, impacting the exposure of users to diverse perspectives and potential security risks. Recommendation systems suggest relevant content, connections, and groups to users, influencing their interactions and information consumption habits. Advertising targeting algorithms analyze user data to deliver personalized ads, raising concerns about privacy infringement and data exploitation. By understanding and regulating the algorithms used by social media platforms, stakeholders can mitigate the risk of algorithmic bias, manipulation, and unintended consequences on user security and privacy.

5.2.4. Specific regulations such as GDPR in Europe, CCPA in the United States, and other international privacy laws play critical roles in safeguarding user security and privacy in the digital age. GDPR, implemented in 2018, mandates stringent requirements for businesses handling personal data of EU residents, including clear consent mechanisms, transparent data practices, and robust data protection measures. It empowers users with rights to access, correct, and erase their data, while imposing severe penalties for non-compliance. Similarly, CCPA, effective from 2020, grants Californian consumers' rights to know, delete, and opt-out of the sale of their personal information. It obligates businesses to disclose data practices, secure personal data, and refrain from discriminatory practices against users exercising their privacy rights. Other international privacy laws, like Australia's Privacy Act 1988 (Cth) and Japan's Act on the Protection of Personal Information (APPI), also enforce strict guidelines on data collection, usage, and protection. These laws reflect global efforts to mitigate risks associated with data breaches, unauthorized data sharing, and privacy infringements, ensuring users' rights are respected across borders in an increasingly interconnected digital landscape.

Social media platform features, policies, and algorithms play integral roles in shaping user security and privacy outcomes. By leveraging effective features, enforcing transparent policies, and regulating algorithms, platforms can promote user empowerment, enhance accountability, and mitigate security and privacy risks. Collaborative efforts from platform providers, policymakers, and users are essential to foster a safer and more privacy-respecting online environment.

5.3. Emerging Threats, Vulnerabilities, and Risks to User Security and Privacy in Social Media Environments

As social media platforms continue to evolve and expand, they face a myriad of emerging threats, vulnerabilities, and risks that pose significant challenges to user security and privacy. Understanding these evolving threats is crucial for developing effective strategies to mitigate risks and protect users in the dynamic online landscape. This analysis explores the key emerging threats, vulnerabilities, and risks to user security and privacy in social media environments.

5.3.1. Cyber Threats

One of the most pressing concerns for users on social media platforms is the risk of cyber threats such as hacking, malware, phishing, and account takeover. Cybercriminals exploit vulnerabilities in platform security mechanisms and user behaviors to gain unauthorized access to accounts, steal sensitive information, or distribute malicious content. As social media platforms become lucrative targets for cyber-attacks, users face increased risks of identity theft, financial fraud, and privacy breaches.

5.3.2. Misinformation and Disinformation

The proliferation of misinformation and disinformation on social media poses significant risks to user security and privacy. Malicious actors exploit the viral nature of social media platforms to spread false or misleading information, manipulate public opinion, and undermine trust in reliable sources. Users are susceptible to misinformation campaigns, conspiracy theories, and propaganda, which can have far-reaching consequences on their beliefs, behaviors, and decision-making processes.

5.3.3. Data Privacy Concerns

Privacy concerns remain a persistent challenge for users on social media platforms, fueled by the collection, storage, and sharing of personal data by platform providers and third-party entities. Users' personal information is often harvested for targeted advertising, data analytics, and algorithmic profiling purposes, raising concerns about privacy infringement, data exploitation, and surveillance. The lack of transparency and control over data practices exacerbates user distrust and anxiety about their privacy on social media.

5.3.4. Cyberbullying and Online Harassment

Cyberbullying and online harassment continue to be prevalent threats to user security and privacy in social media environments. Users, particularly vulnerable groups such as children, teenagers, and marginalized communities, are susceptible to harassment, cyberbullying, and online abuse from peers, strangers, or malicious actors. The anonymity and reach of social media platforms amplify the impact of cyberbullying, causing psychological distress, social isolation, and reputational harm for affected users.

5.3.5. Deepfake and Synthetic Media

The emergence of deepfake technology and synthetic media poses new challenges to user security and privacy on social media platforms. Deepfake videos and manipulated content can deceive users, undermine trust in digital content, and facilitate identity fraud or defamation. As deepfake technology becomes more sophisticated and accessible, users face heightened risks of misinformation, social engineering attacks, and privacy violations on social media.

The evolving landscape of social media presents a multitude of emerging threats, vulnerabilities, and risks to user security and privacy. Cyber threats, misinformation, data privacy concerns, cyberbullying, and deepfake technology are among the key challenges facing users in social media environments. Addressing these emerging threats requires proactive measures from platform providers, policymakers, and users to enhance security measures, promote digital literacy, and foster a safer and more resilient online ecosystem. Collaborative efforts are essential to mitigate risks and protect user rights in the dynamic and evolving landscape of social media.

5.4. Consolidated Statements From Different Social Media Users Regarding Privacy and Security Threats

"As a parent, I worry about my child's safety on social media. With cyberbullying, predators, and inappropriate content circulating, it's challenging to ensure their privacy and security. I constantly monitor their accounts, but I wish there were better safeguards in place to protect young users." - Concerned Parent

"As a freelancer, I rely on social media for networking and promoting my work. However, I'm wary of data breaches and hacking incidents that could compromise my clients' information or intellectual property. I take precautions like using strong passwords and two-factor authentication, but the constant threat of cyber attacks is unsettling." - Freelancer

"Privacy is a fundamental right that's increasingly under threat in the digital age. Social media platforms collect vast amounts of personal data, often without clear consent or transparency. As users, we need to be vigilant about protecting our privacy and advocating for stronger regulations to hold platforms accountable for data misuse." - Privacy Advocate

"Running a small business, social media is crucial for reaching customers and driving sales. However, I'm concerned about the security of our company's social media accounts. Phishing scams, account takeovers, and fake reviews pose significant risks to our reputation and financial security. We invest in cybersecurity measures, but the evolving nature of threats keeps us on edge." - Small Business Owner

"Social media has become a powerful tool for organizing grassroots movements and raising awareness about social issues. However, it's also a breeding ground for misinformation and targeted harassment. As activists, we face threats to our safety and privacy from online trolls, doxxing, and surveillance. It's a constant battle to protect ourselves while amplifying our voices for positive change." - Political Activist

"Growing up in the digital age, I'm aware of the privacy risks associated with social media. I'm cautious about what I share online and regularly review my privacy settings. Still, I'm concerned about data tracking, algorithmic manipulation, and the potential for my information to be exploited by advertisers or malicious actors. Staying informed and proactive is essential for safeguarding my online identity." - Tech-Savvy Teenager

The statements from various social media users illustrate a spectrum of concerns regarding privacy and security threats. Parents express worry about their children's safety amidst cyberbullying and predatory behavior, emphasizing the need for enhanced safeguards. Freelancers and small business owners highlight the constant threat of data breaches and hacking incidents, impacting their clients' information and financial security. Privacy advocates stress the importance of transparency and user vigilance in protecting personal data from exploitation by social media platforms. Political activists face risks such as harassment and surveillance while utilizing social media for advocacy, underscoring the dual nature of these platforms as tools for both empowerment and vulnerability. Even tech-savvy teenagers acknowledge the pervasive dangers of data tracking and algorithmic manipulation, emphasizing the importance of proactive measures to safeguard their online identities. Together, these statements emphasize the multifaceted nature of privacy and security threats on social media, urging for collective action to mitigate risks and protect user rights effectively.

5.5. *Illustrative Case Studies*

Case studies and examples of successful technological interventions in social media security provide practical insights and strengthen theoretical discussions on user security and privacy:

5.5.1. End-to-End Encryption in Messaging Apps

Platforms like WhatsApp and Signal have implemented end-to-end encryption, ensuring that messages sent between users are encrypted and only readable by the sender and recipient. This technological intervention enhances user privacy by preventing unauthorized access to message contents, even by the platform provider.

5.5.2. Two-Factor Authentication (2FA)

Social media platforms such as Facebook, Twitter, and Instagram have adopted 2FA as a security measure. By requiring users to verify their identity through a second method (e.g., a code sent to their phone), 2FA significantly reduces the risk of unauthorized access to user accounts, thereby enhancing security.

5.5.3. AI-Powered Content Moderation

Platforms like YouTube and Facebook utilize AI algorithms to detect and remove harmful or inappropriate content. This intervention not only improves user experience by maintaining a safe environment but also addresses privacy concerns related to the dissemination of sensitive or harmful content.

5.5.4. Privacy-Enhancing Technologies (PETs)

PETs encompass a range of technologies designed to protect user privacy while using digital services. For example, Tor Browser and VPNs (Virtual Private Networks) anonymize users' internet traffic, shielding their online activities from surveillance and unauthorized access.

5.5.5. Blockchain for Data Integrity

Some platforms explore blockchain technology to enhance data integrity and security. For instance, Steemit uses blockchain to securely store and validate user-generated content, ensuring transparency and reducing the risk of content manipulation or censorship.

These case studies demonstrate how technological interventions can effectively address user security and privacy concerns in social media environments. By implementing such technologies, platforms not only mitigate risks but also foster trust among users, thereby enhancing their overall digital experience. These practical examples provide valuable insights for theoretical discussions on the intersection of technology, security, and user privacy in social media.

6. CONCLUSIONS AND RECOMMENDATIONS

6.1. Conclusion

Theoretical Insights into User Security and Privacy in Social Media Environments has provided a comprehensive understanding of the complex dynamics shaping user experiences in online spaces. Through the exploration of theoretical frameworks and empirical research, this study has illuminated the multifaceted nature of security and privacy concerns on social media platforms. The analysis has revealed the interplay between sociocultural factors, platform features, and algorithmic processes in influencing user perceptions, behaviors, and outcomes. Moreover, the examination of emerging threats and vulnerabilities has underscored the urgency of addressing systemic challenges to enhance user protection and promote a safer online ecosystem.

6.2. Recommendations

Here are more specific suggestions for policy improvements regarding user security and privacy on social media platforms:

- *Develop targeted educational initiatives:* Implement comprehensive educational programs that focus on enhancing user awareness and digital literacy specifically tailored to security and privacy risks on social media platforms. These initiatives should equip users with practical skills and knowledge to recognize threats, manage privacy settings effectively, and practice responsible online behavior.
- *Advocate for enhanced transparency and accountability:* Push for social media platforms to adopt greater transparency in their data handling practices, content moderation policies, and algorithmic governance. Establish clear guidelines for disclosing how user data is collected, used, and shared, alongside mechanisms for users to access and control their personal information. Ethical standards should prioritize user rights and ensure fair treatment in content moderation decisions.
- *Promote interdisciplinary collaboration:* Foster collaboration among researchers, policymakers, industry stakeholders, and civil society organizations to tackle the multifaceted challenges of user security and privacy in social media environments. Encourage joint efforts to develop comprehensive solutions that integrate technological innovation with ethical considerations and user well-being.
- *Advocate for robust regulatory frameworks:* Advocate for the implementation of robust regulatory frameworks that prioritize user protection, data privacy, and digital rights on social media platforms. Strengthen enforcement mechanisms to ensure compliance with existing laws such as GDPR and CCPA, and explore the need for new regulations that address emerging challenges like algorithmic transparency and online misinformation.
- *Support ongoing research and evaluation:* Allocate resources to support continuous research and evaluation efforts focused on monitoring evolving trends, identifying emerging threats, and understanding user behaviors in social media environments. Regular assessments will inform evidence-based policymaking and enable stakeholders to adapt strategies effectively to evolving security and privacy challenges.

These specific policy recommendations aim to empower users, enhance platform accountability, foster collaboration across sectors, strengthen regulatory oversight, and support continuous learning and adaptation in addressing the complex landscape of social media security and privacy.

REFERENCES

Abbas, J., Aman, J., Nurunnabi, M., & Bano, S. (2019). The impact of social media on learning behaviour for sustainable education: Evidence of students from selected universities in Pakistan. *Sustainability (Basel)*, 11(6), 1683. DOI: 10.3390/su11061683

Acquisti, A. (2010). *The economics of personal data and the economics of privacy*. Background Paper for OECD Joint WPISP-WPIE Roundtable.

Adu Michael, K., & Adewale Olumide, S. (2014). Mitigating Cybercrime and Online Social Networks Threats in Nigeria. *Proceedings of the World Congress on Engineering and Computer Science*, 1

Al-Qurishi, M., Alrubaian, M., Rahman, S. M. M., Alamri, A., & Hassan, M. M. (2018). A prediction system of Sybil attack in social network using deep-regression model. *Future Generation Computer Systems*, 87, 743–753. DOI: 10.1016/j.future.2017.08.030

Alguliyev, R., Aliguliyev, R., & Yusifov, F. (2018). Role of Social Networks in Government: Risks and Security Threats. *Online Journal of Communication and Media Technologies*, 8(4), 363–376.

Bailey, M., Cooke, E., Jahanian, F., Xu, Y., & Karir, M. (2009, March). A survey of botnet technology and defenses. In 2009 Cybersecurity Applications & Technology Conference for Homeland Security (pp. 299-304). IEEE.

Barnes, S. (2006). A privacy paradox: Social networking in the United States. *First Monday*, 11(9). Advance online publication. DOI: 10.5210/fm.v11i9.1394

Bennet, C. J., & Raab, C. D. (2017). *The Governance of Privacy: Policy Instruments in Global Perspective*. MIT Press. DOI: 10.4324/9781315199269

Boyd, D. (2014). *It's Complicated: The Social Lives of Networked Teens*. Yale University Press.

Chaffey, D. (2016). Global social media research summary 2016. Smart Insights: Social Media Marketing.

Chan, C. K., & Virkki, J. (2014). Perspectives for sharing personal information on online social networks. *Social Networking*, 3(1), 2014. DOI: 10.4236/sn.2014.31005

Edosomwan, S., Prakasan, S. K., Kouame, D., Watson, J., & Seymour, T. (2011). The history of social media and its impact on business. *The Journal of Applied Management and Entrepreneurship*, 16(3), 79–91.

Vakamullu, G., Misra, N. R., & Venugopal, K. (2021). Critical Success Factors of Online Shopping: Rural Perscpective. Asian Journal of Economics. *Business and Accounting*, 21(24), 34–45.

Hogben, G. (2007). Security issues and recommendations for online social networks. *ENISA Position Paper*, 1, 1–36.

Kim, H. J. (2012). Online Social Media Networking and Assessing Its Security Risks. *International Journal Of Security & Its Applications*, 6(3), 11–18. DOI: 10.14257/ijsia.2016.10.3.02

Kontaxis, G., Polakis, I., Ioannidis, S., & Markatos, E. P. (2011). Detecting social network profile cloning. In IEEE International Conference on Pervasive Computing and Communications Workshops (PERCOM Workshops) (pp. 295-300). IEEE. DOI: 10.1109/PERCOMW.2011.5766886

Kraut, R. E., & Resnick, P. (2012). *Building Successful Online Communities: Evidence-Based Social Design*. MIT Press. DOI: 10.7551/mitpress/8472.001.0001

Kumar, A., Tewari, N., & Kumar, R. (2019). Study towards the analytic approach for human-computer interaction using machine learning. *The International Journal of Analytical and Experimental Modal Analysis*, 11, 1456–1466.

Kumar, R., & Sharma, M. K. (2016). Advanced neuro-fuzzy approach for social media mining methods using cloud. *International Journal of Computer Applications*, 137(10), 56–58. DOI: 10.5120/ijca2016908927

Kumar, S., & Kumar, R. (2022). Intelligent model to image enrichment for strong night-vision surveillance cameras in future generation. *Multimedia Tools and Applications*, 81(12), 1–17. DOI: 10.1007/s11042-022-12496-w

Kumar, S., & Somani, V. (2018). Social Media Security Risks, Cyber Threats And Risks Prevention And Mitigation Techniques. *International Journal of Advance Research in Computer Science and Management*, 4(4), 125–129.

Mahammad, A. B., & Kumar, R. (2023). Scalable and security framework to secure and maintain healthcare data using blockchain technology. In 2023 International Conference on Computational Intelligence and Sustainable Engineering Solutions (CISES) (pp. 417-423). Greater Noida, India. IEEE. DOI: 10.1109/CISES58720.2023.10183494

McCarroll, N., & Curran, K. (2013). Social networking in education. [IJIDE]. *International Journal of Innovation in the Digital Economy*, 4(1), 1–1. DOI: 10.4018/jide.2013010101

Meenu, S., Kumar, E. E. P., Panchal, V. K., & Kumar, R. (2019). Evolution of new integrated haze removal algorithm based on haze line. [IJEAT]. *International Journal of Engineering and Advanced Technology*, 8(06), 184–189.

Murlikrishna, P. N., Gupta, D. V., & Venugopal, D. K. (2020). Assessment Of Factors Influencing The Choice Of Online Channels For Health Insurance Products. *Journal of Interdisciplinary Cycle Research*, 12(12), 178–194.

Nissenbaum, H. (2010). *Privacy in Context: Technology, Policy, and the Integrity of Social Life*. Stanford University Press.

Ortiz-Ospina, E. (n.d.). The rise of social media. Our World in Data., Retrieved February 1, 2020, from.

Oxley, A. (2011). *A best practices guide for mitigating risk in the use of social media*. IBM Center for the Business of Government Washington.

Rathore, S., Loia, V., & Park, J. H. (2018). SpamSpotter: An efficient spammer detection framework based on intelligent decision support system on facebook. *Applied Soft Computing*, 67, 920–932. DOI: 10.1016/j.asoc.2017.09.032

Sahoo, S. R., & Gupta, B. B. (2020) Popularity-based detection of malicious content in facebook using machine learning approach. In: *First international conference on sustainable technologies for computational intelligence*. Springer, Singapore, pp 163–17618 DOI: 10.1007/978-981-15-0029-9_13

Siddiqui, M. H. F., & Kumar, R. (2020). Interpreting the nature of rainfall with AI and big data models. In *2020 International Conference on Intelligent Engineering and Management (ICIEM)* (pp. 306-310). London, UK. IEEE. DOI: 10.1109/ICIEM48762.2020.9160322

Vakamullu, G., Misra, N. R., & Venugopal, K. (2023). *Critical Factors for the Affluence of Online Shopping: Rural Perspective ATLAS Skilltech University from 23rd - 29th March 2023* (1st ed.). Eureka Publications.

Venugopal, K., & Das, S. (2022). Social Media Habits of Rural Consumers Influencing on Online Consumption. *Horizon J. Hum. Soc. Sci. Res*, 4, 39–47.

Venugopal, K., Das, S., Manoj, K. P., & Dey, S. (2020). Impact of Efficacious and Detrimental Factors of Social Media on Public Usage Behaviour in the Age of Covid-19 Pandemic: In Case of Srikakulam, A.P. PalArch's Journal of Archaeology of Egypt/Egyptology, 17(9), pp. 2288-2302

Venugopal, K., Das, S., & Vakamullu, G. (2023). *Critical Factors for the Upscale of Online Shopping: A Rural Perspective. Chapter book entitled "Influencer Marketing Applications within the Metaverse". A volume in the Advances in Marketing, Customer Relationship Management, and E-Services (AMCRMES) Book Series*. IGI Global. DOI: 10.4018/978-1-6684-8898-0.ch016

Venugopal, K., Vakamullu, G., & Mishra, N. R. (2022). Social Media Habits of Rural Consumers Influencing on Online Consumption in an edited book entitled Business Perspectives in Reviving Workforce Productivity in the current Volatile and Uncertain Times.

Verma, A., Kshirsagar, D., & Khan, S. (2013). Privacy and Security: Online Social Networking. *International Journal of Advanced Computer Research*, 3(8), 310–315.

Zhang, Z., & Gupta, B. B. (2018). Social media security and trustworthiness: Overview and new direction. *Future Generation Computer Systems*, 86, 914–925. DOI: 10.1016/j.future.2016.10.007

Zuboff, S. (2019). *The Age of Surveillance Capitalism: The Fight for a Human Future at the New Frontier of Power*. PublicAffairs.

Compilation of References

. Li, Y., & Hu, R. (2019). The development of smart homes in China: An analysis of recent trends, drivers and challenges.

. Saha, S. (2024). SECURITY IN IOT USING ARTIFICIAL INTELLIGENCE. *The Fusion of Artificial Intelligence and Soft Computing Techniques for Cybersecurity*.

"Number of social network users worldwide from 2010 to 2021 (in billions)," Statista Inc., available at: https://www.statista.com/statistics/278414/number-of-worldwide-social-network-users/ (last accessed: 16 December 2019)

"The Top 20 Valuable Facebook Statistics," Zephoria Digital Marketing, available at: https://zephoria.com/top-15-valuable-facebook-statistics/ (last accessed: 16 December 2019). "2019 Top 5 Facebook Video Statistics Infographics," available at: https://www.everincreasingcircles.com/2019-top-5-facebook-video-statistics-infographics/ (last accessed: 16 December 2019).

Ababneh, M., & Aljarrah, A. (2024). cybersecurity: malware multi-attack detector on android-based devices using deep learning methods. *Journal of Theoretical and Applied Information Technology*, 102(1).

Abbas, J., Aman, J., Nurunnabi, M., & Bano, S. (2019). The impact of social media on learning behaviour for sustainable education: Evidence of students from selected universities in Pakistan. *Sustainability (Basel)*, 11(6), 1683. DOI: 10.3390/su11061683

Abbas, S., Bouazzi, I., Ojo, S., Al Hejaili, A., Sampedro, G. A., Almadhor, A., & Gregus, M. (2024). Evaluating deep learning variants for cyber-attacks detection and multi-class classification in IoT networks. *PeerJ. Computer Science*, 10, e1793. DOI: 10.7717/peerj-cs.1793 PMID: 38259893

Abdalrdha, Z. K., Al-Bakry, A. M., & Farhan, A. K. (2023). A Survey on Cybercrime Using Social Media. *Iraqi Journal for Computers and Informatics*, 49(1), 52–65. DOI: 10.25195/ijci.v49i1.404

Abdelsadeq, Z. A., Omar, S. N., Basir, N., & Rafei, N. F. N. B. M. (2019). Unintentional Insider Threats Countermeasures Model (UITCM). *2019 International Conference on Cybersecurity (ICoCSec)*, 53–58. https://ieeexplore.ieee.org/abstract/document/8970986/

Abdulhussein, M. (2024). The Impact of Artificial Intelligence and Machine Learning on Organizations Cybersecurity.

Abebe, R., Barocas, S., Kleinberg, J., Levy, K., Raghavan, M., & Robinson, D. G. (2020, January). Roles for computing in social change. In *Proceedings of the 2020 conference on fairness, accountability, and transparency* (pp. 252-260). DOI: 10.1145/3351095.3372871

Abraham, S., & Chengalur-Smith, I. (2010). An overview of social engineering malware: Trends, tactics, and implications. *Technology in Society*, 32(3), 183–196. DOI: 10.1016/j.techsoc.2010.07.001

Acquisti, A. (2010). *The economics of personal data and the economics of privacy.* Background Paper for OECD Joint WPISP-WPIE Roundtable.

Acquisti, A., Gross, R., & Stutzman, F. (2014). Privacy in the Age of Augmented Reality. *IEEE Security and Privacy.*

Adu Michael, K., & Adewale Olumide, S. (2014). Mitigating Cybercrime and Online Social Networks Threats in Nigeria. *Proceedings of the World Congress on Engineering and Computer Science*, 1

Afrifa, S., Varadarajan, V., Appiahene, P., & Zhang, T. (2023). Using Machine Learning to Classify Network Abnormalities into Legitimate or Assault in IoT-based Cyber Physical System. *Sensors and Electronic Instrumentation Advances*, 150.

Agarwal, A. K., & Jain, A. (2019). Synthesis of 2D and 3D NoC mesh router architecture in HDL environment. *Journal of Advanced Research in Dynamical and Control Systems*, 11(4), 2573–2581.

Ahmed, Y. A., Maarof, M. A., Hassan, F. M., & Abshir, M. M. (2014). Survey of Keylogger technologies. International journal of computer science and telecommunications, 5(2).

Ahmed, M. B., Shoikot, M., Hossain, J., & Rahman, A. (2019). Key logger detection using memory forensic and network monitoring. *International Journal of Computer Applications*, 975, 8887.

Alabdulkreem, E., Alotaibi, S. S., Alamgeer, M., Marzouk, R., Hilal, A. M., Motwakel, A., & Rizwanullah, M. (2023). Intelligent Cybersecurity Classification Using Chaos Game Optimization with Deep Learning Model. *Computer Systems Science and Engineering*, 45(1), 971–983. DOI: 10.32604/csse.2023.030362

Alazab, M., Soman, K. P., Srinivasan, S., Venkatraman, S., & Pham, V. Q. (2023). Deep learning for cyber security applications: A comprehensive survey. *Authorea Preprints*.

AL-Dosari, K., Fetais, N., & Kucukvar, M. (2024). Artificial intelligence and cyber defense system for banking industry: A qualitative study of AI applications and challenges. *Cybernetics and Systems*, 55(2), 302–330. DOI: 10.1080/01969722.2022.2112539

Alguliyev, R., Aliguliyev, R., & Yusifov, F. (2018). Role of Social Networks in Government: Risks and Security Threats. *Online Journal of Communication and Media Technologies*, 8(4), 363–376.

AlHuwaishel, N., & Zaghloul, S. S. (2013, September). A technique for load-balanced management of security tasks load in grids. In 2013 Africon (pp. 1-5). IEEE.

Ali, B., & Farooq, A. (2023, May). Ensemble Based AI Detector for Cyber Crimes. In *2023 6th International Conference on Electronics Technology (ICET)* (pp. 619-623). IEEE. DOI: 10.1109/ICET58434.2023.10211904

Ali, H. H., Naif, J. R., & Humood, W. R. (2024, March). Deep learning algorithms for IoT security (survey). In *AIP Conference Proceedings* (Vol. 2885, No. 1). AIP Publishing.

Ali, M., Shahroz, M., Mushtaq, M. F., Alfarhood, S., Safran, M., & Ashraf, I. (2024). Hybrid Machine Learning Model for Efficient Botnet Attack Detection in IoT Environment. *IEEE Access : Practical Innovations, Open Solutions*, 12, 40682–40699. DOI: 10.1109/ACCESS.2024.3376400

Aljuhani, A., Kumar, P., Alanazi, R., Albalawi, T., Taouali, O., Islam, A. N., & Alazab, M. (2023). A deep learning integrated blockchain framework for securing industrial iot. *IEEE Internet of Things Journal*.

Al-Quayed, F., Ahmad, Z., & Humayun, M. (2024). A situation based predictive approach for cybersecurity intrusion detection and prevention using machine learning and deep learning algorithms in wireless sensor networks of industry 4.0. *IEEE Access : Practical Innovations, Open Solutions*, 12, 34800–34819. DOI: 10.1109/ACCESS.2024.3372187

Al-Qurishi, M., Alrubaian, M., Rahman, S. M. M., Alamri, A., & Hassan, M. M. (2018). A prediction system of Sybil attack in social network using deep-regression model. *Future Generation Computer Systems*, 87, 743–753. DOI: 10.1016/j.future.2017.08.030

Alrubayyi, H., Alshareef, M. S., Nadeem, Z., Abdelmoniem, A. M., & Jaber, M. (2024). Security Threats and Promising Solutions Arising from the Intersection of AI and IoT: A Study of IoMT and IoET Applications. *Future Internet*, 16(3), 85. DOI: 10.3390/fi16030085

Alruwaili, F. F. (2023). Optimal hybrid deep learning enabled attack detection and classification in IoT environment. *Computers, Materials & Continua*, 75(1), 99–115. DOI: 10.32604/cmc.2023.034752

Alsharif, M., Mishra, S., & AlShehri, M. (2022). Impact of Human Vulnerabilities on Cybersecurity. *Computer Systems Science and Engineering*, 40(3), 1153–1166. DOI: 10.32604/csse.2022.019938

Ambika, N. (2024). Early Detection of Darknet Traffic in Internet of Things Applications. *Automated Secure Computing for Next-Generation Systems*, 139-153.

Anderson, J., & Brown, L. (2018). Emerging cybersecurity challenges in the age of digital transformation. *Journal of Cybersecurity Research*, 2(1), 45–58. DOI: 10.1000/jcr.2018.045

Anderson, T. (2018). Security Challenges in the Internet of Things: A Case Study of Smart Home Devices. *IEEE Security and Privacy*, 16(5), 26–35.

Ani, U. D., He, H., & Tiwari, A. (2019) Human factor security: evaluating the cybersecuritycapacity of the industrial workforce. Journal of Systems and Information Technology, 21(1). pp. 2-35. ISSN 1328-7265https://doi.org/DOI: 10.1108/JSIT-02-2018-0028

Anis, G. M., Aboutabl, A. E., & Galal, A. (2023). MACHINE LEARNING FOR DETECTING CYBERCRIME IN THE BANKING SECTOR. *Journal of Southwest Jiaotong University*, 58(5).

Anonymous. (2020). Cybersecurity Risk Report for Businesses, Cybint Solutions, https://www.cybintsolutions.com/2020-cybersecurity-risk-report-for-businesses

Anonymous. (2021). IBM X-Force Threat Intelligence Index 2021 https://enterprise.verizon.com/resources/reports/2020-data-breach-investigations-report.pdf

Ansari, J. A. N., & Khan, N. A. (2020). Exploring the Role of Social Media in Collaborative Learning the New Domain of Learning. *Smart Learning Environments*, 7(1), 9. DOI: 10.1186/s40561-020-00118-7

Anwar, A., & Raychowdhury, A. (2020). Masked face recognition for secure authentication. *arXiv preprint arXiv:2008.11104*.

Appel, G., Grewal, L., Hadi, R., & Stephen, A. T. (2020). The Future of Social Media in Marketing. *Journal of the Academy of Marketing Science*, 48(1), 79–95. DOI: 10.1007/s11747-019-00695-1 PMID: 32431463

Asuamah Yeboah, S. (2023). Sustaining Change: Unravelling the Socio-cultural Threads of Sustainable Consumption.

Atami, A., & Al-Namanny, A. (2021). Security and Privacy Concerns of IoT in Smart Home Environments: A Comprehensive Survey. *IEEE Access : Practical Innovations, Open Solutions*, 9, 36627–36646.

Attaran, M., & Deb, P. (2018). Machine learning: The new'big thing'for competitive advantage. *International Journal of Knowledge Engineering and Data Mining*, 5(4), 277–305. DOI: 10.1504/IJKEDM.2018.095523

August, V. (2022). Network Concepts in Social Theory: Foucault and Cybernetics. *European Journal of Social Theory*, 25(2), 271–291. DOI: 10.1177/1368431021991046

Awajan, A. (2023). A novel deep learning-based intrusion detection system for IOT networks. *Computers*, 12(2), 34. DOI: 10.3390/computers12020034

Aziz, L. A. R., & Andriansyah, Y. (2023). The Role Artificial Intelligence in Modern Banking: An Exploration of AI-Driven Approaches for Enhanced Fraud Prevention, Risk Management, and Regulatory Compliance. *Reviews of Contemporary Business Analytics*, 6(1), 110–132.

Bae, I.-H., & Muhammad, F. Y. Z. (2018). CHALLENGE OF SOCIAL MEDIA MARKETING & EFFECTIVE STRATEGIES TO ENGAGE MORE CUSTOMERS: SELECTED RETAILER CASE STUDY. *International Journal of Business & Society*, 19(3).

Bailey, M., Cooke, E., Jahanian, F., Xu, Y., & Karir, M. (2009, March). A survey of botnet technology and defenses. In 2009 Cybersecurity Applications & Technology Conference for Homeland Security (pp. 299-304). IEEE.

Bailey, T., Kolo, B., Rajagopalan, K., & Ware, D. (2018). Insider threat: The human element of cyberrisk. *The McKinsey Quarterly*, 1–8.

Baker, D. J., & Robinson, P. H. (Eds.). (2020). *Artificial Intelligence and the Law: Cybercrime and Criminal Liability*. Routledge. DOI: 10.4324/9780429344015

Balkrishna, B. B., & Deshmukh, A. A. (2017). A study on role of social media in agriculture marketing and its scope. International Journal of Management. *IT and Engineering*, 7(4), 416–423.

Bao, Y., Hilary, G., & Ke, B. (2022). Artificial intelligence and fraud detection. *Innovative Technology at the Interface of Finance and Operations*, I, 223–247. DOI: 10.1007/978-3-030-75729-8_8

Barnes, S. (2006). A privacy paradox: Social networking in the United States. *First Monday*, 11(9). Advance online publication. DOI: 10.5210/fm.v11i9.1394

Barocas, S., Hardt, M., & Narayanan, A. (2023). *Fairness and machine learning: Limitations and opportunities*. MIT Press.

Behiry, M. H., & Aly, M. (2024). Cyberattack detection in wireless sensor networks using a hybrid feature reduction technique with AI and machine learning methods. *Journal of Big Data*, 11(1), 16. DOI: 10.1186/s40537-023-00870-w

Belyaev, M., & Gaivoronski, S. (2014, October). Towards load balancing in SDN-networks during DDoS-attacks. In 2014 international science and technology conference (modern networking technologies)(MoNeTeC) (pp. 1-6). IEEE.

Bennet, C. J., & Raab, C. D. (2017). *The Governance of Privacy: Policy Instruments in Global Perspective*. MIT Press. DOI: 10.4324/9781315199269

Berk, R., Heidari, H., Jabbari, S., Kearns, M., & Roth, A. (2021). Fairness in criminal justice risk assessments: The state of the art. *Sociological Methods & Research*, 50(1), 3–44. DOI: 10.1177/0049124118782533

Bhardwaj, A., & Goundar, S. (2020). Keyloggers: Silent cyber security weapons. *Network Security*, 2020(2), 14–19.

Bhatia, A., Kumar, A., Jain, A., Kumar, A., Verma, C., Illes, Z., Aschilean, I., & Raboaca, M. S. (2022). Networked control system with MANET communication and AODV routing. *Heliyon*, 8(11), 11. DOI: 10.1016/j.heliyon.2022.e11678 PMID: 36439715

Bhatia, P., GRD-IMT, D., Bhatia, A., & India, U. (2023). POTENTIAL ROLE OF ICTS IN. *Social Development*.

Bhusal, C. S. (2021). Systematic review on social engineering: Hacking by manipulating humans. *Journal of Information Security*, 12(1), 104–114. DOI: 10.4236/jis.2021.121005

Bhuvaneshwari, A. J., & Kaythry, P. (2023). A review of deep learning strategies for enhancing cybersecurity in networks: Deep learning strategies for enhancing cybersecurity. [JSIR]. *Journal of Scientific and Industrial Research*, 82(12), 1316–1330.

Bhuvaneshwari, A. J., & Kaythry, P. (2023). A Review of Deep Learning Strategies for Enhancing Cybersecurity in Networks: DEEP LEARNING STRATEGIES FOR ENHANCING CYBERSECURITY. [JSIR]. *Journal of Scientific and Industrial Research*, 82(12), 1316–1330.

Boyd, D. (2014). *It's Complicated: The Social Lives of Networked Teens*. Yale University Press.

Brain, J. (2021). Social Media in the Workplace: What Every Executive Should Know. Retrieved from https://everyonesocial.com/blog/social-media-in-the-workplace

Bright, L. F., Lim, H. S., & Logan, K. (2021). "Should I Post or Ghost?": Examining how privacy concerns impact social media engagement in US consumers. *Psychology and Marketing*, 38(10), 1712–1722. DOI: 10.1002/mar.21499

Brotcke, L. (2022). Time to assess bias in machine learning models for credit decisions. *Journal of Risk and Financial Management*, 15(4), 165. DOI: 10.3390/jrfm15040165

Bui, H. T., Aboutorab, H., Mahboubi, A., Gao, Y., Sultan, N. H., Chauhan, A., Parvez, M. Z., Bewong, M., Islam, R., Islam, Z., Camtepe, S. A., Gauravaram, P., Singh, D., Ali Babar, M., & Yan, S. (2024). Agriculture 4.0 and Beyond: Evaluating Cyber Threat Intelligence Sources and Techniques in Smart Farming Ecosystems. *Computers & Security*, 140, 103754. DOI: 10.1016/j.cose.2024.103754

Bullée, J.-W. H., Montoya, L., Pieters, W., Junger, M., & Hartel, P. H. (2015). The persuasion and security awareness experiment: Reducing the success of social engineering attacks. *Journal of Experimental Criminology*, 11(1), 97–115. DOI: 10.1007/s11292-014-9222-7

Buvaneswari, M., Loganathan, M. P., & Sangeetha, S. (2017, February). Cloud challenges of load balancing and security issues using ICLoS algorithm. In 2017 2nd International Conference on Computing and Communications Technologies (ICCCT) (pp. 103-105). IEEE.

Cai, X., Wang, C., Xiao, B., Chen, X., & Zhou, J. (2012). Deep nonlinear metric learning within dependentsubspace analysis for face verification. *Proceedings of the20th ACM International Conference on Multimedia, ACM*, 749–752. DOI: 10.1145/2393347.2396303

Cao, D. M., Sayed, M. A., Islam, M. T., Mia, M. T., Ayon, E. H., Ghosh, B. P., & Raihan, A. (2024). Advanced Cybercrime Detection: A Comprehensive Study on Supervised and Unsupervised Machine Learning Approaches Using Real-world Datasets. *Journal of Computer Science and Technology Studies*, 6(1), 40–48. DOI: 10.32996/jcsts.2024.6.1.5

Cao, L., Yang, Q., & Yu, P. S. (2021). Data science and AI in FinTech: An overview. *International Journal of Data Science and Analytics*, 12(2), 81–99. DOI: 10.1007/s41060-021-00278-w

Capodieci, N., Hart, E., & Cabri, G. (2013, September). Designing self-aware adaptive systems: from autonomic computing to cognitive immune networks. In 2013 IEEE 7th International Conference on Self-Adaptation and Self-Organizing Systems Workshops (pp. 59-64). IEEE.

Cardoso, P. (2022, June 20). Internet of Things: Security Challenges and Solutions. DOI: 10.31224/2420

Catarinucci, L., De Donno, D., Mainetti, L., Palano, L., & Patrono, L. (2015). M. L. Ste- fanizzi, and L. Tarricone. An iot-aware architecture for smart healthcare sys- tems. *Internet ofThings Journal, IEEE*, 2(6), 515–526. DOI: 10.1109/JIOT.2015.2417684

Chaffey, D. (2016). Global social media research summary 2016. Smart Insights: Social Media Marketing.

Chan, C. K., & Virkki, J. (2014). Perspectives for sharing personal information on online social networks. *Social Networking*, 3(1), 2014. DOI: 10.4236/sn.2014.31005

Chandy, K. M., & Misra, J. (1984, October). The Drinking Philosophers Problem. *ACM Transactions on Programming Languages and Systems*, 6(4), 632–646. DOI: 10.1145/1780.1804

Charanya, R., & Aramudhan, M. (2016). Survey on access control issues in cloud computing. *1st International Conference on Emerging Trends in Engineering, Technology and Science, ICETETS 2016 - Proceedings*. DOI: 10.1109/ICETETS.2016.7603014

Chaurasia, V., & Gupta, M. (2020). Analyzing Smart Home Adoption through the Lens of Indian Culture: An Empirical Investigation.

Cheng, X., Liu, S., Sun, X., Wang, Z., Zhou, H., Shao, Y., & Shen, H. (2021). Combating emerging financial risks in the big data era: A perspective review. *Fundamental Research (Beijing)*, 1(5), 595–606. DOI: 10.1016/j.fmre.2021.08.017

Chen, M., Gonzalez, S., & Leung, V. (2007). Applications and design issues for mobile agents in wireless sensor networks. *IEEE Wireless Communications*, 14(6), 20–26. DOI: 10.1109/MWC.2007.4407223

Chen, R., Liu, C. M., & Chen, C. (2012). An artificial immune-based distributed intrusion detection model for the internet of things. *Advanced Materials Research*, 366, 165–168.

Chen, X., An, L., Yang, S., & Wu, W. (2017). Kinship verification in multi-linear coherent spaces. *Multimedia Tools and Applications*, 76(3), 4105–4122. DOI: 10.1007/s11042-015-2930-9

Chen, Z., Van Khoa, L. D., Teoh, E. N., Nazir, A., Karuppiah, E. K., & Lam, K. S. (2018). Machine learning techniques for anti-money laundering (AML) solutions in suspicious transaction detection: A review. *Knowledge and Information Systems*, 57(2), 245–285. DOI: 10.1007/s10115-017-1144-z

Chertov, R., Fahmy, S., & Shroff, N. B. (2006, March). Emulation versus simulation: A case study of TCP-targeted denial of service attacks. In 2nd International Conference on Testbeds and Research Infrastructures for the Development of Networks and Communities, 2006. TRIDENTCOM 2006. (pp. 10-pp). IEEE.

Chess, D., Harrison, C., & Kershenbaum, A. (1996, July). Mobile agents: Are they a good idea? In International Workshop on Mobile Object Systems (pp. 25-45). Berlin, Heidelberg: Springer Berlin Heidelberg.

Chetty, M., Sung, J.-Y., & Grinter, R. E. How smart homes learn: The evolution of the networked home and household. In *International Conference on Ubiquitous Computing*, pages 127–144. Springer, 2007. DOI: 10.1007/978-3-540-74853-3_8

Chi, P. W., & Lei, C. L. (2018). Audit-Free Cloud Storage via Deniable Attribute-Based Encryption. *IEEE Transactions on Cloud Computing*, 6(2), 414–427. DOI: 10.1109/TCC.2015.2424882

Chohan, M. N., Haider, U., Ayub, M. Y., Shoukat, H., Bhatia, T. K., & Hassan, M. F. U. (2023). Detection of Cyber Attacks using Machine Learning based Intrusion Detection System for IoT Based Smart Cities. *EAI Endorsed Transactions on Smart Cities*, 7(2), e4–e4.

Chu, H. N., Glad, A., Simonin, O., Sempe, F., Drogoul, A., & Charpillet, F. Swarm approaches for the patrolling problem, information propagation vs. pheromone evaporation. In *19th IEEE International Conference on Tools with Artificial Intelligence(ICTAI 2007)*, volume 1, pages 442–449, Oct 2007. DOI: 10.1109/ICTAI.2007.80

Clark, R., & Turner, S. (2017). An overview of intrusion detection systems. *Cybersecurity Review*, 5(2), 78–92. DOI: 10.1000/csr.2017.078

Coello, C. A. C., Rivera, D. C., & Cortes, N. C. Use of an artificial immune system for job shop scheduling. In *International Conference on Artificial Immune Systems*, pages 1–10. Springer, 2003. DOI: 10.1007/978-3-540-45192-1_1

Coffman, E. G., Elphick, M., & Shoshani, A. (1971, June). System deadlocks. *ACM Computing Surveys*, 3(2), 67–78. DOI: 10.1145/356586.356588

Cohen, F. (1999). Simulating Cyber Attacks, Defences, and Consequences Modeling, Simulation, and Data Limitations in Information Protection. *Computers & Security*, 18(6), 479–518. DOI: 10.1016/S0167-4048(99)80115-1

Cohen, L. E., & Felson, M. (1979). Social change and crime rate trends: A routing activity approach. *American Sociological Review*, 44(4), 588–608. DOI: 10.2307/2094589

Contel, N. Y., & Schmick, P. J. (2016). Cybersecurity: Risks, Vulnerablities and countermeasures to prevent social engineering attacks. *International Journal of Advanced Computer Research*, 6(23), 31–38. DOI: 10.19101/IJACR.2016.623006

Costa, M. B., & Sofikitis, D. (2024). Applying Deep Learning and Data Analytics to identify Malware Attacks.

Cusumano, M. (2010). Cloud computing and saas as new computing platforms. *Communications of the ACM*, 53(4), 27–29. DOI: 10.1145/1721654.1721667

Dangerfield, J., McCarthy, T., & Ellery, W. (1998). The mound-building termite macrotermes michaelseni as an ecosystem engineer. *Journal of Tropical Ecology*, 14(4), 507–520. DOI: 10.1017/S0266467498000364

Darwish, M., Ouda, A., & Capretz, L. F. (2013, June). Cloud-based DDoS attacks and defenses. In International Conference on Information Society (i-Society 2013) (pp. 67-71). IEEE.

Dasari, S., & Kaluri, R. (2024). An Effective Classification of DDoS Attacks in a Distributed Network by Adopting Hierarchical Machine Learning and Hyperparameters Optimization Techniques. *IEEE Access : Practical Innovations, Open Solutions*, 12, 10834–10845. DOI: 10.1109/ACCESS.2024.3352281

Dasgupta, D. (1999). *An Overview of Artificial Immune Systems and Their Applications*. Springer.

Dash, B., Sharma, P., & Ali, A. (2022). Federated learning for privacy-preserving: A review of PII data analysis in Fintech. [IJSEA]. *International Journal of Software Engineering and Its Applications*, 13(4).

Das, S., Balmiki, A. K., Mazumdar, K., & Bhowmick, P. (2023). Cyber-Physical Security Issues and Challenges Using Machine Learning and Deep Learning Technologies. In *Artificial Intelligence in Cyber-Physical Systems* (pp. 105–123). CRC Press. DOI: 10.1201/9781003248750-7

Daugherty, P. R., & Wilson, H. J. (2018). *Human+ machine: Reimagining work in the age of AI*. Harvard Business Press.

Davarpanah Jazi, M., Ciobotaru, A. M., & Barati, E. (2014). An introduction to undetectable keyloggers with experimental testing. [IJCCN]. *International Journal of Computer Communications and Networks*, 4(3), 1–5.

Davis, M., & Smith, P. (2016). Understanding the role of firewalls in network security. *Journal of Network Security*, 12(3), 210–225. DOI: 10.1000/jns.2016.210

de Castro, L. N., & Timmis, J. (2002). Artificial immune systems: a novel approach to pattern recognition.

De Castro, L. N., & Von Zuben, F. J. (2002). Learning and optimization using the clonal selection principle. *IEEE Transactions on Evolutionary Computation*, 6(3), 239–251. DOI: 10.1109/TEVC.2002.1011539

Deliri, S., & Albanese, M. (2015). *Security and privacy issues in social networks*. Data Management in Pervasive Systems. DOI: 10.1007/978-3-319-20062-0_10

Dell, C. (2017). Today's Massive Ransomware Attack Was Mostly Preventable; Here's How To Avoid It. Gizmodo. https://www.gizmodo.com.au/2017/05/todays-massive-ransomware-attack-was-mostly-preventable-heres-how-to-avoid-it. Retrieved 13 May 2017.

Demir, B., & Serkan, A. (2024). Cyber Vigilantes: A Deep Dive into the Art and Science of Digital Defense. *Integrated Journal of Science and Technology, 1*(2).

Deshpande, K., Dam, L. B., & Pandey, N. (2022). *Cyberattack at cosmos bank: Regaining customer trust*. SAGE Publications: SAGE Business Cases Originals. https://sk.sagepub.com/cases/cyberattack-at-cosmos-bank-regaining-customer-trust

Devan, A. M., Raghul, V., Dhasmana, U., Rath, A., & Jacob, L. (2024). 6 Deep Support Learning Model Decision for Police Investigation. *Artificial Intelligence for Cyber Defense and Smart Policing*, 76.

Dhenakaran, S. S., & Parvathavarthini, A. (2013). An overview of routing protocols in mobile ad-hoc network. *International Journal of Advanced Research in Computer Science and Software Engineering*, 3(2).

Dhillon, A. (2014). Social Media & Revolution: The Importance of the Internet in Tunisia's Uprising.

Dhingra, M., & Mudgal, R. K. (2019, March). Historical evolution of social media: An overview. In *International Conference on Advances in Engineering Science Management & Technology (ICAESMT)*-2019, Uttaranchal University, Dehradun, India.

Dhoni, P., & Kumar, R. (2023). Synergizing generative ai and cybersecurity: Roles of generative ai entities, companies, agencies, and government in enhancing cybersecurity. *Authorea Preprints*.

Di Minin, E., Fink, C., Hausmann, A., Kremer, J., & Kulkarni, R. (2021). How to address data privacy concerns when using social media data in conservation science. *Conservation Biology*, 35(2), 437–446. DOI: 10.1111/cobi.13708 PMID: 33749044

Dias, M. B., & Stentz, A. A free market architecture for distributed con- trol of a multirobot system. In *6th International Conference on Intelligent Autonomous Systems (IAS-6)*, pages 115–122, 2000.

Dillahunt, T., Mankoff, J., & Paulos, E. (2019). Understanding conflict in the smart home through role-play. *Proceedings of the 2019 CHI Conference on Human Factors in Computing Systems*, 1-13.

Din, N. U., Javed, K., Bae, S., & Yi, J. (2020). A novel GAN-based network for unmasking of masked face. *IEEE Access : Practical Innovations, Open Solutions*, 8, 44276–44287. DOI: 10.1109/ACCESS.2020.2977386

Din, S. M. U., Sharma, R., Rizvi, F., & Sharma, N. (2024). Detection of botnet in IoT network through machine learning based optimized feature importance via ensemble models. *International Journal of Information Technology : an Official Journal of Bharati Vidyapeeth's Institute of Computer Applications and Management*, 16(2), 1203–1211.

Dixit, R., & Rajaura, S. (2023). The Impact of Social Media on Mental Health: Understanding the Effects and Finding Balance. *Research in Multidisciplinary Subjects*, 12, 50.

Djenna, A., Barka, E., Benchikh, A., & Khadir, K. (2023). Unmasking Cybercrime with Artificial-Intelligence-Driven Cybersecurity Analytics. *Sensors (Basel)*, 23(14), 6302. DOI: 10.3390/s23146302 PMID: 37514596

Dobkin, D. M. (2012). *The RF in RFID: UHF RFID in Practice*. Newnes.

Doja, M. N., & Kumar, N. (2008, August). Image authentication schemes against key-logger spyware. In *2008 Ninth ACIS International Conference on Software Engineering, Artificial Intelligence, Networking, and Parallel/Distributed Computing* (pp. 574-579). IEEE.

Douligeris, C., & Mitrokotsa, A. (2003, December). DDoS attacks and defense mechanisms: a classification. In Proceedings of the 3rd IEEE International Symposium on Signal Processing and Information Technology (IEEE Cat. No. 03EX795) (pp. 190-193). IEEE.

Du, Y., & Fan, H. (2020). Exploring the impact of cultural dimensions on smart home technology adoption.

Duan, X., Tan -H. Z. (2015). A feature subtraction method for image-based kinship verificationunder uncontrolled environments.*2015 IEEE International Conference on Image Processing (ICIP)*,1573–1577. DOI: 10.1109/ICIP.2015.7351065

Duarte, M., Gomes, J., Oliveira, S. M., & Christensen, A. L. Evorbc: Evolu- tionary repertoire-based control for robots with arbitrary locomotion complex- ity. In *Proceedings of the Genetic and Evolutionary Computation Conference 2016*, GECCO '16, pages 93–100, 2016. DOI: 10.1145/2908812.2908855

Duarte, M., Oliveira, S. M., & Christensen, A. L. Hybrid control for large swarms of aquatic drones. In *Proceedings of the 14th International Conference on the Synthesis & Simulation of Living Systems.MIT Press,Cambridge, MA*, pages 785–792. Citeseer, 2014.

Duarte, M., Oliveira, S., & Christensen, A. L. Hierarchical evolution of robotic controllers for complex tasks. In *Development and Learning and Epigenetic Robotics (ICDL),2012IEEE International Conference on*, pages 1–6. IEEE, 2012. DOI: 10.1109/DevLrn.2012.6400828

Edosomwan, S., Prakasan, S. K., Kouame, D., Watson, J., & Seymour, T. (2011). The history of social media and its impact on business. *The Journal of Applied Management and Entrepreneurship*, 16(3), 79–91.

Eikenberry, S. E., Mancuso, M., Iboi, E., Phan, T., Eikenberry, K., Kuang, Y., & Gumel, A. B. (2020). To mask or not to mask: Modeling the potential for face mask use by the general public to curtail the COVID-19 pandemic. *Infectious Disease Modelling*, 5, 293–308. DOI: 10.1016/j.idm.2020.04.001 PMID: 32355904

Elluri, L., Mandalapu, V., Vyas, P., & Roy, N. (2023). Recent Advancements in Machine Learning for Cybercrime Prediction. *Journal of Computer Information Systems*, •••, 1–15. DOI: 10.1080/08874417.2023.2270457

Escorcia-Gutierrez, J., Gamarra, M., Leal, E., Madera, N., Soto, C., Mansour, R. F., Alharbi, M., Alkhayyat, A., & Gupta, D. (2023). Sea turtle foraging algorithm with hybrid deep learning-based intrusion detection for the internet of drones environment. *Computers & Electrical Engineering*, 108, 108704. DOI: 10.1016/j.compeleceng.2023.108704

Evans, T., & Jones, K. (2019). The impact of emerging technologies on network security. *Journal of Information Security*, 8(4), 300–315. DOI: 10.1000/jis.2019.300

Fang, R., Gallagher, C. A., Chen, T., & Loui, A. (2013), Kinship classification by modeling facialfeature heredity.*IEEE International Conference on Image Processing*, 2983–2987. DOI: 10.1109/ICIP.2013.6738614

Fang, R., Tang, D. K., Snavely, N., & Chen, T. (2010). Towards computational models of kinshipVerification.*IEEE International Conference on Image Processing*,1577–1580. DOI: 10.1109/ICIP.2010.5652590

Faragher, R., & Harle, R. An analysis of the accuracy of bluetooth low energy for indoor positioning applications. In *Proceedings of the 27th International Technical Meeting of the Satellite Division of the Institute of Navigation (ION GNSS+ '14)*, 2014.

Farmer, J. D., Packard, N. H., & Perelson, A. S. (1986). The immune system, adaptation, and machine learning. *Physica D. Nonlinear Phenomena*, 22(1), 187–204. DOI: 10.1016/0167-2789(86)90240-X

Farooq, K.. (2021). The Study on the Role of Social Media in Social Change in Society. *International Journal of Innovation, Creativity and Change.*, 15(2), 1298. www.ijicc.net

Fife, L. D., & Gruenwald, L. (2003, June). Research Issues for Data Communication in Mobile Ad-hoc Network Database Systems. *SIGMOD Record*, 32(2), 42–47. DOI: 10.1145/776985.776991

Fire, M., Goldschmidt, R., & Elovici, Y. (2014). Online social networks: Threats and solutions. *IEEE Communications Surveys and Tutorials*, 16(4), 2019–2036. DOI: 10.1109/COMST.2014.2321628

Floreano, D., & Mondada, F. Automatic creation of an autonomous agent: Genetic evolution of a neural-network driven robot. 1994. In *Proceedings of the Third International Conference on Simulation of Adaptive behavior: From Animals to Animats*, volume 3.

Floridi, L., Cowls, J., Beltrametti, M., Chatila, R., Chazerand, P., Dignum, V., & Luetge, C. (2018). AI4People—An ethical framework for a good. *AI & Society*. PMID: 30930541

Franklin, S., & Graesser, A. (1996). Is it an agent, or just a program?: A taxonomy for autonomous agents. In *Intelligent agents III agent theories, architectures, and languages* (pp. 21–35). Springer.

Freitas, A. A. (2004). A critical review of multi-objective optimization in data mining: A position paper. *SIGKDD Explorations*, 6(2), 77–86. DOI: 10.1145/1046456.1046467

Friedman, B., & Kahn, P. H., Jr. (2003). Human values, ethics, and design. Handbook of human-computer interaction, 1177-1201.

Funk, R. J., & Owen-Smith, J. (2017). A Dynamic Network Measure of Technological Change. *Management Science*, 63(3), 791–817. DOI: 10.1287/mnsc.2015.2366

Gaber, J., & Bakhouya, M. Mobile Agent-Based Approach for Resource Dis- covery in Peer-to-Peer Networks. In *Agents and Peer-to-Peer Computing*, pages 63–73, 2008.

Gangula, R., Vutukuru, M. M., & Kumar, R. (2024). Hybridization of Bottlenose Dolphin Optimization and Artificial Fish Swarm Algorithm with Efficient Classifier for Detecting the Network Intrusion in Internet of Things (IoT). *International Journal of Intelligent Systems and Applications in Engineering*, 12(6s), 220–232.

Gangwar, N., Semwal, T., & Nair, S. B. Care: An iot based system for passenger service and comfort in railways. In *Communication Systems and Networks (COMSNETS),20179th International Conference on*, pages 55–62. IEEE, 2017.

Ganji, K., & Afshan, N. (2024). A bibliometric review of Internet of Things (IoT) on cybersecurity issues. *Journal of Science and Technology Policy Management*.

Gao, H., Hu, J., Huang, T., Wang, J., & Chen, Y. (2011, July-August). Security issues in online social networks. *IEEE Internet Computing*, 15(4), 56–63. DOI: 10.1109/MIC.2011.50

Garg, H. (2022). Financial Regulators and the Need for Data Privacy and Protection-Issues, Opportunities and Challenges. *International Journal Of Legal Developments And Allied Issues*, 8(1), 290–301.

Gartner. Gartner says 6.4 billion connected "things" will be in use in 2016, up 30 percent from 2015, (2015). [Online; accessed 20-February-2016].

Gerkey, B. P., & Mataric, M. J. (2003, September). Multi-robot task allocation: Analyzing the complexity and optimality of key architectures. In 2003 IEEE international conference on robotics and automation (Cat. No. 03CH37422) (Vol. 3, pp. 3862-3868). IEEE.

Gerkey, B. P., & Matarić, M. J. (2001). *Principled communication for dynamic multi-robot task allocation*. Springer Berlin Heidelberg.

Ghafir, I., Hammoudeh, M., & Prenosil, V. (2018, June 15). Defending against the advanced persistent threat: Detection of disguised executable files. DOI: 10.7287/peerj.preprints.2998v2

Ghosh, A., Ratasuk, R., Mondal, B., Mangalvedhe, N., & Thomas, T. (2010). Lte- advanced: Next-generation wireless broadband technology. *IEEE Wireless Communications*, 17(3), 10–22. DOI: 10.1109/MWC.2010.5490974

Gill, H. (2022, June 21). Malware: Types, Analysis and Classifications. DOI: 10.31224/2423

Girma, A., Garuba, M., Li, J., & Liu, C. (2015, April). Analysis of DDoS attacks and an introduction of a hybrid statistical model to detect DDoS attacks on cloud computing environment. In 2015 12th International Conference on Information Technology-New Generations (pp. 212-217). IEEE.

Godfrey, W. W., & Nair, S. B. A Pheromone Based Mobile Agent Migration Strategy for Servicing Networked Robots. In *Bio-Inspired Models of Network, Information, and Computing Systems*, pages 533–541. Springer, 2012. DOI: 10.1007/978-3-642-32615-8_52

Godfrey, W. W., Jha, S. S., & Nair, S. B. On a mobile agent framework for an internet of things. In *International Conference on Communication Systems and Network Technologies (CSNT),2013*, pages 345–350. IEEE, 2013. DOI: 10.1109/CSNT.2013.79

Godfrey, W. W., Jha, S. S., & Nair, S. B. (2014). On stigmergically controlling a population of heterogeneous mobile agents using cloning resource. In *Trans- actions on Computational Collective Intelligence XIV* (pp. 49–70). Springer. DOI: 10.1007/978-3-662-44509-9_3

Godfrey, W. W., & Nair, S. B. (2008). An immune system based multi-robot mobile agent network. In *Artificial Immune Systems* (pp. 424–433). Springer. DOI: 10.1007/978-3-540-85072-4_37

Godfrey, W. W., & Nair, S. B. (2010). Mobile agent cloning for servicing networked robots. In *Principles and Practice of Multi-Agent Systems* (pp. 336–339). Springer.

Godfrey, W. W., & Nair, S. B. A Mobile Agent Cloning Controller for Ser- vicing Networked Robots. In *International Conference on Future Information Technology IPCSIT*, volume 13, pages 81–85. IACSIT Press, 2011.

Goh, E., Al-Tabbaa, O., & Khan, Z. (2023). Unravelling the Complexity of the Video Game Industry: An Integrative Framework and Future Research Directions. *Telematics and Informatics Reports*, 12(August), 100100. DOI: 10.1016/j.teler.2023.100100

Gomez, C., Oller, J., & Paradells, J. (2012). Overview and evaluation of bluetooth low energy: An emerging low-power wireless technology. *Sensors (Basel)*, 12(9), 11734–11753. DOI: 10.3390/s120911734

Goring, S. P., Rabaiotti, J. R., & Jones, A. J. (2007). Anti-keylogging measures for secure Internet login: an example of the law of unintended consequences. computers & security, 26(6), 421-426.

Gosain, M. S., Aggarwal, N., & Kumar, R. (2023, April). A study of 5G and edge computing integration with IoT-A Review. In *2023 International Conference on Computational Intelligence and Sustainable Engineering Solutions (CISES)* (pp. 705-710). IEEE. DOI: 10.1109/CISES58720.2023.10183438

Gragg, D. (2003). A multi-level defense against social engineering. *SANS Reading Room*, 13, 1–21.

Gray, R. S. Agent tcl: A transportable agent system. In *Proceedings of the ciKM Workshop on intelligent information Agents, Fourth international conference on information and Knowledge Management (ciKM 95), Baltimore, Maryland*, 1995.

Greitzer, F. L., Strozer, J., Cohen, S., Bergey, J., Cowley, J., Moore, A., & Mundie, D. (2014). Unintentional insider threat: Contributing factors, observables, and mitigation strategies. *2014 47th Hawaii International Conference on System Sciences*, 2025–2034. https://ieeexplore.ieee.org/abstract/document/6758854/

Grimm, P. W., Grossman, M. R., & Cormack, G. V. (2021). Artificial intelligence as evidence. *Nw. J. Tech. & Intell. Prop.*, 19, 9.

Gubbi, J., Buyya, R., Marusic, S., & Palaniswami, M. (2013). Internet of things (iot): A vision, architectural elements, and future directions. *Future Generation Computer Systems*, 29(7), 1645–1660. DOI: 10.1016/j.future.2013.01.010

Guirguis, M., Bestavros, A., Matta, I., & Zhang, Y. (2007, May). Reduction of quality (RoQ) attacks on dynamic load balancers: Vulnerability assessment and design tradeoffs. In IEEE INFOCOM 2007-26th IEEE International Conference on Computer Communications (pp. 857-865). IEEE.

Gunavathi, R., & Bharathi, K. M. (2024). 2 Cybercrimes in the. *Artificial Intelligence for Cyber Defense and Smart Policing*, 21.

Guo, H. *Algorithm Selection for Sorting and Probabilistic inference: A ma- chine learning approach.* PhD thesis, Department of Computing and Informa- tion Sciences, College of Engineering, Kansas State University, 2003.

Guo, Y., Dibeklioglu, H., & Van der Maaten, L. (2014). Graph-based kinship recognition. *2014 22nd International Conference on Pattern Recognition, IEEE.*DOI: 10.1109/ICPR.2014.735

Gupta, S., Singhal, A., & Kapoor, A. (2016). A literature survey on social engineering attacks: Phishing attack. *2016 International Conference on Computing, Communication and Automation (ICCCA)*, 537–540. https://ieeexplore.ieee.org/abstract/document/7813778/

Hadnagy, C. (2010). *Social engineering: The art of human hacking*. John Wiley & Sons. https://books.google.com/books?hl=en&lr=&id=9LpawpklYogC&oi=fnd&pg=PT7&dq=Social+Engineering&ots=vdfsJTf3VP&sig=4U3wYfau3ptMGpQSR4cDFUTIC1E

Hadzilacos, V. A note on group mutual exclusion. In *Proceedings of the Twentieth Annual ACM Symposium on Principles of Distributed Computing*, PODC '01, pages 100–106, New York, NY, USA, 2001. ACM. DOI: 10.1145/383962.383997

Hagendorff, T. (2019). From privacy to anti-discrimination in times of machine learning. *Ethics and Information Technology*, 21(4), 331–343. DOI: 10.1007/s10676-019-09510-5

Hamad, S. I. (2023). A review of deep learning applied to cyber security. *Texas Journal of Engineering and Technology*, 22, 49–57.

Hariri, W. (2022). Efficient masked face recognition method during the covid-19 pandemic. *Signal, Image and Video Processing*, 16(3), 605–612. DOI: 10.1007/s11760-021-02050-w PMID: 34804243

Harmer, P. K., Williams, P. D., Gunsch, G. H., & Lamont, G. B. (2002, June). An arti- ficial immune system architecture for computer security applications. *IEEE Transactions on Evolutionary Computation*, 6(3), 252–280. DOI: 10.1109/TEVC.2002.1011540

Harris, B., & White, A. (2020). AI-driven incident response: Challenges and solutions. *Journal of Incident Response*, 7(2), 150–167. DOI: 10.1000/jir.2020.150

Harshita, H. (2017). Detection and prevention of icmp flood ddos attack. *International Journal of New Technology and Research*, 3(3), 263333.

Hart, E., Davoudani, D., & McEwan, C. Immunological inspiration for building a new generation of autonomic systems. In *Proceedings of the 1st international conference on Autonomic computing and communication sys- tems*, page 9. ICST (Institute for Computer Sciences, Social-Informatics and Telecommunications Engineering), 2007. DOI: 10.4108/ICST.AUTONOMICS2007.2229

Hasan, M. A.. (2019). Smart Homes for Elderly Healthcare—Recent Advances and Research Challenges. *Sensors (Basel).*

Heinerman, J., Zonta, A., Haasdijk, E., & Eiben, A. E. On-line evolution of foraging behaviour in a population of real robots. In *European Conference on the Applications of Evolutionary Computation*, pages 198–212. Springer, 2016. DOI: 10.1007/978-3-319-31153-1_14

He, J. (2022). [Retracted] Cloud Computing Load Balancing Mechanism Taking into Account Load Balancing Ant Colony Optimization Algorithm. *Computational Intelligence and Neuroscience*, 2022(1), 3120883.

Hemamalini, V., Mishra, A. K., Tyagi, A. K., & Kakulapati, V. (2024). Artificial Intelligence–Blockchain-Enabled–Internet of Things-Based Cloud Applications for Next-Generation Society. *Automated Secure Computing for Next-Generation Systems*, 65-82.

Hogben, G. (2007). Security issues and recommendations for online social networks. *ENISA Position Paper*, 1, 1–36.

Hoijtink, M., & Planqué-van Hardeveld, A. (2022). Machine learning and the platformization of the military: A study of google's machine learning platform TensorFlow. *International Political Sociology*, 16(2), olab036. DOI: 10.1093/ips/olab036

Holz, T., Engelberth, M., & Freiling, F. (2009). Learning more about the underground economy: A case-study of keyloggers and dropzones. In Computer Security–ESORICS 2009: 14th European Symposium on Research in Computer Security, Saint-Malo, France, September 21-23, 2009. [Springer Berlin Heidelberg.]. *Proceedings*, 14, 1–18.

Hörmann, S., Knoche, M., & Rigoll, G. (2020). A multi-task comparator framework for kinship verification.*15th IEEE International Conference on Automatic Face and GestureRecognition(FG 2020)*, 863–867. DOI: 10.1109/FG47880.2020.00106

Huang, G. B., Lee, H., & Learned-Miller, E. (2012, June). Learning hierarchical representations for face verification with convolutional deep belief networks. In 2012 IEEE conference on computer vision and pattern recognition (pp. 2518-2525). IEEE.

Huang, C., Yan, K., Wei, S., Zhang, G., & Lee, D. H. (2017). Efficient anonymous attribute-based encryption with access policy hidden for cloud computing. *Proceedings of 2017 International Conference on Progress in Informatics and Computing, PIC 2017*, 266–270. DOI: 10.1109/PIC.2017.8359555

Hupperich, T., Löhr, H., Sadeghi, A. R., & Winandy, M. (2012). Flexible patient-controlled security for electronic health records. *IHI'12 - Proceedings of the 2nd ACM SIGHIT International Health Informatics Symposium*, 727–731. DOI: 10.1145/2110363.2110448

I. Goodfellow, Y. Bengio, A. Courville, and Y. Bengio. *Deep learning*, vol- ume 1. MIT press Cambridge, 2016.

Ignatiev, K. (2019) "Statistics on Parental Control Alerts for Various Countries," https://securelist.com/page/107/?calendar=2010-12&chapter=8 (last accessed: 16 December 2019)

Irfan, M., Elmogy, M., & El-Sappagh, S. (Eds.). (2023). *The impact of AI innovation on financial sectors in the era of industry 5.0.* IGI Global.

Ishiguro, A., Kondo, T., Watanabe, Y., & Uchikawa, Y. Dynamic behavior arbitration of autonomous mobile robots using immune networks. In *IEEE International Conference on Evolutionary Computation*, volume 2, pages 722– 727. IEEE, 1995. DOI: 10.1109/ICEC.1995.487474

Ismail, W. B. W., & Widyarto, S. (2022). *A Classification Of Human Error Factors In Unintentional Insider Threats*. 667–676. DOI: 10.15405/epms.2022.10.63

Ismail, W. B. W., & Yusof, M. (2018). Mitigation strategies for unintentional insider threats on information leaks. *International Journal of Security and Its Applications*, 12(1), 37–46. DOI: 10.14257/ijsia.2018.12.1.03

Itani, M., Basheer, H., & Eddine, F. (2023, July). Attack Detection in IoT-Based Healthcare Networks Using Hybrid Federated Learning. In *2023 International Conference on Smart Applications, Communications and Networking (SmartNets)* (pp. 1-7). IEEE. DOI: 10.1109/SmartNets58706.2023.10216144

Iyengar, N. C. S. N., Ganapathy, G., Mogan Kumar, P., & Abraham, A. (2014). A multilevel thrust filtration defending mechanism against ddos attacks in cloud computing environment. *International Journal of Grid and Utility Computing*, 5(4), 236–248. DOI: 10.1504/IJGUC.2014.065384

J. Wielemaker, T. Schrijvers, M. Triska, and T. Lager. SWI-Prolog. *Theory and Practice of Logic Programming*, 12:67–96, 1 2012.

Jabbour, D., Masri, J. E., Nawfal, R., Malaeb, D., & Salameh, P. (2023). Social media medical misinformation: impact on mental health and vaccination decision among university students. Irish Journal of Medical Science (1971-), 192(1), 291-301.

Jain, A. K., Sahoo, S. R., & Jyoti, K. (2021). Online social networks security and privacy: Comprehensive review and analysis. *Complex & Intelligent Systems*, 7(5), 2157–2177. DOI: 10.1007/s40747-021-00409-7

Jaiswal, A., & Kumar, R. (2023). Breast cancer diagnosis using stochastic self-organizing map and enlarge C4. 5. *Multimedia Tools and Applications*, 82(12), 18059–18076. DOI: 10.1007/s11042-022-14265-1

Jakobi, N. (1997). Evolutionary robotics and the radical envelope-of-noise hypothesis. *Adaptive Behavior*, 6(2), 325–368. DOI: 10.1177/105971239700600205

Jernejcic, T., & Kettani, H. (2019, October 23). On the Intersection of Big Data and Privacy. *Proceedings of the 4th International Conference on Big Data and Internet of Things*. DOI: 10.1145/3372938.3372939

Jerne, N. K. (1974). Toward a network theory of immune system. *Annales d'Immunologie*, 125(1), 373–389.

Jha, S. S. (2016). On mobile agents for learning and coordination in a networked robotics milieu.

Jha, S. S., & Nair, S. B. (2012, March). A logic programming interface for multiple robots. In 2012 3rd National Conference on Emerging Trends and Applications in Computer Science (pp. 152-156). IEEE.

Jha, S. S., & Nair, S. B. (2015, December). An Idiotypic Solution Sieve for Selecting the Best Performing Solutions in Real-World Distributed Intelligence. In 2015 3rd International Conference on Artificial Intelligence, Modelling and Simulation (AIMS) (pp. 71-76). IEEE.

Jha, S. S., Shrivastava, K., & Nair, S. B. (2013). On emulating real-world distributed intelligence using mobile agent based localized idiotypic networks. In Mining Intelligence and Knowledge Exploration: First International Conference, MIKE 2013, Tamil Nadu, India, December 18-20, 2013. Proceedings (pp. 487-498). Springer International Publishing.

Jha, S. S., Godfrey, W. W., & Nair, S. B. (2014, June). Stigmergy-Based Synchronization of a Sequence of Tasks in a Network of Asynchronous Nodes. *Cybernetics and Systems*, 45(5), 373–406. DOI: 10.1080/01969722.2014.917235

Jha, S. S., & Nair, S. B. (2015). On a multi-agent distributed asynchronous intelligence-sharing and learning framework. In *Transactions on Computational Collective Intelligence XVIII* (pp. 166–200). Springer Berlin Heidelberg.

Jha, S. S., & Nair, S. B. (2018). Tansa: Task allocation using nomadic soft agents for multirobot systems. *IEEE Transactions on Emerging Topics in Computational Intelligence*, 2(4), 308–318. DOI: 10.1109/TETCI.2017.2764113

Jignesh Chowdary, G., Punn, N. S., Sonbhadra, S. K., & Agarwal, S. (2020). Face mask detection using transfer learning of inceptionv3. In *Big Data Analytics: 8th International Conference, BDA 2020, Sonepat, India, December 15–18, 2020* [Springer International Publishing.]. *Proceedings*, 8, 81–90.

Jin, L., Chen, Y., Wang, T., Hui, P., & Vasilakos, A. V. (2013, September). Understanding user behavior in online social networks: A survey. *IEEE Communications Magazine*, 51(9), 144–150. DOI: 10.1109/MCOM.2013.6588663

Jin, X., Lin, X., Vasilakos, A. V., Hou, Y. T., & Liu, L. (2014). The architecture of the internet of things (IoT) for enabling ubiquitous healthcare monitoring and management. *IEEE Network*, 28(6), 6–14.

Johansen, D., van Renesse, R., & Schneider, F. B. (1996, September). Supporting broad internet access to TACOMA. In Proceedings of the 7th workshop on ACM SIGOPS European workshop: Systems support for worldwide applications (pp. 55-58).

Johnson, B.. (2020). Privacy Perceptions in Smart Home Environments: A Survey of User Attitudes and Behaviors. *Proceedings of the ACM Conference on Human Factors in Computing Systems*, 112-125.

Jones, R., & Patel, S. (2019). Enhancing network security with AI: A review. *International Journal of Artificial Intelligence in Network Security*, 6(3), 180–195. DOI: 10.1000/ijains.2019.180

Junglas, I., Watson, R. T., & Robinson, S. (2020). An analysis of smart home development: Evidence from the USA.

Kadena, E., & Gupi, M. (2021). Human factors in cybersecurity: Risks and impacts. Security science journal, 2(2), 51-64.

Kahn, A. B. (1962). Topological sorting of large networks. *Communications of the ACM*, 5(11), 558–562. DOI: 10.1145/368996.369025

Kahneman, D., & Tversky, A. (2013). Prospect theory: An analysis of decision under risk. In *Handbook of the fundamentals of financial decision making: Part I* (pp. 99–127). World Scientific. DOI: 10.1142/9789814417358_0006

Kambayashi, Y., Tsujimura, Y., Yamachi, H., Takimoto, M., & Yamamoto, H. (2009, January). Design of a multi-robot system using mobile agents with ant colony clustering. In 2009 42nd Hawaii International Conference on System Sciences (pp. 1-10). IEEE.

Kambayashi, Y., & Takimoto, M. (2005). Higher-order mobile agents for controlling intelligent robots. [IJIIT]. *International Journal of Intelligent Information Technologies*, 1(2), 28–42. DOI: 10.4018/jiit.2005040103

Kamei, K., Nishio, S., Hagita, N., & Sato, M. (2012). Cloud networked robotics. *IEEE Network*, 26(3), 28–34. DOI: 10.1109/MNET.2012.6201213

Kant, K., & Mohapatra, P. (2000). Scalable internet servers: Issues and challenges. *Performance Evaluation Review*, 28(2), 5–8. DOI: 10.1145/362883.362891

Katyal, S. K. (2019). Private accountability in the age of artificial intelligence. *UCLA Law Review. University of California, Los Angeles. School of Law*, 66, 54.

Kaushik, K. (2024). Leveraging Deep Learning Techniques for Securing the Internet of Things in the Age of Big Data. *Applying Artificial Intelligence in Cybersecurity Analytics and Cyber Threat Detection*, 309.

Kaviarasan, R., Balamurugan, G., & Kalaiyarasan, R. (2023). *Venkata Ravindra Reddy Effective load balancing approach in cloud computing using Inspired Lion Optimization Algorithm-Prime - Advances in Electrical Engineering* (Vol. 6). Electronics and Energy.

Kayes, I., & Iamnitchi, A. (2015). A survey on privacy and security in online social networks. arXiv preprint arXiv:1504.03342.

Khaluf, Y., & Rammig, F. Task Allocation Strategy for Time-Constrained Tasks in Robots Swarms. In *European Conference on Artificial Life*, number 2009, pages 737–744, 2013.

Khan, R., Khan, S. U., Zaheer, R., & Khan, S. (2012, December). Future internet: the internet of things architecture, possible applications and key challenges. In 2012 10th international conference on frontiers of information technology (pp. 257-260). IEEE.

Khan, F., Salah, K., & Al-Fuqaha, A. (2018). Toward efficient data collection in smart cities using edge and fog computing. *IEEE Internet of Things Journal*, 5(3), 1596–1605.

Khan, M. K., & Matloob Ullah Khan, D. M. U. (2022). Analysis the Growth & Linkage b/w Crypto-currency and Stock Market Indices: Evidence from the US and Indian Stock Market. *CEMJP*, 30(4), 1912–1920.

Kim, H. J. (2012). Online Social Media Networking and Assessing Its Security Risks. *International Journal Of Security & Its Applications*, 6(3), 11–18. DOI: 10.14257/ijsia.2016.10.3.02

Kim, K.-D., & Kumar, P. (2013). An overview and some challenges in cyber-physical systems. *Journal of the Indian Institute of Science*, 93(3), 341–352.

Kim, S., Sung, M. K., & Chung, Y. D. (2014). A framework to preserve the privacy of electronic health data streams. *Journal of Biomedical Informatics*, 50, 95–106. DOI: 10.1016/j.jbi.2014.03.015 PMID: 24704716

Kinnunen, J., Krishnamurthy, G., Huhtanen, K., Jussila, P., & Ratschunas, K. (2004). U.S. Patent No. 6,813,501. Washington, DC: U.S. Patent and Trademark Office.

Kishore, K., Kumar, N., & Krishna, V. (2020). Smart Home Systems: Opportunities and Challenges in India.

Klusch, M., Lodi, S., & Moro, G. (2003). Agent-based distributed data mining: The KDEC scheme. Intelligent Information Agents: The AgentLink Perspective, 104-122.

Kochhar, S. K., Bhatia, A., & Tomer, N. (2023). Using Deep Learning and Big Data Analytics for Managing Cyber-Attacks. In *New Approaches to Data Analytics and Internet of Things Through Digital Twin* (pp. 146–178). IGI Global.

Kongsorot, Y., Musikawan, P., Aimtongkham, P., You, I., Benslimane, A., & So-In, C. (2023). An Intrusion Detection and Identification System for Internet of Things Networks Using a Hybrid Ensemble Deep Learning Framework. *IEEE Transactions on Sustainable Computing*, 8(4), 596–613. DOI: 10.1109/TSUSC.2023.3303422

Kontaxis, G., Polakis, I., Ioannidis, S., & Markatos, E. P. (2011). Detecting social network profile cloning. In IEEE International Conference on Pervasive Computing and Communications Workshops (PERCOM Workshops) (pp. 295-300). IEEE. DOI: 10.1109/PERCOMW.2011.5766886

Kordzadeh, N., & Ghasemaghaei, M. (2022). Algorithmic bias: Review, synthesis, and future research directions. *European Journal of Information Systems*, 31(3), 388–409. DOI: 10.1080/0960085X.2021.1927212

Korst, P., & Velthuis, H. (1982). The nature of trophallaxis in honeybees. *Insectes Sociaux*, 29(2), 209–221. DOI: 10.1007/BF02228753

Kraut, R. E., & Resnick, P. (2012). *Building Successful Online Communities: Evidence-Based Social Design*. MIT Press. DOI: 10.7551/mitpress/8472.001.0001

Kridera, S., & Kanavos, A. (2024). Exploring Trust Dynamics in Online Social Networks: A Social Network Analysis Perspective. *Mathematical & Computational Applications*, 29(3), 37.

Krombholz, H. H., Huber, M., & Weippl, E. (2015). Advanced social engineering attacks. *Journal of Information Security and Applications*, 22, 113–122. DOI: 10.1016/j.jisa.2014.09.005

Kumar Shukla, R., Das, D., & Agarwal, A. (2016, March). A novel method for identification and performance improvement of Blurred and Noisy Images using modified facial deblur inference (FADEIN) algorithms. In *2016 IEEE Students' Conference on Electrical, Electronics and Computer Science (SCEECS)* (pp. 1-7). IEEE.

Kumar Shukla, R., & Kumar Tiwari, A. (2021). Comparative analysis of machine learning based approaches for face detection and recognition. *Journal of Information Technology Management*, 13(1), 1–21.

Kumar, A. (2024). Cybersecurity Threat Detection using Machine Learning and Network Analysis. *Journal of Artificial Intelligence General science (JAIGS) ISSN: 3006-4023, 1*(1), 38-46.

Kumar, A., Bhatia, A., Kashyap, A., & Kumar, M. (2023). LSTM Network: A Deep Learning Approach and Applications. In *Advanced Applications of NLP and Deep Learning in Social Media Data* (pp. 130-150). IGI Global. DOI: 10.4018/978-1-6684-6909-5.ch007

Kumar, A., Bhatia, A., Khan, I., & Kumar, V. (2011). Performance comparison of EW and Genetic Algorithm for Dynamic CMST. International Transactions in Applied Sciences, 3(3).

Kumar, P., Gowda, D. Y., & Prakash, A. M. (2024). Machine Learning in Cybersecurity: A Comprehensive Survey of Data Breach Detection, Cyber-Attack Prevention, and Fraud Detection. *Pioneering Smart Healthcare 5.0 with IoT, Federated Learning, and Cloud Security*, 175-197.

Kumar, A. K., Vadivukkarasi, K., & Dayana, R. (2023, February). A Novel Hybrid Deep Learning Model for Botnet Attacks Detection in a Secure IoMT Environment. In *2023 International Conference on Intelligent Systems for Communication, IoT and Security (ICISCoIS)* (pp. 44-49). IEEE. DOI: 10.1109/ICISCoIS56541.2023.10100396

Kumar, A., & Jain, A. (2021). Image smog restoration using oblique gradient profile prior and energy minimization. *Frontiers of Computer Science*, 15(6), 156706. DOI: 10.1007/s11704-020-9305-8 PMID: 34221535

Kumar, A., Tewari, N., & Kumar, R. (2019). Study towards the analytic approach for human-computer interaction using machine learning. *The International Journal of Analytical and Experimental Modal Analysis*, 11, 1456–1466.

Kumar, R., & Sharma, M. K. (2016). Advanced neuro-fuzzy approach for social media mining methods using cloud. *International Journal of Computer Applications*, 137(10), 56–58. DOI: 10.5120/ijca2016908927

Kumar, R., & Singh, T. (2021). Quantum computing and its impact on network security. *Future Technologies Journal*, 4(1), 65–80. DOI: 10.1000/ftj.2021.065

Kumar, S., Jain, A., Kumar Agarwal, A., Rani, S., & Ghimire, A. (2021). [Retracted] Object-Based Image Retrieval Using the U-Net-Based Neural Network. *Computational Intelligence and Neuroscience*, 2021(1), 4395646. DOI: 10.1155/2021/4395646 PMID: 34804141

Kumar, S., & Kumar, R. (2022). Intelligent model to image enrichment for strong night-vision surveillance cameras in future generation. *Multimedia Tools and Applications*, 81(12), 16335–16351. DOI: 10.1007/s11042-022-12496-w

Kumar, S., & Singh, S. K. (2016). Monitoring of pet animal in smart cities using animal biometrics. *Future Generation Computer Systems*.

Kumar, S., & Somani, V. (2018). Social Media Security Risks, Cyber Threats And Risks Prevention And Mitigation Techniques. *International Journal of Advance Research in Computer Science and Management*, 4(4), 125–129.

Kumar, V., Rus, D., & Sukhatme, G. S. (2008). Networked robots. In *Springer Handbook of Robotics* (pp. 943–958). Springer. DOI: 10.1007/978-3-540-30301-5_42

Kuwahara, H. (1997, April). Experiences teach us the future of autonomous decentralized systems. In *Proceedings of the Third International Symposium on Autonomous Decentralized Systems. ISADS 97* (pp. 169-175). IEEE.

L. E. Parker. Alliance: An architecture for fault tolerant multirobot coopera- tion. *Robotics and Automation, IEEE Transactions on*, 14(2):220–240, 1998.

Lange, D. B., & Oshima, M. (1999, March). Seven good reasons for mobile agents. *Communications of the ACM*, 42(3), 88–89. DOI: 10.1145/295685.298136

Lange, T., & Kettani, H. (2019). On Security Challenges of Future Technologies. *Journal of Communication*, •••, 1002–1008. DOI: 10.12720/jcm.14.11.1002-1008

Latif, S., Boulila, W., Koubaa, A., Zou, Z., & Ahmad, J. (2024). DTL-IDS: An optimized Intrusion Detection Framework using Deep Transfer Learning and Genetic Algorithm. *Journal of Network and Computer Applications*, 221, 103784. DOI: 10.1016/j.jnca.2023.103784

Lee, I., & Shin, Y. J. (2020). Machine learning for enterprises: Applications, algorithm selection, and challenges. *Business Horizons*, 63(2), 157–170. DOI: 10.1016/j.bushor.2019.10.005

Lee, J. H.. (2019). The Internet of Things (IoT): Applications, investments, and challenges for enterprises. *Business Horizons*.

Lee, J., Bagheri, B., & Kao, H.-A. (2015). A cyber-physical systems architecture for industry 4.0-based manufacturing systems. *Manufacturing Letters*, 3, 18–23. DOI: 10.1016/j.mfglet.2014.12.001

Lee, K., Lee, Y., & Kim, Y. (2015). Smart home ecosystems: A holistic approach. *IEEE Access : Practical Innovations, Open Solutions*.

Lee, W. P. (1999). Evolving complex robot behaviors. *Information Sciences*, 121(1-2), 1–25.

legislation.gov.uk. (1990). Computer Misuse Act [online] Available at: http://www.legislatin.gov.uk/ukpga/1990/18/sectin/3ZA

Leis, R., Badillo-Urquiola, K., Caulkins, B. D., & Bockelman, P. (2016). Modeling and Simulation Education for Behavioral Cybersecurity. In Interservice/Industry, Training, Simulation and Education Conference (I/ITSEC), in review, Orlando, FL.

Leppänen, T. (2018). Resource-oriented mobile agent and software framework for the Internet of Things.

Liang, J., Guo, J., Lao, S., & Li, J. (2017). Using deep relational features to verify kinship.*CCF Chinese Conference on Computer Vision*.DOI: 10.1007/978-981-10-7299-4_47

Lightbody, D., Ngo, D. M., Temko, A., Murphy, C. C., & Popovici, E. (2024). Dragon_Pi: IoT Side-Channel Power Data Intrusion Detection Dataset and Unsupervised Convolutional Autoencoder for Intrusion Detection. *Future Internet*, 16(3), 88. DOI: 10.3390/fi16030088

Li, H., & Dong, S. (2024). Image steganalysis algorithm based on deep learning and attention mechanism for computer communication. *Journal of Electronic Imaging*, 33(1), 013015–013015. DOI: 10.1117/1.JEI.33.1.013015

Li, L., Zhao, T., Xie, Y., & Feng, Y. (2020). Interpretable machine learning based on integration of nlp and psychology in peer-to-peer lending risk evaluation. In *Natural Language Processing and Chinese Computing: 9th CCF International Conference, NLPCC 2020, Zhengzhou, China, October 14–18, 2020* [Springer International Publishing.]. *Proceedings*, 9(Part II), 429–441.

Li, P., & Chen, Y. (2022). Research into an image inpainting algorithm via multilevel attention progression mechanism. *Mathematical Problems in Engineering*, 2022(1), 8508702. DOI: 10.1155/2022/8508702

Lipsa, S., & Dash, R. K. (2023). A novel intrusion detection system based on deep learning and random forest for digital twin on IOT platform. *Int. J. Sch. Res. Eng. Technol*, 2, 51–64.

Liu, C., Chen, B., Shao, W., Zhang, C., Wong, K., & Zhang, Y. (2024). Unraveling Attacks in Machine Learning-based IoT Ecosystems: A Survey and the Open Libraries Behind Them. arXiv preprint arXiv:2401.11723.

Liu, C., Yang, J., Chen, R., Zhang, Y., & Zeng, J. (2011, July). Research on immunity-based intrusion detection technology for the Internet of Things. In 2011 Seventh International conference on natural computation (Vol. 1, pp. 212-216). IEEE.

Liu, Q., Puthenputhussery, A., & Liu, C. (2016). A novel inheritable color space with application tokinship verification.*2016 IEEE Winter Conference on Applications of Computer Vision (WACV)*, 1–9. DOI: 10.1109/WACV.2016.7477667

Li, W., Liu, B. M., Liu, D., Liu, R. P., Wang, P., Luo, S., & Ni, W. (2019). Unified fine-grained access control for personal health records in cloud computing. *IEEE Journal of Biomedical and Health Informatics*, 23(3), 1278–1289. DOI: 10.1109/JBHI.2018.2850304 PMID: 29994490

Li, W., Wang, S., Lu, J., Feng, J., & Zhou, J. (2021). Meta-mining discriminative samples for kinship verification. *2021 IEEE/CVF Conference on Computer Vision and Pattern Recognition (CVPR)*.DOI: 10.1109/CVPR46437.2021.01587

Li, W., Zhang, Y., Lv, K., Lu, J., Feng, J., & Zhou, J. (2020). Graph-based kinship reasoning network. *(2020)IEEE International Conference on Multimedia and Expo (ICME)*. DOI: 10.1109/ICME46284.2020.9102823

Li, Y., Guo, K., Lu, Y., & Liu, L. (2021). Cropping and attention based approach for masked face recognition. *Applied Intelligence*, 51(5), 3012–3025. DOI: 10.1007/s10489-020-02100-9 PMID: 34764581

Lone, A. N., Mustajab, S., & Alam, M. (2023). A comprehensive study on cybersecurity challenges and opportunities in the IoT world. *Security and Privacy*, 6(6), e318. DOI: 10.1002/spy2.318

Lui, A., & Lamb, G. W. (2018). Artificial intelligence and augmented intelligence collaboration: Regaining trust and confidence in the financial sector. *Information & Communications Technology Law*, 27(3), 267–283. DOI: 10.1080/13600834.2018.1488659

Lu, J., Hu, J., & Tan, Y.-P. (2017). Discriminative deep metric learning for face and kinship verification. *IEEE Transactions on Image Processing*, 26(9), 4269–4282. Advance online publication. DOI: 10.1109/TIP.2017.2717505 PMID: 28644806

Lu, J., Hu, J., Zhou, X., Shang, Y., Tan, Y.-P., & Wang, G. (2012). Neighborhood repulsed metric learning for kinship verification.*IEEE Conference on Computer Vision and Pattern Recognition*. DOI: 10.1109/CVPR.2012.6247978

Lu, J., Zhou, X., Tan, Y.-P., Shang, Y., & Zhou, J. (2013). Neighborhood repulsed metric learning for kinship verification. *IEEE Transactions on Pattern Analysis and Machine Intelligence*, 36(2), 331–345. Advance online publication. DOI: 10.1109/TPAMI.2013.134 PMID: 24356353

Luo, W., Liu, J., Liu, J., & Fan, C. "An Analysis of Security in Social Networks," *2009 Eighth IEEE International Conference on Dependable, Autonomic and Secure Computing (DASC'09)*, 12-14 Dec. 2009, Chengdu, China. DOI: 10.1109/DASC.2009.100

Maalem Lahcen, R. A., Caulkins, B., Mohapatra, R., & Kumar, M. (2020). Review and insight on the behavioral aspects of cybersecurity. *Cybersecurity*, 3, 1–18.

Machado, R. B., Boukerche, A., Sobral, J. B. M., Jucá, K. R. L., & Notare, M. S. M. A. (2005, April). A hybrid artificial immune and mobile agent intrusion detection based model for computer network operations. In 19th IEEE international parallel and distributed processing symposium (pp. 8-pp). IEEE.

Maes, P. (1995). Artificial life meets entertainment: Lifelike autonomous agents. *Communications of the ACM*, 38(11), 108–114. DOI: 10.1145/219717.219808

Maes, P., Guttman, R. H., & Moukas, A. G. (1999). Agents that buy and sell. *Communications of the ACM*, 42(3), 81–91. DOI: 10.1145/295685.295716

Mahammad, A. B., & Kumar, R. (2023, April). Scalable and security framework to secure and maintain healthcare data using blockchain technology. In *2023 International Conference on Computational Intelligence and Sustainable Engineering Solutions (CISES)* (pp. 417-423). IEEE. DOI: 10.1109/CISES58720.2023.10183494

Manimaran, M., Dhar, M., Norabuena-Figueroa, R., Mahaveerakannan, R., Saraswathi, S., & Selvakumarasamy, K. (2023). Implementing Machine Learning-based Autonomic Cyber Defense for IoT-enabled Healthcare Devices. *Journal of Artificial Intelligence and Technology*, 3(4), 162–172. DOI: 10.37965/jait.2023.0209

Matani, J., & Nair, S. B. (2011). Typhon - A Mobile Agents Framework for Real World Emulation in Prolog. In *Multi-disciplinary Trends in Artificial Intelli- gence* (pp. 261–273). Springer. DOI: 10.1007/978-3-642-25725-4_23

McCarroll, N., & Curran, K. (2013). Social networking in education. [IJIDE]. *International Journal of Innovation in the Digital Economy*, 4(1), 1–1. DOI: 10.4018/jide.2013010101

McKendrick, K. (2019). Artificial intelligence prediction and counterterrorism. *London: The Royal Institute of International Affairs-Chatham House, 9.*

McLaughlin, N., Weir, D., & Argyros, A. (2013). Security Analysis of Emerging Smart Home Applications. *IEEE Security and Privacy.*

Meenu, S., Kumar, E. E. P., Panchal, V. K., & Kumar, R. (2019). Evolution of new integrated haze removal algorithm based on haze line. [IJEAT]. *International Journal of Engineering and Advanced Technology*, 8(06), 184–189.

Mehendele, D. K., Masurekar, R. S., Takawale, N., & Kulkarni, S. (2017). Review of Phishing Attacks and Anti Phishing Tools. [IJRCCE]. *International Journal Of Innovative Research In Computer And Communication Engineering*, 5, 15132.

Messai, M. L., & Seba, H. (2023, June). POSTER: Activity Graph Learning for Attack Detection in IoT Networks. In *2023 IEEE 24th International Symposium on a World of Wireless, Mobile and Multimedia Networks (WoWMoM)* (pp. 320-322). IEEE.

Messai, M. L., & Seba, H. (2023, August). IoT Network Attack Detection: Leveraging Graph Learning for Enhanced Security. In *Proceedings of the 18th International Conference on Availability, Reliability and Security* (pp. 1-7). DOI: 10.1145/3600160.3605053

Mhlanga, D. (2021). Financial inclusion in emerging economies: The application of machine learning and artificial intelligence in credit risk assessment. *International journal of financial studies, 9*(3), 39.

Mi, W., Qiu, X., & Zhang, C. (2011, December). The analysis of security threats in structured P2P load balancing schemes. In 2011 International Conference on Cloud and Service Computing (pp. 296-301). IEEE.

Michalski, R. S., Carbonell, J. G., & Mitchell, T. M. (2013). *Machine learning: An artificial intelligence approach*. Springer Science & Business Media.

Mijwil, M., & Aljanabi, M. (2023). Towards artificial intelligence-based cybersecurity: The practices and ChatGPT generated ways to combat cybercrime. *Iraqi Journal For Computer Science and Mathematics*, 4(1), 65–70.

Mijwil, M., Salem, I. E., & Ismaeel, M. M. (2023). The significance of machine learning and deep learning techniques in cybersecurity: A comprehensive review. *Iraqi Journal For Computer Science and Mathematics*, 4(1), 87–101.

Minar, N., Kramer, K. H., & Maes, P. (1998, May). Cooperating mobile agents for mapping networks. MIT Media Lab, to appear in Proceedings of the First Hungarian National Conference on Agent Based Computing.

Minar, N., Gray, M., Roup, O., Krikorian, R., & Maes, P. (2000). Hive: Distributed agents for networking things. *IEEE Concurrency*, 8(2), 24–33. DOI: 10.1109/4434.846191

Minerva, R., Biru, A., & Rotondi, D. (2015). Towards a definition of the internet of things (iot). *IEEE Internet Initiative*, 1, 1–86.

Mishra, A. K., Hemamalini, V., & Tyagi, A. K. (2024). Digital Forensics with Emerging Technologies: Vision and Research Potential for Future. *Conversational Artificial Intelligence*, 675-697.

Miskelly, F. G. (2001). Assistive technology in elderly care. *Age and Ageing*, 30(6), 455–458. DOI: 10.1093/ageing/30.6.455 PMID: 11742772

Misra, N. R., Kumar, S., & Jain, A. (2021, February). A review on E-waste: Fostering the need for green electronics. In *2021 international conference on computing, communication, and intelligent systems (ICCCIS)* (pp. 1032-1036). IEEE.

Mitchell, R., & Chen, R. (2014). Behavior rule specification-based intrusion detection for safety critical medical cyber physical systems. *IEEE Transactions on Dependable and Secure Computing*, 12(1), 16–30.

Mittal, H. (2024). Software security: Threats, solutions and challenges. *Computer Software and Media Applications*, 6(1), 3769. DOI: 10.24294/csma.v6i1.3769

Mliki, H., Dammak, S., & Fendri, E. (2020). An improved multi-scale face detection using convolutional neural network. *Signal, Image and Video Processing*, 14(7), 1345–1353. DOI: 10.1007/s11760-020-01680-w

Mohapatra, H. (2021, September). Socio-technical challenges in the implementation of smart city. In 2021 international conference on innovation and intelligence for informatics, computing, and technologies (3ICT) (pp. 57-62). IEEE.

Mohapatra, H., & Mishra, S. R. (2024). Unlocking Insights: Exploring Data Analytics and AI Tool Performance Across Industries. In Singh, P., Mishra, A. R., & Garg, P. (Eds.), *Data Analytics and Machine Learning. Studies in Big Data* (Vol. 145). Springer., DOI: 10.1007/978-981-97-0448-4_13

Moioli, R. C., Vargas, P. A., Von Zuben, F. J., & Husbands, P. (2008, June). Towards the evolution of an artificial homeostatic system. In 2008 IEEE Congress on Evolutionary Computation (IEEE World Congress on Computational Intelligence) (pp. 4023-4030). IEEE.

Montasari, R. (2024). Machine Learning and Deep Learning Techniques in Countering Cyberterrorism. In *Cyberspace, Cyberterrorism and the International Security in the Fourth Industrial Revolution: Threats, Assessment and Responses* (pp. 135–158). Springer International Publishing. DOI: 10.1007/978-3-031-50454-9_8

Moustafa, N., Koroniotis, N., Keshk, M., Zomaya, A. Y., & Tari, Z. (2023). Explainable intrusion detection for cyber defences in the internet of things: Opportunities and solutions. *IEEE Communications Surveys and Tutorials*, 25(3), 1775–1807. DOI: 10.1109/COMST.2023.3280465

Mouton, F., Leenen, L., & Venter, H. S. (2016). Social engineering attack examples, templates and scenarios. *Computers & Security*, 59, 186–209. DOI: 10.1016/j.cose.2016.03.004

Moyer, S., Maples, D., Tsang, S., & Ghosh, A. (2002). Service portability of networked appliances. *IEEE Communications Magazine*, 40(1), 116–121. DOI: 10.1109/35.978058

Mühlhoff, R. (2021). Predictive privacy: Towards an applied ethics of data analytics. *Ethics and Information Technology*, 23(4), 675–690. DOI: 10.1007/s10676-021-09606-x

Murlikrishna, P. N., Gupta, D. V., & Venugopal, D. K. (2020). Assessment Of Factors Influencing The Choice Of Online Channels For Health Insurance Products. *Journal of Interdisciplinary Cycle Research*, 12(12), 178–194.

Musa, N. S., Mirza, N. M., Rafique, S. H., Abdallah, A. M., & Murugan, T. (2024). Machine Learning and Deep Learning Techniques for Distributed Denial of Service Anomaly Detection in Software Defined Networks—Current Research Solutions. *IEEE Access : Practical Innovations, Open Solutions*, 12, 17982–18011. DOI: 10.1109/ACCESS.2024.3360868

Nandan, M., & Dey, S. (2023). Cybersecurity: Techniques and Applications to Combat Vicious Threats in Modern-Era Indices. In *AI-Aided IoT Technologies and Applications for Smart Business and Production* (pp. 248-270). CRC Press.

Narayana, Y. V., & Sreedevi, M. (2023, October). DDCATF: Deep Learning Approach for Detection of Cybercrime Activities Based on Temporal Features. In *2023 International Conference on Self Sustainable Artificial Intelligence Systems (ICSSAS)* (pp. 462-469). IEEE. DOI: 10.1109/ICSSAS57918.2023.10331644

Nassar, A., & Kamal, M. (2021). Ethical Dilemmas in AI-Powered Decision-Making: A Deep Dive into Big Data-Driven Ethical Considerations. *International Journal of Responsible Artificial Intelligence*, 11(8), 1–11.

National Institute of Standards and Technology. (2020). NIST Special Publication 800-213: Security Guidance for IoT Device Manufacturers.

Nehinbe, J. O., Benson, J. A., & Chibuzor, L. (2023). The classification of the investigations and punishment for crime syndicates that relate to intrusions against IoT-based healthcare systems. In *Blockchain Technology Solutions for the Security of IoT-Based Healthcare Systems* (pp. 113–131). Academic Press. DOI: 10.1016/B978-0-323-99199-5.00010-0

Nelson, A. L., Barlow, G. J., & Doitsidis, L. (2009). Fitness functions in evolutionary robotics: A survey and analysis. *Robotics and Autonomous Systems*, 57(4), 345–370. DOI: 10.1016/j.robot.2008.09.009

Nguyen, H., Nawara, D., & Kashef, R. (2024). Connecting the Indispensable Roles of IoT and Artificial Intelligence in Smart Cities: A Survey. *Journal of Information and Intelligence*.

Nguyen, H., & Lee, J. (2020). Leveraging AI for network security: Opportunities and challenges. *Journal of AI Applications in Cybersecurity*, 2(2), 85–100. DOI: 10.1000/jaics.2020.085

Nisha, S. R., & Muthurajkumar, S. (2023). Semantic Graph Based Convolutional Neural Network for Spam e-mail Classification in Cybercrime Applications. *International Journal of Computers, Communications & Control*, 18(1).

Nissenbaum, H. (2010). *Privacy in Context: Technology, Policy, and the Integrity of Social Life*. Stanford University Press.

Niu, T., Li, W., & Liu, Y. (2024). DarkGuardNet: A deep learning framework for imbalanced dark web traffic identification and application classification.

Nkoro, E. C., Njoku, J. N., Nwakanma, C. I., Lee, J. M., & Kim, D. S. (2024). Zero-Trust Marine Cyberdefense for IoT-Based Communications: An Explainable Approach. *Electronics (Basel)*, 13(2), 276. DOI: 10.3390/electronics13020276

Nolfi, S. (1998). Evolutionary robotics: Exploiting the full power of self-organization. *Connection Science*, 10(3-4), 167–184.

Norman, D. A. (2013). *The Design of Everyday Things*. Basic Books.

Novak, E., & Li, Q. "A Survey of Security and Privacy in Online Social Networks," available at: https://pdfs.semanticscholar.org/f602/caa6f711f57369246fefa0d608d10bc7e35e.pdf (last accessed: 16 December 2019)

Null, L., & Lobur, J. (2014). *The essentials of Computer Organization and Architecture*. Jones & Bartlett Publishers.

Nyarko, B. N. E., Bin, W., Zhou, J., Odoom, J., Danso, S. A., & Addai, G. E. S. (2024). Forensic detection of heterogeneous activity in data using deep learning methods. *Intelligent Systems with Applications*, 21, 200303. DOI: 10.1016/j.iswa.2023.200303

Odeh, A., & Abu Taleb, A. (2023). Ensemble-Based Deep Learning Models for Enhancing IoT Intrusion Detection. *Applied Sciences (Basel, Switzerland)*, 13(21), 11985. DOI: 10.3390/app132111985

Olan, F., Jayawickrama, U., Arakpogun, E. O., Suklan, J., & Liu, S. (2024). Fake News on Social Media: The Impact on Society. *Information Systems Frontiers*, 26(2), 443–458. DOI: 10.1007/s10796-022-10242-z PMID: 35068999

Ortiz-Ospina, E. (n.d.). The rise of social media. Our World in Data., Retrieved February 1, 2020, from.

Ortiz-Ruiz, E., Bermejo, J. R., Sicilia, J. A., & Bermejo, J. (2024). Machine Learning Techniques for Cyberattack Prevention in IoT Systems: A Comparative Perspective of Cybersecurity and Cyberdefense in Colombia. *Electronics (Basel)*, 13(5), 824. DOI: 10.3390/electronics13050824

Ortolani, S., Giuffrida, C., Crispo, A. B., & Member, S. (2013, January-February). IEEE. *IEEE Transactions on Dependable and Secure Computing*, 10(1).

Outtagarts, A. (2009). Mobile agent-based applications: A survey. *International Journal of Computer Science and Network Security*, 9(11), 331–339.

Oxley, A. (2011). *A best practices guide for mitigating risk in the use of social media*. IBM Center for the Business of Government Washington.

Paddalwar, S., Ragha, L., & Mane, V. (2023). Cyber threat mitigation using machine learning, deep learning, artificial intelligence, and blockchain. In *Intelligent Approaches to Cyber Security* (pp. 163–179). Chapman and Hall/CRC. DOI: 10.1201/9781003408307-14

Paliwal, R., & Sultania, S. (2021). Data Protection and Privacy in Smart Homes: Challenges and Solutions.

Papazoglou, M. P. (2001). Agent-oriented technology in support of e-business. *Communications of the ACM*, 44(4), 71–77. DOI: 10.1145/367211.367268

Parolini, L., Tolia, N., Sinopoli, B., & Krogh, B. H. (2010, April). A cyber-physical systems approach to energy management in data centers. In *Proceedings of the 1st acm/ieee international conference on cyber-physical systems* (pp. 168-177).

Pathan, A. S. K. (Ed.). (2014). *The state of the art in intrusion prevention and detection* (Vol. 44). CRC press.

Pathirana, P. N., Bulusu, N., Savkin, A. V., & Jha, S. (2005). Node localization using mobile robots in delay-tolerant sensor networks. *IEEE Transactions on Mobile Computing*, 4(3), 285–296. DOI: 10.1109/TMC.2005.43

Patil, S., & Javali, P. (2018). A review on smart home present and future. *Materials Today: Proceedings*, 5(1), 1518–1523.

Peine, H., & Stolpmann, T. (1997). The architecture of the Ara platform for mobile agents. In Mobile Agents: First International Workshop, MA'97 Berlin, Germany, April 7–8, 1997 Proceedings 1 (pp. 50-61). Springer Berlin Heidelberg.

Pham, V. A., & Karmouch, A. (1998, July). Mobile software agents: An overview. *IEEE Communications Magazine*, 36(7), 26–37. DOI: 10.1109/35.689628

Pieterse, J. N. (2021). *Connectivity and Global Studies*. Springer Nature. DOI: 10.1007/978-3-030-59598-2

Pilkington, M. (2016). Blockchain technology: principles and applications. In *Research handbook on digital transformations* (pp. 225–253). Edward Elgar Publishing.

Pipattanasomporn, M., Feroze, H., & Rahman, S. (2009, March). Multi-agent systems in a distributed smart grid: Design and implementation. In 2009 IEEE/PES Power Systems Conference and Exposition (pp. 1-8). IEEE.

Plageras, A., Stergiou, C. L., & Psannis, K. (2024). Secure Edge Communications Over the IoT.

Pocher, N., Zichichi, M., Merizzi, F., Shafiq, M. Z., & Ferretti, S. (2023). Detecting anomalous cryptocurrency transactions: An AML/CFT application of machine learning-based forensics. *Electronic Markets*, 33(1), 37. DOI: 10.1007/s12525-023-00654-3

Pokharel, M., Lillie, H. M., Nagatsuka, K., Barbour, J. B., Ratcliff, C. L., & Jensen, J. D. (2023). Social Media Narratives Can Influence Vaccine Intentions: The Impact of Depicting Regret and Character Death. *Computers in Human Behavior*, 141, 107612. DOI: 10.1016/j.chb.2022.107612

Poler, R., Molina, A., & Giret, A. (2012). A survey of models for the Internet of Things. *Journal of Systems and Software*.

Pollini, A., Callari, T. C., Tedeschi, A., Ruscio, D., Save, L., Chiarugi, F., & Guerri, D. (2022). Leveraging human factors in cybersecurity: An integrated methodological approach. *Cognition Technology and Work*, 24(2), 371–390.

Posadas, J., Poza, J., Simó, J., Benet, G., & Blanes, F. (2008, September). Agent-based distributed architecture for mobile robot control. *Engineering Applications of Artificial Intelligence*, 21(6), 805–823. DOI: 10.1016/j.engappai.2007.07.008

Pritee, Z. T., Anik, M. H., Alam, S. B., Jim, J. R., Kabir, M. M., & Mridha, M. F. (2024). Machine learning and deep learning for user authentication and authorization in cybersecurity: A state-of-the-art review. *Computers & Security*, 140, 103747. DOI: 10.1016/j.cose.2024.103747

Priyadarshini, I., Mohanty, P., Alkhayyat, A., Sharma, R., & Kumar, S. (2023). SDN and application layer DDoS attacks detection in IoT devices by attention-based Bi-LSTM-CNN. *Transactions on Emerging Telecommunications Technologies*, 34(11), e4758. DOI: 10.1002/ett.4758

Qin, B., & Li, D. (2020). Identifying facemask-wearing condition using image super-resolution with classification network to prevent COVID-19. *Sensors (Basel)*, 20(18), 5236. DOI: 10.3390/s20185236 PMID: 32937867

Raggo, M. "Anatomy of a Social Media Attack," available at: https://www.darkreading.com/analytics/anatomy-of-a-social-media-attack/a/d-id/1326680 (last accessed: 16 December 2019).

Rai, R., & Sahu, C. K. (2020). Driven by data or derived through physics? a review of hybrid physics guided machine learning techniques with cyber-physical system (cps) focus. *IEEE Access : Practical Innovations, Open Solutions*, 8, 71050–71073. DOI: 10.1109/ACCESS.2020.2987324

Rajkumar, S., Sheeba, S. L., Sivakami, R., Prabu, S., & Selvarani, A. (2023). An IoT-Based Deep Learning Approach for Online Fault Detection Against Cyber-Attacks. *SN Computer Science*, 4(4), 393. DOI: 10.1007/s42979-023-01808-y

Rakha, M. A., Khan, I. U., Ouaissa, M., Ouaissa, M., & Ayub, M. Y. (2024). Hybrid Model for IoT-Enabled Intelligent Towns Using the MQTT-IoT-IDS2020 Dataset. In *Cyber Security for Next-Generation Computing Technologies* (pp. 159-176). CRC Press.

Ramprasath, J., Krishnaraj, N., & Seethalakshmi, V. (2022). Mitigation services on SDN for distributed denial of service and denial of service attacks using machine learning techniques. *Journal of the Institution of Electronics and Telecommunication Engineers*, (Nov), 1–12.

Rasmussen, J. (1983). Skills, Rules, and Knowledge: Signals, Signs, and Symbols, and other Distinctions in Human Performance Models. *IEEE Transactions on Systems, Man, and Cybernetics*, 13(3), 257–266. DOI: 10.1109/TSMC.1983.6313160

Rathee, G., Iqbal, R., Kerrache, C. A., & Song, H. (2024). TrustNextGen: Security Aspects of Trustworthy Next Generation Industrial Internet of Things (IIoT). *IEEE Internet of Things Journal*, 11(15), 25568–25576. DOI: 10.1109/JIOT.2024.3361801

Rathore, S., Loia, V., & Park, J. H. (2018). SpamSpotter: An efficient spammer detection framework based on intelligent decision support system on facebook. *Applied Soft Computing*, 67, 920–932. DOI: 10.1016/j.asoc.2017.09.032

Rathore, S., Shamra, P. K., Loia, V., Jeong, Y.-S., & Park, J. H. (2017, December). Social network security: Issues, challenges, threats, and solutions. *Information Sciences*, 421, 43–69. DOI: 10.1016/j.ins.2017.08.063

Raynal, M. (1986). *Algorithms for mutual exclusion*. The MIT Press.

Raza, A., & Fernández, B. R. (2018). A multi-tier immuno-inspired framework for heterogeneous mobile robotic systems. *Applied Soft Computing*, 71, 333–352. DOI: 10.1016/j.asoc.2018.06.041

Reddy, B. B., Pasha, S. G., Kameswari, M., Chinkera, R., Fatima, S., Bhargava, R., & Shrivastava, A. (2024). Classification Approach for Face Spoof Detection in Artificial Neural Network Based on IoT Concepts. *International Journal of Intelligent Systems and Applications in Engineering*, 12(13s), 79–91.

Ren, W., Beard, R. W., & Atkins, E. M. (2005, June). A survey of consensus problems in multi-agent coordination. In *Proceedings of the 2005, American Control Conference*, 2005. (pp. 1859-1864). IEEE.

Rezaeibagha, F., & Mu, Y. (2016). Distributed clinical data sharing via dynamic access-control policy transformation. *International Journal of Medical Informatics*, 89, 25–31. DOI: 10.1016/j.ijmedinf.2016.02.002 PMID: 26980356

Rimal, B. P., Choi, E., & Lumb, I. (2009, August). A taxonomy and survey of cloud computing systems. In 2009 fifth international joint conference on INC, IMS and IDC (pp. 44-51). Ieee.

Rishi, I.(2020). Twitter accounts of Joe Biden, Barack Obama, Elon Musk, Bill Gates, and others apparently hacked. CNN Business. Archived from the original on July 16, 2020. Retrieved July 15, 2020.

Robles, T., Alcarria, R., de Andrés, D. M., Navarro, M., Calero, R., Iglesias, S., & López, M. (2015). An iot based reference architecture for smart water manage- ment processes. *JoWUA*, 6(1), 4–23.

Rone, J. (2022). Fake Profiles, Trolls, and Digital Paranoia: Digital Media Practices in Breaking the Indignados Movement. *Social Movement Studies*, 21(1–2), 25–41. DOI: 10.1080/14742837.2019.1679108

Roshanaei, M. (2024). Enhancing Mobile Security through Comprehensive Penetration Testing. *Journal of Information Security*, 15(2), 63–86. DOI: 10.4236/jis.2024.152006

Rowe, N. C. (1988). *Artificial Intelligence Through Prolog*. Prentice-Hall, Inc.

Rubenstein, M., Ahler, C., & Nagpal, R. (2012, May). Kilobot: A low cost scalable robot system for collective behaviors. In 2012 [IEEE.]. *IEEE International Conference on Robotics and Automation*, •••, 3293–3298.

Rubenstein, M., Cornejo, A., & Nagpal, R. (2014). Programmable self-assembly in a thousand-robot swarm. *Science*, 345(6198), 795–799. DOI: 10.1126/science.1254295 PMID: 25124435

Sadiq, W., & Cummins, F. A. (1998). *Developing Business Systems with CORBA with CD-ROM: The Key to Enterprise Integration* (Vol. 13). Cambridge University Press.

Sahi, A., Lai, D., Li, Y., & Diykh, M. (2017). An efficient ddos tcp flood attack detection and prevention system in a cloud environment. *IEEE Access : Practical Innovations, Open Solutions*, 5, 6036–6048. DOI: 10.1109/ACCESS.2017.2688460

Sahingoz, O. K., Buber, E., & Kugu, E. (2024). DEPHIDES: Deep Learning Based Phishing Detection System. *IEEE Access : Practical Innovations, Open Solutions*, 12, 8052–8070. DOI: 10.1109/ACCESS.2024.3352629

Sahoo, S. R., & Gupta, B. B. (2020) Popularity-based detection of malicious content in facebook using machine learning approach. In: *First international conference on sustainable technologies for computational intelligence*. Springer, Singapore, pp 163–17618 DOI: 10.1007/978-981-15-0029-9_13

Saiyed, M. F., & Al-Anbagi, I. (2024). A Genetic Algorithm-and t-Test-Based System for DDoS Attack Detection in IoT Networks. *IEEE Access : Practical Innovations, Open Solutions*, 12, 25623–25641. DOI: 10.1109/ACCESS.2024.3367357

Sakthibalan, P., Saravanan, M., Ansal, V., Rajakannu, A., Vijayalakshmi, K., & Vani, K. D. (2024). A Federated Learning Approach for ResourceConstrained IoT Security Monitoring. In *Handbook on Federated Learning* (pp. 131–154). CRC Press.

Salahdine, F., & Kaabouch, N. (2019). Social engineering attacks: A survey. *Future Internet*, 11(4), 89. DOI: 10.3390/fi11040089

Saleem, M., & Chawla, C. (2023). Blockchain-Powered Decentralized Finance (DeFi): Transforming Financial Inclusion & Investment Landscapes. *2023 12th International Conference on System Modeling & Advancement in Research Trends (SMART)*, 342–346. https://ieeexplore.ieee.org/abstract/document/10428666/

Saleem, M., & Khan, M. U. (2021). Green finance for sustainable development: A bibliometric review of current status, development and prospects. *International Journal of Advanced Research in Commerce* [IJARCMSS]. *Management & Social Science*, 4(4), 1–9.

Saleem, M., Khan, M. U., & Ather, D. (2021). Fintech startups and banks: Adoption, incentives, competition, and regulations. *International Journal on Global Business Management & Research*, 10(2), 21–28.

Saltz, J., Skirpan, M., Fiesler, C., Gorelick, M., Yeh, T., Heckman, R., & Beard, N. (2019). Integrating ethics within machine learning courses. [TOCE]. *ACM Transactions on Computing Education*, 19(4), 1–26. DOI: 10.1145/3341164

Sambasivan, N., Arnesen, E., Hutchinson, B., Doshi, T., & Prabhakaran, V. (2021, March). Re-imagining algorithmic fairness in india and beyond. In *Proceedings of the 2021 ACM conference on fairness, accountability, and transparency* (pp. 315-328). DOI: 10.1145/3442188.3445896

Samsudeen, S., & Thomas, L. (2024). Cybersecurity Warning System Using Diluted Convolutional Neural Network Framework for IOT Attack Prevention. *International Journal of Intelligent Engineering & Systems*, 17(1).

Sandeep, G. P., Prashanth, P., Sreenivasulu, M., & Madhavilata, A. (2020). Social Media in Agriculture–A Profile Analysis. *International Journal of Current Microbiology and Applied Sciences*, 9(7), 2727–2736. DOI: 10.20546/ijcmas.2020.907.322

Scharlach, R., Hallinan, B., & Shifman, L. (2023). Governing principles: Articulating values in social media platform policies. new media & society, 14614448231156580.

Schmitt, M. (2020). Artificial intelligence in business analytics, capturing value with machine learning applications in financial services.

Schreyer, P. (2000). The contribution of information and communication technology to output growth: a study of the G7 countries.

Sebbar, A., & Zkik, K. (2023). "Enhancing Resilience against DDoS Attacks in SDN -based Supply Chain Networks Using Machine Learning," 2023 9th International Conference on Control, Decision and Information Technologies (CoDIT), Rome, Italy. DOI: 10.1109/CoDIT58514.2023.10284387

Segovia-Vargas, M. J. (2024). Money Laundering in the Age of Cybercrime and Emerging Technologies.

Selbst, A. D., & Barocas, S. (2018). The intuitive appeal of explainable machines. *Fordham Law Review*, 87, 1085.

Semwal, T., Bode, M., Singh, V., Jha, S. S., & Nair, S. B. (2015, July). Tartarus: a multi-agent platform for integrating cyber-physical systems and robots. In *Proceedings of the 2015 Conference on Advances in Robotics* (pp. 1-6).

Semwal, T., Jha, S. S., & Nair, S. B. (2016, May). Tartarus: A multi-agent platform for bridging the gap between cyber and physical systems. In *Proceedings of the 2016 International Conference on Autonomous Agents & Multiagent Systems* (pp. 1493-1495).

Semwal, T., Jha, S. S., & Nair, S. B. (2017). On ordering multi-robot task executions within a cyber physical system. [TAAS]. *ACM Transactions on Autonomous and Adaptive Systems*, 12(4), 20. DOI: 10.1145/3124677

Semwal, T., & Nair, S. B. (2016). Agpi: Agents on raspberry pi. *Electronics (Basel)*, 5(4), 72. DOI: 10.3390/electronics5040072

Sethi, S., Kathuria, M., & Kaushik, T. (2021). Face mask detection using deep learning: An approach to reduce risk of Coronavirus spread. *Journal of Biomedical Informatics*, 120, 103848. DOI: 10.1016/j.jbi.2021.103848 PMID: 34171485

Shah, I. (2020). *Analysis of Cyber Crime in Banking Sector*. http://103.85.141.163:8071/jspui/bitstream/123456789/182/1/46%20%20IMTISHAL%201190997022.pdf

Shah, M. U., Iqbal, F., Rehman, U., & Hung, P. C. (2023). A comparative assessment of human factors in cybersecurity: Implications for cyber governance. *IEEE Access : Practical Innovations, Open Solutions*.

Shaikh, J., Butt, Y. A., & Naqvi, H. F. (2024). Effective Intrusion Detection System Using Deep Learning for DDoS Attacks. *The Asian Bulletin of Big Data Management*, 4(1). Advance online publication. DOI: 10.62019/abbdm.v4i1.113

Sharma, A., Mansotra, V., & Singh, K. (2023). Detection of Mirai Botnet Attacks on IoT devices Using Deep Learning. *Journal of Scientific Research and Technology*, 174-187.

Sharma, N., & Annaboina, K. (2024). Analytical Study On Prevention And Detection Of Financial Cybercrime And Frauds Using Transaction Pattern Generation Tool. *Journal of Scientific Research and Technology*, 9-31.

Sharma, N., Chakraborty, C., & Kumar, R. (2023). Optimized multimedia data through computationally intelligent algorithms. *Multimedia Systems*, 29(5), 2961–2977. DOI: 10.1007/s00530-022-00918-6

Shi, J., Wan, J., Yan, H., & Suo, H. (2011, November). A survey of cyber-physical systems. In 2011 international conference on wireless communications and signal processing (WCSP) (pp. 1-6). IEEE.

Shi, W., Cao, J., Zhang, Q., Li, Y., & Xu, L. (2016). Edge computing: Vision and challenges. *IEEE Internet of Things Journal*, 3(5), 637–646. DOI: 10.1109/JIOT.2016.2579198

Shrivastava, K., Jha, S. S., & Nair, S. B. (2013, July). Autonomous mobile robot navigation using artificial immune system. In *Proceedings of Conference on Advances In Robotics* (pp. 1-7).

Shukla, R. K., Prakash, V., & Pandey, S. (2020, December). A perspective on Internet of Things: Challenges & applications. In *2020 9th International Conference System Modeling and Advancement in Research Trends (SMART)* (pp. 184-189). IEEE.

Shukla, R. K., Sengar, A. S., Gupta, A., & Chauhan, N. R. (2022, December). Deep Learning Model to Identify Hide Images using CNN Algorithm. In *2022 11th International Conference on System Modeling & Advancement in Research Trends (SMART)* (pp. 44-51). IEEE. DOI: 10.1109/SMART55829.2022.10047661

Shukla, R. K., Sengar, A. S., Gupta, A., Jain, A., Kumar, A., & Vishnoi, N. K. (2021, December). Face recognition using convolutional neural network in machine learning. In *2021 10th International Conference on System Modeling & Advancement in Research Trends (SMART)* (pp. 456-461). IEEE. DOI: 10.1109/SMART52563.2021.9676308

Shukla, R. K., Tiwari, A. K., & Ranjan Mishra, A. (2024). Face Recognition Using LBPH and CNN. *Recent Advances in Computer Science and Communications (Formerly: Recent Patents on Computer Science), 17*(5), 48-58.

Shukla, R. K., & Tiwari, A. K. (2020). A Machine Learning Approaches on Face Detection and Recognition. *Solid State Technology*, 63(5), 7619–7627.

Shukla, R. K., & Tiwari, A. K. (2023). Masked face recognition using mobilenet v2 with transfer learning. *Computer Systems Science and Engineering*, 45(1).

Shukla, R. K., & Tiwari, A. K. (2024). Security Analysis of the Cyber Crime. In *The Ethical Frontier of AI and Data Analysis* (pp. 257–271). IGI Global. DOI: 10.4018/979-8-3693-2964-1.ch016

Shukla, R. K., Tiwari, A. K., & Jha, A. K. (2023). An Efficient Approach of Face Detection and Prediction of Drowsiness Using SVM. *Mathematical Problems in Engineering*, 2023(1), 2168361. DOI: 10.1155/2023/2168361

Shuo, W. (2018, September). Design and Verification of Outbound Mode Strategy Based on EIQ Analysis. In *2018 International Symposium in Sensing and Instrumentation in IoT Era (ISSI)* (pp. 1-6). IEEE.

Siano, P. (2014). Demand response and smart grids—A survey. *Renewable & Sustainable Energy Reviews*, 30, 461–478. DOI: 10.1016/j.rser.2013.10.022

Sicari, S., Rizzardi, A., Grieco, L., & Coen-Porisini, A. (2015). Security, privacy and trust in internet of things: The road ahead. *Computer Networks*, 76, 146–164. DOI: 10.1016/j.comnet.2014.11.008

Siddiqui, M. H. F., & Kumar, R. (2020). Interpreting the nature of rainfall with AI and big data models. In *2020 International Conference on Intelligent Engineering and Management (ICIEM)* (pp. 306-310). London, UK. IEEE. DOI: 10.1109/ICIEM48762.2020.9160322

Silva e Silva, F. J. D., Endler, M., & Kon, F. (2003). A framework for building adaptive distributed applications. In Proceedings.

Silva, A., Da Silva, M. M., & Delgado, J. (1998). An overview of agentspace: a next- generation mobile agent system. In *Mobile Agents* (pp. 148–159). Springer. DOI: 10.1007/BFb0057655

Silva, F., Duarte, M., Correia, L., Oliveira, S. M., & Christensen, A. L. (2016). Open is- sues in evolutionary robotics. *Evolutionary Computation*, 24(2), 205–236. DOI: 10.1162/EVCO_a_00172 PMID: 26581015

Sim, K., Hart, E., & Paechter, B. (2015). A lifelong learning hyper-heuristic method for bin packing. *Evolutionary Computation*, 23(1), 37–67. DOI: 10.1162/EVCO_a_00121 PMID: 24512321

Simoes, E. D., & Dimond, K. R. (2001, October). Embedding a distributed evolutionary system into a population of autonomous mobile robots. In 2001 IEEE International Conference on Systems, Man and Cybernetics. e-Systems and e-Man for Cybernetics in Cyberspace (Cat. No. 01CH37236) (Vol. 2, pp. 1069-1074). IEEE.

Simplicio, M. A., Iwaya, L. H., Barros, B. M., Carvalho, T. C. M. B., & Naslund, M. (2015). Secour health: A delay-tolerant security framework for mobile health data collection. *IEEE Journal of Biomedical and Health Informatics*, 19(2), 761–772. DOI: 10.1109/JBHI.2014.2320444 PMID: 24801629

Singh, B. (2023). Blockchain Technology in Renovating Healthcare: Legal and Future Perspectives. In *Revolutionizing Healthcare Through Artificial Intelligence and Internet of Things Applications* (pp. 177-186). IGI Global.

Singh, B., & Kaunert, C. (2024). Future of Digital Marketing: Hyper-Personalized Customer Dynamic Experience with AI-Based Predictive Models. *Revolutionizing the AI-Digital Landscape: A Guide to Sustainable Emerging Technologies for Marketing Professionals*, 189.

Singh, B., & Kaunert, C. (2024). Harnessing Sustainable Agriculture Through Climate-Smart Technologies: Artificial Intelligence for Climate Preservation and Futuristic Trends. In *Exploring Ethical Dimensions of Environmental Sustainability and Use of AI* (pp. 214-239). IGI Global.

Singh, C., Singh, R., Tiwari, M., & Hazela, B. (2024). Analyse and Predict the Detection of the Cyber-Attack Process by Using a Machine-Learning Approach. *EAI Endorsed Transactions on Internet of Things, 10.*

Singh, A., & Choudhary, P. (2021, August). Keylogger detection and prevention. []. IOP Publishing.]. *Journal of Physics: Conference Series*, 2007(1), 012005.

Singh, B. (2023). Federated Learning for Envision Future Trajectory Smart Transport System for Climate Preservation and Smart Green Planet: Insights into Global Governance and SDG-9 (Industry, Innovation and Infrastructure). *National Journal of Environmental Law*, 6(2), 6–17.

Singh, B. (2023). Tele-Health Monitoring Lensing Deep Neural Learning Structure: Ambient Patient Wellness via Wearable Devices for Real-Time Alerts and Interventions. *Indian Journal of Health and Medical Law*, 6(2), 12–16.

Singh, B. (2023). Unleashing Alternative Dispute Resolution (ADR) in Resolving Complex Legal-Technical Issues Arising in Cyberspace Lensing E-Commerce and Intellectual Property: Proliferation of E-Commerce Digital Economy. *Revista Brasileira de Alternative Dispute Resolution-Brazilian Journal of Alternative Dispute Resolution-RBADR*, 5(10), 81–105. DOI: 10.52028/rbadr.v5i10.ART04.Ind

Singh, B. (2024). Lensing Legal Dynamics for Examining Responsibility and Deliberation of Generative AI-Tethered Technological Privacy Concerns: Infringements and Use of Personal Data by Nefarious Actors. In Ara, A., & Ara, A. (Eds.), *Exploring the Ethical Implications of Generative AI* (pp. 146–167). IGI Global., DOI: 10.4018/979-8-3693-1565-1.ch009

Singh, B. (2024). Social Cognition of Incarcerated Women and Children: Addressing Exposure to Infectious Diseases and Legal Outcomes. In Reddy, K. (Ed.), *Principles and Clinical Interventions in Social Cognition* (pp. 236–251). IGI Global., DOI: 10.4018/979-8-3693-1265-0.ch014

Singh, B., & Kaunert, C. (2024). Integration of Cutting-Edge Technologies such as Internet of Things (IoT) and 5G in Health Monitoring Systems: A Comprehensive Legal Analysis and Futuristic Outcomes. *GLS Law Journal*, 6(1), 13–20. DOI: 10.69974/glslawjournal.v6i1.123

Singh, B., Kaunert, C., & Vig, K. (2024). Reinventing Influence of Artificial Intelligence (AI) on Digital Consumer Lensing Transforming Consumer Recommendation Model: Exploring Stimulus Artificial Intelligence on Consumer Shopping Decisions. In Musiolik, T., Rodriguez, R., & Kannan, H. (Eds.), *AI Impacts in Digital Consumer Behavior* (pp. 141–169). IGI Global., DOI: 10.4018/979-8-3693-1918-5.ch006

Singh, N. J., Hoque, N., Singh, K. R., & Bhattacharyya, D. K. (2023). Botnet-based IoT network traffic analysis using deep learning. *Security and Privacy*, •••, 355.

Singh, V. P., & Srivastava, R. (2018). Automated and effective content-based mammogram retrieval using wavelet based CS-LBP feature and self-organizing map. *Biocybernetics and Biomedical Engineering*, 38(1), 90–105. DOI: 10.1016/j.bbe.2017.09.003

Siwakoti, Y. R., Bhurtel, M., Rawat, D. B., Oest, A., & Johnson, R. C. (2023). Advances in IOT security: Vulnerabilities, enabled Criminal Services, attacks and countermeasures. *IEEE Internet of Things Journal*, 10(13), 11224–11239. DOI: 10.1109/JIOT.2023.3252594

Smith, A. (2019). The Impact of Smart Home Devices on Family Dynamics: A Qualitative Study. *Journal of Human-Computer Interaction*, 25(3), 345–362.

Smith, D.. (2020). The future of AI in cybersecurity. *Cybersecurity Futures*, 3(3), 210–225. DOI: 10.1000/cf.2019.210

Solairaj, A., Prabanand, S. C., Mathalairaj, J., Prathap, C., & Vignesh, L. S. (2016, January). Keyloggers software detection techniques. In 2016 10th International Conference on Intelligent Systems and Control (ISCO) (pp. 1-6). IEEE.

Soliman, S., Oudah, W., & Aljuhani, A. (2023). Deep learning-based intrusion detection approach for securing industrial Internet of Things. *Alexandria Engineering Journal*, 81, 371–383. DOI: 10.1016/j.aej.2023.09.023

Song, C., & Yan, H. (2020).Kinmix: A data augmentation approach for kinship verification. *IEEE International Conference on Multimedia and Expo (ICME)*, 1–6. DOI: 10.1109/ICME46284.2020.9102891

Sowmya, B. J., Hanumantharaju, R., Kumar, D. P., & Srinivasa, K. G. (2023). Identification of authorship and prevention of fraudulent transactions/cybercrime using efficient high performance machine learning techniques. *International Journal of Business Intelligence and Data Mining*, 22(1-2), 144–169. DOI: 10.1504/IJBIDM.2023.127312

Stellefson, M., Paige, S. R., Chaney, B. H., & Chaney, J. D. (2020). Evolving Role of Social Media in Health Promotion: Updated Responsibilities for Health Education Specialists. *International Journal of Environmental Research and Public Health*, 17(4), 1153. DOI: 10.3390/ijerph17041153 PMID: 32059561

Stempel, J., & Finkle, J. (2017). *Yahoo Says All Three Billion Accounts Hacked in 2013*. Data Theft.

Sudhakar, & Kumar, S. (2023, April). ABBDIoT: Anomaly-based botnet detection using machine learning model in the Internet of Things network. In *International Conference on IoT, Intelligent Computing and Security: Select Proceedings of IICS 2021* (pp. 235-245). Singapore: Springer Nature Singapore.

Suhaimin, M. S. M.. (2023). Social Media Sentiment Analysis and Opinion Mining in Public Security: Taxonomy, Trend Analysis, Issues and Future Directions. *Journal of King Saud University. Computer and Information Sciences*, 35(9), 101776. DOI: 10.1016/j.jksuci.2023.101776

Sun, Y., Wang, X., & Tang, X. (2014). Deep learning face representation from predicting10,000 classes.*Proceedings of the IEEE Conference on Computer Vision and Pattern Recognition*, 1891–1898.DOI: 10.1109/CVPR.2014.244

Swami, D., & Gupta, P. (2019). Internet of Things (IoT) and Smart Home Technology: Awareness and Perception among Indian Consumers.

Swiątkowska, J. (2020). Tackling cybercrime to unleash developing countries' digital potential. *Pathways for Prosperity Commission Background Paper Series*, 33, 2020–01.

Tai, H., & Kosaka, K. (1999). The Aglets project. *Communications of the ACM*, 42(3), 100–101. DOI: 10.1145/295685.295882

Takabi, H., Hashem, Y., & Dantu, R. (2018). Prediction of human error using eye movements patterns for unintentional insider threat detection. *2018 IEEE 4th International Conference on Identity, Security, and Behavior Analysis (ISBA)*, 1–8. https://ieeexplore.ieee.org/abstract/document/8311479/

Takimoto, M., Mizuno, M., Kurio, M., & Kambayashi, Y. (2007). Saving energy consumption of multi-robots using higher-order mobile agents. In Agent and Multi-Agent Systems: Technologies and Applications: First KES International Symposium, KES-AMSTA 2007, Wroclaw, Poland, May 31–June 1, 2007. [Springer Berlin Heidelberg.]. *Proceedings*, 1, 549–558.

Tan, L., Pan, Y., Wu, J., Zhou, J., Jiang, H., & Deng, Y. (2020). A new framework for DDoS attack detection and defense in SDN environment. *IEEE Access : Practical Innovations, Open Solutions*, 8, 161908–161919. DOI: 10.1109/ACCESS.2020.3021435

Tarau, P. (1992). BinProlog: a continuation passing style Prolog engine. In Programming Language Implementation and Logic Programming: 4th International Symposium, PLILP'92 Leuven, Belgium, August 26–28, 1992 Proceedings 4 (pp. 479-480). Springer Berlin Heidelberg.

Tarau, P. (1999). Jinni: Intelligent mobile agent programming at the intersection of java and prolog. In *Proc. of PAAM* (Vol. 99, pp. 109-123).

Tatomur, I. (2020, March). UNIVERSITY CYBER SECURITY AS A METHOD FOR ANTI-FISHING FRAUD. *The Economic Discourse*, 1(1), 59–67. DOI: 10.36742/2410-0919-2020-1-7

Tayfour, O., & Marsono, M. N. (2020). Collaborative Detection and Mitigation of Distributed Denial-of-Service Attacks on Software-Defined Network. *Mobile Networks and Applications*, 25(4), 1338–1347. Advance online publication. DOI: 10.1007/s11036-020-01552-0

Tehaam, M., Ahmad, S., Shahid, H., Saboor, M. S., Aziz, A., & Munir, K. (2022, October). A Review of DDoS Attack Detection and Prevention Mechanisms in Clouds. In 2022 24th International Multitopic Conference (INMIC) (pp. 1-6). IEEE.

TEJASVI, K., BEGUM, R., & JABBAR, M. (2024). SECURITY IN IOT: SYSTEMATIC REVIEW. *The Fusion of Artificial Intelligence and Soft Computing Techniques for Cybersecurity*, 217.

Teke, K., Manjare, A., & Jamdar, S. (2021). Survey on face mask detection using deep learning. *International Journal on Data Science and Machine Learning with Applications*, 1(1), 1–9.

Tetri, P., & Vuorinen, J. (2013). Dissecting social engineering. *Behaviour & Information Technology*, 32(10), 1014–1023. DOI: 10.1080/0144929X.2013.763860

Thakur, K., Shan, J., & Pathan, A.-S. K. (2018, April). Innovations of Phishing Defense: The Mechanism, Measurement and Defense Strategies. *International Journal of Communication Networks and Information Security*, 10(1), 19–27.

Thapaliya, S., & Sharma, P. K. (2023). Cyber Forensic Investigation in IoT Using Deep Learning Based Feature Fusion in Big Data. *International Journal of Wireless Information Networks*, 30(1), 16–29.

Thapaliya, S., & Sharma, P. K. (2023). Optimized deep neuro fuzzy network for cyber forensic investigation in big data-based IoT infrastructures. [IJISP]. *International Journal of Information Security and Privacy*, 17(1), 1–22. DOI: 10.4018/IJISP.315819

Theraulaz, G., & Bonabeau, E. (1995). Modelling the collective building of complex architectures in social insects with lattice swarms. *Journal of Theoretical Biology*, 177(4), 381–400. DOI: 10.1006/jtbi.1995.0255

Timmis, J., Neal, M., & Hunt, J. (2000). An artificial immune system for data analysis. *Bio Systems*, 55(1), 143–150. DOI: 10.1016/S0303-2647(99)00092-1 PMID: 10745118

Tippins, N. T., Oswald, F. L., & McPhail, S. M. (2021). Scientific, legal, and ethical concerns about AI-based personnel selection tools: A call to action. *Personnel Assessment and Decisions*, 7(2), 1. DOI: 10.25035/pad.2021.02.001

Tiwari, A. K., & Shukla, R. K. (2019, March). Machine learning approaches for face identification feed forward algorithms. In *Proceedings of 2nd International Conference on Advanced Computing and Software Engineering (ICACSE)*. DOI: 10.2139/ssrn.3350264

Tok, Y. C., & Chattopadhyay, S. (2023). Identifying threats, cybercrime and digital forensic opportunities in Smart City Infrastructure via threat modeling. *Forensic Science International Digital Investigation*, 45, 301540. DOI: 10.1016/j.fsidi.2023.301540

Tomás, J., Rego, A., Viciano-Tudela, S., & Lloret, J. (2021, August). Incorrect facemask-wearing detection using convolutional neural networks with transfer learning. [). MDPI.]. *Health Care*, 9(8), 1050. PMID: 34442187

Tortonesi, M., Morelli, A., Govoni, M., Michaelis, J., Suri, N., Stefanelli, C., & Russell, S. (2016, December). Leveraging Internet of Things within the military network environment—Challenges and solutions. In 2016 IEEE 3rd World Forum on Internet of Things (WF-IoT) (pp. 111-116). IEEE.

Tripathi, S., Vardhan Reddy Baddam, S., Kumar Dhadige, P., Singh, S., Abhishek, T., Vijendar Reddy, G., & Kumar Singla, A. (2024). Cyber Watch an Comprensive Security Tool. MATEC Web of Conferences, 392, 01094. DOI: 10.1051/matecconf/202439201094

Tripathi, D., Singh, L. K., Tripathi, A. K., & Chaturvedi, A. (2021). Model based security verification of Cyber-Physical System based on Petrinet: A case study of Nuclear power plant. *Annals of Nuclear Energy*, 159, 108306. DOI: 10.1016/j.anucene.2021.108306

Triplett, W. J. (2022). Addressing human factors in cybersecurity leadership. *Journal of Cybersecurity and Privacy*, 2(3), 573–586.

Tsipenyuk, G. Y. (2018). *Evaluation of decentralized email architecture and social network analysis based on email attachment sharing (No. UCAM-CL-TR-918)*. University of Cambridge, Computer Laboratory.

Tuli, P., & Sahu, P. (2013). System monitoring and security using keylogger. *International Journal of Computer Science and Mobile Computing*, 2(3), 106–111.

Tyagi, A. K., Rekha, G., & Sreenath, N. (2018). Is your privacy safe with Aadhaar?: An open discussion. *2018 Fifth International Conference on Parallel, Distributed and Grid Computing (PDGC)*, 318–323. https://ieeexplore.ieee.org/abstract/document/8745836/

Tyagi, A. K., Aswathy, S. U., & Abraham, A. (2020). Integrating blockchain technology and artificial intelligence: Synergies perspectives challenges and research directions. *Journal of Information Assurance and Security*, 15(5), 1554.

Upadhyay, D., & Sampalli, S. (2020). SCADA (Supervisory control and data acquisition) systems: Vulnerability assessment and security recommendations. *Computers & Security*, 89, 1–18. DOI: 10.1016/j.cose.2019.101666

Utami, S. H., Purnama, A. A., Hidayanto, A. N., Utami, S. H., Purnama, A. A., & Hidayanto, A. N. (2022). Fintech Lending in Indonesia: A Sentiment Analysis, Topic Modelling, and Social Network Analysis using Twitter Data. *International Journal of Applied Engineering & Technology*, 4(1), 50–56.

Vakamullu, G., Misra, N. R., & Venugopal, K. (2021). Critical Success Factors of Online Shopping: Rural Perscpective. Asian Journal of Economics. *Business and Accounting*, 21(24), 34–45.

Vakamullu, G., Misra, N. R., & Venugopal, K. (2023). *Critical Factors for the Affluence of Online Shopping: Rural Perspective ATLAS Skilltech University from 23rd - 29th March 2023* (1st ed.). Eureka Publications.

Vandenbosch, L., Fardouly, J., & Tiggemann, M. (2022). Social Media and Body Image: Recent Trends and Future Directions. *Current Opinion in Psychology*, 45, 101289. DOI: 10.1016/j.copsyc.2021.12.002 PMID: 35030460

Vaquero, L. M., & Rodero-Merino, L. (2014, October). Finding your way in the fog: Towards a comprehensive definition of fog computing. *Computer Communication Review*, 44(5), 27–32. DOI: 10.1145/2677046.2677052

Varghese, S. (2024). Dynamics of Social Media Networks in the Post-Truth Era. In *Handbook of Digital Journalism: Perspectives from South Asia* (pp. 419–429). Springer. DOI: 10.1007/978-981-99-6675-2_36

Varma, P., Nijjer, S., Sood, K., Grima, S., & Rupeika-Apoga, R. (2022). Thematic Analysis of Financial Technology (Fintech) Influence on the Banking Industry. *Risks*, 10(10), 186. DOI: 10.3390/risks10100186

Vasan, D., Hammoudeh, M., & Alazab, M. (2024). Broad Learning: A GPU-Free Image-based Malware Classification. *Applied Soft Computing*, 154, 111401. DOI: 10.1016/j.asoc.2024.111401

Vatambeti, R., & Mamidisetti, G. (2023). Routing attack detection using ensemble deep learning model for IIoT. *Inf. Dyn. Appl*, 2(1), 31–41. DOI: 10.56578/ida020104

Velliangiri, S., Karthikeyan, P., & Kumar, V. V. (2021). Detection of distributed denial of service attack in cloud computing using the optimization-based deep networks. *Journal of Experimental & Theoretical Artificial Intelligence*, 33(3), 405–424. DOI: 10.1080/0952813X.2020.1744196

Venkatasubramanian, M., Lashkari, A. H., & Hakak, S. (2023). Iot malware analysis using federated learning: A comprehensive survey. *IEEE Access : Practical Innovations, Open Solutions*, 11, 5004–5018. DOI: 10.1109/ACCESS.2023.3235389

Venugopal, K., Das, S., Manoj, K. P., & Dey, S. (2020). Impact of Efficacious and Detrimental Factors of Social Media on Public Usage Behaviour in the Age of Covid-19 Pandemic: In Case of Srikakulam, A.P. PalArch's Journal of Archaeology of Egypt/Egyptology, 17(9), pp. 2288-2302

Venugopal, K., Vakamullu, G., & Mishra, N. R. (2022). Social Media Habits of Rural Consumers Influencing on Online Consumption in an edited book entitled Business Perspectives in Reviving Workforce Productivity in the current Volatile and Uncertain Times.

Venugopal, K., & Das, S. (2022). Social Media Habits of Rural Consumers Influencing on Online Consumption. *Horizon J. Hum. Soc. Sci. Res*, 4, 39–47.

Venugopal, K., Das, S., & Vakamullu, G. (2023). *Critical Factors for the Upscale of Online Shopping: A Rural Perspective. Chapter book entitled "Influencer Marketing Applications within the Metaverse". A volume in the Advances in Marketing, Customer Relationship Management, and E-Services (AMCRMES) Book Series.* IGI Global. DOI: 10.4018/978-1-6684-8898-0.ch016

Verma, A., Kshirsagar, D., & Khan, S. (2013). Privacy and Security: Online Social Networking. *International Journal of Advanced Computer Research*, 3(8), 310–315.

Virmani, D., Ravishankar, T. N., & Tesfayohanis, M. (2023). 6 IoT attack detection using quantum deep learning in large-scale networks. *Quantum-Safe Cryptography Algorithms and Approaches: Impacts of Quantum Computing on Cybersecurity*, 67.

Vu, H. N., Nguyen, M. H., & Pham, C. (2022). Masked face recognition with convolutional neural networks and local binary patterns. *Applied Intelligence*, 52(5), 5497–5512. DOI: 10.1007/s10489-021-02728-1 PMID: 34764616

Wajahat, A., Imran, A., Latif, J., Nazir, A., & Bilal, A. (2019, January). A novel approach of unprivileged keylogger detection. In 2019 2nd International Conference on Computing, Mathematics and Engineering Technologies (iCoMET) (pp. 1-6). IEEE.

Wang, S., Balarezo, J. F., Chavez, K. G., Al-Hourani, A., Kandeepan, S., Asghar, M. R., & Russello, G. (2022). Detecting flooding DDoS attacks in software defined networks using supervised learning techniques. Engineering science and technology, an international journal, 35, 101176.

Wang, Z., Huang, B., Wang, G., Yi, P., & Jiang, K. (2023). Masked face recognition dataset and application. *IEEE Transactions on Biometrics, Behavior, and Identity Science*, 5(2), 298–304. DOI: 10.1109/TBIOM.2023.3242085

Watanabe, Y., Ishiguro, A., & Uchikawa, Y. (1999). Decentralized behavior arbitration mechanism for autonomous mobile robot using immune network. In *Artificial immune systems and their applications* (pp. 187–209). Springer. DOI: 10.1007/978-3-642-59901-9_10

Watkins, A., Timmis, J., & Boggess, L. (2004). Artificial Immune Recognition System (AIRS): An immune-inspired supervised learning algorithm. *Genetic Programming and Evolvable Machines*, 5(3), 291–317. DOI: 10.1023/B:-GENP.0000030197.83685.94

Watson, R. A., Ficici, S. G., & Pollack, J. B. (2002). Embodied evolution: Dis- tributing an evolutionary algorithm in a population of robots. *Robotics and Autonomous Systems*, 39(1), 1–18. DOI: 10.1016/S0921-8890(02)00170-7

Wazid, M., Katal, A., Goudar, R. H., Singh, D. P., Tyagi, A., Sharma, R., & Bhakuni, P. (2013, January). A framework for detection and prevention of novel keylogger spyware attacks. In 2013 7th International Conference on Intelligent Systems and Control (ISCO) (pp. 433-438). IEEE.

Wei, J., Liu, W., & Hu, X. (2018). Secure data sharing in cloud computing using revocable-storage identity-based encryption. *IEEE Transactions on Cloud Computing*, 6(4), 1136–1148. DOI: 10.1109/TCC.2016.2545668

Werfel, J., Petersen, K., & Nagpal, R. (2014). Designing collective behavior in a termite-inspired robot construction team. *Science*, 343(6172), 754–758. DOI: 10.1126/science.1245842 PMID: 24531967

Whitbrook, A. M., Aickelin, U., & Garibaldi, J. M. (2007). Idiotypic immune networks in mobile-robot control. *IEEE Transactions on Systems, Man, and Cybernetics. Part B, Cybernetics*, 37(6), 1581–1598. DOI: 10.1109/TSMCB.2007.907334 PMID: 18179075

Whitbrook, A. M., Aickelin, U., & Garibaldi, J. M. (2010). Two-timescale learning using idiotypic behaviour mediation for a navigating mobile robot. *Applied Soft Computing*, 10(3), 876–887. DOI: 10.1016/j.asoc.2009.10.005

Whitbrook, A., Aickelin, U., & Garibaldi, J. (2008). An idiotypic immune network as a short-term learning architecture for mobile robots. In *International Con-ference on Artificial Immune Systems* (pp. 266–278). Springer. DOI: 10.1007/978-3-540-85072-4_24

Whitley, L. D. (1991). Fundamental principles of deception in genetic search. In *Foundations of genetic algorithms* (Vol. 1, pp. 221–241). Elsevier.

Williams, P., Dutta, I. K., Daoud, H., & Bayoumi, M. (2022). A survey on security in internet of things with a focus on the impact of emerging technologies. *Internet of Things : Engineering Cyber Physical Human Systems*, 19, 100564. DOI: 10.1016/j.iot.2022.100564

Witten, I. H., Frank, E., Hall, M. A., & Pal, C. J. (2016). *Data Mining: Practical machine learning tools and techniques*. Morgan Kaufmann.

Wolfson, O., Chamberlain, S., Kalpakis, K., & Yesha, Y. (2001). Modeling moving objects for location based services. In *Developing an Infrastructure for Mobile and Wireless Systems* (pp. 46–58). Springer.

Wolfson, O., Sistla, P., Xu, B., Zhou, J., Chamberlain, S., Yesha, Y., & Rishe, N. (1999). Tracking moving objects using database technology in domino. In *Next Gen- eration Information Technologies and Systems* (pp. 112–119). Springer. DOI: 10.1007/3-540-48521-X_9

Wood, C., & Raj, R. (2010, July). Keyloggers in Cybersecurity Education. In Se-curity and Management (pp. 293-299).

Wright, A., & Thomas, G. (2019). *Human and organisational factors incyberse-curity: applying STAMP to explorevulnerabilities.Contemporary Ergonomics and Human Factors* (Charles, R., & Golightly, D., Eds.). CIEHF.

Wu, L., Peng, Q., & Lembke, M. (2023). Research trends in cybercrime and cybersecurity: A review based on web of science core collection database. *International Journal of Cybersecurity Intelligence & Cybercrime*, 6(1), 5–28. DOI: 10.52306/2578-3289.1154

Xia, R., Chen, Y., & Ren, B. (2022). Improved anti-occlusion object tracking algorithm using Unscented Rauch-Tung-Striebel smoother and kernel correlation filter. *Journal of King Saud University. Computer and Information Sciences*, 34(8), 6008–6018. DOI: 10.1016/j.jksuci.2022.02.004

Xia, S., Shao, M., Luo, J., & Fu, Y. (2012). Understanding kin relationships in a photo. *IEEE Transactions on Multimedia*, 14(4), 1046–1056. Advance online publication. DOI: 10.1109/TMM.2012.2187436

Xue, K., & Yuan, D. (2021). Review of the development of intelligent home and intelligent hardware industry in China under the background of "New Infrastructure".

Yadav, V. K., Trivedi, M. C., & Mehtre, B. M. (2016). DDA: an approach to handle DDoS (Ping Flood) attack. In Proceedings of International Conference on ICT for Sustainable Development: ICT4SD 2015 Volume 1 (pp. 11-23). Springer Singapore.

Yang, J., Lee, Y., & McDonald, A. P. (2022). SolarWinds Software Supply Chain Security: Better Protection with Enforced Policies and Technologies. In Yang, J., Lee, Y., & McDonald, A. P. (Eds.), *Cyber*. Supply Chain Security. DOI: 10.1007/978-3-030-92317-4_4

Yan, H., Lu, J., Deng, W., & Zhou, X. (2014). Discriminative multimetric learning for kinship verification. *IEEE Transactions on Information Forensics and Security*, 9(7), 1169–1178. Advance online publication. DOI: 10.1109/TIFS.2014.2327757

Zargar, S. T., Joshi, J., & Tipper, D. (2013). A survey of defense mechanisms against distributed denial of service (ddos) flooding attacks. *IEEE Communications Surveys and Tutorials*, 15(4), 2046–2069. DOI: 10.1109/SURV.2013.031413.00127

Zhang, J., Zou, X., Kuang, L. D., Wang, J., Sherratt, R. S., & Yu, X. (2022). CCTSDB 2021: a more comprehensive traffic sign detection benchmark. *Human-centric Computing and Information Sciences, 12*.

Zhang, K., Huang, Y., & Song, C., WuH., WangL. (2015). Kinship verification with deep convolutionalneural networks.*British Machine Vision Conference 2015*. DOI: 10.5244/C.29.148

Zhang, A., Lipton, Z. C., Li, M., & Smola, A. J. (2023). *Dive into deep learning*. Cambridge University Press.

Zhang, L.. (2021). Vulnerability Analysis of Smart Home Devices: A Systematic Review. *Computers & Security*, 90, 102038.

Zhang, L., Duan, Q., Zhang, D., Jia, W., & Wang, X. (2020). Advkin: Adversarial convolutionalnetworkfor kinship verification. *IEEE Transactions on Cybernetics*. Advance online publication. DOI: 10.1109/TCYB.2019.2959403 PMID: 31945005

Zhang, X., Liu, L., Lan, M., Song, G., Xiao, L., & Chen, J. (2022). Interpretable machine learning models for crime prediction. *Computers, Environment and Urban Systems*, 94, 101789. DOI: 10.1016/j.compenvurbsys.2022.101789

Zhang, Y., Suleiman, B., Alibasa, M. J., & Farid, F. (2024). Privacy-Aware Anomaly Detection in IoT Environments using FedGroup: A Group-Based Federated Learning Approach. *Journal of Network and Systems Management*, 32(1), 20. DOI: 10.1007/s10922-023-09782-9

Zhang, Y., Xiong, F., Xie, Y., Fan, X., & Gu, H. (2020). The impact of artificial intelligence and blockchain on the accounting profession. *IEEE Access : Practical Innovations, Open Solutions*, 8, 110461–110477. DOI: 10.1109/ACCESS.2020.3000505

Zhang, Z., Al Hamadi, H., Damiani, E., Yeun, C. Y., & Taher, F. (2022). Explainable artificial intelligence applications in cyber security: State-of-the-art in research. *IEEE Access : Practical Innovations, Open Solutions*, 10, 93104–93139. DOI: 10.1109/ACCESS.2022.3204051

Zhang, Z., & Gupta, B. B. (2018). Social media security and trustworthiness: Overview and new direction. *Future Generation Computer Systems*, 86, 914–925. DOI: 10.1016/j.future.2016.10.007

Zhou, T., Yang, L., & Cheng, Y. (2019). Understanding Smart Home Acceptance in Urban China: An Empirical Study.

Zhuang, L., Zhou, F., & Tygar, J. D. (2009). Keyboard acoustic emanations revisited. *ACM Transactions on Information and System Security*, 13(1), 1–26. DOI: 10.1145/1609956.1609959

Zhu, L., Zhang, C., Xu, C., Liu, X., & Huang, C. (2018). An Efficient and Privacy-Preserving Biometric Identification Scheme in Cloud Computing. *IEEE Access : Practical Innovations, Open Solutions*, 6(c), 19025–19033. DOI: 10.1109/ACCESS.2018.2819166

Ziwei, H., Dongni, Z., Man, Z., Yixin, D., Shuanghui, Z., Chao, Y., & Chunfeng, C. (2024). The applications of internet of things in smart healthcare sectors: A bibliometric and deep study. *Heliyon*, 10(3), e25392. DOI: 10.1016/j.heliyon.2024.e25392 PMID: 38356528

Zuboff, S. (2019). *The Age of Surveillance Capitalism: The Fight for a Human Future at the New Frontier of Power*. PublicAffairs.

About the Contributors

Rajeev Kumar is a distinguished academician and academic administrator with over 15 years of experience in fostering excellence in professional education. He is currently serving as a Professor in the Computer Science and Engineering Department at Moradabad Institute of Technology, Moradabad, Uttar Pradesh, India. Prof. Kumar holds a Ph.D. in Computer Science, a D.Sc. (Post-Doctoral Degree) in Computer Science, and a Postdoctoral Fellowship from Malaysia. His academic credentials are further bolstered by certifications in Data Science and Machine Learning using Python and R Programming from IIM Raipur, as well as additional certifications from IBM and Google. A senior member of IEEE, he actively participates in the IEEE Young Professional Committee and holds memberships in the Computer Society of India (CSI) and SMIEEE. His academic areas of interest and specialization include Artificial Intelligence, Cloud Computing, e-Governance, and Networking.

Saurabh Srivastava is an Assistant Professor of Department of Computer Science & Engineering (Data Science) at Moradabad Institute of Technology, Moradabad, India. He received P.hD. from Integral University Lucknow in 2023, and Master of Computer Application (MCA) from Dr. A.P.J. Abdul Kalam Technical University Lucknow in 2015. He is associated with research after MCA, and he has approx. 9 years of experience in research including Computer Vision & Image Processing, Satellite Image Interpretation and Analysis, Land Cover Mapping, Time Series Analysis, Requirement Engineering, Multi-Agent System, Cyber Security, Social Engineering etc. He has published extensively in renowned journals and has presented his research at numerous national and international conferences. Dr. Saurabh Srivastava is dedicated to fostering critical thinking and innovation among students and actively engages in mentoring emerging scholars.

Ahmed A. Elngar is an Associate Professor and Head of the Computer Science Department at the Faculty of Computers and Artificial Intelligence, Beni-Suef University, Egypt. Dr. Elngar is also, an Associate Professor of Computer Science at the College of Computer Information Technology, American University in the Emirates, United Arab Emirates. Also, Dr. AE is Adjunct Professor at School of Technology, Woxsen University, India. Dr. AE is the Founder and Head of the Scientific Innovation Research Group (SIRG). Dr. AE is a Director of the Technological and Informatics Studies Center (TISC), Faculty of Computers and Artificial Intelligence, Beni-Suef University. Dr. AE has more than 150 scientific research papers published in prestigious international journals and over 35 books covering such diverse topics as data mining, intelligent systems, social networks, and smart environment. Dr. AE is a collaborative researcher He is a member of the Egyptian Mathematical Society (EMS) and International Rough Set Society (IRSS). His other research areas include the Internet of Things (IoT), Network Security, Intrusion Detection, Machine Learning, Data Mining, and Artificial Intelligence. Big Data, Authentication, Cryptology, Healthcare Systems, Automation Systems. He is an Editor and Reviewer of many international journals around the world. Dr. AE won several awards including the Young Researcher in Computer Science Engineering", from Global Outreach Education Summit and Awards 2019, on 31 January 2019 (Thursday) in Delhi, India.

* * *

Syed Adnan Afaq has a PhD in computer application and working as an Assistant Professor in the department of Computer application at Integral University. He has more than 6+ years of experience in academics and research.

Abhay Bhatia is working as Assistant Professor in Department of Computer Science and Engineering at Roorkee Institute of Technology, Roorkee, Haridwar Uttarakhand. He is having 12+ years of academic experience and worked with various reputed engineering institutions. He has completed his B.Tech in Computer Science and Engineering from AKTU (formely UPTU), M.Tech in Computer Science and Engineering from Rajasthan and Ph.D. in Wireless Sensor Networks. He is currently an active member of IEEE as well as a reviewer for several journals too. He is having distinguish record of research papers with 17+ Indexed, Scopus, IEEE and SCI papers. He also visited many institutes for guest lecture on various upcoming research. Moreover 4 patents with 5 book chapters are also in his bucket, he is also author to a book on IoT, as a researcher with research area of Artificial Intelligence, Machine Learning, Image Processing and Wireless Sensor Network his work is up heading to great research.

Aparna Datta holds an MCA and MTech degree from Maulana Abul Kalam Azad University of Technology, West Bengal. She is currently an Assistant Professor in the Department of Computer Application of Meghnad Saha Institute of Technology. Her research interests include medical image processing and machine learning.

Shweta Dwivedi has done PhD in computer application. She has more than 17+ years experience. Currently, she is working as an Assistant Professor in the department of Computer Application, Integral University, Lucknow.

Mohammad Faisal is currently working as Professor and Head, Department of Computer Application, Integral University, Lucknow-India with more than 17 years of teaching and research experience. His areas of interest are Requirement Engineering, Cyber Security, and Blockchain. He has published 2 authored books, 3 edited books and a number of quality book chapters, research papers and technical articles in National/International Books/Journals/Conferences of high repute. He is actively serving the research and academic community by contributing his knowledge and experience as member of Editorial Board/Advisory committee/ Reviewer and TPC in various International Journals/Conferences Dr. Mohammad Faisal is an active member of various professional bodies ISTE, IAENG, CSTA, EASST, UACEE and many more.

Ravi Gugulothu is an Assistant Professor in the Department of CSE-Artificial Intelligence and Machine Learning at Sreenidhi Institute of Science and Technology (SNIST) in Hyderabad, India. He earned his Bachelor of Technology degree in Computer Science and Engineering from Kamala Institute of Science and Technology (KITS(S)) in 2005, followed by a Master of Technology in Software Engineering from Sreenidhi Institute of Science and Technology in 2007. He is pursuing his Ph.D. in Computer Science and Engineering from KL University, Vijayawada. With Seventeen years of teaching experience, Ravi has taught a variety of undergraduate and postgraduate courses, including Web Technologies, Operating Systems, Data Warehousing and Data Mining, Artificial intelligence, Software Requirements and Estimation, Service Oriented Architecture, and Internet Technologies. He has guided over 40 B.Tech and 12 M.Tech projects and actively participated in numerous workshops and conferences. His research interests lie in Cloud Computing, Artificial intelligence, machine learning, and data mining.

Christian Kaunert is Professor of International Security at Dublin City University, Ireland. He is also Professor of Policing and Security, as well as Director of the International Centre for Policing and Security at the University of South Wales. In addition, he is Jean Monnet Chair, Director of the Jean Monnet Centre of Excellence and Director of the Jean Monnet Network on EU Counter-Terrorism (www.eucter.net).

Syed Khalida Izhar is a research scholar in microbiology. She has submitted PhD thesis on microbiology.

Sumana Kundu received her B.E. and M.Tech degree in Computer Science & Engineering in the years of 2008 and 2010. She worked as a Research Scholar (Full Time) at Computer Science & Engineering department of National Institute of Technology, Durgapur and obtained her PhD degree in the year of 2018. Dr. Sumana Kundu was an Assistant Professor at Siliguri Institute of Technology, Techno India Group. Thereafter she was an Associate Professor and Head of the Department at Haldia Institute of Technology. Presently she is an Associate Professor at Computer Science & Engineering department of Dr. B. C. Roy Engineering College, Durgapur. Her Research area of interest includes Pattern Recognition, Machine Learning, Data Security using Steganography.

Hitesh Mohapatra received the B.E. degree in Information Technology from Biju Patnaik University of Technology (BPUT), Odisha in 2006, and the MTech. Degree in CSE from Odisha University of Technology and Research (OUTR) University, Odisha in 2009. He received his Ph.D. in Computer Science & Engineering in 2021 from Veer Surendra Sai University of Technology (VSSUT), Burla, India. He has contributed 30 SCI and Scopus indexed research papers, 21 international/national conferences and books on Software Engineering and C Programming respectively. He has 15 years of teaching experience both in industry and academia. He has served the research community with various capacities like session chair, technical chair, keynote speaker etc. His research interests include wireless sensor network, smart city, smart grid and smart water. Currently he is working as Associate professor at School of Computer Engineering, KIIT DU, Bhubaneswar, and Odisha.

Akash Mondal is a final year student at Meghnad Saha Institute of Technology from the department of Master of Computer Application. He also holds a Bachelor's degree in Computer Science(Honours) from Acharya Prafulla Chandra College, New Barrackpore, under West Bengal State University. He is interested in domains like, Cybersecurity, Block chain and Machine Learning.

RadhikaPulyala works as an Assistant Professor in the Department of Computer Science and Engineering - Cyber Security. With seven years of academic experience, Pursuing Ph.D. from NIT, Warangal, India. She specializes in Machine Learning, Artificial Intelligence, and Cyber Security. She presented a research paper at an IEEE conference with proceedings indexed in Scopus. Additionally, she authored a research paper that was published in the Scopus-indexed journal. She has done Google Cloud Computing Foundations Certification program and also been an instructor to the students for the same certification course. As an Assistant Professor she handled various undergraduate and postgraduate courses like Design and Analysis of Algorithms, Data Warehousing and Data Mining, Artificial Intelligence, Software Quality Assurance and Testing and Web Services Testing. She is also a member of IAENG. Dedicated to both research and teaching, she is passionate about advancing the fields of machine learning and cyber security. She is also fond of various Cyber Security tools like Wireshark, Burp Suite, Nmap, etc. She is committed to sharing her expertise and fostering a collaborative learning environment for the students.

Arunima Sarkar is a final year student from the Department of Master of Computer Application at Meghnad Saha Institute of Technology. Also she holds a Bachelor's degree in Computer Science (Honours) from Acharya Prafulla Chandra College, New Barrackpore, under West Bengal State University. She has interests in the domain of Cybersecurity and Machine Learning.

Sanchayan Sen is a final year student at Meghnad Saha Institute of Technology from the department of Master of Computer Application. He also holds a Bachelor's degree in Computer Science (Honours) from Vivekananda College. He is interested in domains like, Cybersecurity, AI and Machine Learning.

Qudsia Shahab is pursuing PhD in computer application from Integral University, Lucknow. Her research area is IOT.

Bhupinder Singh is working as Professor at Sharda University, India. Also, Honorary Professor in University of South Wales UK and Santo Tomas University Tunja, Colombia. His areas of publications as Smart Healthcare, Medicines, fuzzy logics, artificial intelligence, robotics, machine learning, deep learning, federated learning, IoT, PV Glasses, metaverse and many more. He has 3 books, 139 paper publications, 163 paper presentations in international/national conferences and seminars, participated in more than 40 workshops/FDP's/QIP's, 25 courses from international universities of repute, organized more than 59 events with international and national academicians and industry people's, editor-in-chief and co-editor in journals, developed new courses. He has given talks at international universities, resource person in international conferences such as in Nanyang Technological University Singapore, Tashkent State University of Law Uzbekistan; KIMEP University Kazakhstan, All'ah meh Tabatabi University Iran, the Iranian Association of International Criminal law, Iran and Hague Center for International Law and Investment, The Netherlands, Northumbria University Newcastle UK.

Devendra Sood is working as assistant professor in Tulas Institute Dehradun Uttarakhand India. He did MCA from SRHU Dehradun after which pursued his M.Tech in OOS. Currently he is pursuing PhD in Computer Application. Moreover, he had been member of several committees, and currently worked with the team for NBA accreditation to CSE department of his institution.

Saurabh Srivastava has done PhD in computer application. He is working as assistant professor in MIT Moradabad.

Dheeraj Sundaragiri is an Associate Professor in the Department of Computer Science and Engineering at Sreenidhi Institute of Science and Technology (SNIST) in Hyderabad, India. He earned his Bachelor of Technology degree in Information Technology from Kakatiya Institute of Science and Technology in 2005, followed by a Master of Technology in Software Engineering from Sreenidhi Institute of Science and Technology in 2007. He completed his Ph.D. in Computer Science and Engineering from Sri Satya Sai University of Technology & Medical Sciences in 2021. With sixteen years of teaching experience, Dheeraj has taught a variety of undergraduate and postgraduate courses, including Web Technologies, Python Programming, Data Warehousing and Data Mining, and Linux Programming. He has guided over 60 B.Tech and 9 M.Tech projects and actively participated in numerous workshops and conferences. Dheeraj is also a member of the IEEE, ACM, SNIST Alumni Association and serves as a faculty advisor for CodeChef SNIST Chapter. His research interests lie in artificial intelligence, machine learning, and data mining.

Lingala Thirupathi has 17 years of experience in the Teaching and IT industry. B.Tech, M.Tech. Published 13+ Scopus-indexed national and international journals and 1- SCI indexed journal. He is passionate about advancing the fields of AI, ML, and cyber security. He is committed to sharing his expertise and fostering a collaborative learning environment for the students. He has co-authored 3 textbooks on AI, ML, and Cyber Security.

Arvind Kumar Tiwari received his B.E. degree in Computer Science & Engineering from CCS University, Meerut, India, and M.Tech in CSE from UPTU, Lucknow, and Ph.D. in CSE from IIT(BHU), Varanasi, India. He has worked as Professor and Vice Principal in GGS College of Modern Technology, Kharar, Punjab, India. and currently working as an Associate Professor in KNIT Sultanpur, U.P. India. He is a member of IEEE & IEEE computer society ACM. He has published more than 20 research papers in reputed international journals including Thomson Reuters (SCI & Web of Science) and conferences including IEEE. His main research work focuses on Big Data Analytics, Computational Intelligence, Pattern Recognition. He has more than 10 years of teaching experience and 4 years of Research Experience.

B. Vasundara, an aspiring engineer and technology enthusiast, was born and raised in Hyderabad, India. From a young age, Vasundara exhibited a keen interest in science and technology, often engaging in activities that fueled her curiosity about how things work. Her early education laid a strong foundation for her analytical and problem-solving skills, which would later become pivotal in her academic pursuits. Vasundara excelled in her coursework, demonstrating a profound understanding of AI and machine learning concepts. She was particularly interested in the applications of AI in healthcare, finance, and education, aiming to leverage technology to create impactful solutions. Her research work often received commendations from her professors and peers, earning her a reputation as a diligent and innovative thinker. Vasundara's dedication to her field extended beyond the classroom, as she actively participated in seminars and workshops, constantly seeking to expand her knowledge.

Koppala Venugopal, a professor in Management Studies at Aditya Institute of Technology and Management at Srikakulam, A.P., has had an adroit experience of academic, Research and community service. He has contributed 5 Projects, 2 patents, 10 books, 70 publications, 48 paper presentations, 56 resource talks and 12 memberships. He is guiding 4 scholars from various universities. His exceptional interest industry interface has made his efforts dexterous.

Gausiya Yasmeen is a research scholar. Her research area is image processing.

Index

E

F

H

I

K

L

M

N

P

S

T

U

www.ingramcontent.com/pod-product-compliance
Lightning Source LLC
LaVergne TN
LVHW080340011026
849161LV00009B/2140